SAMS Teach Yourself

Adobe®
Creative Suite

All in One

Mordy Golding

SAMS   *800 East 96th Street, Indianapolis, Indiana, 46240 USA*

Sams Teach Yourself Adobe Creative Suite All in One

Copyright © 2005 by Sams Publishing

International Standard Book Number: 0-672-32591-8

Library of Congress Catalog Card Number: 2003092925

Printed in the United States of America

First Printing: July 2004

07   06   05   04   4   3   2   1

Trademarks

Warning and Disclaimer

Bulk Sales

Sams Publishing offers excellent discounts on this book when ordered in quantity for bulk purchases or special sales. For more information, please contact

U.S. Corporate and Government Sales

1-800-382-3419

corpsales@pearsontechgroup.com

For sales outside of the U.S., please contact

International Sales

1-317-428-3341

international@pearsontechgroup.com

Acquisitions Editor
Betsy Brown

Development Editor
Jonathan Steever

Managing Editor
Charlotte Clapp

Project Editor
Matthew Purcell

Copy Editor
Cheri Clark

Indexer
Chris Barrick

Proofreader
Juli Cook

Technical Editor
Kate Binder

Publishing Coordinator
Vanessa Evans

Designer
Gary Adair

Page Layout
Stacey Richwine-DeRome
Kelly Maish

Table of Contents

Contents at a Glance

About the Author

Mordy Golding has played an active role in the design and publishing environment since 1990. A production artist for both print and the Web for many years, Mordy, an Adobe Certified Expert and Adobe Certified Print Specialist, has served as a hands-on trainer and has spoken at worldwide events and seminars including Macworld, Seybold, NAB, and PhotoshopWorld.

Mordy worked at Adobe as the product manager for Adobe Illustrator 10 and Adobe Illustrator CS, and is currently a consultant specializing in the Adobe Creative Suite and Mac OS X migration.

You can often find Mordy hanging around the Adobe User to User forums or the Print Planet forums online and you can reach him at mordy@mordy.com. Other books published by Mordy Golding include *The Web Designer's Guide to Color* and *Sams Teach Yourself Adobe Illustrator in 24 Hours*.

Dedication

*To Zaidy, who always wanted to know what you
could do with a computer anyway. I miss you.*

Acknowledgments

Books don't just appear on the bookshelves by themselves. Thanks to all the folks at Sams Publishing, and to Betsy Brown, Jon Steever, Kate Binder, Cheri Clark and Matt Purcell for their professional and untiring help in publishing this book.

Writing this book was a huge task and I couldn't have done it without the help and expertise of Steve Samson, Jen Alspach and Lynn Grillo. I am privileged to count them among my friends.

This book is a work that finds its words shaped from years of experience and friendship. Thanks to Sharon Steuer, Sandee Cohen, David Blatner, Deke McClelland, and Bert Monroy for your continued support.

There's no way that I could have possibly completed a project of this magnitude without the support from my peers at Adobe. While it's impossible to list everyone, there are some friends for which a blanket "thanks to everyone at Adobe" statement simply won't do. Thank you Lydia Varmazis, Leon Brown, Margot McClaughry, Shane Tracy, Will Eisley, Tricia Gellman, Lonn Lorenz, Bob Schaffel, John Nack, Addy Roff, Kevin Connor, Gray Knowlton, Mark Asher, George Arriola, Caleb Belohavek, Hans Grande, Ginna Baldasarre, Annick Baudot, Julieanne Kost and Daniel Brown.

Additionally, special thanks go to Dave Burkett, Jim Heeger and Shantanu Narayen of Adobe for helping to make this book—and the Creative Suite—a reality.

To the members of the Graphics Offsite Leadership Forum—Ted Alspach, Rob Sargent, Barry Hills, and Mike Abbott.

To the Wrotslavsky family, who welcomed me as one of their own over ten years ago (and who still willingly admit to that fact today).

For all the times I asked him silly questions like why the sky is blue, my father has forever earned the right to ask me how to create a mask in Photoshop (and other assorted technical support questions). My mother continues to serve as my role model for everything I do.

Of course, this book would not have been possible without the love and support of my wife Batsheva and my children, Chayala, Simcha Bunim and Chavi. I'm one lucky man.

:) Mordy

We Want to Hear from You!

As the reader of this book, *you* are our most important critic and commentator. We value your opinion and want to know what we're doing right, what we could do better, what areas you'd like to see us publish in, and any other words of wisdom you're willing to pass our way.

You can email or write me directly to let me know what you did or didn't like about this book—as well as what we can do to make our books stronger.

Please note that I cannot help you with technical problems related to the topic of this book, and that due to the high volume of mail I receive, I might not be able to reply to every message.

When you write, please be sure to include this book's title and author as well as your name and phone or email address. I will carefully review your comments and share them with the author and editors who worked on the book.

E-mail: graphics@samspublishing.com

Mail: Mark Taber
Associate Publisher
Sams Publishing
800 East 96th Street
Indianapolis, IN 46240 USA

Reader Services

For more information about this book or others from Sams Publishing, visit our Web site at www.samspublishing.com. Type the ISBN (excluding hyphens) or the title of the book in the Search box to find the book you're looking for.

Introduction

Welcome to *Sams Teach Yourself Adobe Creative Suite All in One*. This book is designed to give you a fast and easy start with Adobe's powerhouse of creativity, design, and production tools. Adobe's Creative Suite brings together the industry-standard Photoshop, Illustrator, and Acrobat software; the award-winning InDesign and GoLive software; and a new innovative file management tool called Version Cue. Together, these tools can create a smooth workflow for professional print or Web design, taking into account all aspects of the design and production process.

A recent quick search at Amazon.com came back with more than 30 books on Photoshop CS alone. Considering that the Adobe Creative Suite contains the fully functional versions of Photoshop, Illustrator, InDesign, GoLive, and Acrobat, it's a wonder this book is anything smaller than *War and Peace*. The goal of this book isn't to overwhelm you with needless information about every single feature in every application, but rather to help you learn how to use the Adobe Creative Suite as a whole to get your work done.

I've broken the book down into three parts, each taking a different approach to the Adobe Creative Suite:

Part I: The Creative Suite—An overall introduction to the different applications in the Creative Suite, as well as an overview of each application's strengths and weaknesses. You'll learn when to use which application, as well as get an understanding of how each application works with the others to produce a complete product. You'll also see how each application in the Suite integrates with the others and how certain features are similar across the entire Suite.

Part II: The Applications—An in-depth look at each individual application in the Adobe Creative Suite. Part I of the book gave you an understanding of when to use a particular application, and now Part II goes into detail about the features, functionality, and uses for Photoshop, ImageReady, Illustrator, InDesign, GoLive, Acrobat, and Version Cue.

Part III: The Projects—A collection of projects you can re-create using all the tools in the Creative Suite. After becoming familiar with the workflow process and the applications themselves in Part I and Part II, you will now create a series of projects that will not only give you real-world working experience with the Creative Suite, but also offer tips and tricks you can apply as you are working on the projects themselves. All art and files necessary to complete the projects are already installed with the Creative Suite, so you can follow along to create a corporate identity, a brochure, an ad campaign, a Web banner, a Web site, and a business presentation.

If you have some familiarity with the applications in the Suite, you can read Part I and then jump to Part III to work on the projects, using Part II as a reference when you need more information about a particular feature in an application. In either case, the three sections will present the Creative Suite in a way that is not overwhelming, and before you know it you'll be creating professional-quality art and having fun at the same time!

That said, we've got a lot of ground to cover, so let's get started using the Adobe Creative Suite!

PART I

The Creative Suite

CHAPTER 1

Overview: The Creative Process

Every child is an artist. The problem is how to remain an artist once he grows up.

Pablo Picasso

A Creative Mind

We're all creative.

It doesn't matter what job we do, but we all manage to be creative in one way or another—either doing our job or just as a hobby. You don't have to be a graphic designer or an artist to be creative either. Lawyers put together graphic presentations to demonstrate a part of a case in court. Doctors use diagrams to describe medical procedures to patients. Business professionals create snazzy charts and graphs to demonstrate future growth of their company. Parents create scrapbooks for their kids about their trip to Disney World, and grandparents distribute cute photos of all the kids to the family.

It wasn't that many years ago that professional layouts for books and magazines could only be set on special expensive typesetting machines and then mechanically put together using X-ACTO blades and wax or rubber cement. Photo retouching was a costly expense that required the use of an airbrush, and printing your final art required a lengthy task of creating film color separations manually.

These days, the process is quite different. Pages for magazines are now completely laid out on a computer, incorporating hi-end typography. Photographs can be combined or adjusted to just about anything, and digital presses can take files directly from the screen to the printed page. Additionally, the emergence of the Internet brings a new level of publishing and creativity to the forefront.

Technology plays a large part in the way people are creative. There are digital cameras, scanners, computers, digital printers, pressure-sensitive graphics tablets, and more. These technologies open the door to allow people to explore news ways of expressing their creativity. We all have a creative mind inside of us, and these items—along with the software that takes the most advantage of them—can help us to not only express those ideas, but do it faster and more efficiently, and maybe even have some fun in the process.

The catch, of course, is learning to how to use the technology available to you to express your creativity. Think of design software as a set of tools you can use. Just as an artist may have paintbrushes, pastels, pencils, erasers, scissors, glue, or glitter (my favorite messy creative item), the Adobe Creative Suite serves as the tools to express your creativity on your computer. As a creative individual, you'll find that this knowledge gives you an edge over the competition.

Throughout this book you'll learn what these tools are, when you should use them (and when you shouldn't), and how to use them.

The Right Tools for the Job

Take a good look at any successful company and you'll find a team of people who all work together toward a common goal. The employees, each with his or her own strengths, are coordinated by a masterful president or CEO. Successful sports teams share similar traits—take basketball, for example.

A basketball team has five players: a center, whose primary job is to score; two guards, whose primary job is to get the ball to the center; and two forwards, whose primary job is to be an alternative option to score (see Figure 1.1). There is also a coach who coordinates plays and aids in communication between players. Each player possesses specific talents to do his or her job.

With good communication and leadership, a team like we just described could take advantage of each team member's abilities to score every time. Because each team member has diverse skills, the team could score in any number of ways depending on what challenge or situation they were facing. In contrast, a team that had only one kind of player might be able to do one certain play very well, but might fail if other kinds of plays were required.

So why are we talking about basketball here? Well, interestingly enough, you can look at a group of design tools in the very same way. At the center you have page layout where your page comes together. You have two elements, photographs and illustrations, being fed into the page layout (and text), and you have two ways to publish your work, either on the Web or in print.

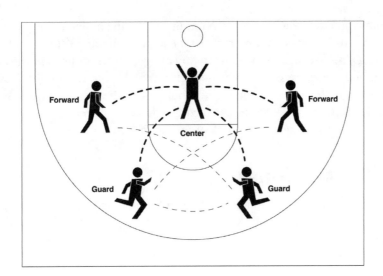

FIGURE 1.1
The five players on a basketball team.

Think of the Adobe Creative Suite as the dream team of software (see Figure 1.2). Illustrator and Photoshop feed photos and graphics to InDesign, the page layout software. GoLive represents Web publishing, and Acrobat, print publishing. Version Cue acts like the coach, bringing the whole team together.

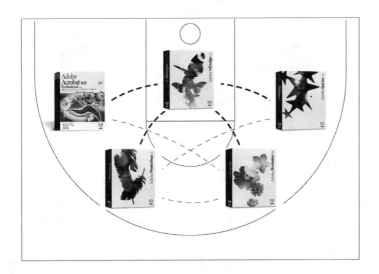

FIGURE 1.2
The five players on the Adobe Creative Suite team.

What makes the Adobe Creative Suite unique is that the individual programs in the suite are all professional programs that can perform various tasks on their own. In fact, some tasks can be done in any of several applications in the Suite. For example, a business card can be done in InDesign or Illustrator (or a combination of both). We'll discuss when you should use each of the applications in Chapter 2, "So Many Applications: Which One to Use?" Before we get to that stage, however, let's take a closer look at the components in the Creative Suite.

The Dream Team

The Adobe Creative Suite is made up of several components, each with its own set of tools that excel at specific tasks. To get a better understanding of what's included in the Adobe Creative Suite, let's discuss each of the components and what its primary function is.

Adobe Photoshop CS and Adobe ImageReady CS

Photoshop is a pixel-based program (we'll talk more about this in Chapter 2) that excels at working with photographs and illustrations with painterly effects. Most noted for its capability to manipulate photos (see Figure 1.3), it is also used for designing Web graphics. Although most people don't know it, Adobe ImageReady is a part of Photoshop that is geared specifically to Web graphics. It's more of a production tool that lets you specify optimizations, rollovers, animations, and more. Competitors to Photoshop have come and gone, but Macromedia Fireworks is similar in many ways to ImageReady.

FIGURE 1.3
A photograph before and after it was edited in Photoshop.

Adobe Illustrator CS

Illustrator is a vector-based program (more on this in Chapter 2) that excels at creating illustrations (see Figure 1.4), logos, maps, signs, and more. Illustrator can also serve as a single-page layout tool for creating ads and posters, and for designing Web pages. Competing programs similar to Illustrator are Macromedia's FreeHand and Corel's CorelDRAW.

FIGURE 1.4
An illustration created with Illustrator.

Adobe InDesign CS

InDesign is a page layout program that allows you to composite or put together entire brochures or booklets (see Figure 1.5). Robust tools such as table editors and master pages allow for designers to easily compose pages and designs. Competing programs similar to InDesign are QuarkXPress and Microsoft Publisher.

FIGURE 1.5
A typical page spread designed in InDesign.

Adobe GoLive CS

GoLive is a Web publishing program that allows you to publish and manage Web sites (see Figure 1.6). You can use the HTML editor to lay out individual pages of a site as well as set up complex database-driven pages. Server management tools and FTP functionality let you easily update and maintain your Web sites. Competing programs similar to GoLive are Macromedia Dreamweaver and Microsoft FrontPage.

FIGURE 1.6
A typical Web site designed in GoLive.

Adobe Acrobat 6.0 Professional

Acrobat is a tool used for working with PDF (Portable Document Format) files. You can mark up and review PDF files with useful annotation tools, making it easy to get feedback from clients or coworkers (see Figure 1.7). Acrobat can also be used for filling out forms, applying digital signatures, preflighting files for printing, and previewing color separations onscreen.

By the Way

There are actually several programs in the Acrobat family (as Adobe likes to call it), which is always a cause for confusion. Each product has different levels of functionality.

Adobe Reader (once called Acrobat Reader) is a free program and browser plug-in that allows anyone to view and print PDF documents. This is the version most people have—with more than 700 million downloads worldwide. In fact, whenever you hear people say, "Yeah, I have Adobe on my computer," they are most likely referring to the free Adobe Reader.

Adobe Acrobat Standard gives users the ability to mark up and review PDF files as well as fill out forms, apply digital signatures, and perform some other basic functions. This version is useful for people who often work with PDF files, but usually do the same simple tasks.

Adobe Acrobat Elements enables users to view and print PDF files as well as fill out forms and apply digital signatures. This version is available only for Windows computers and can be purchased only with 1,000 user licenses or more (it's mostly meant for large corporations that use PDF forms for processing).

Adobe Acrobat Professional is the version that ships in the Creative Suite and offers the most robust toolset of all the versions listed here, including everything mentioned previously plus preflight tools, separations preview, editing tools, and more.

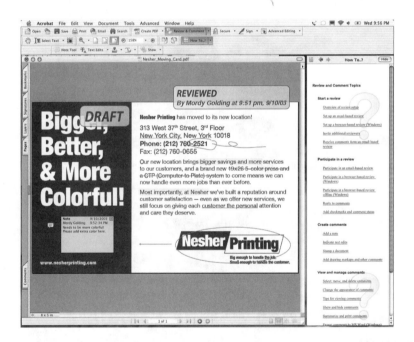

FIGURE 1.7
A marked-up PDF with comments in Acrobat.

There aren't any programs that compete significantly or directly with Acrobat, although Microsoft has recently announced a technology called X-Docs (currently in development) that is clearly targeted at competing with Acrobat and PDF files. In Chapter 3, "The Game Plan: Developing a Workflow," we'll talk a lot more about PDF files and how they are used.

Adobe Version Cue

Version Cue is a database server product that tracks files and versions of project files (see Figure 1.8). Intended for smaller workgroups (anywhere from 1 to 20 users), it allows users to easily find images or other assets used in a particular project. The database also stores multiple versions of files, meaning that you can easily keep track of what changes were made on a project and even go back to previous versions effortlessly. Version Cue is available only as part of the Adobe Creative Suite—you can't buy it separately—and at the time of this writing, there are no products that compete with it.

FIGURE 1.8
Viewing file meta-data with Version Cue.

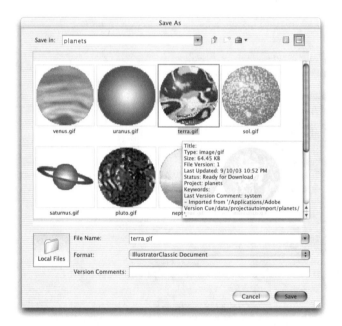

Premium Edition Versus Standard Edition

The Adobe Creative Suite is available in two configurations. The Premium Edition contains five applications (Photoshop CS and ImageReady CS, Illustrator CS, InDesign CS, GoLive CS, and Acrobat 6.0 Professional) and Version Cue, the file management and retrieval system we just discussed. The Standard Edition does not include GoLive CS or Acrobat 6.0 Professional, but it does contain Version Cue. Both versions contain a full-color workflow guide and a 90-minute Total Training CD.

So which one do you need? If you plan to publish Web sites, you'll want to have GoLive CS, so the Premium Edition is the right choice. If you need to do more with PDF files than just create them, you'll also need Acrobat Pro, so again the Premium Edition is what you'll need.

Although this book does cover the Premium Edition of the Suite, it also will prove useful to owners of the Standard Edition because many of the tasks and projects listed here don't necessarily require GoLive or Acrobat Pro. Reading about those tools throughout the book will also give you a better understanding of the workflows and uses for those applications.

A New Look

If you've used any of the Adobe products in the Suite before (older versions of Photoshop or Illustrator for example), you'll notice that all the applications have new packaging and icons, quite different from what they've had in the past. Photoshop's icon always had some kind of eye, and Illustrator's icon was Botticelli's Venus; but all the Adobe images have been replaced with elements of nature, all clean-cut against white backgrounds. This approach clearly defines the integration among all the applications in the suite while offering a clean, organic approach to design.

> The Adobe Creative Suite Premium Edition has a plant with five leaves as its image because it contains five products. The Standard Edition has a plant with three leaves as its image because it contains three products.

By the Way

CHAPTER 2

So Many Applications: Which One to Use?

Quality is never an accident; it is always the result of high intention, sincere effort, intelligent direction and skillful execution; it represents the wise choice of many alternatives.

William A. Foster

Do I Have to Use Them All?

I recently began playing golf. (I've come to realize that up until a certain age, golf is the most boring, idiotic sport in the world, but suddenly one day it becomes this spectacular sport and you become infatuated with getting this little ball in a hole.) As a beginner, here I was with a bag full of different golf clubs all with different numbers or names, and I had absolutely no idea when I was supposed to use which one. I also had no idea whether I was supposed to use all of them in any specific order. It was actually quite confusing.

As it turns out, each golf club is made for a specific purpose. A sand wedge is used to hit golf balls out of sand traps, drivers are used to hit balls long off the tee, and various irons can be used to give the ball just the right amount of lift or distance. A good golfer knows exactly which club to use in each situation.

Likewise, when using the Adobe Creative Suite, a good designer knows exactly which program to use for each situation or task.

Some jobs will call for using all the tools you've got. Yet some projects might require only one or two of them. The important thing to realize is that just because you have all of these tools, it doesn't mean you have to use all of them for every project. Knowing each and every feature of each and every program is also something you may not need (at least not right away), so don't get frustrated if learning all of these applications seems like an insurmountable task. Getting a basic understanding of what each of these applications can do for you is enough to get you started—the rest will come in time.

Taking a First Glance at the Applications

Before you can start making decisions about which application to use for each kind of job, you have to know how each application works, what tools it has, and what its strengths are. The more you know about the tools you use, the easier it will be for you to decide how best to use them to your advantage.

In this section we're going to focus on each application by itself and the tasks that each can do (and ones that they can't). In Chapter 3, "The Game Plan: Developing a Workflow," we'll discuss how to use all the Adobe Creative Suite applications together to complete full projects.

Adobe Photoshop CS and Adobe ImageReady CS

Adobe Photoshop CS and Adobe ImageReady CS would have been Photoshop version 8 and ImageReady version 8, respectively, if Adobe had not renamed them to CS for the Creative Suite.

Where Photoshop and ImageReady Came From

What started out as a personal project for Thomas Knoll and his brother John in the late 1980s turned into Adobe Photoshop—an image editing program that has since redefined how we look at computer graphics. Photoshop has since become a verb ("I just photoshopped his head in the picture..."). And Adobe has created other products such as Photoshop Elements (a consumer version of Photoshop) and Photoshop Album (a digital photo album), an endeavor that almost makes the name Photoshop into a franchise itself.

What Photoshop Does

Adobe Photoshop is what's generally called a pixel-based (or raster-based) paint program. A raster is a matrix of dots, called *pixels*, that form to make a picture or an image (see Figure 2.1). The number of pixels in a raster image is what defines the *resolution* of that image. The resolution is usually specified as dpi (dots per inch) or ppi (pixels per inch)—you've probably heard of images being described as 300dpi, for example. This means that for every inch in the raster image, there are 300 pixels or dots. Think of it as a level of detail—to fit 300 pixels in one inch, you have to make them a lot smaller than the size of pixels you would need to fit 72 pixels in an inch. Having more and smaller pixels gives you better detail (see Figure 2.2). That's why when you hear people talk about professional-quality images, they refer to them as high-resolution images.

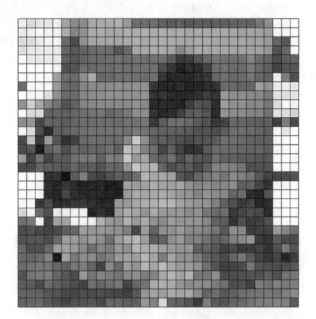

FIGURE 2.1
A low-resolution raster, each square representing one pixel.

36 pixels per inch   300 pixels per inch

FIGURE 2.2
The more pixels, the better the detail.

I know what you're thinking—if higher resolution images look better, let's crank up the resolution to something like 1000dpi everywhere. Well, it's a bit more complicated than that. First of all, the resolution of an image is determined when the image is created. When you scan an image using an image scanner, it gets scanned at a resolution that you set; when you take a photo with a digital camera, the photo is taken at a specific resolution; when you create a new Photoshop document, you're asked to determine what resolution you want the document to be (see Figure 2.3). After a resolution is set for an image, it can't be changed. This means that if I enlarge a 300dpi photo to be twice its size (200%), the resulting image will be 150dpi—the pixels themselves get enlarged when you scale the photo, resulting in bigger pixels. What you get is usually less than ideal, resulting in a block-like jagged-edge image. When an image is such that you can see the individual pixels, it is called *pixelated* (see Figure 2.4).

FIGURE 2.3
Setting the document resolution in Photoshop's New dialog.

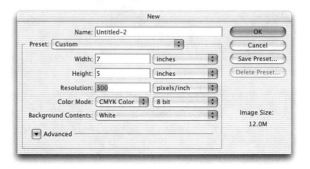

FIGURE 2.4
A pixelated image.

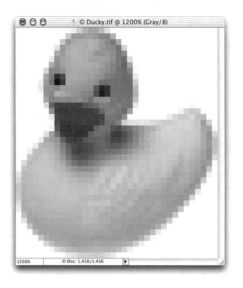

> Okay, so I lied. You *can* change the resolution of an image, using a process called resampling. Luckily, you have the best tool to resample with: Photoshop. *Downsampling* an image means you're reducing the number of pixels, such as reducing a 300dpi image to 72dpi for use on the Web. Basically, extra pixels are thrown out of the image to bring the resolution down. *Upsampling* occurs when you increase the number of pixels in an image. Photoshop uses a process called interpolation to create the necessary extra pixels—but increasing the number of pixels won't necessarily increase the detail or make for a better image.

By the *Way*

Photoshop may rely on resolution, but its power lies in how it can manipulate those individual pixels. A wide range of pixel-based tools and effects gives you complete control over any image. By control, I mean the capability to change each and every pixel in your image. The following is just a sample of the kinds of tools and effects Photoshop provides:

- ▶ Color correction and tonal filters to adjust the overall look of an image or to add special color effects, such as sepia tones.

- ▶ Cloning tools to manipulate or retouch images, such as adding or removing items from a photo.

- ▶ Blur and smudge effects to smooth out parts of an image or to add a sense of motion.

- ▶ Layers and alpha channels to assist in compositing multiple images into a single image, as in a photomontage or collage.

- ▶ A Magic Wand tool and other selection tools to choose which parts of an image you want to adjust or work with.

I'd like to focus on that last item for a moment. The one thing you'll do most often with the Adobe Creative Suite is select things. Until the day comes when computers can read our minds (and I constantly live in fear, knowing that day will come), we have to tell Photoshop—or any program, for that matter—what it is we want to do. More specifically, we need to indicate what part of the image (or the page, the illustration, and so on) we want to work with. As you'll come to see, your options of what kinds of functions you can apply depend on your selection. It's hard to change the font for some text if you have a blue circle selected. We'll discuss how to make selections as we learn about each of the programs, throughout Part II, "The Applications."

What ImageReady Does

Something we haven't touched on yet is Web design. Although Photoshop has the tools to create Web graphics, it does one better by including an entire program suited for just that purpose. Adobe ImageReady was once a standalone product but has shipped as part of Adobe Photoshop since version 5.5. ImageReady does one thing and one thing only: creates Web graphics. A handy Jump To button (see Figure 2.5) lets you easily move images from Photoshop to ImageReady (and vice versa).

FIGURE 2.5
The Jump To button in Photoshop that opens your file in ImageReady.

Following is a list of some of the kinds of tools and functions you'll find in ImageReady:

- ▶ Optimization settings and Web previews to easily specify image formats such as GIF, JPEG, and SWF.

- ▶ Slice tools to cut up images into HTML tables for better and more flexible design options.

- ▶ An intuitive Rollover palette that allows you to specify interactive rollovers.

- ▶ An animation palette to help create graphics that move on the Web.

- ▶ Many Photoshop-like tools and effects to make adjustments to your Web graphics.

Now that you have a better understanding of what Photoshop and ImageReady can do, let's discuss when you should use these tools.

When to Use Photoshop and ImageReady

Photoshop and ImageReady are perfect for various tasks, including the following:

▶ If a photograph is too yellow, too dark, too blurry, or just needs adjustments in the highlights or shadows, you can access all kinds of tools and functions to make it just the way you need it—like the cool Shadow/Highlight feature, for example. Likewise, blemished photos (ones with fingerprints, scratches, or cracks) or old damaged photographs can be repaired with cloning tools or Photoshop's spectacular Healing Brush tool.

▶ Photo compilations such as collages and montages are perfect for Photoshop. With layers, masks, alpha channels, and more, Photoshop is well-equipped to combine multiple images into single compositions.

▶ Photoshop excels at Web design. A large majority of the Web sites you see on the Web every day are designed using Photoshop. Because Photoshop allows for such precise control over the individual pixels of an image, designers can tweak pixel-based Web graphics to perfection.

▶ Web design is only half of the job. Preparing graphics for the Web, such as optimizing, slicing, adjusting the number of colors—otherwise called Web production—is just as important. Photoshop combined with ImageReady is perfect for this kind of work.

▶ Do you consider yourself an artist? Photoshop is often used for digital painting and fine art. Attach a pressure-sensitive graphics tablet (such as a Wacom tablet) to your computer, and you can take advantage of Photoshop's powerful brush engine to create paintings and original art.

▶ Final art preparation and production is a necessary task in just about every project. Whether it's resizing a photo, converting an image from RGB to CMYK or from a JPEG to a TIFF, or specifying spot colors for a duotone, Photoshop is up to the task. A perfect utility tool, Photoshop can both open and export a wide range of file formats.

▶ Sometimes photos or images need that special touch, such as vignettes or soft drop shadows. Photoshop's powerful selection tools and feather commands make it the perfect tool to add these popular effects.

▶ Photoshop is a great tool for capturing digital images from peripheral hardware such as a scanner or a digital camera. Photoshop's File Browser makes it easy to find the images you need, and the File Info dialog enables you to add metadata to a file.

As you can see, Photoshop can be used to perform a wide range of tasks, but keep in mind that there are certain things you don't want to use Photoshop for. Because it's pixel-based, you want to avoid using Photoshop for art that will be scaled to different sizes (logos, for instance). Things that may require a lot of editing or changes, such as text headlines, should also be avoided because it's time-consuming to make those changes in Photoshop.

Adobe Illustrator CS

Adobe Illustrator CS would have been Illustrator version 11 if Adobe had not renamed it to CS for the Creative Suite.

Where Illustrator Came From

After inventing PostScript, a computer language specifically tailored for printing graphics on laser printers, John Warnock devised a program that would allow people to draw in PostScript—which became Adobe Illustrator. The first software program that Adobe sold, Illustrator was released in 1987 and has since come a long way from being a simple vector drawing program. It now does great 3D effects, transparency, Web graphics, and more.

What Illustrator Does

Described as a vector-based drawing program, Illustrator uses mathematical outlines (called Bézier curves) to define paths and shapes. Unlike Photoshop, which works with individual pixels, Illustrator is object-based, meaning that you work with things such as shapes, lines, and text objects instead of a bunch of little dots. Don't get the idea that Illustrator is a kids' drawing program, though—nothing could be farther from the truth. Illustrator has the capability to create art that is so photo-realistic, you'd think it was created in Photoshop (see Figure 2.6).

FIGURE 2.6
This image was created in Adobe Illustrator (it's included as a sample file with Illustrator CS).

Let's take a deeper look at what vector graphics are and how they work. In the early 1960s, a fellow by the name of Pierre Bézier developed a computer drawing system that consisted of points and paths to help design aircraft and cars (those paths would come to be known as Bézier paths). Think of the points and paths like those connect-the-dots exercises you did as a kid (although if you're anything like me, you still enjoy doing them). There are dots, which we call anchor points, and the lines that connect them, which we call paths. In the world of vectors, there are two kinds of paths, closed and open (see Figure 2.7). A closed path is one in which the path starts at one anchor point and then finishes at that same anchor point, whereas an open path doesn't.

FIGURE 2.7
An open vector path and a closed one.

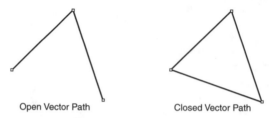

Open Vector Path   Closed Vector Path

At a basic level, every vector object has two attributes, a fill and a stroke (see Figure 2.8). The fill is the part that fills up the area inside the path, and the stroke is the actual path itself. You can apply colors and settings to the fill of an object, the stroke, or both.

FIGURE 2.8
The stroke and fill of a vector object.

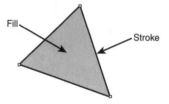

Fill

Stroke

You're probably asking yourself how Illustrator can create complex artwork if all it does is connect straight paths between all of these anchor points. Good question. Well, it turns out that not all anchor points are created equal. In fact, Illustrator employs three kinds of anchor points (see Figure 2.9)—corner points, smooth points, and combination points—and each one controls how the paths that connect to it are drawn.

FIGURE 2.9
The three kinds of anchor points.

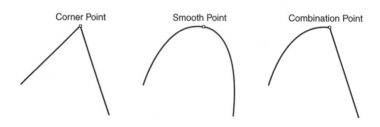

Corner Point   Smooth Point   Combination Point

A good way to quickly grasp the concept of drawing with Bézier paths is to understand that you don't draw the paths. What you are really drawing are the anchor points—the dots—and Illustrator does the rest, automatically connecting the dots with paths, based on how you place those anchor points.

A vector shape can be made up of any combination of anchor points, so you can already get an idea of how precise vector graphics can be (see Figure 2.10). Illustrator's Pen tool allows you to draw these vector shapes, as well as edit existing vector paths.

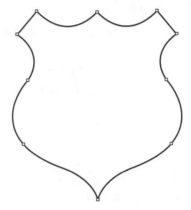

FIGURE 2.10
A complex vector path made of different kinds of anchor points.

You'll find a lot more than just the Pen tool in Illustrator, however. Here's a small sample of the kinds of tools and features you'll find in Illustrator CS:

▶ Illustrator has spectacular 3D and artwork mapping capabilities, making it easy to not only create the coolest art but also create realistic packaging mockups.

▶ Many designs utilize parts of artwork repeatedly (logos, design elements, and so on), and Illustrator manages these artfully with the Symbols palette. Special tools let you spray symbols on your page, taking creativity to a new level.

▶ A Save for Web feature enables you to export Web graphics in just about any Web format you might need, such as GIF, JPEG, SWF, and SVG.

▶ A seemingly endless supply of vector drawing tools makes it as easy as possible to help you draw art, including Pen, Pencil, and Brush tools. There are also a Polygon tool, a Line tool, an Arc tool, and a Grid tool—even a vector Flare tool.

▶ A wide range of what Illustrator calls Live Effects, such as Drop Shadow for adding those nice soft shadows, Feather for giving vector shapes a nice soft edge, and many other effects—even Photoshop ones such as Gaussian Blur.

▶ Illustrator's Pathfinder palette makes editing vector shapes a breeze by giving you a plethora of options that let you combine shapes, cut holes in them, and more, all at the click of a button.

▶ Illustrator contains a wealth of text options that allow you to set the perfect line or paragraph of type, as well as have text run along a freeform path.

▶ Powerful Enveloping, Warp, and Liquefy tools to twist, squeeze, bend, and distort art to your heart's desire.

▶ A Mesh tool and a Blend tool that allow you to achieve painterly effects and smooth blends and gradations between colors—all vector, all the time.

▶ Illustrator has an innovative Variables palette for helping to generate artwork automatically using scripting and a database.

Now that you have a better understanding of what Illustrator can do, let's discuss when you should use it.

By the Way

> You'll also find the vector Pen tool in Photoshop and in InDesign. In fact, many of the applications in the Adobe Creative Suite share similar tools, which we'll discuss in detail in Chapter 4, "The Key That Makes It All Work: Integration."

When to Use Illustrator

Illustrator is perfect for various tasks, including the following:

▶ Most people use Illustrator for logo design and corporate identity. Because logos are continually scaled to different sizes (anywhere from a button on a Web site to a highway billboard or the side of a blimp), creating them as vector artwork is a must.

▶ As if the name of the program wasn't enough of a hint, Illustrator is the tool of choice for fine art and illustration. Illustrator's diverse and flexible toolset allows for a wide variety of stylized artwork. Many of Illustrator's tools also have support for pressure-sensitive tablets to allow artists to put their ideas on screen easier, with more control.

▶ With a full selection of text tools and the capability to place raster images into a file, Illustrator is a great single-page layout tool for creating flyers, advertisements, or sales sheets.

▶ Walk down the aisle of your favorite supermarket and take a look at all the packages on the shelves. Chances are that just about every package you see was created with Illustrator. Package design demands unlimited creative options, custom color support, and reliable printing—all attributes of Illustrator.

▶ Because most graphics on the Web are rasters, most people don't think of Illustrator when they think of Web Design. The truth is that Illustrator is a great tool for designing Web graphics. Illustrator's Save for Web feature lets you export optimized Web graphics directly, or you can bring art directly into Photoshop or ImageReady. An added benefit is that if you ever need to use those graphics for print, you don't need to re-create the art at a higher resolution—you can use it right from Illustrator for just about any task.

▶ In Illustrator you can open and edit Illustrator files, EPS files (PostScript), PDF files, SVG files (Scalable Vector Graphics), DXF/DWG files (AutoCAD)— even native FreeHand and CorelDRAW files. Illustrator can also export files in all kinds of formats, making it a valuable production and utility tool. Between Photoshop and Illustrator, you'll be able to open and work with just about any kind of file you might get your hands on.

▶ Graphs and charts are used to graphically represent numbers or other data that may be hard to grasp just by looking at a bunch of numbers. Illustrator's Graph tool allows designers to quickly create eye-catching and appealing infographics that can be incorporated into annual reports, newsletters, and business presentations.

▶ Going beyond the static image, Illustrator can convert layered and blended art into art that animates or moves when exported as a Flash (SWF) file. Illustrator is also used for creating art that is used in traditional animation such as television cartoons and animated motion pictures.

▶ Maps, environmental graphics (such as signs), and architectural drawings require Illustrator's precise vector tools and unique capability to structure art using layers, sublayers, groups, and subgroups.

It quickly becomes obvious that Illustrator is a powerful application that can perform a wide range of tasks. Keep in mind, however, that Illustrator can contain only one page per document, so it isn't ideal for layouts like newsletters, books, magazines, and other documents that require several pages. Although you can place raster images into an Illustrator document, you can't edit the individual pixels, such as taking the red-eye out of a photo.

Adobe InDesign CS

Adobe InDesign CS would have been InDesign version 3 if Adobe had not renamed it to CS for the Creative Suite.

Where InDesign Came From

There is a lot of history behind InDesign. It started way back in 1986, when a company called Aldus introduced PageMaker, a ground-breaking program (most likely responsible for the era that would define the term *desktop publishing*) that allowed users to lay out pages on a computer screen and set type. As PageMaker evolved, it lost ground in the professional design community to competitor QuarkXPress. Adobe took ownership of PageMaker in 1994, but the technology that it was based on was limited in what it could do. Adobe began work on what it dubbed "the Quark Killer," which was code-named K2. When K2 was finally named InDesign 1.0 and launched in 1999, it was greeted with little fanfare. Sure, there was hype, but being a version 1.0 product, it simply had too many issues that prevented people from using it. When Adobe released InDesign 2.0 in January of 2001, it was a whole new ballgame.

Fast-forward to the present and the battle ensues between QuarkXPress 6 and InDesign CS—although if you read the press reviews or the various forums on the Internet, the battle seems to have already been won by Adobe. There is a definite turn of the tide in today's industry as both designers and printers continue to move to adopt InDesign.

What InDesign Does

InDesign is what is generally called a page layout program. Also dubbed an aggregate tool, InDesign basically allows you to gather content that was created in other applications and position the elements on a page to create a completed design. For example, to create a page of a catalog, you'd set up a page in InDesign, place a product photo you touched up in Photoshop, place the company logo you created in Illustrator, and import some text from Microsoft Word (see Figure 2.11). After the elements are on the page, you can experiment with your design, moving the items around and adjusting them to complete your page design.

Whether you're producing a magazine, a newsletter, or a brochure, nothing is more important than the way the text looks on your page. InDesign has many strengths but typography is definitely first on that list, because it was built to set perfect type quickly and consistently.

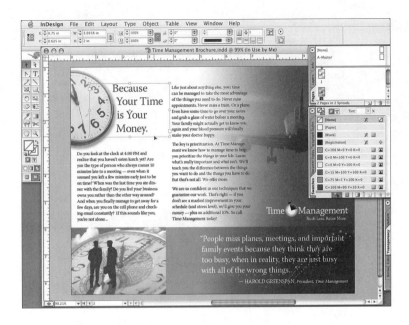

FIGURE 2.11
Working with different elements on a page in InDesign.

A professional designer pays close attention to how a paragraph of text reads. Things such as kerning and tracking (the amount of spacing between letters and words), justification (how text lines up to the margins), leading (pronounced "ledding," the amount of space between lines), and the number of hyphens can make the difference between a block of text that's easy to read and one that gives the reader a headache (see Figure 2.12). Various special characters such as curly quotes and ligatures (special character combinations such as fi, ffi, fl, and ffl) can really make an impact on the visual appearance of text as well.

Adobe InDesign offers features such as Paragraph Styles that allow you to store all the information we just talked about, as well as specify font attributes, size, color, and more—all in a setting you can apply with one click of a button. For example, you can have paragraph styles (see Figure 2.13) set up for how you want a headline, body text, or a caption to look—and have any text in your document match those attributes instantly.

What really makes InDesign shine above the competition is how it fits with all the things you need to do in the design process—something called workflow—which we'll talk about in intimate detail in Chapter 3. But just to give you an idea of what we're talking about, InDesign understands native files from other applications in the Creative Suite, so you can easily drop native Illustrator, Photoshop, and PDF files into your InDesign layout. InDesign also exports PDF files directly, letting you effortlessly send proofs to clients or co-workers for review and approval.

FIGURE 2.12
The difference between good (right) and bad (left) typography.

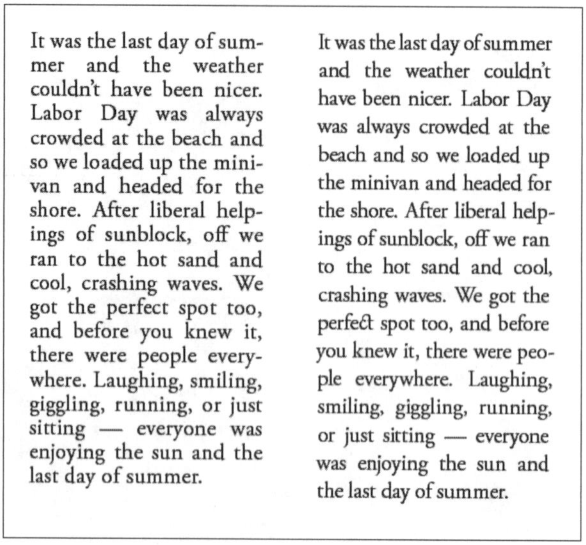

It was the last day of summer and the weather couldn't have been nicer. Labor Day was always crowded at the beach and so we loaded up the minivan and headed for the shore. After liberal helpings of sunblock, off we ran to the hot sand and cool, crashing waves. We got the perfect spot too, and before you knew it, there were people everywhere. Laughing, smiling, giggling, running, or just sitting — everyone was enjoying the sun and the last day of summer.

It was the last day of summer and the weather couldn't have been nicer. Labor Day was always crowded at the beach and so we loaded up the minivan and headed for the shore. After liberal helpings of sunblock, off we ran to the hot sand and cool, crashing waves. We got the perfect spot too, and before you knew it, there were people everywhere. Laughing, smiling, giggling, running, or just sitting — everyone was enjoying the sun and the last day of summer.

FIGURE 2.13
InDesign's Paragraph Styles palette.

Of course, InDesign contains a lot more than professional type tools. Here's a sample of the kinds of tools and features you'll find in InDesign CS:

▶ InDesign has a powerful table editor for quickly laying out tables that can flow from one page to another.

▶ Text wrap controls can help create designs in which text follows the irregular shape of images, as well as other creative options.

▶ InDesign's story editor allows you to make quick edits by displaying text in a word processor–like window, while it updates live in your layout.

▶ To make it easy, fast, and reliable to set type consistently, InDesign has paragraph and character style sheets.

▶ You don't have to worry about how good your spelling is, because InDesign contains a handy Spell Checker.

▶ InDesign is currently the only professional page layout tool to offer the capability to apply such transparency effects as Photoshop-style blend modes and soft drop shadows.

▶ OpenType is a new standard for type, and InDesign can take full advantage of all the features that OpenType brings. InDesign also has a handy Glyph palette to help you find just the glyph (or character) you need from any font.

▶ InDesign saves you time with an innovative Edit Original feature, which allows you to quickly edit and update art that was placed into a layout.

▶ When it comes time to print your file, InDesign has a full-featured Print dialog box allowing you to print color separations. InDesign even has an onscreen Separation Preview feature.

▶ InDesign features an Export command for quickly creating PDFs that you can send to others for review.

Now that you have a better understanding of what InDesign can do, let's discuss when you should use it.

When to Use InDesign

InDesign is perfect for various tasks, including the following:

▶ Product brochures and folders are perfect layout tasks for InDesign. These types of jobs normally include placing content from Photoshop and Illustrator and demand consistent typography and table layouts.

▶ InDesign has specific long-document support that makes it great for designing and laying out books. Besides all the benefits you get with professional-looking typography, InDesign can generate a table of contents automatically, can assist in generating indexes, and has a feature that will "stitch" several files together (individual chapters) to create an entire book with correct page numbering throughout.

▶ Magazines and newspapers usually require quick assembly but also demand the capability to create eye-catching designs that will generate interest by subscribers and readers. InDesign gives designers creative features such as transparency effects, resulting in more creative options.

▶ Most advertisements you see out there don't have much text (people just don't seem to have time to read anymore), but that doesn't mean you can't use InDesign to design great ads. InDesign can export files directly in the PDF/X-1a standard, which is used in the advertising industry.

▶ InDesign's layout and alignment features can be used to design and lay out forms. Integration with Adobe Acrobat also makes InDesign the perfect tool for designing electronic forms (or *eForms*, as they are often called).

▶ Some documents such as newsletters and periodicals are based on templates and are published very often, something perfect for the powerful text features in InDesign. The built-in Story Editor makes these specific tasks easy to do, because you don't need to scroll through complex layouts to change a few words of text.

▶ Catalogs—like the ones you receive in the mail almost daily—utilize just about every aspect of what InDesign can do (complex layouts, tables, text treatments, and more). And InDesign's high-resolution preview mode allows you to position photos and art precisely, as well as allowing you to get a better idea of what the entire page will look like when printed.

▶ Whether you're designing a CD cover for the latest best-selling pop sensation or creating a DVD cover for your recent family vacation to San Jose (to visit Adobe, of course), InDesign helps you specify custom page sizes, bleeds, trim marks, fold marks, and more to ensure that your job prints as it should.

▶ As technology pushes the publishing industry forward, standards such as XML are becoming even more important. InDesign's capability to automatically flow and maintain structured content makes it perfect for XML-based workflows.

▶ At the end of the day, printing your job flawlessly is most important. InDesign contains a wealth of features to ensure quality output every time, including the capability to preview color separations. InDesign makes for a wonderful print production tool.

After discussing how InDesign is used, you should have a better understanding of why it's called an aggregate tool—gathering content from different sources to complete a layout. Although InDesign is also capable of handling complete projects from scratch on its own, it is usually better to use InDesign's Edit Original feature to link graphics and edit them in the apps that handle specialized tasks better. Although InDesign does have an innovative feature called *Package for GoLive* that can help you repurpose content from a print job to be used on a Web site (which we'll discuss in detail in Chapter 9, "Using Adobe GoLive CS"), don't mistake InDesign for a Web design tool.

Adobe GoLive CS

Adobe GoLive CS would have been GoLive version 7 if Adobe had not renamed it to CS for the Creative Suite.

Where GoLive Came From

Whether or not you believe that the Internet was invented by Al Gore, the World Wide Web has pushed professional publishing and design to a new level. The tools to help publish rich Web experiences have evolved as well. Back in the day (um, like several years ago), creating Web graphics and publishing Web sites of any kind required an intimate knowledge of HTML, Unix-based systems and commands, and more. HTML (Hypertext Markup Language) is the code that defines how a Web page should appear. (We'll talk in more detail about HTML later in this book.) At the time when Internet IPOs meant instant wealth and early retirement, a slew of WYSIWYG (What You See Is What You Get) HTML editors were released. Similar in concept to PageMaker or Quark, these programs, such as Adobe PageMill, attempted to allow designers to easily lay out pages without having to learn or know how to code HTML. There weren't many success stories. A promotional QuarkXPress poster at the time proclaimed: *"HTML is just like typesetting—yeah, like typesetting from 20 years ago."*

One HTML editor that was particularly geared toward designers, called GoLive CyberStudio, allowed users not only to design pages, but also to manage Web sites. Adobe bought CyberStudio and called it, simply, Adobe GoLive. Facing similar challenges to that of InDesign with QuarkXPress, GoLive competes with Macromedia Dreamweaver, which is considered the preferred tool for Web site development and management.

What GoLive Does

At first glance, GoLive seems like an incredibly complex program, but on closer inspection it begins to make a lot of sense. That's because GoLive takes care of just about every aspect of the process, from planning a Web site, to designing it, and to publishing it to the Internet. If you had to make a comparison with a program like InDesign, you'd have to give InDesign storyboards for planning your entire project, and then you'd need to add a printing press to boot.

Let me explain. One of the most incredible aspects of the World Wide Web is how quickly you can distribute information. After the world-changing events on

September 11, 2001, the number of hits to news sites on the Internet increased tremendously. That's because the Web is a medium that offers the capability to publish information so quickly—even in real-time—to anywhere in the world. This can happen because the information is electronic—publishing information on the Web is as simple as copying a file from your computer to another computer (a server or "host"). GoLive possesses the tools to perform all the steps involved in this process; there are site layout tools to help you plan your Web site, a full range of Web page layout tools, and a complete set of tools to upload your site to a server.

Let's take things one step at a time, shall we? Before you begin to create a Web site, you create what's called a site architecture—basically a layout of all the pages in your site and how they link together. A Web site isn't like a printed booklet in which everything is linear, one page after another. A Web site is nonlinear—a user can jump to different pages as needed, or on impulse. A Web site requires planning, or you end up doing triple the work later in the process. GoLive can assist in the planning process with the Site Diagram feature, which allows you to set up how pages will link to each other, and even export the site as a PDF to get approval from a client or a manager (see Figure 2.14). When you have the site design approved, GoLive can automatically convert the site design to an actual site where you can begin the next process—designing the pages.

FIGURE 2.14
A site design in GoLive.

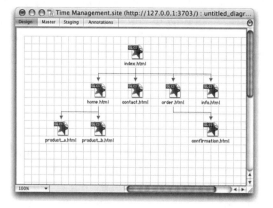

GoLive is a graphic artist's Web design program. You can place native Photoshop and Illustrator files right into your Web layouts (see Figure 2.15), you can position items precisely on your page (down to the pixel), and, most important, you don't have to know HTML. GoLive works much like a page layout tool, in which you position items on a page—but you also have the ability to add fun stuff such as sounds, buttons, links, movies, and rollovers. GoLive even handles all the scary stuff—such as adding JavaScripts and setting up scripts—which we'll talk more in detail about in Chapter 9. GoLive also has a feature called Components for managing the many design elements or parts of a Web site that are used often, such as navigation elements that appear on every page. GoLive makes managing these repeating elements easy—update one and they update everywhere.

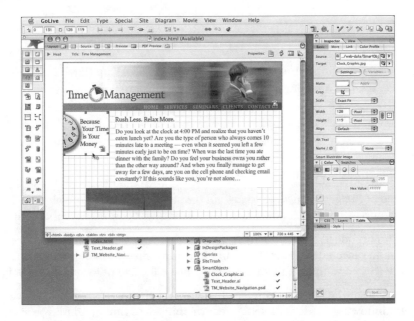

FIGURE 2.15
Laying out items on a Web page in GoLive.

The final part of the Web publishing process involves uploading your Web site to a server—a process called taking your site "live." GoLive has a full range of site management features (see Figure 2.16) that make it easy to track changes across your entire site, as well as manage updates and modifications. Basically, GoLive knows exactly what needs to be uploaded when you modify your Web site and can do so at the click of a button. GoLive also makes it easy to administer a site so that you can have several people contributing or updating different parts of your site simultaneously.

FIGURE 2.16
GoLive's Site window helps you manage your Web site.

It's important to realize that some Web design firms break up these three processes into completely different departments. Site designs are done by information architects, Web designers create the look of the site, and Web developers oversee the technical aspects of coding and maintaining the site. GoLive can handle all of these tasks if you're a department of one, but if you are part of a team, you can focus on just the part of GoLive that you need. Of course, GoLive has a whole range of features, some of which we'll mention here:

▶ One of the powerful ways to lay out graphics and text on a Web page is by using HTML tables, and GoLive has powerful yet easy-to-use table controls.

▶ With an added level of integration, GoLive's Smart Object feature allows you to place native Photoshop and Illustrator files into your layout and allows you to update them easily (just like Edit Original works in InDesign).

▶ For those who still feel compelled to write their own HTML code, GoLive has an innovative code completion feature that saves time (and maybe even helps combat carpal tunnel syndrome).

▶ For those publications published simultaneously to print and the Web, GoLive can use content directly from InDesign with the innovative *Package for GoLive* feature.

▶ Never guess at how your Web page will look. GoLive offers both HTML and PDF Preview modes, giving you real-time feedback as you design.

▶ For items that are used repeatedly throughout a Web site (such as a navigation interface, headers, footers, or legal blurbs), GoLive can store these in a single location as something called a Component. Update a Component and it gets updated wherever it appears throughout the entire site.

▶ GoLive has full FTP (File Transfer Protocol) capabilities, allowing you to upload your site directly to your Web server.

▶ A Web site has many components, such as HTML pages, scripts, and linked graphics. GoLive allows you to keep track of all of these in a single Site window.

▶ Using a feature called Co-Author, you can set up administration rights and have other people perform updates to the Web site.

Now that you have a better understanding of what GoLive can do, let's discuss when you should use it.

When to Use GoLive

GoLive is perfect for various tasks, including the following:

▶ When planning your Web site, you can use GoLive's Site Design tools to plan how each page of your site will link to the others. GoLive maintains dynamic links between the pages you create, so you can easily move elements around to adjust how your Web site will flow. GoLive can also automatically convert a site design into a full site after everything is approved and ready to go.

▶ Web site management is an extremely important part of maintaining a Web site. GoLive does this exceptionally well by keeping track of links. For example, say you change the name of a Web page. Any link that may already link to that page needs to be updated with the new name. GoLive automatically updates these links for you (free of charge, I might add).

▶ As alluded to earlier, GoLive excels at giving the designer the ability to lay out Web pages, allowing for the placement of native Photoshop, ImageReady, and Illustrator files. This makes it possible to take your Web designs that you created in those other programs and implement them quickly in GoLive.

▶ Although you can use Photoshop, ImageReady, and Illustrator to create high-impact designs for the Web, you can use GoLive alone to create more straightforward and simple Web designs. This is helpful for creating quick sites for internal purposes or for Web sites where getting a specific look isn't a requirement.

▶ Have a Web site already? GoLive can create new Web sites from scratch (or a site design), or it can import a Web site that already exists, allowing you to take advantage of GoLive's site management features.

▶ For those who still like to write their own HTML code, GoLive can serve that purpose as well. With features such as code completion and HTML preview to see how your code looks, GoLive is a great tool not only for HTML coding but for writing scripts as well.

▶ GoLive has a full complement of tools for creating forms, including adding value fields, pop-up lists, submit buttons, and more, making it a snap to create feedback forms, order forms, and the like.

▶ Even if you aren't creating Web sites, you can use GoLive as an FTP client to perform file transfers and downloads. Many printers these days maintain FTP sites where users can upload jobs or corrections to files instantly, and if needed, GoLive can perform these file transfers.

If you've never been involved with Web design before, it may take some getting used to, but overall, the concepts are similar to those you've seen in the print world. Of course, just because GoLive can export PDF files and works with XML, that doesn't mean you should use it to design your next print brochure. A specialized tool for all that the Web brings to the table, GoLive will fit your needs today and for the future as well.

Adobe Acrobat 6.0 Professional

Adobe Acrobat doesn't have the same CS moniker as the other applications in the Suite, mainly due to the fact that it was released several months before the Suite was released.

Where Acrobat Came From

In an effort to be able to view a document—as it was carefully designed—on just about any computer in the world, John Warnock and the folks at Adobe came up with the *Portable Document Format* (PDF). Acrobat would be the name of the product that could display these PDF files, which would look right, fonts and all, on any computer. Adobe created a version of Acrobat called Acrobat Reader, which it gave away free of charge. You still needed the full version of Acrobat to *create* PDF files (a process called *distilling*), so the company made money selling the full version of Acrobat—and people who created these documents were assured that anyone could view those documents with the free reader. Nice concept, eh?

What Acrobat Does

Chances are that you've seen a PDF file before. Of course, the initial benefit of working with PDF files is that you're safe knowing that what you are creating on your screen will look right on someone else's computer. There are many other benefits, such as the capability to password-protect your PDF file so that only the people who are supposed to see it are able to. Adobe Acrobat 6.0 Professional basically enables you to take control of your PDF files.

Let's start from the beginning. Acrobat allows you to create PDF files in any of several ways:

► You can print your file from any application to an "Acrobat Printer," which was installed when you installed Acrobat.

► You can use the Distiller part of Acrobat (it's a separate application that comes with Acrobat) to create PDF files from any PostScript file.

► You can open a PDF file in Acrobat Pro and export it as a PDF (you would do this if you wanted to save the PDF with different settings than it already had).

Of course, you can also export or save PDF files directly from any of the other applications in the Adobe Suite.

After you have a PDF file, there are many things Acrobat can do with it. What's interesting to note is that many people aren't aware of even half of the things Adobe Acrobat can do. Most people use it like the free Adobe Reader—to view and print PDF files.

But let's explore how we use PDF files today and see how we can use tools like Acrobat Pro to make our lives easier (I'm sure you've heard *that* one before...). You create a PDF to send to a client or a co-worker for approval. Inevitably, there will be corrections, comments, changes, and such, and so the one reviewing the document prints out the file, makes some comments, and faxes it or hand-delivers it back to you. Or the person might send you an email describing the desired changes. This process might repeat itself several times before the job is ready to go. But who are we kidding here? If your job is anything like mine, at least 5—maybe even 10—people need to review that document. The next thing you know, you have e-mails and faxes out the wazoo and you can't even keep track of who said what.

Acrobat has a set of commenting and reviewing tools that allow users to make comments directly in the PDF file (see Figure 2.17). For example, you can highlight or strikethrough text, add sticky notes, draw arrows, and add scribbles, as well as add dynamic "stamps" such as "APPROVED" or "REJECTED," with time and date stamps that note exactly when the file was approved or rejected. The client simply indicates changes in the PDF and sends the file back to you. What's better is that Acrobat will let you merge the comments of several files into a single file. So if your document is being reviewed by 10 people, you can look at a single PDF file that has comments from everyone. Each comment is identified by who created it and when it was created (see Figure 2.18). You can even print out a summary of all the comments in a specific PDF—great for billing purposes.

FIGURE 2.17
Acrobat's annotation toolbar.

FIGURE 2.18
Comments are identified by who made them and when.

By the Way

Comments are stored in a separate "layer" on a PDF file, called Annotations. This not only keeps the original data intact, but also allows you to save the comments into a separate file (called an FDF file). This is extremely useful when dealing with large PDF files. For example, say I send a 10MB PDF file of a catalog to a client for comments. The client can make comments and then send back just the FDF file (see Figure 2.19), saving the time it would take to keep sending that 10MB file back and forth over e-mail.

FIGURE 2.19
The icon of an Acrobat PDF file and that of an FDF file.

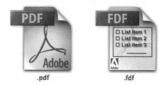

Commenting and reviewing are just a sample of the many features you'll find in Adobe Acrobat 6.0 Professional. Here's a partial list of the tools and features you'll soon find yourself using in Acrobat Pro:

▶ Acrobat has a fantastic feature that allows you to kick off a review process via e-mail that automatically tracks comments and makes it easier for people who prefer to do things via e-mail.

▶ With a full-featured Print dialog, Acrobat can print any PDF file (with correct authorization), including creating color separations for prepress.

▶ Acrobat Pro has a Preflight tool that helps ensure that your PDF file is ready for print, and that highlights the problematic areas based on preset criteria.

▶ For electronic forms and to indicate approvals, Acrobat has the capability to add digital signatures to a file.

▶ You can export PDF files to conform with any of several PDF standards, such as PDF/X-1a and PDF/X-3.

▶ Acrobat contains *touch-up* editing tools that allow you to modify text and perform certain edits to PDF files.

▶ For creating eForms, Acrobat has the capability to create form fields, buttons, and more.

▶ Acrobat has the capability to link or even embed interactive content into your PDF files, such as QuickTime movies and Flash (SWF) files.

▶ A Search tool allows you to quickly find the text you're looking for throughout an entire PDF file.

▶ Acrobat can encrypt files with passwords that allow you to control whether the document can be printed or changed. You can even use a process called Certification that allows you to specify even higher levels of security.

Now that you have a better understanding of what Acrobat Professional can do, let's discuss when you should use it.

When to Use Acrobat

Acrobat is perfect for various tasks, including the following:

▶ Acrobat is used for the viewing of PDF files (of course!).

▶ Acrobat is the best tool for creating or resaving PDF files for various purposes, such as for PDF/X-1a or PDF/X-3 compliance, or for Web-optimized viewing.

▶ With the capability to select and edit text as well as art elements, Acrobat is a great tool for making small edits or for "touching up" PDF files.

▶ As we mentioned earlier, Acrobat is just the tool you need for commenting and reviewing, getting approvals, and more. The e-mail–based review process makes it easier than ever to get people involved in the process as well.

▶ How can you be sure that your PDF files are ready to print? You can create your own Preflight profiles and check each PDF, as well as use Acrobat's onscreen Separation Preview feature to ensure that your color separations are correct. Of course, you can (and should) use Acrobat to print all of your PDF files.

▶ As eForms become more and more popular, you can use Acrobat to fill out PDF-based forms. Not only is Acrobat a great way to work with internal forms in your company (job tickets, for example), but you also can use Acrobat to fill out forms online, such as tax and insurance forms.

▶ Use Acrobat to digitally sign documents or authorize PDFs by certifying them. In the United States, laws have been passed to allow such signatures to be legally binding, enabling people to digitally sign mortgage documents, contracts, tax forms, and more.

▶ Protect your files by assigning passwords to limit how your PDF files can be used. Different levels of security allow for either printing the file only as a low-resolution proof, or not allowing printing or copying at all.

Chances are that you're probably a bit surprised (if not overwhelmed) at just how much Acrobat Pro can do. Don't worry, we'll go into a lot more detail about each of these features in Chapter 10, "Using Adobe Acrobat 6.0 Professional." Although Acrobat can perform certain edits to PDF files, if you have more complex editing to do, you'll want to make those changes in the application the file was originally created in, if at all possible. As a last resort, you can always open a PDF in Adobe Illustrator CS (one page at a time).

Adobe Version Cue

Adobe Version Cue is new (it's at version 1.0). It was released specifically—and only—as a part of the Adobe Creative Suite (it is not currently available as a standalone product).

Where Version Cue Came From

As designers generated more and more files, as workflows became more complex, and as design departments collaborated with each other on more projects, Adobe realized that it was increasingly important to not only keep track of files, but also track versions of files. This technology first appeared as the Adobe Workgroup Server that was included free with GoLive 6.0. Adobe Version Cue builds on that by adding integrated support across more Adobe applications and by adding better functionality.

What Version Cue Does

Basically, Version Cue is a scaled-down asset management system. If you're wondering what that means, think about each element in your project as an asset, for example, your Photoshop, Illustrator, and InDesign files. Version Cue helps you manage and keep track of all these files.

How many times has this happened to you? You create a design for a client or a creative director (I'm not sure which one is worse) and they want a change made. So you make the change and they want yet another change. This happens several times, and then they say, "You know, I think I liked one of the first ones you showed me better." If you were smart, you saved a separate version of your file each time you made a change (otherwise, good luck). But you are then tasked with trying to figure out where that version is, what you named the file, and so on. Chances are that you spend your lunch break at your desk looking for the right file.

Version Cue is a database that allows you to save versions of files along with descriptive information that you can add to that version of the file (such as a description of what changes were made and why). The difference is that all of these versions are saved transparently in the database—so you're always working on the same file. At any time, you can go back to a previous version of your file and make that the current version (see Figure 2.20). Think of it as Undo on steroids, in a way. Because the descriptive information that is saved in each version (called metadata) is accessible within Version Cue, you can you easily search for just the right version or file. Version Cue will also display thumbnails of the versions, so you can visually choose the correct one as well.

Version Cue can also keep track of who is working on a file. In design departments where several people might be working on the same overall project, it's possible to copy files from a server without knowing that someone else may be updating the file. Version Cue allows you to check in and check out files, meaning that if one designer is working on a file, another can't make edits until the first one is done. Users are also able to see who is working on that file (see Figure 2.21).

FIGURE 2.20
Viewing the version
history of a file.

FIGURE 2.21
Seeing who is
using a file. In this
example, one file is
shown as "in use
by me."

What makes Version Cue so different and refreshing is how it's integrated into the
Adobe Creative Suite—so well, in fact, that you hardly notice it's there. To open a
file from a Version Cue project, you choose File, Open from any of the applications in the Creative Suite. You don't have to learn anything new at all (see
Figure 2.22).

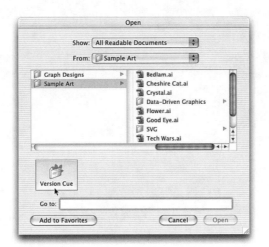

FIGURE 2.22
Accessing Version
Cue from the Open
dialog box in
Illustrator.

When to Use Version Cue

Version Cue can be installed on a server or it can be installed on a local machine. In either case, it's specifically geared toward individuals or groups of 10 to 20 people. If you're working on a project that consists of only one or two files, it may not pay to turn it into a Version Cue project, but if you're working on a project that contains several elements and has an assortment of photos, illustrations, logos, or more, it certainly makes sense to take advantage of what Version Cue has to offer.

We'll discuss how to set up a Version Cue project and how to use it to your advantage in Chapter 11, "Using Version Cue."

Bringing It All Together

You should now have a clear understanding of what each of the individual applications in the Creative Suite does. In our next chapter, we'll discuss how all of these programs work together to help you complete projects (and spend your weekends at home instead of at the office).

CHAPTER 3

The Game Plan: Developing a Workflow

If you can't describe what you are doing as a process, you don't know what you're doing.

W. Edwards Deming

What Is a Workflow?

A workflow is a process of how something gets done. It's a map that gets you from point A to point B. In other words, it's the roadmap for a project. In most cases, there are several ways to get to where you're going. Some ways might have more traffic, others nice scenery—but they all basically get you to your destination. In the business world, though, you want to get to your destination in the shortest amount of time, using the least amount of gas, and having a bit of fun at the same time— which makes your job rewarding, successful, and, most important, profitable.

In graphic design, a workflow comprises all the necessary steps that have to happen for a particular job to be completed. Obviously, whatever your final result is supposed to be is going to determine what the workflow is. If you're designing a piece that will be output to the Web, it's going to a have a different workflow, or process, than a project that will end up on a printing press.

Right off the bat, it's important to realize that every workflow is different—mostly, of course, because every project has different goals, but also because there is usually more than just one way to accomplish a task. Workflows are also affected by factors you might not necessarily think about. For example, if you're a designer who is putting together a newspaper, you might be incorporating some photographs into your layout that came from prints from your local photographer. Another paper might have overseas photographers who need to submit their images digitally.

More so, there are organizations or design firms that handle nearly all the aspects of a project, and there are designers who may work on only one portion of a project. Some firms offer services from concept all the way through design. Some people are just photographers. Even so, photographers who understand the entire workflow not only can provide better services to their clients, but also can be more efficient and avoid having to redo work later in the process.

Traditionally, one was required to possess and learn several software tools, each one working differently. A tremendous amount of work was required to make sure that all of these tools worked together in some useful way. And maintaining them was challenging (to say the least), because each of the tools had different upgrade cycles, causing constant workflow changes.

What is unique about the Adobe Creative Suite is that it provides all the tools necessary for a design workflow. Because of the integration between the applications in the Suite, it's easy to move your project along each step of the process. And because these applications all work in the same way, you don't have to tear your hair out learning about all kinds of programs to get your work done. Most important, Adobe has aligned each of the products in the Suite to release at the same time, making it easier to develop a workflow and maintain it.

By the Way

The workflows you'll find here are guidelines to give you a better idea of how the applications work together, and what the process might be for different kinds of projects. They will work in a majority of cases; however, specialized tasks or functions might require a modified workflow. By all means, feel free to customize and expand on the workflows mentioned here to achieve just the workflow required for your particular needs.

As you read through the rest of this chapter, you may feel the urge to skip particular areas because they don't pertain to the kinds of things you are doing today. For example, you may skip anything related to the Web because you work primarily in print-related materials. My advice (if you're willing to take it) is to at least get a basic understanding of other workflows because you never know what might come your way. This way, if you end up getting an opportunity to do such work—even if you're going to outsource it—you'll have a complete understanding of the process and what needs to happen. If I had a nickel for every time I've heard someone say, "I lost so much money because I told them I could do it, but I had no idea how much work was involved...," I'd have enough money for one of those speedy G5 computers (and an iPod, of course).

Understanding Print, the Web, and Beyond

In the 1980s, computer technology redefined print publishing. In the 1990s, the Internet and the World Wide Web took center stage as a powerful medium for communication. As we begin to settle into this new millennium, wireless technologies are pushing design and communication even further.

By the Way

Another workflow that is becoming more common as bandwidth increases is creating content for video. Adobe has a separate Video Collection of tools which can be used to create this content. The good news is that these tools, including Premiere Pro (video editing), After Effects (special effects and compositing), Encore DVD (DVD authoring), and Audition (sound editing) are all applications that integrate with the apps you now have in the Adobe Creative Suite (mainly Photoshop and Illustrator). Should the day come when you need to dive into the world of video, you'll already have some of the tools—and the knowledge—to get you started.

As we look at the workflows specific to these different media, I'm going to focus primarily on the aspects that involve working with the Creative Suite directly. Obviously, many different things need to happen in order to communicate your (or your client's) message. For example, concepts are discussed, copy is written, sketches are drawn, and meetings with the client are endured (oh, the agony)— all before you even start working on the project. This book, however, focuses mainly on the technical aspects of doing your job, not necessarily the conceptual ones. I'm going to make the assumption here that the initial concept is done and that you have copy written.

Designing for Print

Say what you want about the future of print, but find me another medium that can provide a designer with the prospect of using an exquisite paper with embossing, foil stamping, custom die-cutting, varnishing, or various other effects that pulls a reader in and delivers a message all its own. I've seen art directors who sometimes spend days picking out just the right paper for an Annual Report. Use of custom inks such as metallics, pastels, or even magnetic inks (like what's used for account numbers on bank checks) takes print a step further.

That being said, when you are designing for print, you have to be mindful of such things as image resolution, custom spot colors, transparency flattening, bleed and trim areas, folds, fonts, and color separations. Some jobs also require knowledge of government or postal regulations. Following are three workflows that are common in the area of print design.

Corporate Identity

Corporate Identity includes the creation of a logo and other materials used to identify a company or an organization. Examples are business cards, letterheads, envelopes, notes, and the like. Most corporate identity projects also focus on the branding and positioning of the company. Common applications used in this workflow are Photoshop, Illustrator, and InDesign (see Figure 3.1 shown on pages 54-55).

Brochure

A brochure is used as an informational and marketing tool for businesses and organizations. The simplest type of brochure is printed on a letter-sized page and folded into three panels (commonly referred to as a tri-fold). Common applications used in this workflow are Photoshop, Illustrator, and InDesign. Microsoft Word (or any other word processor) is also commonly used (see Figure 3.2 shown on pages 56-57).

Advertising Campaign

An advertising campaign is an organized effort to publicize a company or an organization. Integrated campaigns often feature a series of ads that share a similar concept, and may include print advertising, direct mail, or other methods of distribution. Common applications used in this workflow are Photoshop, Illustrator, and InDesign. Acrobat may also be used for campaign reviews (see Figure 3.3 shown on pages 58-59).

Designing for the Web

There are two approaches to Web design: create something the same way you would for print, but adapt it to work on the Web; and create a true interactive experience from the ground up. In the early days of the Web, most sites you went to were of the former kind—page after page of large static images, garish colors, and illegible text. Granted, two main reasons for that were a lack of powerful Web authoring tools and a general lack of understanding of the technical capabilities of the medium.

By the Way

I should note that today's dynamic design environment has also caused a reverse of this effect. There are many designers who specialize in Web design but have almost no knowledge of what it takes to create a quality printed piece. Those who have tried going to press with a 72dpi RGB image know what I'm talking about.

A good Web designer will be thinking about what size monitor he expects users to have, how best to build a page that can be updated quickly and easily, how to add interactive elements to draw a reader's attention, how to provide useful navigation and links to help readers find what they're looking for, and, most important, how to communicate all of it with a design concept that delivers the right message. Some jobs may also require knowledge or interfacing with back-end systems and databases. Following are three workflows that are common in the area of Web design.

Web Banner

A Web banner is an advertisement that appears on a Web site. Ever since the Internet became a place that people frequent, companies and organizations have found the Web to be an effective medium to advertise their products and services. Most Web banners have to conform to specific sizes and formats. Common applications used in the creation of Web banners are Photoshop, Illustrator, and ImageReady (see Figure 3.4 shown on pages 60-61).

Web Navigation

When you visit a Web site, there are often buttons you can click on that will take you to other pages in the site. A collection of buttons is called Web navigation, and is nearly an art form in itself. Good Web navigation can help viewers find what they need on a Web site, but bad navigation can frustrate viewers and send them elsewhere. Common applications used in the creation of Web Navigation are Photoshop, Illustrator, and ImageReady (see Figure 3.5 shown on pages 62-63).

Web Site

What started out as a "fad" in many people's eyes has become a way of life today. Web sites are used to sell products, provide information, display family pictures, and present just about anything else you might want to share with other people around the globe. Common applications used in the creation of Web sites are Photoshop, Illustrator, ImageReady, and GoLive (see Figure 3.6 shown on pages 64-65).

Designing for Both Print and the Web

Most people say that print and the Web don't mix. They may be right, but it doesn't mean that print and the Web can't coexist together peacefully. By carefully planning a workflow, you can save significant time developing content that will be published both in print form and electronically on the Web.

Obviously, the goal is to create content once and then share that content between the Web and print elements you are producing. In this way, you avoid having to create and manage two sets of identical content (one for print, one for the Web), and more importantly—if changes need to be made (show me one job where they don't), you only have to change one set of assets instead of two. Save time, make more money, go home early. Nice, eh? Following are two workflows that are common in the area of cross-media (or mixed-media) design.

Print/Online Newsletter

Companies often create newsletters to distribute news to all the employees of the organization. With the advent of the "I need it now" mentality in today's fast-paced world, companies offer online versions of these publications as well. Cross-media (Web and print) workflows are quickly becoming the norm in today's business environment. Common applications used in a cross-media workflow are Photoshop, Illustrator, InDesign, and GoLive (see Figure 3.7 shown on pages 66-67).

Interactive PDF

In a relatively short period, PDF has become a standard in the industry for distributing published information. Lately, capabilities have been built into the PDF format to support interactive content. Businesses and organizations can now deliver rich media content—including hyperlinks, interactivity, and movies—in a single file that nearly everyone can view. Common applications used to create interactive PDF files are Photoshop, Illustrator, InDesign, and Acrobat (see Figure 3.8 shown on pages 68-69).

Moving to a PDF Workflow

Undoubtedly you've seen both Acrobat and PDF appear quite often on the workflows listed here. In fact, one of the biggest benefits of using the Adobe Creative

Suite is that you can take full advantage of PDF—mainly because support for PDF is built into the Creative Suite at almost every level. From PDF creation and placing PDF files into your layouts to opening PDF files and using PDF as a final delivery format, the Creative Suite assures that it all works and fits seamlessly into your workflow.

Think about it. In the past, client reviews consisted of expensive color comps, unclear faxes, low-resolution JPEG images, and forgotten phone conversations. Today, e-mail–based PDF reviews make for an experience that's welcome to clients, because they can review materials faster than ever before, as well as to designers, who can save money and track issues and make changes more efficiently than ever.

This isn't to say that moving to a complete PDF workflow is easy. There are still issues that have to be dealt with, including color management issues (making sure that what you see on *your* screen is the same as what the client sees on *his* screen), software compatibilities (making sure that clients are using the right version of Acrobat), and more.

Switching to PDF overnight probably won't happen, but one thing is sure: After you establish a workflow and get comfortable with using the Adobe Creative Suite, you'll be able to help yourself and your clients by taking advantage of PDF where you can. Before you know it, you'll have more PDF files in your inbox than promises of $10,000 a month for working from home (okay, maybe that isn't possible…).

Putting It All in Perspective

So many tasks can be done in any of several programs. People are always asking when Photoshop and Illustrator will combine to become one program, or when Illustrator will support multiple pages (making for less of a need for InDesign). Now that the Creative Suite is out there, it should be obvious that each tool is necessary for certain tasks. No one tool can do it all—nor should it. An arsenal of integrated tools such as the Creative Suite offers far more power and options than any single application ever could.

In the next chapter, we'll talk about integration and how all the Suite applications work together as one complete graphics solution.

FIGURE 3.1
An example of a
corporate identity
workflow.

Workflow: Corporate Identity

Adobe Illustrator
The logo for Time Management was
created in Adobe Illustrator and saved
as a native file (.AI), making it simple to
adapt the logo for just about any use.

Adobe Photoshop
The photograph was chosen and edited
in Adobe Photoshop and saved as a native
file (.PSD), giving the designer creative
freedom with the photo.

Adobe InDesign
The letterhead, envelope and business cards were assembled
in 3 separate documents inside InDesign. The photo (.PSD)
and the logo (.AI) were placed into the layouts, and additional text
was then added to complete the design.

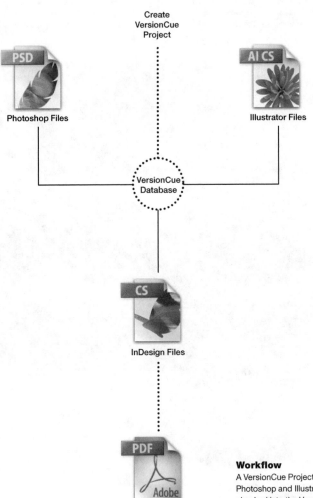

Workflow

A VersionCue Project is created and Photoshop and Illustrator files are checked into the VersionCue database. The native .PSD and .AI files are then placed into an InDesign Document and positioned on the page. Other design elements, including text, are added inside InDesign. A PDF is then created and sent for client approval or to the printer for final output.

FIGURE 3.2
An example of a
brochure workflow.

Workflow: Brochure

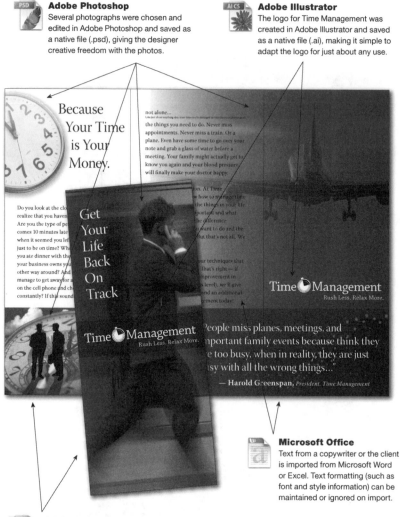

Adobe Photoshop
Several photographs were chosen and edited in Adobe Photoshop and saved as a native file (.psd), giving the designer creative freedom with the photos.

Adobe Illustrator
The logo for Time Management was created in Adobe Illustrator and saved as a native file (.ai), making it simple to adapt the logo for just about any use.

Microsoft Office
Text from a copywriter or the client is imported from Microsoft Word or Excel. Text formatting (such as font and style information) can be maintained or ignored on import.

Adobe InDesign
The brochure was laid out and assembled in a single document inside InDesign. Fold and trim marks help a printer prepare the final printed piece correctly. The photos (.psd) and artwork (.ai) were placed into the layouts, and additional text was then imported from Microsoft Word and styled to complete the design.

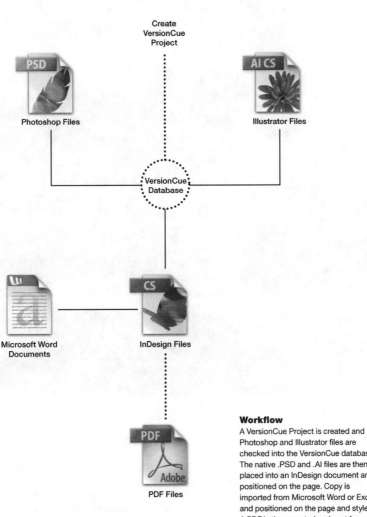

Workflow

A VersionCue Project is created and Photoshop and Illustrator files are checked into the VersionCue database. The native .PSD and .AI files are then placed into an InDesign document and positioned on the page. Copy is imported from Microsoft Word or Excel and positioned on the page and styled. A PDF is then created and sent for client approval or to the printer for final output.

FIGURE 3.3
An example of an
ad campaign work-
flow.

Workflow: Advertising Campaign

Adobe InDesign

The ads were assembled in a single InDesign document, where the designer can specify trim sizes as well as a slug area — a place to include specific job and client information in an area that won't print. The photos (.PSD) were placed into the layout and cropped, copy was added and the logo (.AI) was dropped in place.

Adobe Photoshop

This ad campaign relies on the powerful photos that were carefully chosen. The Photoshop File Browser helps designers and photographers choose the perfect photo for the job.

Adobe Illustrator

The logo for Time Management was created in Adobe Illustrator and saved as a native file (.AI), making it simple to adapt the logo for just about any use.

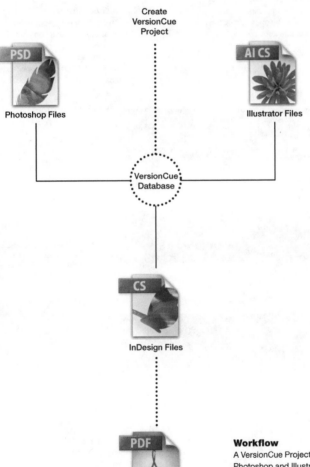

Standard Workflow
Optional Workflow

Create
VersionCue
Project

Photoshop Files

Illustrator Files

VersionCue
Database

InDesign Files

PDF Files

Workflow

A VersionCue Project is created and Photoshop and Illustrator files are checked into the VersionCue database. The native .PSD and .AI files are then placed into an InDesign Document and positioned on the page. Other design elements, including text, are added inside InDesign. A PDFX-1a file is then created (a PDF standard now adopted by many magazines and newspapers) and sent for client approval or to the publisher.

FIGURE 3.4
An example of a Web banner work-flow.

Workflow: Web Banner

 Adobe Photoshop
Stock photography was chosen and edited in Adobe Photoshop. Photoshop files (.PSD) can then be opened or placed into Illustrator or ImageReady (Photoshop contains a "Jump To" button to move files between the two applications).

 Adobe Illustrator
The ad banner was designed in Illustrator, allowing elements of the design to be repurposed for print projects easily. The file was exported as a layered .PSD file and opened in ImageReady.

 Adobe ImageReady
Once the design is created in Photoshop and Illustrator, the art is brought into ImageReady to add interactivity elements like rollovers and animation. The image is also sliced up and optimized for Web-ready graphics.

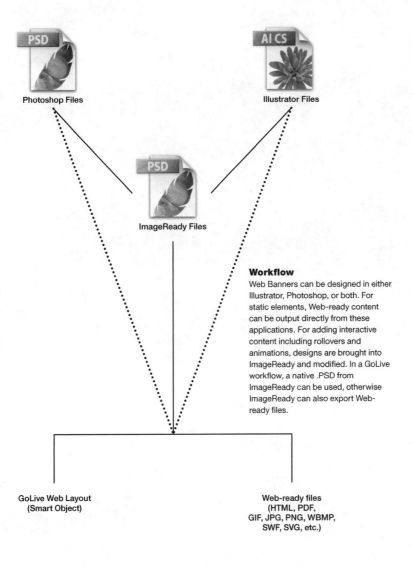

Standard Workflow
Optional Workflow

PSD

Photoshop Files

AI CS

Illustrator Files

PSD

ImageReady Files

Workflow

Web Banners can be designed in either Illustrator, Photoshop, or both. For static elements, Web-ready content can be output directly from these applications. For adding interactive content including rollovers and animations, designs are brought into ImageReady and modified. In a GoLive workflow, a native .PSD from ImageReady can be used, otherwise ImageReady can also export Web-ready files.

GoLive Web Layout
(Smart Object)

Web-ready files
(HTML, PDF,
GIF, JPG, PNG, WBMP,
SWF, SVG, etc.)

FIGURE 3.5
An example of a
Web navigation
workflow.

Workflow: Web Navigation

 Adobe Photoshop
Stock photography was chosen and
edited in Adobe Photoshop to get the look
the designer wanted. Photoshop files (.PSD)
can then be opened or placed into Illustrator
or ImageReady (Photoshop contains a "Jump
To" button to move files between the two
applications).

Adobe Illustrator
The navigation bar was designed in
Illustrator, allowing elements of the
design to be repurposed for print
projects easily. The file was exported as
a layered .PSD file and opened in
ImageReady.

 Adobe ImageReady
Once the design is created in Photoshop and
Illustrator, the art is brought into ImageReady
to add interactivity elements like rollovers
and animation. The image is also sliced up
and optimized for Web-ready graphics.

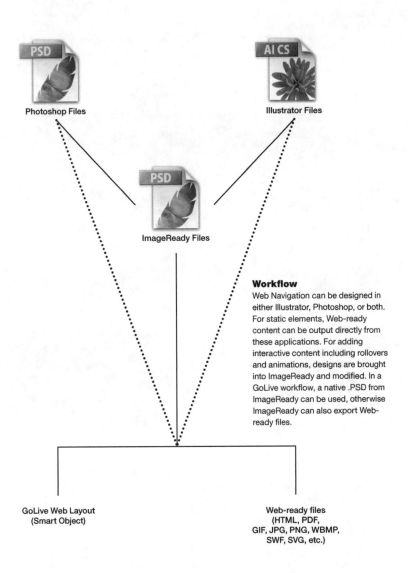

Workflow

Web Navigation can be designed in either Illustrator, Photoshop, or both. For static elements, Web-ready content can be output directly from these applications. For adding interactive content including rollovers and animations, designs are brought into ImageReady and modified. In a GoLive workflow, a native .PSD from ImageReady can be used, otherwise ImageReady can also export Web-ready files.

FIGURE 3.6
An example of a
Web site workflow.

Workflow: Website

 Adobe Illustrator
The logo for Time Management as well
as some text elements for the site were
created in Adobe Illustrator and saved
as native files (.ai). The initial concept for
the site design was also created using
Illustrator and Photoshop.

 Adobe ImageReady
Once the design is created in Photoshop and
Illustrator, the art is brought into ImageReady
to add interactivity elements like rollovers in
the navigation bar and animation in the ad at
the bottom of the page.

 Adobe GoLive
The website was laid out and assembled in GoLive.
Pages and links were set up and then native Illustrator
(.AI), Photoshop (.PSD) and ImageReady (.PSD) were
added using GoLive's Smart Object support. Certain
items, such as the navigation bar, were added as
components, making it easy to manage the same
content across mutliple pages on the site. GoLive also
handled the website management including uploading
the site to the server and checking all of the links.

 Adobe Photoshop
Stock photography was chosen and
edited in Adobe Photoshop to get the look
the designer wanted. Some elements were
then placed directly into the web layout or
sent to ImageReady for further editing.
Photoshop was also used, along with
Illustrator, to provide a comp (design idea) to
the client for approval.

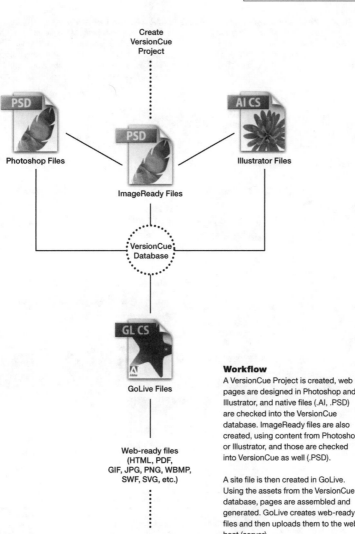

Workflow

A VersionCue Project is created, web pages are designed in Photoshop and Illustrator, and native files (.AI, .PSD) are checked into the VersionCue database. ImageReady files are also created, using content from Photoshop or Illustrator, and those are checked into VersionCue as well (.PSD).

A site file is then created in GoLive. Using the assets from the VersionCue database, pages are assembled and generated. GoLive creates web-ready files and then uploads them to the web host (server).

FIGURE 3.7
An example of a cross-media newsletter workflow.

Workflow: Print/Online Newsletter

 Adobe Photoshop
Several photographs were chosen and edited in Adobe Photoshop and saved as a native file (.psd), giving the designer creative freedom with the photos.

 Adobe Illustrator
The logo for Time Management as well as the masthead was created in Adobe Illustrator and saved as a native file (.ai), making it simple to adapt the logo for just about any use.

XML Content
Structured XML content can be used to move data between the print version and the web version of the newsletter. What that means to you is, make changes once, and see both places updated at once.

 Adobe InDesign
The newsletter is laid out and assembled in InDesign. The photos (.psd) and artwork (.ai) were placed into the layouts, and additional text was then placed from a structured XML file, allowing the text to be shared with GoLive.

 Adobe GoLive
The website was laid out and assembled in GoLive; pages and links were set up, and then native Illustrator (.AI), Photoshop (.PSD) and ImageReady (.PSD) file were added using GoLive's Smart Object support. Using InDesign's "Package for GoLive" feature, assets can be shared between the printed newsletter and the online version.

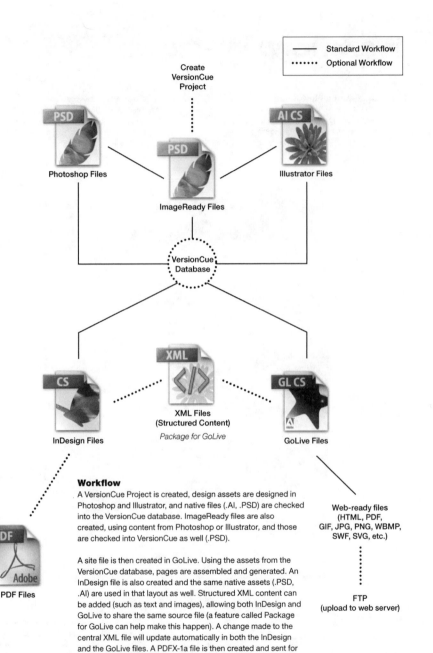

Standard Workflow

Optional Workflow

Create VersionCue Project

PSD — Photoshop Files

PSD — ImageReady Files

AI CS — Illustrator Files

VersionCue Database

CS — InDesign Files

XML — XML Files (Structured Content)
Package for GoLive

GL CS — GoLive Files

PDF Adobe — PDF Files

Web-ready files (HTML, PDF, GIF, JPG, PNG, WBMP, SWF, SVG, etc.)

FTP (upload to web server)

Workflow

A VersionCue Project is created, design assets are designed in Photoshop and Illustrator, and native files (.AI, .PSD) are checked into the VersionCue database. ImageReady files are also created, using content from Photoshop or Illustrator, and those are checked into VersionCue as well (.PSD).

A site file is then created in GoLive. Using the assets from the VersionCue database, pages are assembled and generated. An InDesign file is also created and the same native assets (.PSD, .AI) are used in that layout as well. Structured XML content can be added (such as text and images), allowing both InDesign and GoLive to share the same source file (a feature called Package for GoLive can help make this happen). A change made to the central XML file will update automatically in both the InDesign and the GoLive files. A PDFX-1a file is then created and sent for client approval or to the publisher from InDesign. GoLive creates web-ready files and then uploads them to the web host (server).

FIGURE 3.8
An example of an
interactive PDF
workflow.

Workflow: Interactive PDF

Adobe Photoshop
Several photographs were chosen and
edited in Adobe Photoshop and saved as
a native file (.psd), giving the designer
creative freedom with the photos.

Adobe Illustrator
The logo for Time Management was
created in Adobe Illustrator and saved
as a native file (.ai), making it simple to
adapt the logo for just about any use.

Adobe InDesign
The document was laid out and designed in InDesign,
pulling elements from Illustrator (.AI) and Photoshop (.PSD).
Using structured XML text files means that text will reflow
correctly even if the PDF is viewed on alternative devices
like PDAs and cellphones. InDesign can also add interactive
elements like buttons, rollovers and hyperlinks.

Movie Files
Place movie files directly into
InDesign and specify playback
settings. The PDF 1.5 format
supports the embedding of movie
files, so your movies play back when
viewed in Acrobat.

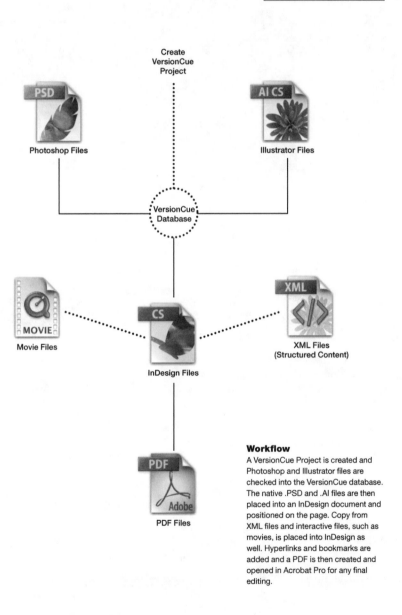

Workflow

A VersionCue Project is created and Photoshop and Illustrator files are checked into the VersionCue database. The native .PSD and .AI files are then placed into an InDesign document and positioned on the page. Copy from XML files and interactive files, such as movies, is placed into InDesign as well. Hyperlinks and bookmarks are added and a PDF is then created and opened in Acrobat Pro for any final editing.

CHAPTER 4

The Key That Makes It All Work: Integration

It is not a question of how well each process works, the question is how well they all work together.

Lloyd Dobens and Clare Crawford-Mason

Getting Started with the Suite

So you know what each application in the Suite is supposed to do. You also have a pretty good understanding of where each application fits in the workflow and when you would use each of them. Now we'll take a look at how the applications work and how they are used.

As you'll find out, many tasks and concepts apply to all the applications in the Suite. One thing that Adobe does extremely well is make its applications look and feel the same way. The different applications also play very well together. These combined aspects of the Creative Suite are referred to as integration. One of the main benefits of working with the Suite is this high level of integration, and we'll talk about many of these aspects in this chapter.

Before we get to the applications themselves, I want to spend a few moments talking about your computer setup. After all, it's what you'll be using to run the Creative Suite.

System Requirements for the Real World

Adobe puts a list of system requirements on the box, but those should be treated as an absolute bare minimum. What I list here are items that I feel are important for the needs of the graphic designer. Use this only as a guideline, of course—your budget most likely dictates what you have at your disposal.

▶ **Computer**—I'm not even going to touch the whole Mac versus Windows issue, because I believe that you should use whatever you're most comfortable with (my own personal preference is a Mac). What's important, though, is that you have a system that can handle whatever you have to throw at it. Hard drive space (storage memory) is always important because graphics files tend to be quite large. It would also be wise to have at least 1GB of RAM (working memory) on your machine because that will allow you to run several applications at the same time (rather than having to continually open and close them). If you're planning to use a digital video camera, you need to get a system with a FireWire (also called "IEEE 1394" or "iLink") port.

▶ **Monitor**—Your monitor is your workspace and can prove to be a very important factor as you design. Remember that as a user of the Creative Suite, you'll have several applications running at the same time, and Adobe's user interface is palette-happy (we'll talk more about palettes later in the chapter); so the more screen real estate you have, the better. From a design standpoint, there's really no difference between flat panel and CRT screens, although I'll admit I'm addicted to my 22-inch flat panel Apple Cinema Display.

▶ **Input Devices**—No doubt your computer came with a mouse and a keyboard, but depending on what kind of work you'll be doing, you might want to explore other options as well. Photoshop CS and Illustrator CS both have built-in support for pressure-sensitive tablets for such tasks as photo retouching, painting, and drawing. Trackballs offer a different feel than a mouse, and mice are available that offer a scroll wheel, several programmable buttons, and other features.

By the Way

Being comfortable with your input devices is essential if you make your living working on a computer. Ergonomic input devices are more than just hype—they can mean the difference between having fun at your job and having painful wrists, a sore neck or back, stressed eyes, headaches, and more. I'm not suggesting buying every product out there with the word "ergonomic" on the box, but doing some research (trying things out at stores, or at a friend's workspace) can prove to be very helpful. I've personally found that switching between a mouse and a pressure-sensitive pen every so often relieves the pressure on my wrists.

▶ **Internet Connection**—A DSL or cable connection is essential for many reasons. The Internet has much to offer today's designer. Stock photography sites allow you to quickly find just the images you're looking for and use them for comps and to download high-resolution versions instantly. User forums and Web sites offer a tremendous resource for tips, tricks, or even help. If you're the type who loves fonts, you can purchase just about anything your heart (or client) desires on-demand, and more. Most important, with a high-speed connection, you can easily download software updates and patches.

▶ **Scanner**—A scanner is important for several reasons. There will always be photo prints or logos you'll need to scan for design jobs. Many people also like to start their designs as sketches on paper (or napkins over a lunch meeting with the client) and may want to scan those in and work from there. Finally, I've found that a scanner can be very useful for experimenting with fabrics and materials for interesting backgrounds, or even from other sources (when it's legal to do so, of course—I'm not advocating copyright infringement). Some scanners require a FireWire connection; most also offer a (slower) USB connection.

▶ **Digital Camera**—A digital camera can do a lot more than just take pictures of the family. It's a great way to get quick concepts onto your screen. You can scout out scenery, take photos for comps to show clients and photographers—even take simple product shots. Just about any camera with at least 2 megapixels should work fine for these tasks.

▶ **Archiving**—After a job is done, you'll want to keep it somewhere that's easy to find and get to (a client will always ask for a small update to a job they did several months ago). I find that copying jobs to CDs or DVDs can be the easiest and cheapest, although there are plenty of other methods. Choose a system that you can be comfortable with and track easily. The reason I like the CD or DVD method is that most computers come with drives that can easily record these, the media is cheap enough, and the technology won't become obsolete anytime soon (remember SyQuest drives?).

▶ **Backup**—Nothing could possibly be worse than losing your data just when you need it the most. You've invested a lot into your work, and the only way to protect it is with a decent backup system. You'll find many different solutions out there (DAT, AIT, CD, DVD, and so on), and you should use whatever fits your budget and your work patterns.

▶ **Work Area**—Sometimes you have no control over where you'll be working— be it a cubicle in an office, a small desk tucked into the corner of your bedroom, a home office, or a decked-out design studio. But there are some things you should take into consideration. Bright sunlight can make it difficult to see your computer screen and can make colors look different on a sunny day than on a cloudy one. Desk space is also important. If you can, try to use as large a workspace as possible. Cramped work areas are the main cause for repetitive strain injuries (such as Carpal Tunnel Syndrome), to say nothing of making it harder to find that fax the client sent you yesterday (one of the reasons I fill my fax machine with yellow paper, by the way).

Enabling Version Cue

In the previous chapters we briefly discussed the role that Version Cue plays. Version Cue is a server that runs constantly in the background (on your computer, on someone else's computer, or on a dedicated server), allowing you to access project files from any of the Suite applications at any time.

You can configure Version Cue to automatically launch every time you start your computer (which is a good thing unless you don't plan on ever using Version Cue in your workflow). One thing to remember is that Version Cue likes memory—and lots of it. It requires a minimum of 128MB, but if you plan on using it to track all of your files (and why not?), you should bump that up to at least 256MB.

Turning On Version Cue for Macintosh

To activate Version Cue on a Mac, launch your System Preferences (you can find this either in the Dock or in the Apple menu). Click on the Adobe Version Cue icon (it will appear in the "Other" category of preferences; see Figure 4.1) and choose "On" from the pop-up list. If you plan to use Version Cue all the time, you can check the "Turn Version Cue On When the Computer Starts" option (see Figure 4.2). This will save you from having to turn on Version Cue manually every time you restart. Click on the Apply Now button to start up Version Cue, and when it has started, you can close System Preferences.

FIGURE 4.1
Version Cue in your System Preferences dialog.

FIGURE 4.2
Setting Version Cue to automatically load each time you start your Macintosh computer.

Turning On Version Cue for Windows

To activate Version Cue on Windows, choose Control Panel from the Start menu. Click on the Adobe Version Cue icon (see Figure 4.3) and choose "On" from the pop-up list. If you plan to use Version Cue all the time, you can check the "Turn Version Cue On When the Computer Starts" option (see Figure 4.4). This will save you from having to turn on Version Cue manually every time you restart. Click on the Apply button to start up Version Cue, and when it's done, you can close Control Panel.

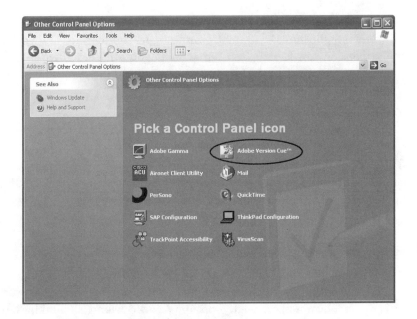

FIGURE 4.3
Version Cue in your Control Panel dialog.

FIGURE 4.4
Setting Version Cue
to automatically
load each time you
start your Windows
computer.

By the Way

> Don't worry about the rest of the settings in the Version Cue window—we'll discuss them in detail in Chapter 11, "Using Version Cue."

Launching the Applications

Even though all the applications in the Suite were installed at the same time, you still have to launch each one individually. In other words, if you need to do a task in Photoshop only, there's no need to launch the rest of the applications in the Suite.

You launch any of the Creative Suite applications the same way you launch just about any other application. You might want to create shortcuts (or aliases) for your applications on your desktop (on Windows XP you can place them in the Quicklaunch Toolbar), or on a Mac you might want to put the applications on your Dock so that you can find and launch them easily.

Did you Know?

> To create a shortcut in Windows, right-click the application's icon and choose Create Shortcut. On a Mac, drag the application's icon onto the Dock.

So what are we waiting for? Let's get started by examining some of the Creative Suite applications and learning about the similarities between them.

Integration: Defined

It's hard enough keeping track of all of my kid's names, let alone trying to remember how to check my spelling in all the applications I use to get my work done. So it's of great comfort for me to find that Check Spelling is found in the same place—the Edit menu—in all Adobe applications (see Figure 4.5). This is just a small example of what integration means, and as you begin to use Adobe's applications more and more, you'll appreciate these "little things" to no end.

FIGURE 4.5
The Check Spelling feature in Adobe InDesign CS.

The remainder of this chapter discusses many of the things that define integration as it pertains to the Creative Suite applications. By learning about the basic functionality in this way, you'll be able to comfortably walk your way through any of the individual Suite applications.

As we walk through the applications in this chapter, we're going to talk mainly about Illustrator, Photoshop and ImageReady, InDesign, and GoLive. Even though Acrobat 6 Professional is a part of the Creative Suite, it doesn't share the same interface as the other applications. Acrobat is also the only application in the Suite that isn't primarily an authoring application (meaning that it's not used to create files from scratch, but usually to work with PDF files that already exist). We'll cover Acrobat in detail in Chapter 10, "Using Adobe Acrobat 6.0 Professional."

Common User Interface

You bought this book (or "borrowed" it from your friend) because you wanted to learn how to use the Adobe Creative Suite. It would be a pain if you had to spend time learning how to use a photo editing program, only to realize that you have to learn a whole new way of using your computer for working in a page layout application. So it's of comfort to know that the applications in the Suite all share the same award-winning Adobe user interface.

In case you aren't familiar with the term, *user interface* describes how a person uses or interacts with software. Examples of these kinds of elements can range from buttons, palettes, and dialog boxes to tools and how they work.

In fact, the interfaces of the Suite applications are so alike, it's sometimes easy to forget which application you're using. Because so many things work the same way in all the individual applications, it's possible to focus on *doing* your work rather than trying to figure out *how* to do it.

The user interface really comprises many things, and we're going to discuss some of them here, including palettes, tools, and more.

Remember that although the Adobe Creative Suite promises untold integration among its parts, it's still a version 1.0 product (the Suite, not the individual components, of course). Each of the apps in the Suite (with the exception of Version Cue) has been around for some time, so there are still parts of the interface that are different between the applications. I imagine that with each release of the Suite over the years, the interface will become more and more consistent among the Suite applications.

Palettes

If you've ever used an Adobe application before, you know what a *palette* is. Certain functions and tools are always at your disposal, and these "float" on top of your document and are called floating palettes (see Figure 4.6). Palettes can be shown or hidden, and some palettes can expand or contract to show more or less information.

As you'll quickly find out, there are a lot of palettes in each application, and your entire screen can quickly get filled with palettes, leaving you with little or no space to view or work with your document. But don't worry, because there are plenty of ways to adjust palettes so that you can best take advantage of them.

Palettes share many similarities. The part where the name of the palette appears is called the palette tab. On the upper-right corner of the palette is a little triangle inside a circle. Clicking on it opens the *palette flyout menu* (see Figure 4.7), where you can choose from several additional options or functions. At the bottom of a palette is usually a row of palette buttons that provide more functionality.

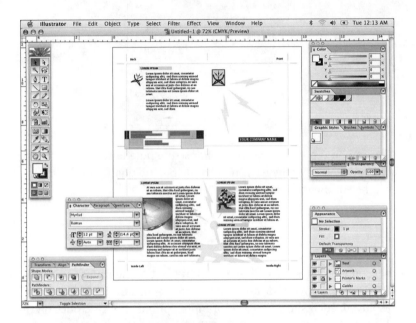

FIGURE 4.6
Floating palettes in Adobe Illustrator CS.

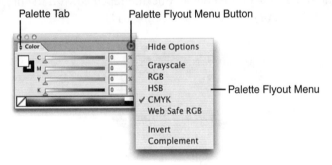

FIGURE 4.7
The Color palette in Adobe Illustrator CS.

You can move palettes around by grabbing their title bar, and you can resize some of them by grabbing the lower-right corner. You'll notice that palettes "snap" to each other and to the edges of your screen.

Showing/Hiding Palettes

The simplest way of working with palettes is showing and hiding them. You'll find all the palettes listed in the Window menu for any of the Suite applications. A check mark next to an item means the palette is open, or showing (see Figure 4.8).

FIGURE 4.8
A check mark indicates that the palette is already open on your screen.

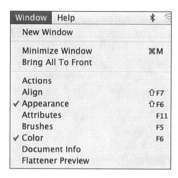

Double-clicking on a palette's tab will collapse the palette so that it takes up less space (see Figure 4.9). Whenever you need the palette again, double-clicking on the tab will reveal the contents of the palette again.

FIGURE 4.9
A collapsed palette.

Notice that some palettes have little arrows in front of the name in the tab (see Figure 4.10). Those arrows indicate that the palette has multiple *states* or ways it can be displayed, each showing fewer or more options. Clicking once on the arrows changes the state of the palette. Clicking repeatedly on the arrows cycles through all the states of the palette (see Figure 4.11).

FIGURE 4.10
You know that a palette has multiple states when you see the up and down arrows in the palette tab.

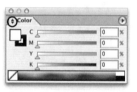

FIGURE 4.11
The three states of the Color palette.

By the Way

Press the Tab key to quickly clear your entire screen of palettes. Press Tab again to restore your palettes onscreen. If you press Shift+Tab, all of your palettes will become hidden except for your toolbox (which we'll cover in detail later in this chapter).

Clustering and Docking Palettes

Palettes can be manipulated, allowing you even more control over how they display (and take up space) on your screen. We discussed before how clicking and dragging on the title bar of the palette will let you move it around your screen, but if you grab your palette by the palette tab instead, you'll notice that when you drag it around, you'll get an outlined "ghost" of your palette (see Figure 4.12).

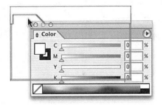

FIGURE 4.12
Dragging a palette from the palette tab gives you a ghost outline.

You can drag this ghost outline *into* another palette to create a *cluster* of palettes. Notice that as you drag the ghost into another open palette, that palette will get a thick black outline around it (see Figure 4.13). In a cluster of palettes, clicking once on the palette tab will bring that palette into focus. For example, if you have the Stroke, Gradient, and Transparency palettes in the same cluster, clicking on the Transparency palette tab will bring that palette to the front (see Figure 4.14). Of course, you can still access the different states of each palette as mentioned earlier. The benefit of creating a cluster of palettes is that you can have multiple palettes on your screen but have them take up the screen space of just one palette.

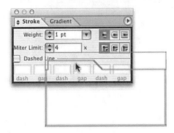

FIGURE 4.13
The black outline indicates that you're about to create a palette cluster.

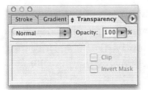

FIGURE 4.14
The Stroke, Gradient, and Transparency palettes clustered in Illustrator CS, with the Transparency palette in front.

If you drag the ghost outline of a palette to the very bottom of another palette, you'll notice that only the bottom of the receiving palette will get a black outline (see Figure 4.15). This indicates that you'll be *docking* the palettes instead of clustering them. Docking a palette attaches it to another so that they act as one palette (see Figure 4.16). Double-clicking on the palette tab of the upper palette will collapse all the docked palettes in one fell swoop. Some palettes allow you to use the keyboard to navigate through them. The Color palette is one such palette where you can enter CMYK values and tab between them. When you have palettes docked to each other, you can also tab between the palettes. So if I had the Stroke palette docked to my Color palette, I'd be able to tab through the CMYK values and then press tab again to edit the Stroke weight value.

FIGURE 4.15
A black line at the bottom of the palette indicates that you're about to dock the palette.

FIGURE 4.16
The Color palette and the Stroke palette in Illustrator CS, docked.

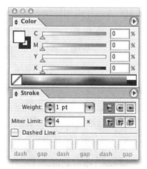

Stashing Palettes

Sure, collapsing, clustering, and docking all of your palettes can be fun and even helpful in making room on your screen; but Adobe is always known for making even cooler features, and you won't be disappointed with this one. It's called Palette Stashing and it's currently available only in InDesign CS and GoLive CS. (Hopefully Adobe will be adding this functionality to Photoshop and Illustrator in their next releases.)

Here's how this feature works. Grab a palette by its tab and drag it to the left or right side of your screen. When you get to the edge of your screen, you'll notice that the tab switches to a vertical orientation (see Figure 4.17). When you let go of the mouse, the palette is now "stashed" along the side of your screen. Click once on the palette tab and the palette slides open, revealing its contents. Click on the tab again and the palette slides back to its stashed position (see Figure 4.18). It's a totally cool way to free up some valuable space on your screen while keeping the palette close at hand. Of course, you can stash palettes that have been clustered together too.

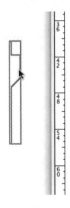

FIGURE 4.17
The vertical outline indicates that you're about to stash your palette.

FIGURE 4.18
The Pages palette in InDesign CS, in both an open and a stashed state.

I know that you're having *way* too much fun right now stashing and unstashing your palettes (I'll admit that it can be quite addictive), but I want to direct your attention to a feature that takes everything we've learned so far about palettes and brings it to the next level: Custom Workspaces.

Custom Workspaces

No doubt by now you're overwhelmed with the plethora of palettes in any one of Adobe's applications. Besides having to understand what each of those palettes is for, you can already tell that your screen is going to be a mess of palettes. Many people spend precious time moving their cursor around the screen looking for a palette they have hidden somewhere under three other palettes. And when you're actually working on your document, all those palettes get in the way, so you're always moving them around (see Figure 4.19). Life would be so much easier if there was just a way to control or manage all of these palettes.

FIGURE 4.19
"Palette's Gone Wild"—a daily occurrence on my computer.

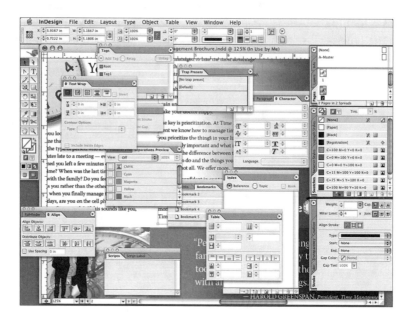

Luckily, there's a feature in the Suite called Custom Workspaces that allows you to save the position of all of your palettes, and reset your screen to that setting at any time. In fact, you can keep multiple workspaces so that you can easily switch between them.

By the Way

Custom Workspaces is a fantastic feature that appears in Photoshop CS, InDesign CS, and GoLive CS, but it seems to have been left out of Illustrator (for now). Hopefully Custom Workspaces will make its way into Illustrator in a future release.

Using this feature is really quite simple. Start by opening the palettes you want, and then position them to your liking on the screen. Cluster them, dock them, stash them—all to your heart's content. After you have everything perfectly positioned and set up, choose Window, Workspace, Save Workspace (see Figure 4.20) and give your new workspace a name. You can create as many workspaces as you like by repeating the process.

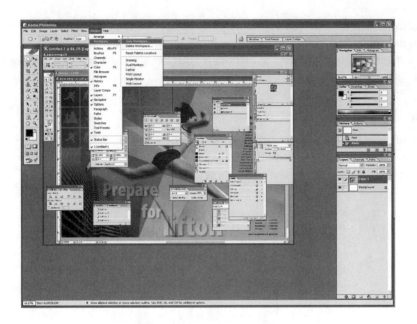

FIGURE 4.20
Saving a work-space.

Whenever you want to switch workspaces, all you have to do is choose one from the Window, Workspace submenu, and like magic, your screen will adjust to the new palette configuration. Just in case you go crazy and define totally wacky workspaces, the kind and thoughtful people at Adobe included a default work-space allowing you to quickly get back to normalcy (see Figure 4.21).

FIGURE 4.21
Choosing the default workspace.

If you're using two monitors, this feature can be extremely helpful in arranging different palette layouts for different tasks. And if you're using a laptop that is sometimes connected to a desktop monitor, Custom Workspaces allows you to easily arrange your palettes for optimal use when you're just on the laptop, or attached to the monitor.

Tools

These tools aren't the kind you buy at the Home Depot, but rather the kind that helps you select objects, draw shapes, create graphs, and perform other functions with the Adobe Creative Suite. Although each application contains a whole slew of tools, the good news is that many of them are the same across applications. We'll discuss these tools here, but before we do, let's first take a look at where the tools live.

The Toolbox

Basically a palette on its own, the toolbox is where you'll find all the tools for any of the Suite applications. With the exception of GoLive CS, the toolboxes are extremely alike across the rest of the Suite (see Figure 4.22).

FIGURE 4.22
The toolboxes in Photoshop CS, ImageReady CS, Illustrator CS, InDesign CS, and GoLive CS.

Photoshop CS   Illustrator CS   GoLive CS

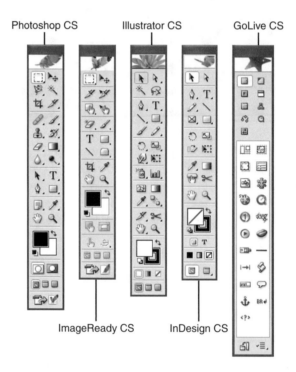

ImageReady CS   InDesign CS

By the Way

As we'll see later, GoLive CS doesn't really use tools because the interface is extremely context sensitive—as you click on parts of your page, your options automatically adapt and change to the needs of the object selected. GoLive CS does utilize the toolbox paradigm for adding objects to your page, making it at least similar in look and feel to its sibling applications.

As with other palettes, you can grab the toolbox from the top and position it to your liking. The top part contains a pretty graphic that helps identify which application you're in (sometimes the apps look so similar that you need to look at this image to tell which of the apps you're actually in). Clicking on this button will launch a dialog giving you the option to connect to the Internet to check for software updates and the like.

InDesign and GoLive allow you to change the look or format of the toolbox to make it easier to position on your screen. For InDesign, you can double-click on the title bar of the toolbox to create a single row of tools rather than the default two-column setup. It saves a few valuable pixels on your screen (see Figure 4.23). GoLive has a small button at the bottom of the toolbox that reformats the bar as a palette—similar to how it appeared in previous versions of the product (see Figure 4.24).

FIGURE 4.23
The single-column configuration of the InDesign CS toolbox in both horizontal and vertical formats.

Button to switch configuration

FIGURE 4.24
GoLive CS's alternative toolbox configuration.

If you take a closer look at the toolbox, you'll notice that some of the tools have a miniscule triangle or arrow at the lower-right corner of the tool. This icon indicates that more tools are "hidden" behind that one (see Figure 4.25). As you'll quickly come to realize, Adobe applications have many tools, and it's impossible to display all of them at once without taking up a tremendous amount of screen real estate. Rather than trying to display them all, Adobe combined them into logical groups. Take Illustrator's Pen tool, for example. Hidden under it are the Add Anchor Point tool, the Delete Anchor Point tool, and the Convert Anchor Point tool. To access these tools, simply press and hold the mouse down on the tool and wait a second as the other tools pop up (see Figure 4.26). You can then choose one of the other tools.

FIGURE 4.25
A little black triangle indicates that there are hidden tools.

Later in the chapter we're going to talk about keyboard shortcuts that can assist you in selecting tools quickly. One of the great things about keyboard shortcuts is that you can use them to select a tool that's hidden behind another one.

By the Way

Sometimes you're continually jumping between tools that are grouped together (such as the Symbolism tools in Illustrator), and it can be quite tedious to continually access the hidden tools. Using a feature found in Illustrator (not in the other Suite apps), if you look to the far right when you click and hold down the mouse to see all the tools in the group, you'll see a narrow button with an arrow in it—

called the tearoff icon (see Figure 4.27). When selected, it actually creates a mini toolbox with all the grouped tools in a row. You can position this anywhere on your screen as needed (see Figure 4.28).

FIGURE 4.26
Accessing the hidden Pen tools in Illustrator CS.

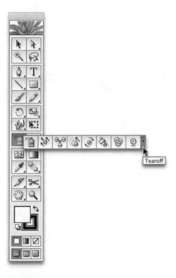

FIGURE 4.27
The tearoff handle.

FIGURE 4.28
A "mini toolbox" of the Symbolism tools in Illustrator CS.

Selection Tools

Back in Chapter 2, "So Many Applications: Which One to Use?" I mentioned the importance of selecting things, and I'd like to clarify that here and explain some of the methods of selections in the Suite apps.

As you use your computer, you'll find that you're basically doing one of two things: creating content, when you're using tools or functions to add elements to your document; or editing content, when you're adjusting or modifying elements in your document. A quick example of what I mean: When drawing a star in Illustrator, first you draw the star itself (creating content), and then you choose a color for it and position it just where you want it (editing content).

To edit content, you need to indicate what it is exactly that you want to edit. This process is called making a selection. Depending on the program, there are many ways to achieve this. For the most part, Illustrator and InDesign are object-based programs, so making selections in those programs is very similar. Photoshop has similar selection tools for its vector shapes, but because it's mainly a pixel-based tool, it also has a range of other selection tools specific to selecting pixels themselves. GoLive is unique in that you don't need any specific tool to select things at all—it's more of a context-sensitive interface. We'll discuss each of these methods when we focus on each of the applications, but I wanted to touch on a few important concepts here.

Selections in Illustrator and InDesign

Both Illustrator and InDesign are primarily object-based programs, so you're usually selecting one of the following:

- ▶ An object
- ▶ Part of an object
- ▶ A group of objects
- ▶ Text

Illustrator and InDesign both have two primary selection tools: the black arrow and the white arrow (okay, so that's what I like to call them; their real names are the Selection tool and the Direct Selection tool). For the most part, the black arrow is used to select objects and groups of objects. The white arrow is used to select parts of objects (see Figure 4.29). In both applications, the Type tool is used to both create and edit text, so you use the Type tool to select text as well.

FIGURE 4.29
The Selection and Direct Selection tools in Adobe InDesign CS.

There are two basic ways to select objects (see Figure 4.30) with the arrow tools. You can either click on the object you want to select, or click and drag over an area to select any objects that fall within that area—a method called marquee selection.

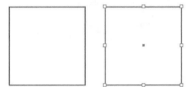

FIGURE 4.30
When an object is selected, it is highlighted (right), indicating so.

Let's start simple and talk about the first method. Using the black arrow, click once on an object to select it. You can then move the object around using the black arrow as well. Click on any empty space on your screen to deselect the object. Click on it again to select it. To select more than one object, you can press and hold the Shift key while clicking on additional objects (see Figure 4.31). You'll notice that with each click, you're adding objects to your selection, and you'll be able to move all the selected objects together at once. If you Shift-click on an object that's already selected, that object will be deselected.

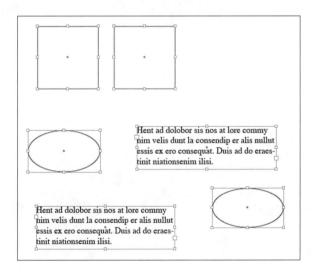

FIGURE 4.31
Multiple objects selected in Adobe InDesign CS.

Did you
Know?

When you think about it, the Shift key toggles a selection on or off. If you Shift-click an object that is not selected, the object will become selected, and if you Shift-click an object that is already selected, it will become deselected.

If you want to select several objects, you can use the marquee method by clicking and holding the mouse button down on a blank area of the screen and then dragging. As you drag the mouse, you'll notice a box being drawn (this is the marquee). When you let go of the mouse, whatever objects fall within the boundaries of the marquee will become selected (see Figure 4.32).

FIGURE 4.32
The three steps to marquee selection: Click the mouse outside the objects; drag over the objects; release the mouse.

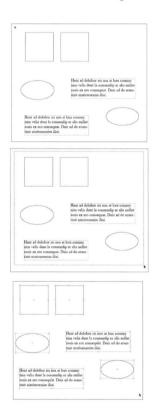

When you're marquee selecting, it's important not to click directly on an object, or you'll simply be selecting and moving that object (as we discussed in the first method).

Sometimes it's useful to use both methods to make your selections. For example, say you had a group of 10 objects and you wanted to select them all except for one in the middle. Using the first method, you might try to select one, then Shift-click each of the other 8 objects to select the ones you want. However, you could use the marquee method to select them all and then Shift-click on the one object you *don't* want—to get the same selection much faster.

Selections in Photoshop

Photoshop is primarily a pixel-based program, so most of the selection tools are focused on selected pixels rather than objects. In other words, you can't just select the "sky" in a photograph—because Photoshop doesn't see it as a single object, but rather a collection of many individual pixels. The three primary selection tools in Photoshop are the Marquee selection tool, the Lasso tool, and the Magic Wand tool. I'm sure you're sitting at home thinking to yourself, *"A magic wand? This guy is pulling my leg…."* Well, before you put this book down to pick up the latest copy of the *National Enquirer* instead, let me explain.

The Marquee selection tool (see Figure 4.33) selects a range of pixels in much the same way we discussed marquee selections before. You drag a box and whatever pixels fall inside the box become selected (see Figure 4.34). There are several variations of the Marquee tool in Photoshop—one for making ellipse-shaped selections, one for selecting a single vertical row of pixels, and one that does the same for horizontal rows of pixels. To add to your selection, press the Shift key to marquee more pixels (see Figure 4.35); to remove pixels from your selection, press the (Option) [Alt] key as you draw your marquee.

FIGURE 4.33
The Marquee selection tool in Photoshop CS.

FIGURE 4.34
An area of pixels
selected.

FIGURE 4.35
As you press the
Shift or (Option)
[Alt] key, the cursor
indicates whether
you are adding or
removing from your
selection.

The Lasso tool (see Figure 4.36) acts exactly like the marquee selection tool with one major difference: It lets you select pixels by drawing a free-form path. Remember that with the Marquee tools, you can select only with rectangular- and elliptical-shaped boundaries, but the Lasso tool lets you draw an irregularly shaped path. For example, the Elliptical Marquee tool might be perfect for selecting the sun in a sky, but the Lasso tool would be perfect for selecting branches of a tree (see Figure 4.37). To use the Lasso tool, you simply click and drag to draw a path around the area of pixels you want to select. If you let go of the mouse before you get back to the point of the path where you started, Photoshop will draw a straight line from the last point your cursor was to the point where the path started, completing the shape for you.

FIGURE 4.36
The Lasso selection tool in Photoshop CS.

FIGURE 4.37
An area of pixels selected with the Lasso tool.

In addition, Photoshop has a Polygonal Lasso tool, which allows you to mark boundaries by clicking repeatedly (almost like connect the dots), as well as a Magnetic Lasso tool, which "magically" detects edges as you drag along them. We'll discuss these in detail when we get to Chapter 5, "Using Adobe Photoshop CS."

Finally, there's the Magic Wand tool (see Figure 4.38). Because of the nature of pixel-based images (photographs), colors are usually painterly, or what we call continuous-tone. So if there's a blue sky in your picture, each blue pixel is probably a slightly different shade of blue. The Magic Wand tool selects regions of the same color, but with a tolerance. That means you can control how close the colors have to match in order to be selected. For example, you click on the blue sky, as we just mentioned, but you don't want white clouds selected, right? The Magic Wand tool can differentiate the colors and select just the blue sky (see Figure 4.39). Why the folks at Adobe called this the Magic Wand tool is beyond me.

FIGURE 4.38
The Magic Wand selection tool in Photoshop CS.

By the Way

You can control the tolerance level (see Figure 4.40) for the Magic Wand in the Tool Options Bar (the context-sensitive bar that sits right under the menu bar). We'll discuss exactly how this works when we delve into Photoshop CS in Chapter 5.

By the Way

If you've used Illustrator before, you might know that Illustrator also has a Lasso and a Magic Wand. Although they work the same way as the Photoshop tools in concept, Illustrator's tools are built to select objects. So the Lasso tool in Illustrator lets you select objects using nonrectangular marquees, and the Magic Wand tool has many options for selecting a range of objects that share similar attributes (such as selecting all objects filled with a "yellowish" color).

FIGURE 4.39
An area of pixels selected with the Magic Wand.

FIGURE 4.40
The Tolerance level setting for the Magic Wand in the Tool Options Bar in Photoshop CS.

Selections in GoLive

As I mentioned earlier, making a selection in GoLive is quite different from doing so in the other applications in the Suite. This is because the user interface is context based. As you click on an object, the options that appear in the interface change to represent the things available to you for that object (see Figure 4.41). At its most basic level, your mouse cursor itself is your one and only selection tool. As we explore GoLive in Chapter 9, "Using Adobe GoLive CS," we'll see exactly how this works.

Drawing Tools

The world of design was forever changed with the introduction of Adobe Illustrator in the late 1980s. Since then, drawing on a computer has become an art form in itself. Illustrator introduced the world to the Pen tool, and since then

Adobe applications have added many more such tools, each for specific tasks. Rectangle, Ellipse, Polygon, Star, and Line tools all give users the ability to quickly and easily draw basic shapes. The Pen, Pencil, and Paintbrush tools give users the freedom of creating more free-form and natural renderings. Many of these tools appear across the apps, and they all work in much the same way.

FIGURE 4.41
The options in GoLive CS change based on what object you click on.

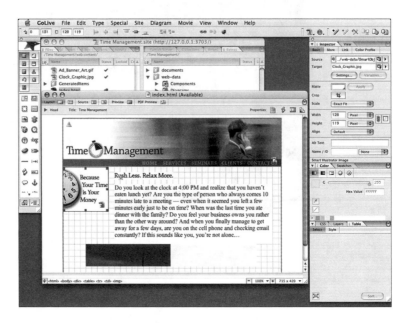

By the Way

> Because some applications address particular tasks, there may be some differences in how the same tool is used between the applications. For example, the Paintbrush tool in Photoshop has different settings and options because it's a pixel-based tool. Illustrator's Paintbrush has other options available pertaining to the object-based nature of vector graphics.

Drawing a rectangle in Photoshop, Illustrator, or InDesign can be accomplished in exactly the same way. You start by selecting the Rectangle tool, and then you click and drag (see Figure 4.42). We'll go into specific details about each of these tools when we talk about the applications themselves, but I wanted to point out how learning even one application in the Suite can give you the basics on using the other apps as well.

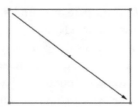

FIGURE 4.42
Drawing a rectangle
in any of the Suite
applications.

Keyboard Shortcuts

The mouse is a wonderful thing (I'm not referring to the squeaky kind that likes cheese), but it can be inefficient for many tasks. For example, to choose the Print command so that you can print your document, you would move the mouse to the File menu, then scan down the list of items and choose Print (see Figure 4.43). Printing can be something you do quite often, and having to navigate back to that File menu each time can be time-consuming.

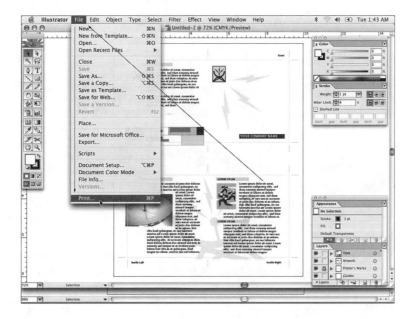

FIGURE 4.43
Using the mouse to
choose the Print
command.

The good news is that there are keyboard shortcuts—or keys you can press on your keyboard to perform specific tasks or functions—that can save a whole lot of time. In the example I gave previously, simply pressing (⌘-P) [Ctrl+P] would invoke the Print command. In fact, there are hundreds of keyboard shortcuts for many different tasks. Power users take advantage of keyboard shortcuts to execute tasks quickly. Keyboard shortcuts can even be used to switch between different tools, allowing you to focus more clearly on the work at hand. You'll find that as you become more adept at using keyboard shortcuts, switching between tools and performing certain functions will become second nature—almost to the point where you won't be consciously aware that you are doing it.

By the Way

It's easy to find out what the keyboard shortcut is for a function or a tool. Menu items have the keyboard shortcut listed to the right (see Figure 4.44), and tools list their shortcut in the tool tip (see Figure 4.45).

FIGURE 4.44
Keyboard shortcuts indicated in the File menu of Illustrator CS.

FIGURE 4.45
Keyboard shortcuts indicated in the toolbox of Photoshop CS.

Now, obviously, if you consider that each program can have a ton of keyboard shortcuts and there are several applications in the Suite, that's a lot of shortcuts to try to learn and remember. It's no coincidence, then, that most of the keyboard shortcuts are consistent across the Suite applications. This means that you can press the "P" key in Photoshop, Illustrator, or InDesign and expect to get the Pen tool in each.

Clearly, learning even one of the applications in the Suite gives you a head start on learning all the others. Even if you've never used InDesign, simply being familiar with Illustrator or Photoshop serves as an introductory course to using these other tools.

But there's more…

Make Your Own Shortcuts

Adobe realizes that their users are unique and that just about every designer wants a keyboard shortcut assigned to the feature or tool that he personally uses most often. At the same time, there are several hundred menu items, tools, and functions in each application, and there are a limited number of possible key combinations you can use on your keyboard. Above that, certain key commands are reserved for use by functions outside the applications. For example, (⌘-Tab) [Ctrl+Tab] is a shortcut used by the operating system (both Windows XP and Mac OS X) to switch between open applications.

Photoshop, Illustrator, InDesign, and GoLive all enable you to customize keyboard shortcuts. That means you can assign your own shortcuts to functions or tools you use most often.

It's important to point out that there are certain keyboard shortcuts that are not consistent between the applications, and there are usually good reasons for it. For example, (⌘-F) [Ctrl+F] in InDesign is the shortcut to bring up the Find and Replace dialog box. However, in Illustrator that same shortcut is used for the Paste in Front command. This is because Find and Replace is something that might be used quite often in InDesign, but not nearly as often in Illustrator. At the same time, Illustrator users may use Paste in Front all the time. Of course, customizable shortcuts now let you make all of these decisions on your own.

By the Way

Customizable keyboard shortcuts is one of those cross-product features that hasn't been "sweetened" yet (sorry, couldn't resist the pun) in that the implementation is slightly different depending on which application you're in (see Figure 4.46).

From Photoshop, InDesign, and Illustrator, choose Edit, Keyboard Shortcuts. In GoLive, choose Keyboard Shortcuts from the GoLive menu (on the Mac). The interfaces are somewhat different, but the concept is the same. You can change or assign keyboard shortcuts to any tool, any menu item, and some palette flyout menus as well. If you try to assign a shortcut that already exists (say, for another tool or function), you'll get a warning telling you so, with the option to keep the older assignment or to adopt the new one you just defined (see Figure 4.47).

Most important of all, you have the ability to save your custom keyboard shortcut settings as an external file. This means you can secretly change all the keyboard shortcuts on your coworker's computer—um, I mean you can easily distribute custom sets to coworkers or take your own sets with you if you regularly work on differentcomputers, or share a different computer with others.

FIGURE 4.46
The Keyboard
Shortcuts dialog for
each of the Suite
applications.

Photoshop CS

Illustrator CS

InDesign CS

GoLive CS

FIGURE 4.47
A warning in
Illustrator CS indi-
cating that a key
combination that
you've assigned
already exists.

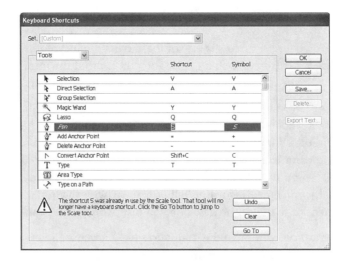

Moving Data Between Apps

As you use the individual applications in the Suite, you'll realize more and more that you have to move information between them—and other applications outside the Suite as well. There are several ways to do this, each method having its own pros and cons.

Copy and Paste

One of the quickest ways to move data between applications—be it text, images, or artwork—is via the copy and paste command. But like most things in life, the quicker way isn't always the best way. In most cases, information is lost when copying and pasting between applications, including text formatting, color information, image resolution, metadata, and more. However, many times a simple copy and paste will save time and provide you with what you need. For example, you may want to draw a shape in Illustrator, taking advantage of the precise drawing tools in that application, and then copy and paste just the path into Photoshop or InDesign.

There is a "richer" format you can use when copying and pasting between some Adobe Suite applications, and that format is PDF. Illustrator will copy using PDF, which even supports transparency when pasting into Photoshop or InDesign, but you won't be able to access the paths in those applications. Make sure that the AICB option is checked in Illustrator's Preferences to get that functionality (see Figure 4.48). InDesign also has a setting where you can specify to prefer PDF when pasting (see Figure 4.49).

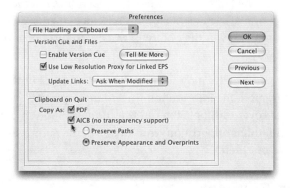

FIGURE 4.48
Turning on the AICB option in Illustrator CS's Preferences.

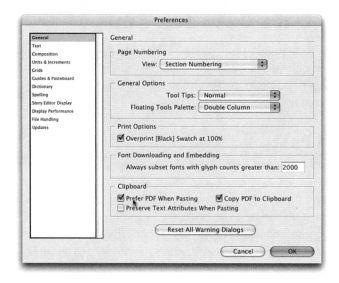

Exporting/Importing

The applications in the Suite can both import and export different file formats. Depending on where your files and documents have to go, you can choose from various formats—each with its own particular strength or use. Some of the more common formats used for print workflows are PDF, TIFF, and EPS. Popular Web formats are GIF, JPEG, SWF, and SVG. Illustrator also has the capability to save files in Photoshop (PSD) format and contains a Save for Microsoft Office command.

Most applications in the Suite can also place or open these formats—along with a long list of other formats, such as Microsoft Office documents, FreeHand files, and QuarkXPress files—giving you the ability to work with just about any file that might come your way.

Exporting and importing files may seem like an extra step, but the formats are richer and support more file information (including important metadata, in many cases—we'll cover this topic later in the chapter). It's also a necessary step when working with other applications that aren't in the Suite (yes, there *is* a whole other world out there).

Native File Support

One of the strengths of using the Creative Suite in your workflow is that all the Suite applications can support the native file formats of each other. This means that I can easily place a native Illustrator file into Photoshop, InDesign, or GoLive, and even open it in Adobe Acrobat. Other applications might require that you export a specific file format from Illustrator, such as EPS.

Of course, this is an extremely valuable benefit. As we discussed back in Chapter 3, "The Game Plan: Developing a Workflow," this allows you to keep just one version of your file (rather than native files as well as EPS, TIFF, and JPEG versions, and so on) and also allows you to take advantage of the rich format that these file formats support. For example, you can access all the layers in a Photoshop file when you open it inside Illustrator. You can view and hide layers from both InDesign and Illustrator files when you're in Acrobat. And GoLive's Smart Object technology allows you to place native Photoshop and Illustrator files right into your Web page layouts—you don't even have to save GIF or JPEG files, because GoLive does that all for you.

When possible, it's best to use native file formats because those file formats retain the most information. An added benefit to this method is that you retain the individual files, making it easy to quickly update different elements in your design. Using the Edit Original command found in each of the applications (see Figure 4.50), you can easily make changes to a graphic—and have that graphic automatically updated throughout all the documents that it is placed in. We'll discuss how to do that from each of the applications in Part II of this book, "The Applications."

FIGURE 4.50
Initiating the Edit Original command via a contextual menu in InDesign CS.

Metadata

Meta-*what?* If you're not familiar with the term, *metadata* refers to data that resides inside a file that provides extra information about the file itself. For example, a file may contain information about who created the file, when it was created, what client or job number it was created for, and so on. Digital photos may contain copyright information and even data about what kind of digital camera was used and what the camera settings were (called EXIF metadata) when the photo was taken.

Some metadata is added automatically to every file (such as which application created it), but you can also add your own. In any of the Adobe Suite applications, you can choose File, File Info to access the File Info dialog box, where you can add specific information to your file (see Figure 4.51).

FIGURE 4.51
The File Info dialog in Photoshop CS.

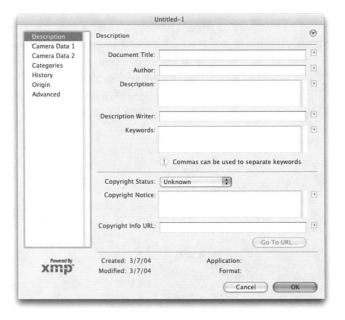

Adobe helped to publish an open standard platform for metadata called XMP, which is basically a way to describe metadata using XML. All Adobe applications write metadata into an XML header in the files they save. This information is available to any application or system that can read it. And although metadata is pretty cool on its own, it takes on a whole new meaning when you consider what Version Cue can do with that information.

Version Cue

We've touched on Version Cue in the first two chapters, and we'll discuss it in detail in Chapter 11. But because Version Cue is the "glue" that holds the Suite together (as Adobe puts it), it really helps define a whole new level of integration never before seen in a collection of applications. In fact, Version Cue paired with the metadata functionality we discussed moments ago is such a powerful benefit that some studios have decided to use the Adobe Creative Suite based on those two features alone.

What makes Version Cue unique is how you interface with it. Rather than your having to learn some new system or method for opening and saving files, Version Cue is seamlessly embedded into all the Adobe Suite applications (with the exception of Acrobat Professional and ImageReady).

We turned on Version Cue back in the beginning of this chapter, but you also need to indicate inside each of the Suite applications that you want to be able to access Version Cue features (with the exception of GoLive, in which Version Cue functionality is always activated). In Preferences, go to the File Handling panel and check the Enable Version Cue option (see Figure 4.52). This will immediately turn on the Version Cue features in that application (although InDesign will require you to relaunch the application for the change to take effect).

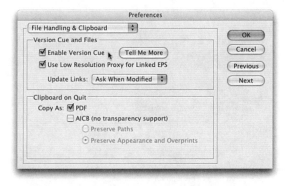

FIGURE 4.52
Activating Version Cue functionality inside the Illustrator CS File Handling & Clipboard Preferences panel.

To open a file from a Version Cue project, you simply choose File, Open from any application and click on the Version Cue button (see Figure 4.53). This is where the metadata that we spoke about earlier really makes a difference. As you mouse over each file in a Version Cue project, you can see the metadata for that file without having to open the file (see Figure 4.54). Beyond that, you can search for files based on their metadata as well, taking much of the guesswork out of your workflow (see Figure 4.55). When you're working with large graphics files over a network, this can save a lot of time when you're trying to find the right file—you can even choose to view image thumbnails to make sure (see Figure 4.56).

FIGURE 4.53
Choosing to open a file from a Version Cue project inside InDesign CS.

FIGURE 4.54
Viewing file info metadata while browsing files in Version Cue.

FIGURE 4.55
Specifying search
criteria inside
Version Cue.

FIGURE 4.56
Viewing image
thumbnails in
Version Cue.

Saving files to a Version Cue project works exactly the same way, and all of this functionality is identical whether you're in Photoshop, Illustrator, InDesign, or GoLive.

Taking on the Applications

By now you have a solid understanding of what all the applications are for, and when they should be used, along with a general understanding of how they work hand-in-hand with each other. All you have left to do now is actually learn each of the applications. Have no fear—if you've gotten this far, you're going to do just fine. In the next part of the book, we'll jump into each of the applications one by one and fully understand the strengths and uses for each of them.

PART II

The Applications

CHAPTER 5

Using Adobe Photoshop CS

Over the past few versions, Photoshop has gotten an impressive facelift, helping to make the traditionally complex program a bit easier to use. Improvements of note are the Tool Options bar that spans to the top of the screen when Photoshop is in use, and the File Browser, which makes it easy to find the files you're looking for. In this chapter we'll learn how to use Photoshop and get familiar with its tools and features.

What's New in Photoshop CS?

If you've used Photoshop before, here's a quick overview of what's new in the CS version of Photoshop: a much-improved File Browser with better performance, more support for metadata, and automation capabilities; full integrated support for the Camera Raw format, which allows you to import images directly from your digital camera in its native format; an amazing Shadow/Highlight filter; an auto straighten and crop feature; a new Match Color feature that allows you to map the colors of one file to another; a Filter Gallery, which allows you to preview and apply artistic filters easily; 16-bit image support throughout most of the application for even better image quality and fidelity; non-square pixel support (for video use); and Layer Comps, a feature that enables you to store several configurations of your design in a single file easily and even export them all as a multipage PDF.

Introduction to Photoshop CS

When you first launch Photoshop, you're greeted with the new Photoshop CS welcome screen (see Figure 5.1). Here you can access some Tutorials from Adobe, as well as some Tips and Tricks from Photoshop professionals. You can also view a very helpful guide to Color Management, as well as an overview of what's new in the CS version of Photoshop.

FIGURE 5.1
The Photoshop CS welcome screen.

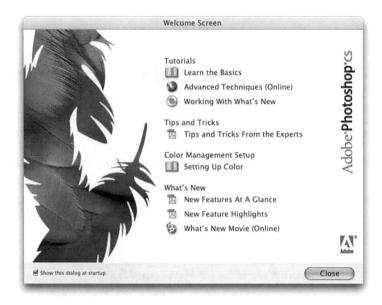

When you first look at Photoshop (see Figure 5.2), you'll see the standard menu bar across the top of the screen. Directly under the menu bar is the Tool Options bar, which is context-sensitive. That means the options listed in this area change depending on what tool you have selected. To the far right of the Tool Options bar is the button used to access the File Browser and the palette well, where you can "store" palettes.

Menu bar

File Browser button

Tools Option bar

Palette Well

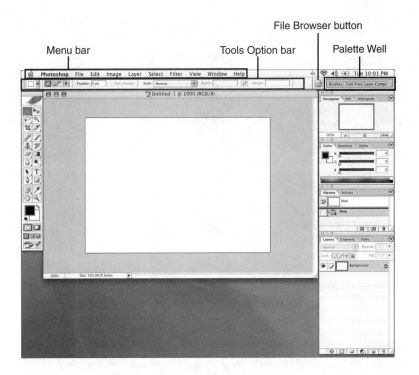

FIGURE 5.2
The Photoshop CS user interface.

Along the left side of the screen is the toolbox (see Figure 5.3), which contains all of Photoshop's tools, as well as several other functions. The color proxies indicate the foreground and background colors (you can also choose colors by clicking on them), and the two icons surrounding the proxies allow you to set the colors to the default black foreground and white background, and to swap the foreground and background colors. Directly below the proxy icons are the Quick Mask mode buttons—we'll talk more about these useful mask buttons later in the chapter— and under those are the different view modes, Standard, Full Screen with Menu Bar, and Full Screen. You can toggle through the view modes by repeatedly pressing the "F" key on your keyboard (the letter *F*, not a Function key). The last button at the bottom of the toolbox allows you to jump to ImageReady directly with the file you're working on.

FIGURE 5.3
The Photoshop CS
toolbox.

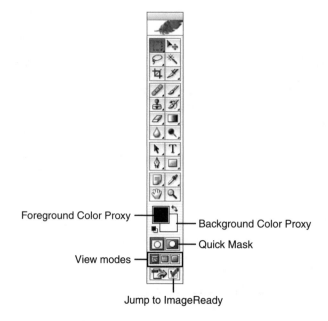

Foreground Color Proxy ———

——— Background Color Proxy

——— Quick Mask

View modes ———

Jump to ImageReady

Did you Know?

Some useful keyboard shortcuts to remember and get used to are the X key to swap the foreground and background colors, and D to set the colors to their default settings.

Along the right side of your screen are some of Photoshop's palettes. We'll discuss what each of them does and how to use them as we go through this chapter.

Did you Know?

If you remember, we talked about custom workspaces in Chapter 4, "The Key That Makes It All Work: Integration," and discussed how you can save your screen setup, including palette locations, which palettes are open or closed, and so forth.

Finally, the document window (see Figure 5.4) is where you work on your file. The gray area is the part of the image that falls outside the image area. Photoshop lists the filename, the view percentage, and the color mode right in the title bar of each file. Along the bottom left of the window, you'll find a zoom indicator, as well as the status bar.

Document Title bar

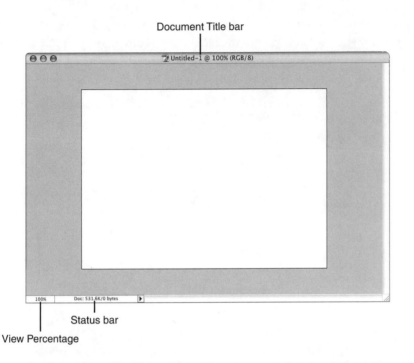

FIGURE 5.4
The Photoshop CS document window.

Status bar

View Percentage

Opening, Creating, and Importing Files

You have to start with something, right? With Photoshop, you have various options: You can open existing files, whether Photoshop files, JPEG images, or any other of Photoshop's laundry list of supported file formats; you can create a new file from scratch (basically a blank document); or you can import files from another source, such as a scanner or a digital camera.

The Open Dialog

As with just about any computer program, you can open a file by choosing File, Open or by pressing (⌘-O) [Ctrl+O] to bring up the standard system Open dialog box. As you highlight files in the dialog, you may or may not see a low-resolution preview, depending on the file type and what your operating system supports. After you've located the file you want to open, click on the Open button to open the file. Photoshop will also let you open several files at once by holding the (⌘) [Ctrl] key as you click on the different files.

If you want to choose a file from a Version Cue project, click on the Version Cue button in the lower-left corner of the dialog (see Figure 5.5). We'll talk more about Version Cue in Chapter 11, "Using Version Cue."

FIGURE 5.5
The Version Cue option in the Photoshop CS Open dialog box.

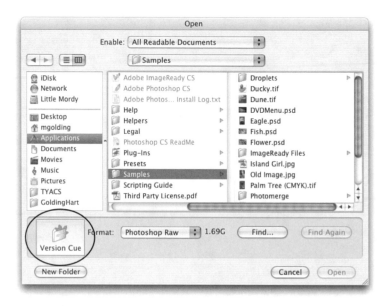

> If you don't see the Version Cue button in your Open dialog, you haven't activated Version Cue in Photoshop yet. In the File Handling screen of the Preferences dialog, check the option Enable Version Cue Workgroup File Management.

By the Way

The File Browser

Back in the day, when you were looking for a particular photograph, you received a stack of chromes from a photographer or agency and laid them all out on a lightbox or light table to choose the right one. The truth is, scrolling through a list of filenames in your Open dialog box isn't the most intuitive way to choose a photo (see Figure 5.6). Especially considering that today's digital cameras give very descriptive names to each photo (DCP00634.JPG, DSCN0521.JPG, and such), one can easily see why root canal would seem to be preferable to choosing just the right image from a list of hundreds of photos.

One of the most useful and time-saving features you'll find in Photoshop is the File Browser, which you can open by choosing File, Browse, or by pressing (⌘-Shift-O) [Ctrl+Shift+O], or by clicking on the File Browser button in the Tool Options bar (see Figure 5.7). Instead of scrolling through files and trying to figure out which is the one you want to open, you can see the files as thumbnails in the File Browser, making it easy to find the file you're looking for.

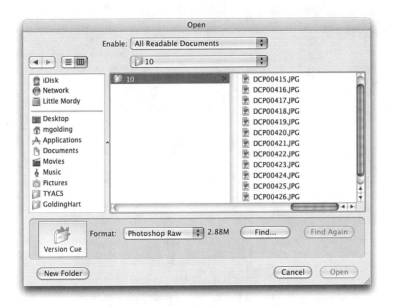

FIGURE 5.6
Choosing images from the Open dialog can be time-consuming and unintuitive.

FIGURE 5.7
The File Browser button in the Tool Options bar.

You can't access Version Cue projects from the File Browser. To access your projects, you need to use the Open dialog method described previously.

Did you Know?

The File Browser (see Figure 5.8) is really *far* more useful than a digital lightbox. Upon closer inspection you'll see that the browser is split into different sections, the first one being a menu bar and a group of icons across the top of the window. I know what you're thinking, and yes, the File Browser actually needs its own menu bar because it performs so many functions, such as batch processing and custom views—and even its own preferences. The buttons to the right of the menu bar allow you to rotate images in the browser (in 90-degree increments), flag images (for easier grouping), perform a search, and put images in the trash.

When you rotate an image using the rotate buttons in the File Browser, the actual image isn't rotated, but when you open that image in Photoshop, a rotate transformation is automatically applied to it.

By the Way

FIGURE 5.8
The Photoshop CS
File Browser.

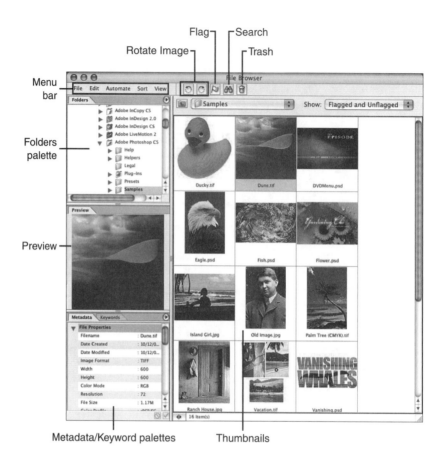

Menu bar

Folders palette

Preview

Metadata/Keyword palettes

Thumbnails

Flag — Search
Rotate Image — Trash

FIGURE 5.8
The Photoshop CS
File Browser.

The right side of the File Browser window displays thumbnails of all the files in the selected folder. The left side of the window is split into three sections. The top section is the Folders palette, which displays the folder or file you have selected. You can navigate in this palette just as you would at the system level, choosing folders, drives, network drives, and so forth. The middle section is the Preview palette, which shows a larger high-resolution preview of the selected image. The bottom section combines the Metadata and Keywords palettes, where you can view and even add or edit the metadata.

Being able to edit metadata in the File Browser can be especially useful when you need to add metadata to JPEG files. That's because every time you open and save a JPEG file, you lose some quality in the file (JPEG uses a lousy compression algorithm). By adding metadata through the File Browser, you can actually accomplish the task without having to open and resave the file—and the file can stay at the same level of quality.

There are many, many metadata fields—and you may or may not need to see them all in the File Browser. In the File Browser's Edit menu you can choose Metadata Display Options and choose just the fields you want to appear.

The palettes that appear in the File Browser act very much like regular palettes—you can double-click on their tabs to change their state, and if you want to shuffle them around for some reason, you can cluster them with one another. At the bottom of the File Browser window, there's a double-arrow icon that will hide the entire left side of the window, using the entire window to display image thumbnails (see Figure 5.9). Within the thumbnail section you also have the option to view all files, all flagged files, or just unflagged files (see Figure 5.10). This makes it easy to choose pictures the same way you might on a light table. You mark several that are good candidates, and then gradually go through a process of removing others until you're left with the one you love (only to have your client ask for a different one...).

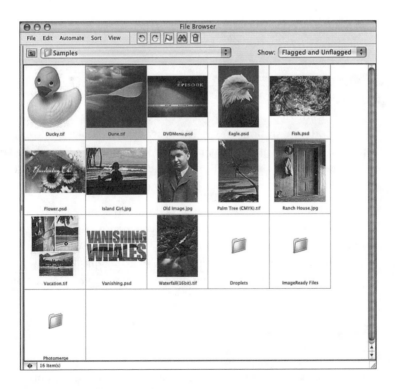

FIGURE 5.9
The File Browser showing thumbnails only.

FIGURE 5.10
Choosing to view
flagged files in the
File Browser.

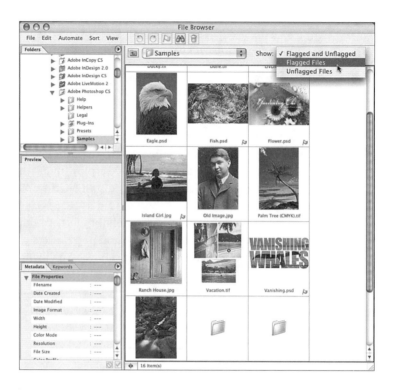

Apparently, the folks at Adobe thought all of this functionality still wasn't enough, so they made the sections in the File Browser adjustable. You can simply grab the separator bars and give yourself a really large preview. Or maybe you want a really large metadata section. Basically, Adobe has given that choice over to you (see Figure 5.11).

After you've found the image you're looking for, you can simply double-click on it to open the file. You can open multiple files at once by Shift-clicking on several thumbnails. Clicking while holding the (⌘) [Ctrl] key will allow you to select non-contiguous images. Additionally, you can (Control-click) [right-click] on an image to bring up a contextual menu with many options that are available for the selected image(s).

Creating a New File

To start from scratch and create a new file, choose File, New or press (⌘-N) [Ctrl+N] to access the New dialog box (see Figure 5.12). Here you can give your file a name (you can do this later when you actually save the file too) and choose a size and resolution for your file. Adobe has also included many preset canvas sizes, and you can choose one of those (for example, a 5×7-inch file). Choosing a resolution is very important when you create a Photoshop file because changing the resolution in the file later may cause degradation or distortion in your file.

FIGURE 5.11
The File Browser adjusted for a larger preview.

FIGURE 5.12
The New document dialog box.

You can also create your own New document presets by choosing the options you want, and then clicking on the Save Preset button.

Did you Know?

There's an option to choose what the default background of your file will be (White, Background Color, or Transparent), and you can click on the Advanced button to choose a color profile or to specify a non-square pixel aspect ratio for video content (see Figure 5.13).

FIGURE 5.13
Choosing a video setting from the Advanced section of the New dialog.

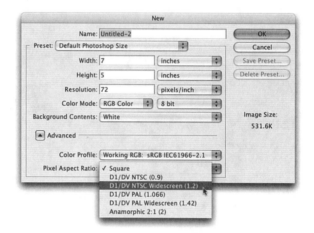

Color Modes

Photoshop lets you create files using any of several color modes, and it's important to know which one to choose. Although you can change color modes later in the process, just about any such change will cause color shifts. Each color mode has a *gamut*, or range of colors that can be produced. Some gamuts are wider, or can contain more colors, than others. For example, there are certain colors that can be displayed in RGB that simply can't be reproduced in CMYK (for example, bright greens or oranges or pastel colors). So converting an RGB file to CMYK might cause some colors to become dull or change color altogether because those colors don't exist in CMYK. Let's take a look at each of the supported color models:

▶ **Bitmap**—Also called 1-bit, a one-bit bitmap image can contain only two colors, black and white (like my favorite kind of cookie). It's useful for certain workflows, such as screen printing or specialized newspaper techniques. Some other programs (Illustrator, for example) can change the black color of a bitmap to a different color, so scanned logos are also sometimes saved as bitmap images. Some cell-phone displays or PDAs also require bitmap images.

▶ **Grayscale**—The Grayscale color model is black and white with a touch of gray—256 levels of gray, that is. Mainly used for single-color artwork such as black-and-white photographs, the Grayscale model is also used to create monotones, duotones, tritones, and quadtones—all of which we'll cover later in the chapter.

▶ **RGB Color**—RGB (Red Green Blue) is a *subtractive* color method. Subtractive means that if you mix all the colors together, the result is white, and if none of the colors are present, the result is black. Televisions, computer monitors, and the like use the RGB color model (when your TV is turned off, the screen is black). When you're working on files that will be used in video, for broadcast, on the Web, or for onscreen presentations, RGB is the format you should use.

▶ **CMYK Color**—Unlike RGB, CMYK is an *additive* color method, which means that if you mix all the colors together, you get black, but if none of the colors are present, you get white. Anything you see in print uses CMYK (a blank piece of paper is white), so obviously when you're designing content that will be printed in color, CMYK is the color model of choice. CMYK stands for Cyan (a shade of blue), Magenta (a shade of red), Yellow, and Key (Black). Black is referred to as Key because that is traditionally the key color; it reinforces and invigorates the other colors (or so a printer once told me).

As I mentioned earlier, the CMYK gamut isn't anywhere near as wide as most designers would like, so designers use spot colors (for example, Pantone colors) that allow designers to pick a specific color ink (including metallic inks, pastels, and the like).

By the Way

▶ **Lab Color**—Almost scientific in nature (as if the other color models weren't), the Lab color model contains a Luminance level called "L" and two channels of color, called "a" and "b" (hence the name Lab). Lab has the widest color gamut of all those listed here, and Photoshop uses this model internally to calculate operations. For example, when you convert an image from RGB to CMYK, Photoshop first internally converts the RGB data to Lab and then converts the Lab data to CMYK. Because very few—if any—applications can use or understand Lab files, I would suggest that you choose this color model only if your image isn't going to be placed into other applications or printed on a press.

Importing Images

Another way to bring images into Photoshop is to import them from another hardware source. There are plenty of scanners, traditional cameras with digital film backs, fully digital cameras, video capture devices, and the like that can be used to capture images which can be directly imported into Photoshop. Each of these devices usually comes with a plug-in for Photoshop to allow this use. For example, my Epson Expression 1600 FireWire scanner has a plug-in that allows me to access my scanner from the File, Import menu (see Figure 5.14).

FIGURE 5.14
Importing an image
from a scanner
directly into
Photoshop.

More popular than almost anything these days are digital cameras. It seems as though just about everyone has one. Some cameras let you import pictures directly into Photoshop as JPEG images; others simply copy the files to your hard drive. Additionally, some cameras support something called camera raw format.

Camera Raw Image Import

Many of the newer digital cameras have the capability to shoot in "raw" format. This means that the camera preserves the image in a native format, rather than storing it as a JPEG file (as most cameras do). The benefit, of course, is that the image is unadulterated and contains every aspect of the data that the camera can capture. Think of it like this: Opening a JPEG photo in Photoshop is like drinking bottled water, but opening a camera raw file is like going to Evian in France and drinking the water right from the spring.

When you open a camera raw file (CRW), you're presented with the Camera Raw dialog box, where you can make adjustments to the image (see Figure 5.15). Any changes you make to the image here do not affect the original raw image—they only take effect as you open the file in Photoshop. Along the right side of the dialog, a color histogram gives you a visual of the tonal range of the image (see Figure 5.16). Below that are the Adjust and Detail palettes. If you choose the Advanced option instead of the Basic option at the top of the dialog, you have the Lens and Calibrate palettes as well.

FIGURE 5.15
The Photoshop CS Camera Raw dialog box.

For some people, it may seem as though all of this functionality (such as adjusting an image's *chromatic aberration*) is overkill. For others, such as professional photographers, having this kind of detailed control over their images is a dream come true. Admittedly, making adjustments to the White Balance setting (in the

Adjust palette) is useful for nearly everyone, because this setting can correct photos that were taken on overly cloudy or sunny days, photos that have odd color casts, and more (see Figure 5.17).

FIGURE 5.16
A color histogram.

FIGURE 5.17
The White Balance setting in the Camera Raw dialog.

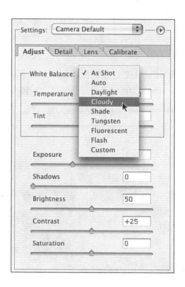

By the Way

If you ever catch me talking about chromatic aberration at a social party, remind me to change careers.

Overall, what makes Photoshop's camera raw support such a big deal is that you can save the changes you make to one file and then automatically apply those adjustments to an entire range of files. For example, if you find that your particular camera needs certain adjustments to all the photos it takes, you can have Photoshop automatically apply certain camera raw settings when it opens files taken with that camera. Or you can use the camera raw settings to fix a photo that you took on a really cloudy day. You can then apply those settings automatically to all other photos you shot on that day. These adjustments can be done via the Settings pop-up and flyout menu.

Working with Selections

In our journey through life, we're always making selections. When we dress in the morning, we select what clothes to wear. When we order a meal at a restaurant, we select an entree from the menu. Selections are especially important in Photoshop due to the pixel-based nature of the program. With the exception of text and vector shapes, everything in Photoshop is just a mass of pixels. If you have a photograph with a blue sky, don't think of it as a sky that's colored blue, but rather many, many blue pixels that together form the image of a sky. If I want to change the sky to a different color, I can't just select the sky; I have to select all the individual pixels that form the sky. At a basic level, if I want to manipulate only *part* of my image, I need to isolate that part so that other parts of my image aren't affected (see Figure 5.18).

FIGURE 5.18
A file with one area of the image selected.

Selections can also be called masks. When professionals used an airbrush to edit photographs in the past, they didn't want to accidentally affect other parts of the photo as they worked, so they cut masks (called friskets) that allowed them to use the airbrush on a specific part of the photo.

By the Way

It may all sound a bit confusing, but as we go through the individual selection tools and the methods used to work with selections, everything will begin to make sense.

Marquee Selection Tools

In our basic introduction to making selections back in Chapter 4, we discussed the Marquee selection tools. They are used whenever you want to select a rectangular or elliptical range of pixels. For example, say you want to darken a rectangular area of a photo so that you can overlay some text. You would use the Rectangular Marquee tool to select an area that you will darken.

You have various options when using the Marquee tools:

▶ Holding the Shift key while dragging will constrain the marquee area to a square or a circle.

▶ Holding the (Option) [Alt] key while dragging will draw the marquee out from the center of where you clicked, rather than from the corner of where you clicked.

▶ Holding the spacebar will "freeze" the marquee and let you position it anywhere in your image.

The options for the Marquee tool can be found in the Tool Options bar. By default, if you currently have a selection on your screen and then you draw a new marquee, you get a new selection and the previous marquee is discarded. You can change this behavior by choosing from the options Add, Subtract, or Intersect (see Figure 5.19). For example, if you draw your first selection, then click on the Add button, and then draw another marquee, both areas will become selected simultaneously. If your new marquee overlaps the previous one, they will be joined together to form a single larger selection.

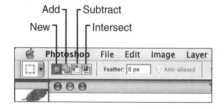

FIGURE 5.19
Choosing marquee options from the Tool Options bar.

I personally find it tedious to have to navigate up to the Tool Options bar to specify Add, Subtract, or Intersect mode—so naturally I use the keyboard shortcuts. Holding the Shift key will add to your selection, holding (Option) [Alt] will subtract from your selection, and holding both Shift and Option (Alt) together will use the intersect mode.

Notice that the Marquee icon in the Tool Options bar is actually a pop-up menu button in itself. See the sidebar "Tool Options for Everyone," later in this section.

At times you may want to draw a marquee that is a specific size. Rather than guessing as you draw the marquee, you can choose one of the options from the Style pop-up in the Tool Options bar: Fixed Aspect Ratio (which will resample the file) and Fixed Size (see Figure 5.20). When either of these two options is chosen, you can enter a Width and Height value, and you'll notice that as you draw with the Marquee tool, your selection will be created or constrained to the dimensions you've specified.

FIGURE 5.20
Choosing the Fixed Aspect Ratio setting in the Tool Options bar.

After you've drawn your selection, you can move the selection around as you like by positioning your cursor anywhere inside the marquee, and then dragging it. You'll notice that only the selection itself moves, not the pixels that are inside it. To move the pixels themselves, switch to the Move tool or press and hold the (⌘) [Ctrl] key before you start dragging the selection. To drag a *copy* of the selected pixels, press and hold the ⌘ (Ctrl) *and* the (Option) [Alt] keys before you click and drag.

Lasso Tools

Although the Marquee selection tools can be quite helpful, chances are there will be plenty of times when you'll need to select something that isn't rectangular or elliptical in shape. The Lasso tool enables you to make irregularly shaped selections. Simply choose the Lasso tool and press the mouse button. As you drag, you'll see a line appear. When you release the mouse button, Photoshop will close the path and turn it into a selection (see Figure 5.21). All the options we spoke about for the Marquee tools are available here as well (adding, subtracting, moving, and so on).

If you're not as comfortable using a mouse, it can be difficult to make clean selections using the Lasso tool (as with anything, practice helps). Don't fret though—Photoshop has two variations of the Lasso tool that might help:

> ▶ **Polygonal Lasso tool**—I personally use this selection tool more than any other, and I find it extremely useful for many tasks, including creating silhouettes (which we'll discuss later in the chapter). Rather than having to press the mouse and drag it all over your screen, you can click once and then move your cursor to the next spot and click again. A "rubber band" follows your cursor around to give you visual feedback of where your

selection path will be drawn (see Figure 5.22). You can either click on the original point to close your path and turn it into a selection or simply double-click to have Photoshop automatically close the path for you.

FIGURE 5.21
A selection created with the Lasso tool.

FIGURE 5.22
Making a selection using the Polygonal Lasso tool.

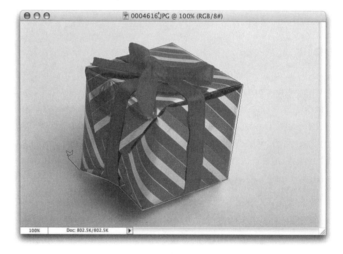

Did you
Know?

Holding the (Option) [Alt] key while using the regular Lasso tool makes it act just like the Polygonal Lasso tool.

▶ **Magnetic Lasso tool**—You spent enough money on your computer and on the software you're using, so why are *you* left doing all the work? Shouldn't the computer be doing the work for you? Well, the Magnetic Lasso tool does it's part—it automatically detects edges as you use it. An edge here is defined as a shift or change between one color and another. As you drag along an edge with the Magnetic Lasso tool, it automatically detects the edge and draws a path along it (see Figure 5.23). Double-clicking with the tool will automatically close the path and turn it into an active selection.

FIGURE 5.23
Making a selection using the Magnetic Lasso tool.

If you look at the Tool Options bar when you have the Magnetic Lasso tool selected, you can see various options that control the sensitivity of the tool (see Figure 5.24). Width refers to how far the tool will look for an edge from where your cursor is. Edge Contrast controls how sensitive the tool is with regard to differences in color. A higher number will find only an edge that is a high-contrast one, whereas a lower number will look for more subtle shifts in color. The Frequency value determines how many points the tool uses to draw out the path. A higher number will yield a path that is more precise, and a lower number will result in a smoother path.

FIGURE 5.24
The settings for the Magnetic Lasso tool.

With Caps Lock turned on, Photoshop will display the cursor for the Magnetic Lasso tool as the size of the Width setting, making it easier to trace over edges of color. Pressing the right or left bracket on your keyboard will increase or decrease the Width setting by one pixel.

Magic Wand

For selecting areas of similar color, you can use the Magic Wand tool. By default, the Magic Wand takes the area that you click on and selects all pixels of similar color adjacent to it. Simply click on an area of your image. If you uncheck the Contiguous option in the Tool Options bar, Photoshop will select all similarly colored pixels throughout the entire document.

You can control how sensitive the Magic Wand tool is by adjusting the Tolerance setting in the Tool Options bar (see Figure 5.25). A low tolerance number means the Magic Wand will select only pixels that are closer to the color that you clicked on. For example, if you click on a dark blue color with a low tolerance, the Magic Wand will select only dark blue pixels—but with a higher tolerance, other shades of blue will be selected as well (see Figure 5.26).

FIGURE 5.25
The Tool Options bar for the Magic Wand tool.

FIGURE 5.26
A selection made with a high tolerance setting (left) and a selection made with a low tolerance setting (right).

If you don't see the Tolerance setting in the Tool Options bar, it means you haven't selected the Magic Wand tool from the toolbox.

As with the other selection tools, you can use the Add, Subtract, and Intersect options with the Magic Wand tool.

Another way to make a selection is by using a feature called Quick Mask, which we'll cover later in the chapter.

Selecting a Range of Colors

Although the Magic Wand tool is cool and all, it doesn't really provide the user (that's you) with any useful feedback. It's basically hit and miss—you click, see what gets selected, deselect, change the tolerance level a bit, and then try again.

Let me direct your attention, if you will, to the Color Range feature (Select, Color Range). Here you can use an Eyedropper tool to click on parts of an image and get a preview so that you can see what will be selected before you actually make the selection (see Figure 5.27). Above that, you have options such as Fuzziness (I love saying that word), which can control how sensitive the feature is to color shifts. Using the Select pop-up menu, you can choose to automatically select ranges of predefined colors, highlights, shadows, midtones, and even out-of-gamut colors (see Figure 5.28).

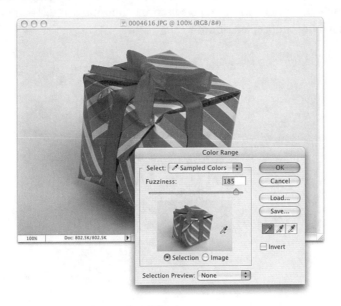

FIGURE 5.27
Using the Color Range dialog.

FIGURE 5.28
Choosing from various selection
options in the Color
Range dialog.

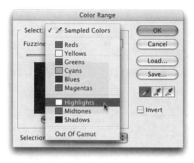

For even better previewing, you can choose to preview your document window
itself with different viewing options that are found in the Selection Preview pop-
up menu. Clicking on the OK button will close the Color Range dialog and return
you to your document with your new selection waiting for you.

Feathering

Ever see a nice vignette photograph with a soft edge (see Figure 5.29) and wonder
how they did that? Wonder no more. Until now, you've been creating selections
that have hard edges. Using a technique called *feathering*, you can specify a grad-
ual edge for your selection instead of a hard one. You can specify how soft your
edges are by indicating how many pixels you want your feather to be. For each of
the selection tools, you can specify a feather amount in the Tool Options bar.
Doing so will apply the feather to your selection as you make it. Alternatively,
you can apply a feather by making a selection, choosing Select, Feather, and then
entering a feather radius (see Figure 5.30).

FIGURE 5.29
A photograph with
a vignette.

FIGURE 5.30
Choosing to specify
a feather for your
selection.

After you apply a feather to a selection, it stays until you discard the selection. Additionally, the feather isn't editable, meaning you can't change the value. So if you apply a 5-pixel feather to a selection, you can't then decide to change it to an 8-pixel feather. You basically have to discard the selection, create a new one, and then apply an 8-pixel feather.

When you're unsure how much of a feather you want, save your selection before you apply a feather (saving selections is covered later in this chapter). This way you can always reapply the feather if necessary.

Did you Know?

Here's an important fact: Feathers are calculated using pixels, not units that are absolute. Because the size of a pixel is dependent on the resolution of your file, a 10-pixel feather might be very soft in a 72ppi file, yet barely recognizable in a 300ppi file (see Figure 5.31). As you get experience in working with feathered selections, you'll get a better feel for how much is right for each task.

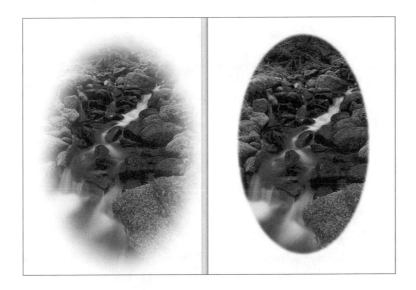

FIGURE 5.31
A 10-pixel feather
in a 72dpi image
(left) and a 300dpi
image (right).

There are many uses for feathering selections. As we mentioned earlier, they can be used to help create soft-edged masks to create vignettes. They can also be used for creating soft cast shadows, for glow effects, for blending photos into each other, and more. I find that they are most useful for selections that you make for purposes of photo retouching. If you have an area that needs an adjustment such as a color shift, doing so with a regular selection will create a visible line that shows where you made the correction. Using a feathered selection, however, will result in a seamless correction that no one will be able to see (see Figure 5.32).

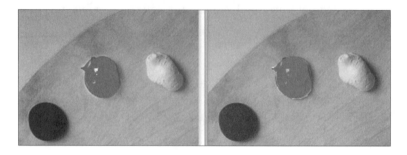

FIGURE 5.32
The paint dab in the middle was adjusted in this photo. The image on the left had a feather applied to the selection before the retouching was done, and the image on the right did not.

By the Way

Tool Options for Everyone

The Tool Options bar is pretty handy and gives quick access to the most commonly used options for each Photoshop tool, but the most *brilliant* part of it is something called Tool Presets, which allow you to save different settings that you use often. For example, say I often use a feathered 4×5 aspect ratio setting for my Rectangular Marquee. I can save that as a Tool Preset and access those settings with one click of a button. You can store many of these tool presets, saving you valuable time as you work on your files.

Of course, these presets aren't limited to the selection tools—you can save tool presets for just about any Photoshop tool. You do so by choosing the settings you want in the Tool Options bar, clicking on the tool icon (the one that looks like a pop-up button), and then clicking on the Create New Tool Preset button. Alternatively, you can choose New Tool Preset from the flyout menu (see Figure 5.33). Give your new tool preset a descriptive name (otherwise you won't remember what each one is), and it will appear in the list from now on (these are application preferences, meaning that even if you close the file you're working on, or open a new or different file, your tool presets will still be present).

Modifying Selections

There are several ways you can modify a selection after it's created. One of the most useful is by using the Select, Inverse command or pressing (⌘-Shift-I) [Ctrl+Shift+I], which basically selects whatever you *don't* have selected (and deselects everything that was selected). Sometimes it's easier to select the one part of an image that you don't want, and then inverse your selection (see Figure 5.34). You can also transform your selection. These transformations that you make (by choosing Select, Transform Selection) apply only to the selection itself and not the pixels inside them. For example, you might use the Rectangular Marquee tool to create a square selection, and then use the Transform Selection command to rotate the square (see Figure 5.35) to effectively get a diamond-shaped selection.

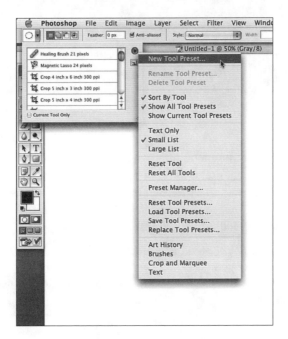

FIGURE 5.33
Defining a new tool preset.

FIGURE 5.34
Choosing to inverse your selection.

FIGURE 5.35
Transforming a
selection.

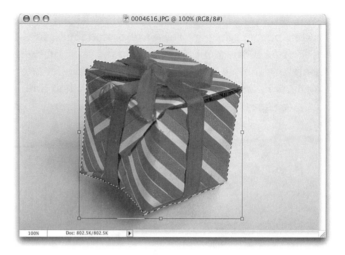

Under the Select, Modify submenu, there are four additional ways you can adjust your selection. All of them are useful and it would be a good idea to experiment with them to fully understand what each one does. In each of these cases, you'll lose your original selection, so you may want to save it before you modify the selection. These are the additional options:

▶ **Border**—Use the Select, Modify, Border command to specify a pixel width for just the edge of your selection (see Figure 5.36), similar to adding a stroke. This command yields a round-cornered selection, which is not appropriate in all cases.

FIGURE 5.36
A selection with the
Border modification
applied to it.

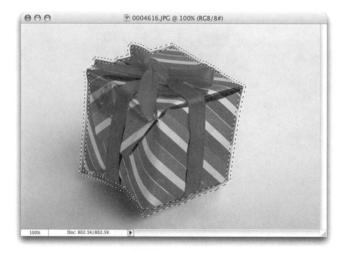

▶ **Smooth**—Not everyone can draw with a mouse as well as they can with a pencil (myself included), so when you're creating selections with the Lasso tools, it's nice to know that you can smooth out your selections by choosing Select, Modify, Smooth. This is also useful when you're making selections with the Magic Wand tool, because it can sometimes create selections with jagged or uneven edges.

▶ **Expand**—At times you will want to enlarge or expand your selection by a specific number of pixels. One such example is if you want to have a border or background around the edges of text. Although you can instead scale your selections using the Transform Selection command I mentioned earlier, many times simply scaling your selection won't work (especially with odd-shaped selections).

▶ **Contract**—There will be times when, rather than expanding your selections, you'll want to contract them. You can do so by choosing Select, Modify, Contract and then specifying the number of pixels you want your selection to shrink.

Saving and Loading Selections

A quick selection is easy enough to make, but many times getting just the perfect selection for your needs can take quite a bit of time (and a double dosage of patience). The last thing you want in that case is to accidentally click somewhere and lose your selection. Or you may want to continue to make adjustments to that selection later. You can save your selections so that you can retrieve them later by choosing Select, Save Selection (see Figure 5.37). It's best to give your selections a descriptive name; otherwise, if you have several of them, it may be difficult to find the right one when you want to load one.

If you want to access the last selection you made, choose Select, Reselect.

Did you **Know?**

In general, it's a good idea to name things carefully, because one day you'll have to edit the file and you'll go crazy trying to remember what you named it. You also never know who else will be working with your file (a co-worker, prepress operator, or client, for example), so naming things that will help people quickly find what they are looking for is important.

Did you **Know?**

When you have selections already saved in a file, you can either continue to save new selections, or add to or modify existing selections (see Figure 5.38). You'll probably get a much better understanding about how selections work when you learn what channels are. Oh, look at that—the next paragraph is about channels!

FIGURE 5.37
Choosing to save
your selection.

FIGURE 5.38
Choosing to modify
an existing selec-
tion.

Channels

No, I'm not referring to the channels on your TV (there are so many of them, yet nothing is ever on). Rather, these channels, also called alpha channels, can be thought of as selections, because in reality that's what they are. You can find them in the Channels palette.

Every file has at least one channel by default, and three or more if it is a color file. For example, an RGB file starts with three channels: one each for red, green, and blue. Photoshop also displays a composite, one for all of the channels combined, although this composite isn't actually a channel itself (see Figure 5.39). You can view and edit each channel individually, giving you total control over your image.

But the real strength here is that you can create your own channels. When you save a selection (as mentioned earlier), Photoshop is creating a channel, and that is how the selection is stored (see Figure 5.40). Channels that you create can contain 256 levels of gray. There are certain file formats that can use the information in channels as well. For example, you can specify that a channel should be a transparency mask when you export a file as a PNG from Photoshop. In contrast to clipping masks (which we'll discuss later in the chapter) that you might save in EPS format, an alpha channel transparency mask can utilize 256 levels of gray.

FIGURE 5.39
The channels of an RGB document.

FIGURE 5.40
A file with several channels saved.

Rather than having to load selections via the Select menu, you can simply (⌘-click) [Ctrl-click] on a channel (in the Channels palette) to load that selection. This is true with any layer, actually—you can select all of a layer's contents this way.

Paths

If you've used Illustrator before, you know what a Bézier path is. We'll learn more about it in Chapter 7, "Using Adobe Illustrator CS," but at a basic level, it's an object-based path that you can draw using Photoshop's Pen tool (see Figure 5.41). It just so happens that Illustrator, InDesign, and Photoshop all have Bézier Pen tools—mainly because these tools are basic drawing tools.

FIGURE 5.41
Drawing a Bézier path with the Pen tool.

The selection tools we've discussed until now aren't really precise drawing tools at all. When you want to draw a high-quality selection, the Pen tool is the way to go. As you draw a path, it automatically creates a vector mask layer (see Figure 5.42). We'll talk about masks later in the chapter, but you're basically creating a vector shape that is filled with colored pixels. A listing also appears in the Paths palette. From the Paths palette, you can choose Save Path from the palette flyout menu to save the path for future use. At any time you can also (⌘-click) [Ctrl-click] on the path in the Paths palette to turn it into an active selection.

FIGURE 5.42
A vector mask layer in the Layers palette.

You can also use paths in the reverse context. You start by creating a selection using any of the methods we've discussed. Then, with the selection active, choose Make Work Path from the Paths palette flyout menu (see Figure 5.43) to turn that selection into a vector path, at which point you can use the Pen tools to further edit that path if necessary.

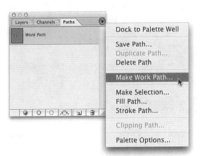

FIGURE 5.43
Creating a work
path from a selec-
tion.

Creating a Clipping Path

A clipping path is basically a mask for an exported EPS image (although the
newer TIFF format supports clipping paths as well). You can save a path with an
image that will define how the image appears in a page layout application, such
as InDesign or QuarkXPress (see Figure 5.44).

FIGURE 5.44
An image as it
appears placed in
InDesign, with (left)
and without (right)
a Photoshop clip-
ping path applied.

Back in Chapter 3, "The Game Plan: Developing a Workflow," we discussed how
InDesign can understand Photoshop's native transparency, so clipping paths
aren't really necessary in a full Adobe workflow. Regardless, it's important to
know about clipping paths in case you need to work with QuarkXPress or send
files to other people.

Begin by creating a path. If you're uncomfortable using the Pen tool, use the
reverse method we mentioned earlier, in which you start with a selection and
then convert it to a path. After the path is created, save it. Then choose Clipping
Path from the Paths palette flyout menu and choose the path you saved. I normally use 2 for my flatness setting (see Figure 5.45).

Finally, for the path to be recognized in a page layout application, choose to save
your file in either Photoshop EPS or TIFF format. See the discussion later in this
chapter for information on how to save files.

FIGURE 5.45
Specifying clipping
path settings.

Layers and Effects

Trying to imagine what Photoshop would be like without layers is like to trying to imagine what a peanut butter and jelly sandwich is like without the bread (everything is just one gooey, sticky mess).

Imagine painting in the traditional method. As you use the brush on the canvas, you're adding paint. If you decide to paint a white cloud over a blue sky, the white paint covers the blue paint under it (some paint might show through, and we'll get to the subject of opacity soon). Theoretically, if you wanted to move that cloud to a different part of the sky, you'd have to cut it out and then glue it elsewhere, leaving a gaping hole in your canvas. It's no different in Photoshop. Let's say I create a blue sky, and then draw a white cloud over a part of it. If I try to select and move that cloud elsewhere, I'll have a hole cut out of the sky where the cloud was originally (see Figure 5.46).

FIGURE 5.46
Moving pixels
leaves a gaping
hole behind.

Now let's talk about layers. Going back to the canvas, imagine that you first painted the sky, and then covered your painting with a clear sheet of acetate (plastic). You then painted the white cloud on the acetate. Think about it: You'd see the same composite result, but if you moved the acetate around, you'd be able to position the cloud independently of the sky under it (see Figure 5.47). In Photoshop, think of a layer as a sheet of acetate—only better. Layers can have opacity values, blend modes, and even special effects such as drop shadows and bevels. As you'll see, Photoshop uses layers extensively to make files more editable and easier to work with.

FIGURE 5.47
Using layers, you can reposition pixels easily.

Layers 101

Let's start with the basics. Layers are controlled via the Layers palette. Every Photoshop file starts with one layer, called a Background layer, which can only be the bottom-most layer in the document (see Figure 5.48). This layer does not support any kind of transparency.

To convert the Background layer so that it acts like any other layer, double-click on it to rename it Layer 0 and click OK.

FIGURE 5.48
The Background
layer of a file.

To add a layer to a file, click on the Create New Layer button in the Layers palette. Alternatively, you can drag an existing layer on top of the Create New Layer icon to create a duplicate layer. You can drag layers up and down to shuffle them within the hierarchy of the Layers palette. Layers at the bottom of the palette are stacked behind those that appear at the top of the palette (see Figure 5.49).

FIGURE 5.49
The same image
with different layer
hierarchies, demon-
strating how layer
order affects the
stacking order of
objects in the docu-
ment.

Viewing and Locking Layers

Besides being able to shuffle the stacking order of objects by moving layers up and down in the Layers palette, you can also choose to show or hide any layer at any time. The little eye icon to the far left of each layer indicates whether a layer is visible (see Figure 5.50). Click once on the eye to hide the layer; click again to show the layer. If you (Option-click) [Alt-click] an eye, Photoshop will automatically hide all the other layers in your document, allowing you to see just the layer you're working on.

FIGURE 5.50
The visibility icon
indicates whether a
layer is shown or
hidden.

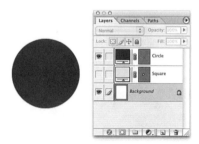

Using the Move tool, you can move the items around on a layer, but sometimes you'll want to move several items together at once—and those items may be on different layers. Because you can select and work with only one layer at a time, one would think that each layer would have to be moved independently. But you, the smart one who is reading this book, know differently. Just to the right of the eye icon is a link box. An icon of a paintbrush indicates that the layer is selected and that any edits to the document will occur on that layer. But when you have a layer selected, you can click on the link boxes of other layers. When you do so, a link icon appears on those layers, indicating that the transform edits you make will occur to those layers as well (see Figure 5.51). Transform edits consist of moving, scaling, and rotating, as well as using the Free Transform tool.

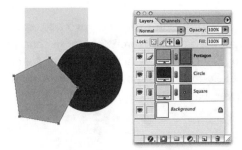

FIGURE 5.51
Several layers linked, indicating that they can be transformed together, all at once.

Layer Opacity and Blend Modes

As we mentioned earlier, you can apply opacity levels to a layer or blend modes that affect the appearance of the pixels on the layer. For example, changing the opacity of the top layer of your document (see Figure 5.52) will allow you to "see through" that layer to the layer underneath—basically allowing the lower layer to show through. Blend modes allow you to specify how the pixels from the upper layer and those from the lower layer mix with each other. For example, if you had two layers and Layer 1 was filled with blue and Layer 2 was filled with yellow, you could set Layer 2 to use the Multiply blend mode to give you a green result.

With the Move tool selected in the toolbox, you can press Shift along with the plus (+) or minus (-) key to step through the different blend modes. This allows you to quickly see how the different blend modes will affect the image's final appearance.

FIGURE 5.52
Specifying a blend
mode and an opaci-
ty value for a
selected layer.

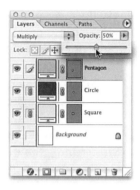

Layer Sets

Managing a lot of layers can be difficult, and having to scroll through a large
number of them is time-consuming as well. Similar in concept to Illustrator,
Photoshop has the capability to create nested layers, or *layer sets*, as they are
called. A layer set is like a folder that has several layers inside it (see Figure 5.53).
You can also put a layer set into another layer set (up to four levels deep), giving
you even more control.

FIGURE 5.53
Several layers
inside a layer set.

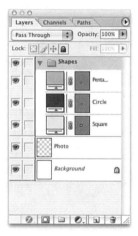

Create new layer sets by clicking on the Create New Set button at the bottom of
the Layers palette, and you can add other layers into a set by dragging them into
the set (see Figure 5.54).

FIGURE 5.54
Dragging a layer
into a layer set.

Layer Styles

Each layer can have several effects applied to it, which Photoshop refers to as
Layer "Styles." You can access the Layer Style dialog by choosing "Blending
Options" from the Layer palette flyout menu. Alternatively, you can double-click
on the layer itself (just not on the actual name of the layer).

To apply a particular effect, check the box for it along the left side of the dialog
(see Figure 5.55). For each effect, there are specific settings you can use to control
how that effect is applied. A layer can have any combination of these effects.

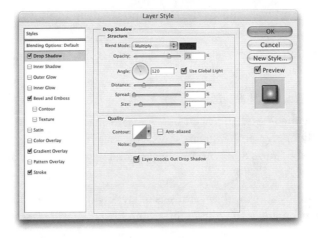

FIGURE 5.55
The Layer Style dia-
log with the Drop
Shadow options
showing.

Did you Know?

> Double-click on a layer's name in the Layers palette to edit the name of the layer. Double-click elsewhere in the layer to open the Layer Style dialog.

Here are some of the functions you can apply in a layer style:

- ▶ **Drop Shadow**—Probably the most over-used effect ever created, the drop shadow is still very useful to make elements seem to pop off the page. This effect creates a soft shadow along the outside of the boundaries of your layer.

- ▶ **Inner Shadow**—Creates a shadow within transparent areas on your layer. The effect causes your image to appear to be cut out of the page.

- ▶ **Outer Glow**—Adds a glow around the perimeter of objects on the selected layer.

- ▶ **Inner Glow**—Applies the reverse effect of the outer glow.

- ▶ **Bevel and Emboss**—Contains several settings that make an image appear as if it were three-dimensional by adding highlighted edges. Used often for making Web buttons.

- ▶ **Satin**—Adds shadows and highlights to make the image appear as if it has the pillowed waves or ripples of satin.

- ▶ **Color Overlay**—Simply adds a color over the entire layer. Colors can be set with an opacity, and this can be used to create color casts or special effects.

- ▶ **Gradient Overlay**—Same as the Color Overlay, but uses gradient fills.

- ▶ **Pattern Overlay**—Same as the Color and Gradient overlays, but with pattern fills.

- ▶ **Stroke**—Can be used to simulate a stroked outline around your layer.

Saving and Reusing Styles

After you've defined a style that you like, you can save it as a style, which you can then easily apply to other layers. After you save a style, it appears in the Styles palette (see Figure 5.56). Alternatively, you can define styles directly from the Styles palette.

Photoshop actually ships with several sets of styles you can use. More important, you can reverse-engineer these styles by seeing how they were created. You can access these sets from the Styles palette flyout menu (see Figure 5.57).

FIGURE 5.56
Choosing a layer
style from the
Styles palette.

FIGURE 5.57
Accessing
Photoshop's prede-
fined styles.

Layer Comps

Because layers can be manipulated so easily in Photoshop, and because they are nondestructive, designers will often use layers to create different variations of a design. By hiding or showing different layers, they can quickly preview several different design ideas—either throughout their own process or to show a client several design possibilities.

Continually hiding and showing layers can be tedious—especially when you're trying to remember which layers were used for which design concept. So the wonderful folks at Adobe added a feature called layer comps, which manages this entire process quite well. Layer comps can save the visibility, position, and appearance (layer style) of each layer in your document. You can then quickly step through different layer comps to see what your designs look like. Because Photoshop is simply remembering the "state" of each layer, if you change an item on a certain layer, that change is automatically made on all of your layer comps; so it's a great time-saver as well.

To create a layer comp, begin first in the Layers palette and hide or show your layers as necessary to show your first design. Then open the Layer Comps palette and click on the Create New Layer Comp button. You'll be presented with a dialog box (see Figure 5.58), where you can name your comp, choose which attributes Photoshop will save, and add a comment (always helpful for those of us who forget easily). Where was I again? Oh, yes, you can create additional layer comps by repeating the process. To preview each of your comps, simply click on the icon along the left side of the Layer Comps palette (see Figure 5.59).

FIGURE 5.58
The New Layer Comp dialog.

FIGURE 5.59
The icon on the left indicates which layer comp is active.

When we discuss scripting later in the chapter, you'll learn how to automatically generate multiple-page PDF files from your layer comps.

Working with Masks

Some superheroes wear masks on their faces. The mask hides certain parts of their face, yet lets other parts show through. Masking in graphic design isn't much different. A mask hides some parts of an image and lets other parts "show through." This is extremely useful when you want to mask parts of an image but don't want to lose any data in your file by having to delete parts of it.

Earlier, we discussed one kind of mask: creating a clipping path for placing images into page layout applications. But there are also needs for masking inside Photoshop itself—such as when you want to have one photo blend into another, or when you want to make a quick selection.

Layer Masks

When it comes to creating a mask for a layer, Photoshop makes the task pretty easy. Using your selection method of choice, choose the layer in the Layers palette, select the area of the image that you want to remain visible, and click on the Add Layer Mask button at the bottom of the Layers palette. This does two things right off the bat: First, it masks the image in your document; second, it creates a second thumbnail in your layer (see Figure 5.60). In fact, let's take a closer look at what's going on in the Layers palette.

FIGURE 5.60
A layer mask applied to a layer.

You'll notice that a masked layer has two thumbnails with a link icon in between them. The thumbnail on the left is the image itself, and the thumbnail on the right is the mask. To edit and work with your image, click on the left icon to highlight it. Any edits you make to that layer will occur to the image itself. If you click and highlight the thumbnail on the right, you can edit the mask itself (see Figure 5.61).

FIGURE 5.61
In this illustration, the mask thumbnail is highlighted.

If you're unsure whether you're in the image editing mode or the mask-editing mode, take a quick look at your document's title bar.

If you move the image with the Move tool, the mask will move along with it, because the link icon between the two thumbnails indicates that they are locked to each other. If you click on the link, it will disappear, allowing you to the move the image and mask independently of each other (see Figure 5.62).

FIGURE 5.62
The image and the layer mask, unlinked.

To remove a mask, drag the mask thumbnail to the Layer's palette Trash icon (in the lower right). You'll get a dialog asking whether you want to apply the mask (which will delete the parts of the image that are masked) or discard it (and the image will return to its full view).

Vector Masks

Although Photoshop has vector tools, it's not a vector-based drawing program. What Photoshop does is use vector outlines to create masks filled with color. For example, when you draw a rectangle using Photoshop's Rectangle tool, it creates a vector mask (which is vector), filled with the color of your choice (which is raster). You can create vector masks by choosing Layer, Add Vector Mask, Reveal All, or by simply drawing a shape with any of Photoshop's vector tools (see Figure 5.63).

FIGURE 5.63
A layer with a vec-
tor mask applied.

Quick Mask Mode

Masks and selections are nearly one and the same. Sometimes you want to create a simple quick selection, and you can best do that by using one of Photoshop's many painting tools. That's where Quick Mask comes into play. Press the Q key on your keyboard to enter Quick Mask mode. You can tell you're in Quick Mask mode because it's indicated in the document's title bar.

When you're in Quick Mask mode, anything you paint or draw shows up in a transparent red color (see Figure 5.64). Press Q again and whatever was not red becomes your selection (see Figure 5.65). This is extremely useful for creating selections that you will use in a layer mask. For example, you want a photo to fade into the layer under it. So you select the layer that the photo is on, press Q, select the Gradient tool, drag a gradient, and press Q again—your selection is now the gradient. Then you click on the New Layer Mask button and you're done.

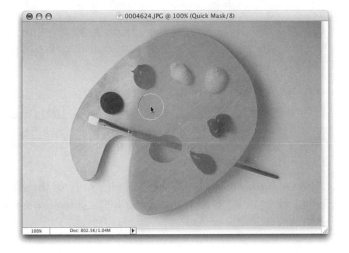

FIGURE 5.64
"Painting" a mask.
Areas that are
painted become a
tint of red.

FIGURE 5.65
Exiting Quick Mask mode converts the painted areas to a selection.

Painting and Drawing

Until now, we've been looking at Photoshop as a tool specifically for working with existing images and photographs, but in reality, there's a whole other side to Photoshop—in which your screen is a canvas and your colors are paints and your pressure-sensitive tablet (or mouse) is your paintbrush.

Choosing Colors

Photoshop allows you to choose colors in just about any way you desire. You can specify colors in RGB, CMYK, HSB, Lab, or Hexadecimal. Additionally, Photoshop also ships with many different industry-standard custom color libraries such as Pantone and TOYO.

You can choose colors in Photoshop in any of several ways:

▶ **Click on the Foreground or Background color proxy in the toolbox—** Photoshop will present you with the Color Picker (see Figure 5.66), where you can choose just about any color, including industry-standard spot colors (by clicking on the Custom button).

▶ **Click on the Foreground or Background color proxy in the Color palette**—Photoshop presents you with the Color Picker, as just described (see Figure 5.67).

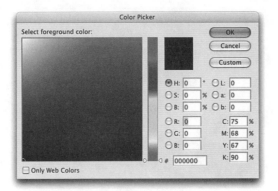

FIGURE 5.66
The Photoshop
Color Picker.

FIGURE 5.67
The Foreground and
Background color
proxies in the Color
palette.

▶ **Click anywhere on the color ramp at the bottom of the Color palette—**
This changes depending on the color mode you have selected and also provides quick shortcuts to black and white (see Figure 5.68).

FIGURE 5.68
The color ramp in
the Color palette.

▶ **Adjust the color sliders in the Color palette—**You can choose to use the
sliders to choose a color by eye, or enter values directly for a specific color.

▶ **Choose a color from the Swatches palette—**You can store your own custom colors as well as access other color libraries, from the Swatches palette
flyout menu (see Figure 5.69).

▶ **Use the Eyedropper tool—**Sample a color from any area on your document
or screen.

FIGURE 5.69
Choosing a color
library from the
Swatches palette.

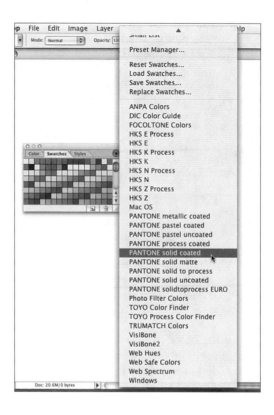

**Did you
Know?**

> To quickly fill an area with the Foreground color, press (Option-Delete) [Alt+Delete].

Gradients

Before soft drop shadows became the latest design fad, there were gradients—fills that fade gradually from one color to another—sometimes with multiple colors (that is, a color spectrum). Gradients can also fade from a color to transparent.

Creating gradients in Photoshop is quite easy, and there are basically two ways to accomplish the task. The first way is to add a Gradient Overlay layer effect as we discussed earlier when talking about layer styles (see Figure 5.70). The second— and far more popular—way is to use the Gradient tool.

With the Gradient tool selected, the Tool Options bar changes to reflect the different options you have for applying gradients. Click on the pop-up arrow to get a list of predefined gradients (see Figure 5.71), and you can choose from any of five types of gradients: linear, radial, angle, reflected, and diamond.

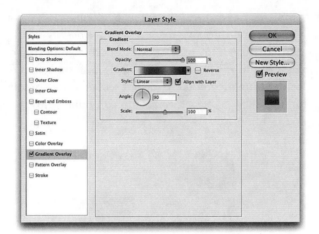

FIGURE 5.70
The Gradient Overlay settings in the Layer Style dialog.

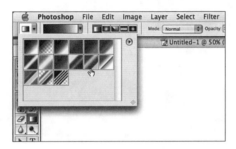

FIGURE 5.71
Choosing a predefined gradient from the Tool Options bar.

To apply a linear gradient, with the Gradient tool selected, position your cursor at the point you want the leftmost color of the gradient to begin. Press the mouse button—and hold it—while you drag to the place where you want the rightmost color of the gradient to end (see Figure 5.72). When you release the mouse, Photoshop will apply the gradient.

> If you don't have a selection made, using the Gradient tool will result in a gradient that fills the entire layer.

By the Way

> You can drag your gradient outside of your selection, or even the document window, so that only a portion of the gradient will be applied.

Did you Know?

You can also create your own gradients by clicking on the gradient proxy in the Tool Options bar to open the Gradient Editor (see Figure 5.73). Click on the New button to define a new gradient. Add a new *color stop* by clicking in an empty area under the gradient. You can edit the colors by double-clicking on the color-stop arrow. Arrows that appear above the gradient are *opacity stops,* and they let you define the transparency of the gradient at a specific point. You can have as many stops as you want in your gradient. The little diamonds that appear in between the color stops are the midpoint of that section of the gradient—meaning that at that point, there's 50% of each color. You can adjust those points by dragging them left and right as well.

FIGURE 5.72
Dragging with the Gradient tool to apply a gradient.

FIGURE 5.73
The Gradient Editor dialog.

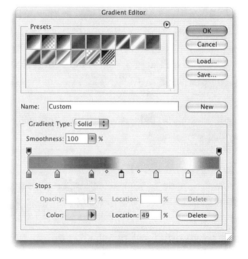

Remember that using the Quick Mask feature along with the Gradient tool can help you create faded selections in the blink of an eye.

The Brush and Pencil Tools

To draw or paint with Photoshop, you can use either the Pencil tool or the Paintbrush tool. The Pencil tool is akin to the speedball inking pens of yesterday, allowing you to lay down solid pixels using different brush shapes (see Figure 5.74). It's great for touching up small areas or for drawing lines and the like. The Paintbrush tool, on the other hand, has more of an organic feel to it, and you can even set it to act and feel like an airbrush (see Figure 5.75). To use these tools, simply choose a brush shape from the pop-up in the Tool Options bar (see Figure 5.76) and have fun painting.

FIGURE 5.74
Drawing with the Pencil tool.

FIGURE 5.75
Drawing with the Paintbrush tool.

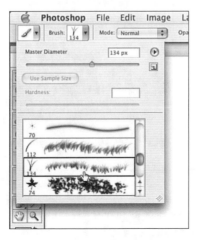

FIGURE 5.76
Choosing a brush from the Tool Options bar.

Pressing the bracket keys on your keyboard—the left [and right] brackets—is a quick way to increase or decrease your brush size.

Obviously, the power of the Brush tool lies in the power behind the brush engine inside Photoshop.

The Brush Engine

Historically, when it came to organic painterly drawing, Photoshop had always played second fiddle to another program called Painter. But that changed when Adobe introduced the new brush engine in Photoshop 7.

Let's take a closer look at this incredibly powerful feature. Click once on the button that appears at the far right of the Tool Options bar when the Brush tool is selected (see Figure 5.77), or choose Window, Brushes to open the Brushes palette. Along the left side of the palette are all the settings you can apply to a brush, the right side contains all the specific controls for each setting, and the bottom features a real-time preview of your brush (see Figure 5.78).

FIGURE 5.77
The Brushes palette icon in the Tool Options bar.

FIGURE 5.78
The Photoshop CS Brushes palette.

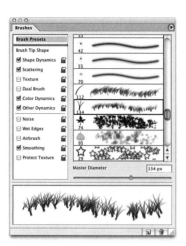

Want more brushes? You can access hundreds of brushes from the Brushes palette flyout menu.

Click on each of the settings along the left to customize the behavior of your brush. With these settings, painters and illustrators can finally get the control they want and need right in Photoshop. For example, the Jitter attributes allow for a level of randomness that gives the brushes a real hand-drawn quality. When you're done finding the right settings for your brush, you can save them to use again later.

Defining Your Own Brush

Photoshop's brush engine lets you define your own custom brush shapes. Start off with a grayscale image and silhouette it. Then select it and choose Edit, Define Brush Preset (see Figure 5.79). Give your custom brush shape a name, and when you choose the Brush tool, you'll see your custom shape appear in the Brush Tip Shape list.

FIGURE 5.79
Defining a custom brush shape.

Vector Shape Tools

Photoshop has a range of vector shape tools that allow you to draw simple elements such as rectangles, ellipses, polygons, and lines (see Figure 5.80). These tools work similarly to those found in InDesign and Illustrator. The main difference is that these tools create vector masks (which we discussed earlier).

FIGURE 5.80
Photoshop's vector drawing tools.

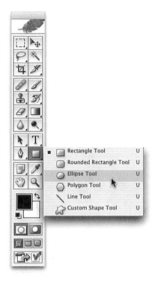

History Brush

Adobe hasn't invented time travel just yet (I'm *sure* it will be in the next version, though), but there *is* a way to go back in time using Photoshop's History brush.

> **Know Your History**
>
> Although Photoshop doesn't have multiple undos (like InDesign and Illustrator do, for example), it does have something called the History palette, which records each step you make as you work. You can step backward one step at a time, or you can jump to a previous step by clicking on the entries in the History palette (see Figure 5.81). Clicking on the Create New Snapshot button will freeze the state of your document in time. This *snapshot* of your document can be used as a reference for other functions (such as the History Brush). Snapshots are stored near the top of the palette—the bottom part of the palette is a running history of the file itself (since the last time it was opened).

The History brush paints in your current file (or canvas) using pixels from a snapshot or a previous state of the file. For example, say when I first opened my file, the sky in the photo was blue. Then I changed that blue color to orange. If I select the History brush and indicate the source to be the original snapshot, painting with the History brush will produce blue pixels as I paint on the sky. This is one way to get the popular "one splash of color in a black and white photo" effect.

FIGURE 5.81
The top section of the History palette contains snapshots; the lower section takes note of each step you take.

To use the brush, select the History brush from the toolbox (see Figure 5.82) and then open the History palette. To the left of each entry in the History palette is an empty square, and clicking there will select it as the source for the History brush (indicated by an icon).

FIGURE 5.82
Choosing the History Brush tool from the toolbox.

Art History Brush

A variation of the History Brush, the Art History brush lets you paint pixels from a previous history state or snapshot, but with a twist. Instead of just copying the pixels exactly, you can paint with artistic brushes, giving a really creative look to your photos. With the Art History brush's default settings, and using the same method as with the History brush, the brush seems to produce very odd results. To best see the effect, you should create a new blank layer and fill it white. As you paint you can easily see how the Art History brush is re-creating the art that was in the snapshot, yet with a very stylized look (see Figure 5.83).

FIGURE 5.83
Painting with the Art History brush on a new white layer.

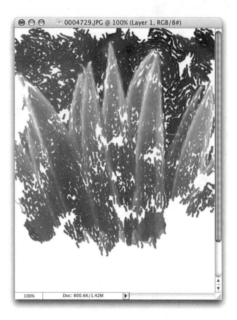

In the Tool Options bar you can adjust any of several options for the Art History brush. It's a good idea to decrease the brush size to 3–5 pixels so you can better see the effect. You'll also want to experiment with the options in the Style pop-up menu (see Figure 5.84). Additionally, you can choose just about any brush shape and size via the Brushes palette.

FIGURE 5.84
Choosing a style from the Art History brush's Tool Options bar.

Remember, if you ever get tool settings just right and you know you're going to want to use that combination of settings again in the future, you can save it as a tool preset.

Photoshop and the Web

We will cover Web graphics extensively in Chapter 6, "Using Adobe ImageReady CS," but for getting graphics ready for the Web quickly, the following basic concepts will serve as an introduction to the world of Web graphics.

Save for Web

The World Wide Web, as we know it today, supports several image formats. Actually, it isn't the Web itself, but the software—or browsers—that people use to view the Web. A Web browser, such as Microsoft Internet Explorer, Netscape Navigator, or Apple's Safari, is a window in which we can view the content of the Web. These browsers support various image formats, mainly GIF and JPEG. There are other formats that are supported through the use of plug-ins—add-on software that you can download (usually free)—which add functionality to your browsers. Formats that are supported by plug-ins are PNG, SWF, and SVG—although the latter two are vector-based formats and don't apply to Photoshop.

If you've ever surfed the Web, you know that speed is everything. Although DSL and cable modems are becoming more and more popular, the majority of people who connect to the Internet still use 56K dial-up connections. That means surfing the Web and viewing Web site pages filled with graphics and images could take a long time. A designer's challenge is to design Web graphics that are small in file size, which would allow their pages to load faster. It's always a balance—you don't want a page that's filled only with text, yet you also don't want a page that contains so many images that a user will skip to the next site because he has to wait too long for your page to load.

The image file formats that are supported in Web browsers have many settings for such things as colors and compression, giving designers some degree of control over the final file size of each graphic. There is a direct correlation between the visual quality of a graphic and its file size. You can choose to make a file size smaller at the expense of how good the image looks. Likewise, a better-looking image will result in a larger file size.

Photoshop's Save for Web feature allows designers to make that decision easily by allowing you to preview an image in any of the supported Web formats, along with all the color and compression settings. The Save for Web feature also lets you know what your final file size will be, giving you all the information you need in order to decide how you want to save your Web graphic—all before you even save the file.

> The Save for Web feature is such an integral feature for Web designers that Adobe has included the entire Save for Web feature inside Illustrator and GoLive as well. We'll cover that specifically when we get to those chapters.

When you're ready to save your image for the Web, you choose File, Save for Web, which will launch a larger-than-life dialog box that features tools, previews, and palettes of its own (see Figure 5.85). We'll cover these settings in detail in the ImageReady and Illustrator chapters.

FIGURE 5.85
The Save for Web dialog in Photoshop CS.

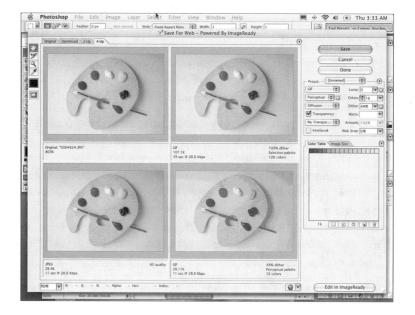

Slicing

In an effort to gain even more control over how images are displayed on the Web, a method called *slicing* was born. By taking a large single image and chopping it up into smaller pieces (called slices), designers found that they could optimize their graphics better (see Figure 5.86).

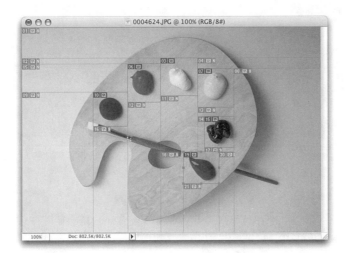

FIGURE 5.86
An image with Web slices indicated.

Photoshop has a Slice tool that lets you indicate how to chop up the image, and you can use Save for Web to optimize each slice individually. There are other benefits to slicing images as well, such as indicating rollovers and animation. We'll cover this subject in detail in the next chapter.

Setting Type

Although you might not need text features to color correct your digital photos, you will most likely need them for doing any kind of Web design. In fact, you never really know when you might need a little bit of text. Although you're better off using Illustrator or InDesign for most text needs, there will be plenty of times when it will make sense to add text in Photoshop.

To add text to your image, choose the Type tool and click in your document. You'll get a blinking insertion mark and you can begin typing. Notice that Photoshop automatically creates a new kind of layer for you—a type layer (see Figure 5.87).

> You can double-click on the thumbnail of a type layer to select the text quickly and easily.

Did you Know?

Use the Move tool to position the type layer in your document. You can also double-click the layer in the Layers palette to apply a layer style, just as you can with any normal layer (remember to click anywhere in the layer except on the name of the layer itself).

FIGURE 5.87
A type layer in the
Layers palette.

Styling Text

With the Type tool selected, you'll notice that the Tool Options bar will update to offer text-specific settings such as font, size, justification (left, centered, right), and color. You can also choose from several antialiasing options (see Figure 5.88).

FIGURE 5.88
Choosing an
antialiasing method
from the Tool
Options bar.

Did you Know?

Antialiasing is a method used to make graphics appear smoother onscreen. With small text especially, antialiasing can make some words blurry or unreadable. Various algorithms are available for antialiasing and Photoshop lets you choose from among them to get the best result. As you change algorithms, you'll see a live preview of your text.

Choose Window, Character and Window, Paragraph to access even more text controls (see Figure 5.89). The Character palette lets you specify kerning and tracking values (the spaces between letters), as well as leading (pronounced "ledding"), which is the amount of space between each line of text in a paragraph.

FIGURE 5.89
The Character and
Paragraph palettes.

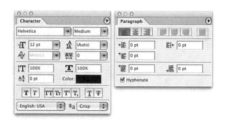

Warping Text

To add cool effects, you can apply warps to text (see Figure 5.90). To do so, select some text and click on the Create Warped Text button in the Tool Options bar (see Figure 5.91) to get the Warp Text dialog. Here you can choose from 15 warp effects, as well as tweak the individual settings of each type of warp (see Figure 5.92).

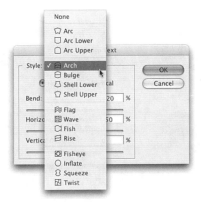

FIGURE 5.90
Text with a warp effect applied to it.

FIGURE 5.91
The Create Warped Text icon in the Tool Options bar.

FIGURE 5.92
Applying a warp from the Warp Text dialog.

> Illustrator has identical warp effects but can apply the effects to any kind of art, as opposed to Photoshop, which is limited to warping only text objects.

By the Way

Adjusting Images

A day will come when a camera will be introduced that can compensate for every possible thing that could go wrong in the fraction of a second it takes to snap a photo. Like the sun going behind the clouds at the just the wrong moment. Like the flash not going on for some reason. Like the bright yellow taxi that just drove by. Like the lights that just went out.

Until that day comes, photos will always need some kind of adjustments made to them so that they reproduce and print the way we want them to. Above that, there are times when we want to purposefully embellish photos, such as give them a specific color cast, or engulf them in shadows.

Photoshop contains a wealth of tools and functions that can help you turn less-than-ideal photos into perfect ones.

Auto Controls

For quick fix-me-ups, Photoshop has three "auto" controls that can make adjustments to files: Auto Levels, Auto Contrast, and Auto Color. All three can be found in the Image, Adjustments submenu (see Figure 5.93). Depending on the photo, these controls can either be "ok" or useless. At times you just want a quick edit and that's fine, but for most other tasks, you'll want to read on....

FIGURE 5.93
The Auto Levels, Auto Contrast, and Auto Color commands in the Image, Adjustments submenu.

Levels

A step above the auto controls is the Levels command. Press (⌘-L) [Ctrl+L] to bring up the Levels dialog. Notice that you are presented with a histogram that shows you the highlight, shadow, and midtone areas of your image (see Figure 5.94). Drag the little triangle sliders to make adjustments.

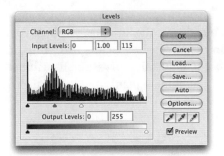

FIGURE 5.94
The Levels dialog.

You can adjust the black and white points of your image by selecting the black Eyedropper tool in the dialog and then clicking on the darkest area of your photo. Repeat again with the white eyedropper, clicking on the lightest point in your image. The histogram will then update as Photoshop makes the adjustments.

I often use levels to "tint back," or lighten, images. Drag the black Output Level triangle (lower left) toward the right until you get what you need.

Did you Know?

What's great about the Levels dialog is that you can apply these changes to the entire image overall, or you can make adjustments to specific color channels by choosing one from the pop-up (see Figure 5.95). After you're happy with the adjustments you've made, click OK.

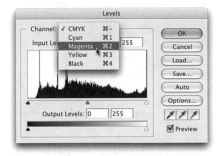

FIGURE 5.95
Choosing to edit the levels of the magenta channel only.

Curves

Although the Levels feature is easy to use and pretty much straightforward, it's limited to applying linear adjustments only. For even more control over the tonal range and values of your images, choose Image, Adjustments, Curves. Here you also have the eyedroppers to choose black and white points, but you have more precision when it comes to making tonal adjustments.

The grid in the center is your image—the region at the upper right is where the highlights are, and the region at the lower left is where your shadows live. Midtones are smack in the middle (see Figure 5.96). You can click in the grid to add a point, and drag it to adjust the curve. The benefit here is that you can open up the shadows, but also add more points and adjust the curve to keep the highlights from getting blown out (see Figure 5.97).

FIGURE 5.96
The different areas of the Curves grid.

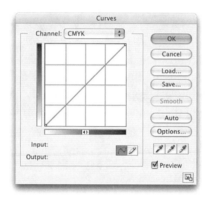

FIGURE 5.97
Adjusting a curve.

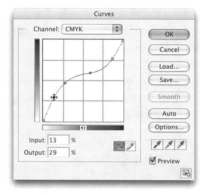

Did you Know?

As you drag in your document, a circle will appear on your curve indicating where that area falls on the curve. You'll see that as you click on the lighter areas of your image, the circle will appear closer to the top right of the grid, whereas darker areas will fall lower and to the left (see Figure 5.98).

Just as with levels, you can apply curves to the entire image as a whole or to individual channels. After you've made your adjustments, you can click OK.

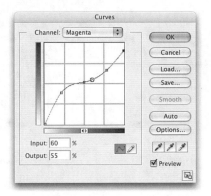

FIGURE 5.98
The circle indicates
where on the curve
your chosen
pixel is.

Shadow/Highlight

Photoshop CS introduces the brand-new Shadow/Highlight command that auto-matically adjusts both the shadows *and* the highlights of a picture while using "smart" intelligence to ensure that the image doesn't lose any detail.

> The Shadow/Highlight command works only on RGB and Grayscale images. It won't work on CMYK images.

By the Way

To use this command, choose Image, Adjustments, Shadow/Highlight (see Figure 5.99). Use the Shadows and Highlights sliders to make adjustments as necessary, and then click OK (see Figure 5.100).

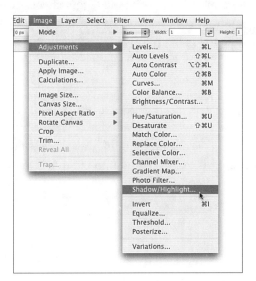

FIGURE 5.99
Choosing
Shadow/Highlight
from the Image,
Adjustments sub-
menu.

FIGURE 5.100
Adjusting the
Shadow/Highlight
sliders.

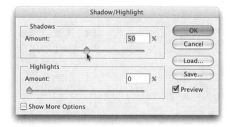

Adjustment Layers

All the adjustments we've spoken about until now are what we call "destructive adjustments," because after these adjustments are applied, the actual pixels in the file are changed and there's no way to go back to the original version of the file.

Although there are times when you know that what you're doing is final (or you have the original backed up if you need it), there are plenty of times when you are required to make multiple adjustments (for example, each time you go back to visit the clients, they change their mind—although I'm *sure* that never happens to you).

So Adobe created something called an *adjustment layer* that allows you to keep certain adjustments "live" and editable—even long after you've saved and closed the file. This is accomplished by adding the adjustment itself as a special kind of layer. To add an adjustment layer for Levels, for instance, click on the Adjustment Layer button at the bottom of the Layers palette and choose Levels (see Figure 5.101). You'll see the normal Levels dialog, as you've seen earlier, but when you click OK, you'll notice that a new layer has been added to your file. Any layer that falls below this adjustment layer will be affected by it (see Figure 5.102).

Adjustment layers are great when you want to make adjustments to only certain layers in your file. Any layers that appear above the adjustment layer won't be affected.

At any time, you can double-click on that adjustment layer to edit it or make changes to it. Of course, you can also drag it to the trash icon in the Layers palette if you want to get rid of it altogether.

FIGURE 5.101
Applying an adjust-ment layer.

FIGURE 5.102
The applied adjust-ment layer, as it appears in the Layers palette.

Match Color

It always ends up that you have several photos from a photo shoot and the light-ing and color are good in some photos, but the person's expression and face are better in another. Using the Match Color feature, you can pull the color from one image and apply it to another one.

First, open both images—the one you want to change, and the one that has the color that is perfect, which we'll call the source image (that's where the color data will be coming from). From the document that has the bad color, choose Image, Adjustments, Match Color (see Figure 5.103) to open the Match Color dialog box. The first step is to look at the Image Statistics area and, from the Source pop-up, choose the source file (see Figure 5.104). Now that you can see the new color applied, you can tweak the settings using the sliders in the Image Options section of the dialog. When you're done, click OK.

FIGURE 5.103
Choosing the
Match Color com-
mand from the
Image, Adjustments
submenu.

FIGURE 5.104
Choosing the
source file in the
Match Color dialog.

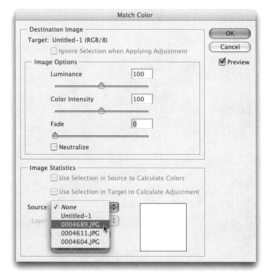

Dodge and Burn Tools

If you've ever spent time in a traditional darkroom before, you know that *dodging* is underexposing film, making it lighter, whereas *burning* film is overexposing it, making the image darker. Photoshop has both Dodge and Burn tools that let you "paint on" these kinds of effects. Simply choose the Dodge or Burn tool (see Figure 5.105), choose a brush size, and go to town.

FIGURE 5.105
Choosing the Burn tool from the tool-box.

While using the Burn tool, you can hold down the (Option) [Alt] key to temporarily access the Dodge tool. The same applies in the reverse.

Did you Know?

Retouching Images

There are some people who make their living doing one thing only—retouching photographs. Although some tasks are complicated and require masterful re-creations of elements in a photo, many retouching jobs simply require getting rid of a few scratches or a stain. Others require removing a person from a photo. In either case, Photoshop has several tools you can use to assist in the task.

The Clone Stamp Tool

Probably the most popular retouching tool of all time, the Clone Stamp tool does what its name implies. You sample one area of your image and then paint with the tool elsewhere. As you paint, a clone of the area that you sampled is painted in the new location. For example, you could sample a single flower and then create many more of them in your photo (see Figure 5.106).

To use the Clone Stamp tool, select it from the toolbox (see Figure 5.107) and hover the mouse cursor over the area you want to sample. Press the (Option) [Alt] key and click once to sample the area. Now move your mouse pointer to hover over the area you want to paint on, and click and press the mouse to clone the area.

FIGURE 5.106
The original photo (left) and the retouched one.

FIGURE 5.107
Choosing the Clone Stamp tool from the toolbox.

Did you Know?

You may want to work on a copied layer when doing retouching—this way you always have the original to go back to if necessary. To duplicate a layer, drag the layer to the New Layer icon in the Layers palette.

Besides being used to duplicate objects, the Clone Stamp tool is very useful for fixing up blemishes and stains, or for repairing parts of a photo—such as removing a telephone wire or removing a mole from a person's face. Just sample a clean area and clone it over the blemished area.

The Healing Brush

I still remember the first time I saw a demonstration of the Healing Brush tool in action, and the only word to describe what it does is "magic." One of the problems with using the Clone Stamp tool is that not every part of an image has the same underlying tonal values. For example, say you want to cover up a mole on a person's face. Because of the lighting in the photo, the right side of the person's face is darker than the left side. If you take a sample for the Clone Stamp tool from one side of the face and try to clone the other side of the face, you'll see a visible change of tone and luminosity where you've painted (see Figure 5.108).

FIGURE 5.108
Sampling from one side of the face to the other using the Clone Stamp tool results in a noticeable difference in tonal values.

The Healing Brush icon looks like a Band-Aid. It makes all of your boo-boos better.

Did you Know?

You use the Healing Brush tool the same way you use the Clone Stamp tool. Find a nice clean area, (Option-click) [Alt-click], and then paint over the area you want to fix. At first, it appears to be painting it all wrong because you clearly see the brush marks (see Figure 5.109). But when you let go, Photoshop examines the luminosity and tonal values of that area and compensates for them. This means you can clone from the dark side of a face to the light side of the face without worrying about the shading (see Figure 5.110).

FIGURE 5.109
The Healing Brush,
as you apply it.

FIGURE 5.110
The final result.

The Patch Tool

Calling on the same underlying technology as the Healing Brush, the Patch tool
provides a different way to quickly clean up or repair parts of your image. The
way it works is you select the Patch tool (see Figure 5.111) and then draw a selection around the blemished area of your photo (just like with the Lasso tool).
When you've selected the area, click inside the selected area and drag the selection to a clean area of your photo (see Figure 5.112).

FIGURE 5.111
Choosing the Patch tool from the toolbox.

FIGURE 5.112
Dragging the patch area to a clean part of the photo.

Note that you can use this tool in the reverse as well. Simply choose the Destination option (see Figure 5.113) in the Tool Options bar (rather than the default Source setting) and select a clean area of your photo. Then drag the selection on top of blemished areas.

Blurring Images

When there are excessive artifacts in your image, you can try applying a Gaussian blur to soften the image, and reduce the effect of the artifacts. Above that, the Gaussian Blur filter can be used for special effects, such as when you want part of an image to appear in soft focus, or even completely out of focus.

Choose Filter, Blur, Gaussian Blur to bring up the dialog, and experiment with different radius values until you achieve the effect you're looking for (see Figure 5.114). This filter can also be helpful when you're trying to clear up moiré patterns that result from scanning photos that have been printed (halftones).

FIGURE 5.114
Applying a
Gaussian blur.

Did you Know?

There are plenty of other blur effects you can apply to achieve special effects, such as motion, radial, and lens blurs.

To blur just a few pixels at a time, you can use the Blur tool. I find it incredibly useful to soften up the edges after I've silhouetted an image.

Sharpening Images

For images that are blurry or out of focus, you can try to sharpen them by choosing Filter, Sharpen, Unsharp Mask. I find that almost every photo that I scan or import requires some level of sharpening—especially images that I will be uploading for viewing on the Web. Sharpening a photo enhances the edges or borders of color, giving a clearer image that seems to have more life to it (see Figure 5.115). You want to be careful not to oversharpen an image, though, because this will introduce visible artifacts (see Figure 5.116).

FIGURE 5.115
Applying the Unsharp Mask filter.

I was always taught to consider the line screen at which the image will be printing to best determine the radius setting for Unsharp Mask. For a 133-line screen, set your radius to 1.3 pixels. A 200-line screen would get a 2.0 radius setting, and so on. Of course, line screens apply only to images that will be used for print purposes.

Alternatively, you can use the Sharpen tool to touch up small parts of your image interactively.

I've found that many times, sharpening will enhance not only the faces of people and objects in the photo, but also dust and scratches in the photo, making them visible. After sharpening, you may need to apply the Dust & Scratches filter to clear up those artifacts.

FIGURE 5.116
Too much sharpen-
ing can add
unwanted artifacts.

Getting Rid of Dust and Scratches

Usually when scanning from photo prints, you'll notice dust or scratches in your scanned image. Sometimes it's because the glass on your scanner is dirty (I clean my scanner glass daily), whereas other times it's because the photo itself has scratches on it. In those cases you can choose Filter, Noise, Dust & Scratches to clear them up (see Figure 5.117). Be careful not to use too high a setting because doing so might blur out parts of your image that should remain sharp.

Rather than applying the Dust & Scratches filter to an entire image, I use the following technique to save time and take advantage of the Dust & Scratches filter while retaining the sharp parts of my image:

Apply the Dust & Scratches filter, and use a setting that is just a bit more than you would ordinarily use. Then click on the Create New Snapshot icon in the History palette to create a snapshot of the blurred image. Press (⌘-Z) [Ctrl+Z] to undo the Dust & Scratches filter. You now have your original file. Select the History Brush, and in the History palette click the box to the left of the snapshot you just took. This sets the History brush to paint from that snapshot. Now paint over the scratched-up areas on the photo (use a big enough soft-edged brush). This allows you to easily and selectively apply the Dust & Scratches filter.

FIGURE 5.117
Applying the Dust &
Scratches filter.

Applying Filters

One of Photoshop's trademarks is the capability to quickly change the appearance of a photograph or an image. Not only does Photoshop ship with a laundry list of filters for this purpose, but you also can buy other third-party filters for even more specialized purposes. Here we'll discuss some of the more widely used filters.

> If you notice that most of Photoshop's filters are grayed out, there's a good chance your document is set to grayscale or CMYK (see Figure 5.118). In reality, many of Photoshop's filters will work only in RGB documents. This is specifically due to the fact that those filters use calculations that can be applied only in RGB. If you need to use one of these filters in a CMYK document, choose Image, Mode, RGB to switch color modes, apply the filter, and then choose Image, Mode, CMYK to go back to your original color space. Be aware that color shift may (and most likely will) occur.

Did you Know?

Filter Gallery

Besides being able to retouch just about any image in Photoshop, you can also stylize or adjust a photo to give it a certain look. For example, Photoshop can apply a filter to a standard photograph to make it appear as if was painted with watercolor or drawn with chalk and charcoal.

FIGURE 5.118
Many filters are grayed out for CMYK images.

Photoshop's filter menu is filled with a plethora of these types of effects (see Figure 5.119), but unless you know exactly what you're looking for, it can be quite time-consuming having to go through them all and see how your selected image will look with a filter applied. So it's with good reason that Photoshop CS introduced a new feature called Filter Gallery that allows you to visually apply any of Photoshop's many artistic and stylistic filters—and even combine them—in a single dialog box.

FIGURE 5.119
Choosing from Photoshop's plethora of stylistic filters.

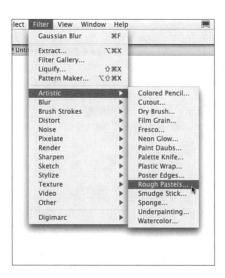

The Filter Gallery feature works only on RGB and grayscale files. To apply a filter to a CMYK file, you'll have to first convert the file to RGB, apply the filter, and then convert the image back to CMYK.

Choose Filter, Filter Gallery and you're presented with a full-screen dialog that consists of four sections (see Figure 5.120). The far-left area gives you a preview of your image, and the middle section is where you choose the kind of filter you want to apply. The upper-right section allows you to tweak the individual settings of the filter that's chosen in the center panel, and the lower-right panel allows you to control multiple filters, and how they are applied to your image.

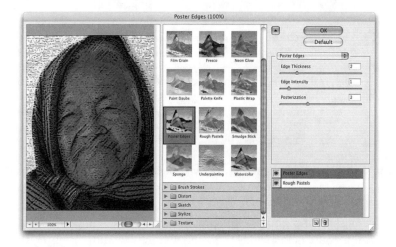

FIGURE 5.120
The Filter Gallery dialog.

Using Filter Gallery is not only easy and useful, but addictive and fun. The possibilities are endless. Why settle for a standard stock photo for that brochure when you can create an entire stylized look by applying filters?

What makes this feature so powerful is how it enables you to experiment and apply multiple filters to your image. On the lower-right section of the dialog, use the New Effect Layer button to add another effect (as many as you like), and choose a different filter from the middle panel (see Figure 5.121). Stacking order is important, so you can also drag the filters up and down to see how the appearance changes depending on which filter is applied last. You can also disable an effect by clicking on the eye icon to the immediate left of the effect listing.

FIGURE 5.121
Applying multiple fil-
ters to an image.

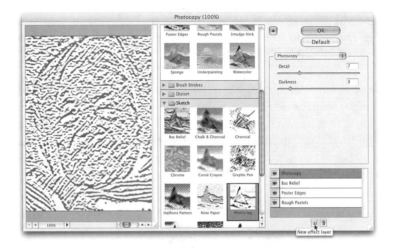

You can also apply filter effects to gradients or patterns that you've created to make interesting and unique backgrounds.

Extract

When we were talking about selections, way back in the beginning of this chapter, we mentioned how you can use tools such as the Magic Wand and the Magnetic Lasso to help make selections. Many times what you're trying to do is remove the background from a photograph (called silhouetting). Depending on the image, this could be a tedious task, and you may want to try using the Extract filter.

When you choose Filter, Extract, you'll be presented with another large dialog, with a large preview of your image in the center (see Figure 5.122). Select the Edge Highlighter tool to trace over the edge of the shape you're trying to silhouette. You can adjust the size of the brush, and the goal here is to have the actual edge you're tracing fall into the highlighted area. Make the brush big enough that you can easily trace the edge, but at the same time, don't make it so big that other elements are being highlighted as well (see Figure 5.123).

When you've highlighted the edge, switch to the Fill tool and click on the part of the image you want to keep. Whatever is not highlighted in your file will be removed by the Extract filter. Click on the Preview button to see what the results will look like (see Figure 5.124). Click OK when you're done.

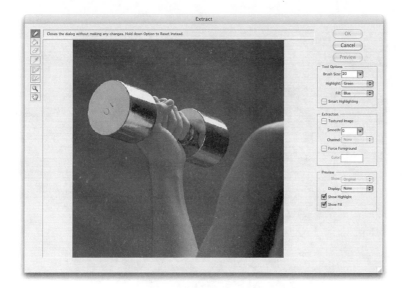

FIGURE 5.122
The Extract dialog.

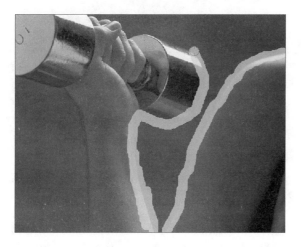

FIGURE 5.123
Tracing over the
edge of your object
with the Edge
Highlighter tool.

In my experience, I've found that at times you want to manually silhouette an image (rather than use the Extract filter), because either the actual shape isn't good, or you want to enhance it. For example, if a person's hair is blowing in the wind and a few strands are flying in odd directions, you'll want to get rid of those strands, not keep them.

Did you
Know?

FIGURE 5.124
A preview of the
object with the
background
extracted.

Liquify

Thinking back, one of the highlights of kindergarten for me was finger painting (hey, it wasn't that long ago). The cool squishy paint, the smell, and, most of all, the ability to mush around and mix the colors to create art worthy of nothing less than my mother's refrigerator door. Although Photoshop can't create bright orange handprints on your classmate's dress, the Liquify feature can come pretty close to adding fun to your day (and Mom will still hang it on the fridge).

Seriously, though, the Liquify filter can be quite useful by allowing you to smudge, pull, and distort your photos. Begin by choosing Filter, Liquify, and once again your entire screen will be filled with a dialog box (see Figure 5.125). Choose any of the liquify tools along the left of the dialog and change the brush size by using the bracket keys on your keyboard. Other options are available in the Tool Options section on the right side of the dialog, and there's an option to use your pressure-sensitive tablet as well (see Figure 5.126).

What's so great about this filter is that you can apply distortions to your file, but you can also reconstruct your image to reverse the effect of your distortions by using the Reconstruct tool. You can also use the Freeze Mask tool to highlight areas you don't want affected by the distortion tools. If you use the Liquify filter on a low-resolution image, you'll see real-time performance and you'll have a fun time distorting your image. But you won't be having as much fun on high-resolution images because applying distortions to them takes a lot of computing power.

FIGURE 5.125
The Liquify dialog.

FIGURE 5.126
Using the Liquify tools to apply distortions to your image.

If you've used Illustrator before, you may be familiar with something called "mesh." Used for gradients and envelopes, a mesh is a matrix of points used to describe a distortion (in it's most basic form). Photoshop incorporated this mesh concept behind the scenes with the Liquify filter in that as you use the tools to create your distortions, Photoshop saves all the information as a mesh. At home, you're thinking, *"Um, glad to hear that—let's get on with the lesson already,"* but what this allows you to do is save your distortion mesh from Photoshop and apply it to other files (see Figure 5.127).

FIGURE 5.127
The Load and Save
Mesh buttons in
the Liquify dialog.

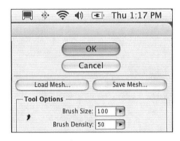

Let's apply the concept to a real-world example. You are working with a low-resolution file in your comps, and then when you get client approval, you'll replace all of your files with high-resolution ones. You can save the mesh from your low-res file and then apply it to your high-res one. To save a mesh, click on the Save Mesh button in the Liquify dialog, and use the Load Mesh button to load one.

Noise

In physics, the word *noise* is defined as "a disturbance, especially a random and persistent disturbance, that obscures or reduces the clarity of a signal." But as with most things in life, you can take something that appears to be negative and turn it around, making it into a positive—something you can use. At times you may have distortion in certain parts of an image, and adding some noise to that area might improve the overall appearance. Here are two examples:

▶ Most digital cameras save pictures in JPEG format, and the pictures can sometimes contain artifacts (random pixels and anomalies, and so forth). Many times these artifacts appear due to distortion in the Blue channel. Applying some noise to just the Blue channel might result in a smoother and cleaner image overall.

▶ Gradients that span large areas (entire pages, spreads, or large documents, such as movie posters) can print with banding—visible shifts or "steps" of color. This is especially evident with light colors, such as yellow. Adding a bit of noise can visually break up these steps and produce a smoother-looking gradient (although more grainy in appearance).

**Did you
Know?**

Adding noise is also a great way to create background textures and special effects.

To add noise to a selection (or, if nothing is selected, an entire image), choose Filter, Noise, Add Noise. Use the Amount slider to control how much noise is added, and choose Uniform or Gaussian distribution (see Figure 5.128). I find that when you're adding smaller doses of noise, Gaussian looks best, but Uniform gives a better appearance when you're adding large amounts of noise. The Monochromatic option adds only black noise (very useful for mezzotint-like effects).

FIGURE 5.128
Applying noise to a selection.

Automating Tasks

We've all made the following statement at some point in our lives: "For the price I paid for this computer, it should be making my coffee too." Well, that may be asking too much, but it isn't too much to ask your computer to do repetitive tasks for you while you're busy refilling your mug with your favorite brew.

You'll be happy to know that Photoshop (along with its sibling apps Illustrator and InDesign) has best-in-class support for scripting and automation. You'll also find plenty of premade scripts and features ready to go right out of the box.

Actions

So you're probably thinking, *"Sure, automation is great and everything, but I don't know—or even want to know—how to write in scripting language,"* right? Have no fear because Photoshop has something called Actions—which require no knowledge of programming languages or any math, for that matter (I'm not a big fan of math).

The way it works is quite simple. You basically perform a set of operations once to show Photoshop what you want to do, and you save that sequence of events as an Action. Then whenever you want to perform that sequence of events again, you play the script and Photoshop performs all the steps for you.

For example, say you have a CD that you use often, which is filled with RGB stock photos. You can't use the photos as-is, so each time you want to use one of these stock photos, you open the file, convert it to CMYK, change the resolution, and then save it as a TIFF. So you open the Actions palette and click the Create New Action button (see Figure 5.129). You name the file and click the Record button. Then you open a file, convert it to CMYK, change the resolution, and then save the file as a TIFF, all as you would normally do. When you are finished, you click on the Stop Recording button in the Actions palette. And you're done.

FIGURE 5.129
Creating a new Action with the Actions palette.

The next time you need to use a photo from that CD, you can use the Action you recorded to do the conversion for you automatically. Now this may sound nice and all, saving you a few keystrokes, but it gets even better. You can apply an Action to an entire group of files at once, called batch processing. In this way, you can apply conversions to all the images on your CD automatically—all while you go and grab some lunch.

To apply a batch Action, choose File, Automate, Batch and then specify the Action and choose a source location (where the files are being opened from) and a destination location (where you want the adjusted files to be saved). This being Adobe Photoshop, of course, you also have many options on how to name new files, and how to deal with dialog boxes and warnings (see Figure 5.130).

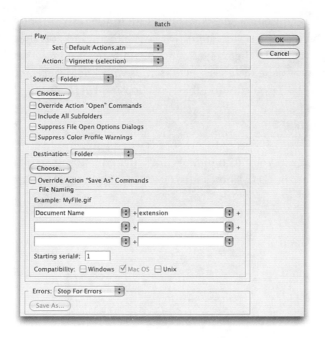

FIGURE 5.130
The Batch dialog.

Scripts

Photoshop has built-in support for both AppleScript (used on Macintosh computers) and Visual Basic Script (used on Windows computers). If you are familiar with either of these scripting languages, you can tell Photoshop to do just about anything.

> Scripts and Actions differ in that Actions are simply a recording of specific keystrokes. Scripts can contain logic and perform functions based on different conditions. For example, in the Actions example mentioned earlier, a script could check what color mode the document is in and perform different functions depending on what the setting is. Scripts can also allow Photoshop to "talk" with other applications. For example, you could have a script do the file conversions and then launch InDesign and place the photos into InDesign and print a catalog of images. Actions are limited to functions within the application.

By the Way

If you're like me, and can write a script as well as you can write a thesis on the advances of brain surgery in the twenty-first century, then you're thinking that this scripting stuff won't be of much help in your everyday life.

Don't despair, because nowhere is it stated that to use a script, you have to write it yourself. There are plenty of people who write them and post them to the Web, sell them, or even make themselves available to write custom scripts for people. More important, Adobe includes several scripts with Photoshop that you can use right out of the box. You can find these by choosing File, Scripts.

Exporting Layers

The Export Layers to Files script is useful for when you want to create a separate file for each layer in your document. What's great about this script is that it can generate files in JPEG, Photoshop, TIFF, PDF, Targa, or BMP formats (see Figure 5.131).

FIGURE 5.131
Running the Export Layers to Files script.

Exporting Layer Comps

We discussed earlier how layer comps can assist in keeping tabs on multiple design ideas within a single Photoshop document. To extend that functionality even further, Photoshop includes three scripts specifically designed for the layer comps feature. You can automatically generate separate files for each of your comps, create a multiple-page PDF file that contains all of your designs, or create a Web photo gallery of your designs (which we'll discuss momentarily)—all with a single command.

Photomerge

Some cameras are designed to shoot photos in panoramic mode, giving you a very wide view of such things as a landscape or a stadium. There's also a technique of using a regular camera to shoot a panoramic view in multiple photographs, which you can then "stitch" together in Photoshop. Photomerge is an automatic feature that takes a range of specified files and attempts to create one single large file by analyzing the edges of each of the pictures and aligning them where they match. Photomerge actually does a very impressive job, and of course you can touch up the final file as necessary, using Photoshop's other retouching tools.

Choose File, Automate, Photomerge to get the Photomerge dialog. After you've chosen the source files (see Figure 5.132), click OK and watch as Photoshop does all the work (see Figure 5.133).

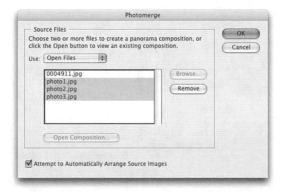

FIGURE 5.132
Specifying the source images to be merged.

FIGURE 5.133
The separate pictures (top) and the final merged image (bottom).

Crop and Straighten Photos

Scripts are cool, and watching scripts work right before your eyes is even cooler. One of the problems with scanning images on a flatbed scanner is that it's a pain to make sure that each photo is perfectly straight. It's also time-consuming to have to scan one picture at a time.

The Crop and Straighten Photos feature solves all of that by allowing you to cram several photos on your scanner at once and scan it as one large image. You also don't need to fret about whether the images are perfectly straight. Scan your photos and choose File, Automate, Crop and Straighten Photos (see Figure 5.134). Then watch as Photoshop magically detects each photo, rotates it perfectly, and then puts each one into its own file.

FIGURE 5.134
Choosing the Crop and Straighten Photos command.

Web Photo Gallery

So you've got a whole bunch of photos that you want to upload to the Web to show a client who is vacationing in some lovely remote village that just happens to have Internet access (if such a thing exists, I have yet to see it). The automation technique called Web Photo Gallery will create an HTML page for you with all the images you specify in the dialog (see Figure 5.135). You can choose from several styles of pages and even specify thumbnails and security options.

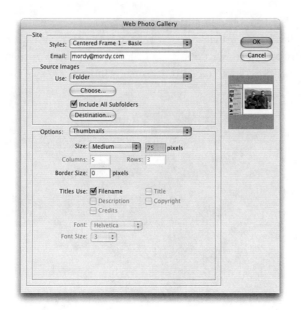

FIGURE 5.135
The Web Photo
Gallery dialog.

Spot Colors

We discussed RGB colors and CMYK inks before, but there is also an additional "color space" called spot colors. A spot color is a specified ink color that printers can use to reproduce a color exactly. There are different ways of specifying colors, and one of the most popular in the United States is the Pantone Color Matching System. Pantone publishes a guide of specific named colors. When you specify a Pantone color, your printer knows exactly what color you want, because he uses the same Pantone guide to know what ink to put on press.

Spot colors play a very specific role in Photoshop (they play a much larger role in applications like InDesign and Illustrator). Photoshop can create spot channels, where a channel is specified as a spot color. Additionally, spot colors are used when one is creating photos that will print entirely in one or several different custom colors—most commonly, duotones.

Spot Channels

Just as there are channels in your document for RGB or CMYK plates, you can also have channels for spot color plates. You can add a spot channel by opening the Channels palette and choosing New Spot Channel from the palette flyout menu (see Figure 5.136). The benefit here is that you can specify an exact color so that you can get a better preview onscreen. From the New Spot Channel dialog box, click on the color proxy to open the Color Picker. You can then choose from any of several standard spot color libraries (see Figure 5.137).

FIGURE 5.136
Creating a spot channel.

FIGURE 5.137
Choosing a Pantone library.

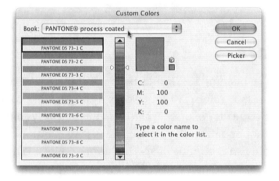

Did you Know?

Anything that appears on a spot channel will separate on its own spot color plate when printed from an application like InDesign CS.

Monotones, Duotones, Tritones, and Quadtones

By far, the most common use of spot color in Photoshop is related to multitone files, which include monotones, or images that are entirely one spot color; duotones, or images that consist of two spot colors; tritones, or images containing three spot colors; and quadtones, which are images that contain—you guessed it—four spot colors.

Duotones are mainly used to add color or style to print jobs that are printing in only two spot colors. Multitone files can also be used to add tonal depth to an image—reason enough that some photographers and printers will print black and white photos as duotones made up of black and gray.

To create a multitone file, you must first make sure that your file is in Grayscale mode. If it isn't already, choose Image, Mode, Grayscale. You can then choose Image, Mode, Duotone, and you'll be presented with the Duotone Options dialog box. From the Type pop-up at the top of the dialog, choose one of the four options (see Figure 5.138).

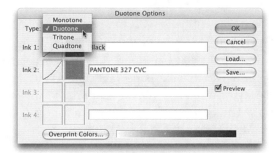

FIGURE 5.138
Choosing to specify a duotone from the Duotone Options dialog.

> For most applications to print duotones correctly, they must be saved as Photoshop EPS files. Illustrator and InDesign will also accept duotones saved as Photoshop PDF files.

By the Way

There are three settings for each ink:

▶ **Curves**—Click on the curves box to edit the duotone curve values for each ink color (the same way we adjusted curves earlier in the chapter).

▶ **Ink Color**—Click on the ink color proxy to choose the ink color.

▶ **Ink Name**—Enter the name for the ink. If you choose a color from the Color Picker, a name will automatically be added for you.

> The ink name is extremely important in spot color workflows. To avoid having multiple plates separate for the same spot color, make sure that the spot color name in Photoshop and the spot color name in your page layout application are the same.

Did you Know?

If fooling around with duotone ink curves isn't your thing, you can use one of several settings that the folks at Adobe were kind enough to include with Photoshop. Click on the Load button in the Duotone Options dialog and navigate to the Adobe Photoshop CS, Presets, Duotones folder, where you can choose from duotones, tritones, and quadtones. Don't worry about the colors that are in these presets—you can easily change the colors yourself—but the valuable parts of these files are the curve settings. Experiment with different presets to find one that suits your needs.

Saving and Printing

When you're done with your file, you can either print it or save it in any of several formats. To print your file, choose File, Print, but you'll get more options when you choose File, Print with Preview (see Figure 5.139). Here you can scale and control the position of the art on your page, and choose color management options, such as specifying a color profile for your printer. You can also click on the pop-up menu (the Show More Options button) to choose output options such as bleeds and registration marks (see Figure 5.140).

FIGURE 5.139
The Print dialog.

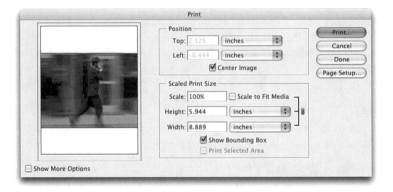

When saving your files, you can choose from many of Photoshop's supported formats, including JPEG, Photoshop PDF, Photoshop EPS, PNG, TIFF, or even Targa files (used for video workflows). Depending on your workflow, you may require different file formats. In Part III of this book, "The Projects," we'll dive deeper into many of these file formats.

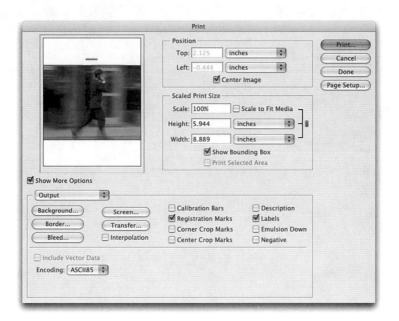

FIGURE 5.140
Specifying other
print-specific
options.

CHAPTER 6

Using Adobe ImageReady CS

Adobe began including the entire ImageReady application in the box along with Photoshop when Photoshop 5.5 was released. And now, many people aren't even aware that ImageReady exists, let alone know that it's already installed on their computer. Although Photoshop (and Illustrator as well) has a robust Save for Web feature for exporting Web graphics, there are many things that ImageReady—a dedicated Web graphics production program—can offer, including animation and rollover effects. In fact, the Save for Web features found in Photoshop, Illustrator, and GoLive all "borrow" their functionality from ImageReady. This is evident because the Save for Web dialog boxes now state, "Save for Web—Powered by ImageReady" in each of these applications.

With the release of the Adobe Creative Suite, Adobe has made a conscious effort to raise awareness around ImageReady, which is an essential tool for anyone doing Web design. Besides the "Powered by ImageReady" notice in other applications, as I just mentioned, Adobe now refers to Photoshop as "Adobe Photoshop CS with Adobe ImageReady CS" in all of its marketing materials. ImageReady CS is a powerful and integral part of the Creative Suite, hence my decision to cover it in its own separate chapter.

What's New in ImageReady CS?

If you've used ImageReady before, here's a quick overview of what's new in the CS version of ImageReady: an updated interface, support for exporting files in the Flash (.SWF) format, a new Web Content palette that makes it easier to add interactivity and remote rollovers, conditional actions and support for variables and data sets to automate the creation of graphics, and the capability to export layers as individual files.

Introduction to ImageReady CS

When you first launch ImageReady, you're greeted with the new ImageReady CS welcome screen (see Figure 6.1). From here you can access some tutorials from Adobe, as well as some tips and tricks from professionals. You can also view PDF files that detail new features. Many of these documents and tutorials are the same as those found in Photoshop CS.

FIGURE 6.1
The ImageReady
CS welcome
screen.

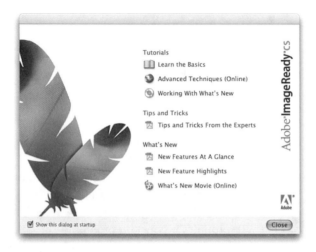

Did you
Know?

> If you're anything like me, you won't want to be bothered by the welcome screen
> every time you launch ImageReady. You can uncheck the Show This Dialog at
> Startup box to keep Photoshop from showing the screen automatically at launch
> time. You can always access the Welcome screen from the Help menu.

Taking a look at the screen when you first start ImageReady (see Figure 6.2), you
have the standard menu bar across the top of the screen. Directly under the menu
bar is the Tool Options bar, which is context-sensitive. That means the options
listed in this area change depending on what tool you have selected. To the far
right of the Tool Options bar is the palette well, where you can "store" palettes
(same as in Photoshop).

Along the left side of the screen is the toolbox (see Figure 6.3), which contains all
of ImageReady's tools, as well as performing several other functions. The color
proxy indicates the foreground and background colors (you can also choose
colors by clicking on them), and the two icons surrounding the proxy allow you
to set the colors to the default black foreground and white background, and to
swap the foreground and background colors. Directly below the proxy icons are
two buttons that toggle the visibility settings for image maps and slices, and two
additional buttons for previewing your image in ImageReady and the Web browser of your choice. Under those are the different view modes, Standard, Full Screen
with Menu Bar, and Full Screen. You can toggle through the view modes by
repeatedly pressing the "F" key on your keyboard (the letter F, not the Function
key). The last button at the bottom of the toolbox allows you to edit your file in
Photoshop.

Menu Bar   Tool Options Bar   Palette Well

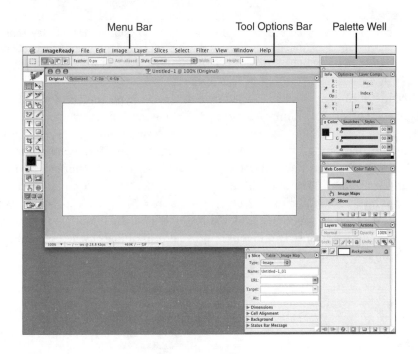

FIGURE 6.2
The ImageReady
CS User Interface.

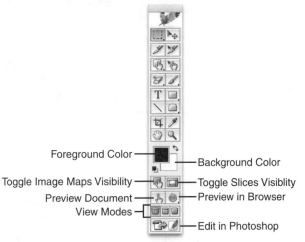

FIGURE 6.3
The ImageReady
CS toolbox.

Foreground Color ———
——— Background Color
Toggle Image Maps Visibility ———
——— Toggle Slices Visiblity
Preview Document ———
——— Preview in Browser
View Modes ———
——— Edit in Photoshop

Along the right side of your screen are some of ImageReady's palettes. We'll discuss what each of them does and how to use them as we go through this chapter.

If you remember, we talked about custom workspaces in Chapter 4, "The Key That Makes It All Work: Integration," and how you can save your screen setup, including palette locations, which palettes are open or closed, and so forth.

Finally, the document window (see Figure 6.4) is where you work on your file. ImageReady lists the filename, the view percentage, and the preview mode right in the title bar of each file. Directly under the title bar are four tabs, each for a different preview mode: Original, for seeing your file in full quality; Optimized, for viewing your file as it would appear in a Web browser; 2-Up, for comparing two different optimized settings simultaneously; and 4-Up, for comparing four different optimized settings simultaneously (see Figure 6.5). In the upper-right corner of the window there's a button that looks just like a palette flyout menu button, which you can use to specify different output settings and easily access the File Info dialog for adding metadata to your file.

FIGURE 6.4
The ImageReady CS document window.

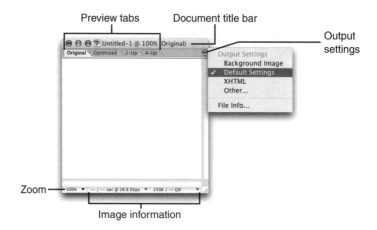

Along the bottom of the window, you'll find a pop-up zoom menu as well as two pop-up image information menus (see Figure 6.6), allowing you to view two types of vital information about your file simultaneously. For example, you could choose to display the image dimensions so that you're readily aware of the size of your graphic. Additionally, you can choose to view an approximation of how long the image will take to download at specific modem speeds.

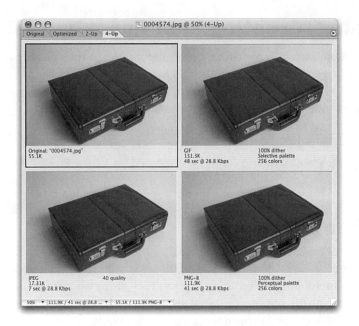

FIGURE 6.5
Comparing three different optimized settings with the original image using the 4-Up view.

FIGURE 6.6
The image information pop-up menus give you instant feedback on various settings and options.

Opening, Creating, and Importing Files

Just as in Photoshop, you can either open existing files in ImageReady or create your own from scratch. In addition, both Photoshop and ImageReady share a feature called Edit in... that allows you to easily transfer a file between the two applications with a single click of a button.

Did you Know? ImageReady also has an Import command (found in the File menu) that allows you to scan images directly, or even create an animated file from a folder of separate images.

The Open Dialog

As with just about any computer program, you can open a file by choosing File, Open or pressing (⌘-O) [Ctrl+O] to bring up the standard system Open dialog box. As you highlight files in the dialog, you may or may not see a preview, depending on the file type and what your operating system supports. After you've located the file you want to open, click on the Open button to open the file. You can also open several files at once by holding the (⌘) [Ctrl] key as you click on the different files.

Did you Know? ImageReady CS can open animated GIF files, JPEG files, and many other file formats.

By the Way ImageReady CS does not support Version Cue directly. If you'd like to open a file in ImageReady from a Version Cue project, open the file in Photoshop CS and then use the Edit in ImageReady button to bring the file into ImageReady CS. Likewise, when you save the file, use the Edit in Photoshop button to bring the file back to Photoshop CS so that you can save a version of the file in your Version Cue project. Using the Edit in Photoshop button is covered later in this section. For more information on Version Cue, see Chapter 11, "Using Version Cue."

Creating a New File

To start from scratch and create a new file, choose File, New or press (⌘-N) [Ctrl+N] to access the New Document dialog box (see Figure 6.7). Here you can give your file a name (you can do this later when you actually save the file too) and choose a size for your file. Because Web graphics are always measured in pixels, you can't specify image sizes in inches or any other measurement system.

Image resolution is also always set to 72dpi for Web use. Adobe has also included many preset image sizes to choose from (see Figure 6.8). Finally, you can choose whether the first layer of your new image is filled with white, filled with the background color, or left transparent by default.

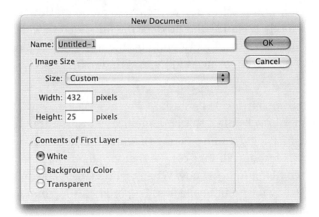

FIGURE 6.7
The New Document dialog box.

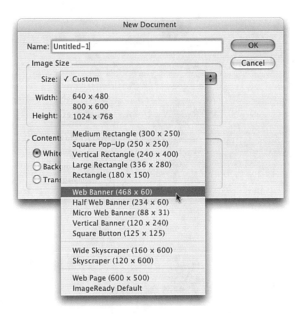

FIGURE 6.8
Choosing from a list of predefined image sizes.

Unlike Photoshop, ImageReady doesn't allow you to create your own custom document presets to appear in the Image Size pop-up menu.

"Jumping" Between Applications

The truth is, ImageReady is less of a design program and more of a production tool. Although you certainly can design graphics in ImageReady, most designers feel more comfortable using the robust functionality and extended toolset of either Photoshop or Illustrator to design their Web graphics. However, when it comes time to actually optimize and produce the final Web files, designers will take advantage of the powerful tools found in ImageReady. Additionally, ImageReady can add certain functionality to Web graphics that Photoshop or Illustrator cannot.

After a design is complete inside Photoshop, you can click on the Edit in ImageReady button (see Figure 6.9) to automatically transfer that file from Photoshop to ImageReady. If ImageReady isn't already launched and running on your computer, Photoshop will take care of that for you as well. You can then edit and work with the file in ImageReady. When you're done, you can either save the file from ImageReady or use ImageReady's Edit in Photoshop button to send the file back to Photoshop.

FIGURE 6.9
Clicking on the Edit in ImageReady button in Photoshop CS.

Edit in ImageReady (Shift+⌘+M)

Did you Know?

Although there's no way to automatically move files between Illustrator and ImageReady, you can export Photoshop files directly from Illustrator, and those files can be opened directly in ImageReady. The advantage of exporting a Photoshop file from Illustrator rather than just opening an Illustrator file in ImageReady directly is that you can preserve layers, transparency, vectors, text, slices, image maps, and a whole lot more through the Photoshop export feature in Illustrator.

With Photoshop CS and ImageReady CS, Adobe has structured the files so that only the changes you make to a file are transferred between the two applications (rather than the entire file). This can save lots of time, especially when you're working with complex files.

Similarity with Photoshop

Photoshop and ImageReady are almost identical twins in that they share not only the same interface, but also much of the same functionality. Many of the tools, such as the selection tools, the type tools, and the shape tools, are exactly alike. Applying a layer style or a layer mask, working with layer comps, and working with layers themselves are also identical. Most important, Photoshop and ImageReady share the exact same file format (Photoshop, .PSD), which allows you to keep one set of files.

Because so many things are similar across the two applications, I'm going to spend the remainder of this chapter focusing on the functionality that is specific to ImageReady. As you use ImageReady, you will undoubtedly find yourself applying techniques you learned in Photoshop CS.

It can be confusing sometimes trying to differentiate between Photoshop and ImageReady. One easy way to quickly tell the difference is by looking at the application icons at the top of the toolbox. Photoshop's icon has one feather, and ImageReady's has two feathers.

Did you
Know?

Optimizing Files for the Web

In the preceding chapter, we briefly spoke about saving Web graphics from Photoshop using the Save for Web command. As you'll see in the following chapter, Illustrator has the same command as well, with extended functionality. In reality, all of this stems from ImageReady itself. Before we begin talking about optimizing Web graphics, I want to take a step back and explain what optimizing really means, why it's important, and how ImageReady can help in the entire process.

First, it's important to understand how Web graphics differ from those created for print. A designer is faced with specific challenges when it comes to creating graphics that will be displayed on the Web. Of course, there are pros and cons to just about everything, but here's a list of some of the things a designer has to keep in mind when designing Web graphics:

▶ **Delivery Medium**—Unlike a printed piece, in which a designer can choose an exact size paper to use, a Web site is displayed on a digital screen—on a computer, a PDA, or a cell phone. These devices have specific screen sizes, and a designer has to create images that will fit on these screens. Scrolling is fine for paragraphs of text, but you don't want a user to have to scroll to see an image. What makes this even more difficult is that a designer never knows what kind of device a person will use to view the Web site, so what might fit nicely on one computer screen may not fit well at all on another.

▶ **Color**—When designing a printed piece, one has the ability to specify exact colors, which can be extremely important when reproducing corporate logos and conveying brand identity. On the Web, however, color isn't so accurate. Some monitors, with modern graphics cards, can display millions of colors. Other monitors can display only up to 256 colors at once. Cell phones and handheld PDA devices have their own color limitations as well. What looks bright red on your computer screen may end up looking like a dull orange on another device.

▶ **Technology**—The Internet as we know it today, with the World Wide Web, has been around for about a decade. In that short time, standards have come and gone, and technology continues to evolve. At one time, Netscape Navigator commanded a huge share of the market, and designers could optimize their Web sites for viewing in that particular browser. Today, Microsoft's Internet Explorer owns that distinction, and Apple's Safari browser adds similar challenges among Macintosh users. Today's Web designers need to be aware of what technologies are in place, what standards are in use, and what file formats are acceptable.

▶ **Speed**—There's no reason to sacrifice quality when it comes to designing a print piece. You can use high-resolution images to reproduce large, clear, and sharp photographs. A variety of fonts are at your disposal to achieve that perfect look and feel. Things are different on the Web however. All graphics on the Web are 72dpi low-resolution images for two main reasons. First, a monitor can display only 72 pixels per inch anyway, and second, high-resolution images are large in file size. Not everyone has a speedy connection to the Internet, and the larger an image is in file size, the longer it will take to download and display on a computer screen. On the Internet, speed is king. As a designer, you want to create great-looking images but not at the expense of a slow-loading Web site.

▶ **Interactivity**—The Web does offer something that no print piece could ever match, and that's interactivity. Designers can create Web graphics that move and change, either on their own or when users interact with them.

Web graphics can also call users to action, and to respond in ways that print simply cannot. Of course, interactive content isn't required on the Web, but a designer should know when he or she can take advantage of technologies that will enhance the messages they need to convey.

In some cases, a designer might know more about the targeted audience for a Web site, and take advantage of that knowledge. For example, when designing an intranet—a Web site that is accessed only by the internal employees of a company—a designer might know that everyone in the company has a monitor that supports more colors, giving the designer freedom to use more colors.

Did you Know?

Optimizing graphics for the Web means preparing images that will display appropriately, taking into account all the issues mentioned previously. Sometimes it means finding the lowest common denominator, making for a graphic that will display correctly on *any* device. On the other hand, a designer may want to weigh the costs of a graphic that looks better, but that might not display on all devices.

The good news is that ImageReady has all the tools necessary to optimize graphics for the Web. Even better, ImageReady CS contains time-saving features and easy-to-use functions to make the process of optimizing graphics for the Web quite painless. And, of course, having the same user interface as Photoshop means you don't have to learn a whole new program to create great-looking Web graphics.

Color on the World Wide Web

As mentioned previously, color on the Web isn't something a designer can rely on—mainly because as carefully as a designer may choose a color, there's no way to guarantee how that color will look on computers, PDAs, and cell phones throughout the world.

That being said, there's still reason to pay close attention to colors when designing Web graphics. First of all, some file formats allow you to control how many colors are saved in a file. The more colors, the larger the file size. If you're smart when choosing colors, you can get significant savings in file size.

Second, when a computer doesn't have enough colors to display an image, the computer uses a process called *dithering* to simulate the colors it doesn't have. For example, if you create an image that uses millions of colors but try to view that image on a computer with 256 colors, the computer will use the colors it has available to create patterns or areas of color to approximate the color it doesn't have (see Figure 6.10). Sometimes, this process produces results that are presentable, but many times, the dithering ends up looking horrible, producing moiré patterns. What's worse, the patterns could interfere with text or graphics and render a Web site illegible.

FIGURE 6.10
An example of what dithering looks like.

Web-Safe Colors

As Douglas Adams would say, "don't panic." You can do a few things to ensure that your art looks great on the Web—on any machine—by using a *Web-safe* color. A Web-safe color is one of 216 colors that will not dither when viewed on any computer screen.

How did someone come up with the number 216? Well, it's like this: Most people out there have monitors that can display 256 colors (VGA is 256 colors). These 256 colors are in what's called the system palette, which is built into your operating system. The Windows system palette and Macintosh system palette, however, differ slightly. To be exact, 40 colors do not match up between the two system palettes. So if you eliminate those 40 colors, you are left with 216 colors that are identical on both platforms.

By using colors from the Web-safe color palette, you can be sure that the colors you choose will not dither. The Color palette inside ImageReady allows you to use Web color sliders, making it easy to choose a Web-safe color. Simply choose Web Color Sliders from the Color palette flyout menu (see Figure 6.11).

FIGURE 6.11
Choosing to use
Web-safe colors in
ImageReady's Color
palette.

Slicing Images

Web slicing is the best thing to come around since sliced bread (I always wanted
to say that—but in reality, I have to think that TiVo deserves that honor). In simple terms, Web slicing is the process of cutting a large image into several smaller
images (see Figure 6.12). There are various reasons why this is desirable.

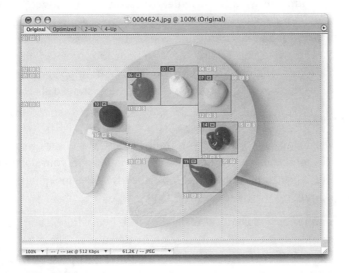

FIGURE 6.12
An image with
slices specified.

First of all, there's perception. If you tried to load a Web page that had one single
large image on it, you would sit there impatiently waiting for it to download and
appear on the page. But when an image is sliced into smaller parts, each smaller
image loads faster, and it feels like the image is loading faster.

On that same note, you can apply different optimization settings to each image slice, which could allow you to save some valuable file size space, making for a faster-loading graphic overall. As you'll see later, these settings will directly impact the final file size (read: download time) of your total image.

Slicing is also helpful if there are parts of a graphic that need to be updated often. Instead of always creating larger images, you can update just a part of the image. Swapping out a slice or two can be more efficient than having to work with one large bulky file all the time.

Because each slice is its own image, you can assign a link, or URL, to it, effectively making it a button. If someone clicks on a sliced part of an image, they'll be linked to another Web page. Of course, you can specify other functionality for such a button as well.

Finally, slices are necessary for creating rollovers, which allow you to specify that a graphic should change when the user interacts with it (like rolling a mouse over it).

Slices Explained

So what exactly happens when you create a slice? In reality, ImageReady is taking a single image and splitting it into multiple images. An HTML table is created, with each cell of the table containing one of these slices, or pieces of the image. In this way, when you display the Web page in a browser, all the sliced-up images appear together, almost like a puzzle. This is an important concept to keep in mind, because you can create only rectangular-shaped slices.

Creating Slices

There are several ways to create slices in ImageReady. The easiest way is to choose the Slice tool from the toolbox and click and drag in your document window (see Figure 6.13). You'll notice that ImageReady's Slice tool snaps to the edges of other slices, making it easy to use.

One thing to notice as you create slices is that when you draw a slice, other dimmed slices may appear automatically in the document. These are called *auto slices* (see Figure 6.14). Slices you create are called *user slices*. Going back to what we discussed earlier about HTML tables, ImageReady will automatically create a table for your entire graphic, so it will create slices as necessary to complete the table. As you continue to create slices, ImageReady will update the auto slices accordingly.

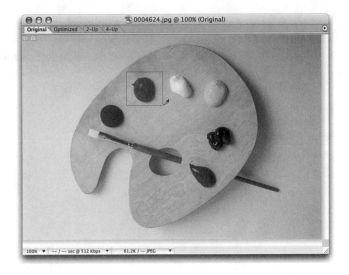

FIGURE 6.13
Drawing a slice with the Slice tool.

User Slices

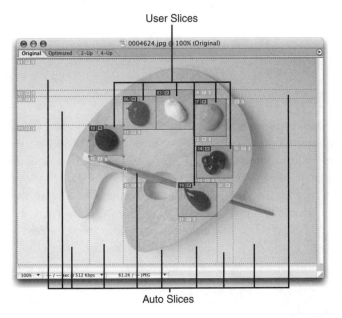

FIGURE 6.14
An image with auto slices and user slices.

Auto Slices

If you want to convert an auto slice to a user slice, you can choose the slice with the Slice Select tool and choose Slices, Promote to User Slice.

Did you **Know?**

Another way to create slices is to drag guides onto the document (you can add guides by dragging them out of the rulers). After you've positioned the guides where you want them, choose Slices, Create Slices from Guides (see Figure 6.15).

It makes sense to create your slices after you've already finished the design process, because after you draw your slices, if your design changes, you may need to readjust your slices. ImageReady does have the capability to create a slice that changes with your design—something called a *layer-based slice*. A layer-based slice is a slice that's automatically created to fit the contents of a layer. So if, for example, a layer had some text on it, defining that layer as a layer-based slice would create a slice the exact size of the text. If you would change the text at any point after that, the slice would update accordingly. To create a layer-based slice, highlight a layer in the Layers palette and choose Layer, New Layer Based Slice (see Figure 6.16).

Slice Attributes

You can specify certain attributes for a slice. Remember that a slice is really a cell in an HTML table. So, for example, a slice can have its own background color or URL link. Settings for each slice are specified via the Slice palette (see Figure 6.17), which you can access from the Window menu.

FIGURE 6.16
Choosing to create
a new layer-based
slice.

FIGURE 6.17
The Slice palette.

Web File Formats

Images can be saved for the Web in various formats. Each format has its own strengths and weaknesses. Depending on the use and functionality of your graphics, you can choose the format that's right for the task at hand. Remember that when you slice up an image, you can choose to optimize slices using different file formats. Feel free to mix and match file formats as you see necessary.

In ImageReady, you can choose a file format from the Optimize palette (see Figure 6.18). Start by selecting a slice, and then choose a file format from the pop-up menu in the Optimize palette (see Figure 6.19). Each file format has specific settings, which you can access by clicking on the disclosure triangles in the Optimize palette.

FIGURE 6.18
The Optimize
palette.

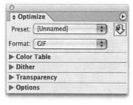

FIGURE 6.18
The Optimize
palette.

FIGURE 6.19
Selecting a file for-
mat from the
Optimize palette.

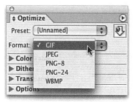

GIF

Probably the most common image file format present on the Web, the GIF format
was developed by the people at CompuServe—one of the pioneers of the Internet
and the World Wide Web, though you hardly hear of them today. Seeing the need
to send graphics files across modem connections (which in those days were quite
slow), they developed a file format that contained a limited number of colors and
that was compressed. GIF files can contain a maximum of 256 colors, and they
use a *lossless* method of compression. Lossless compression means that no information is lost in the compression process and the quality of the image remains
intact. The way a GIF saves space is by looking for large areas of contiguous solid
color, which makes the format perfect for logos, backgrounds, text headlines, and
the like.

There are some other capabilities that the GIF format supports, including the
capability to control the exact number of colors present in the file, transparency,
and the capability to store multiple images in a single GIF file—commonly
referred to as an animated GIF file. An animated GIF file displays each image in
the file one after the other, giving the appearance of movement, much like a
movie. Each image in an animated GIF file is called a frame, and we'll talk about
how to create frames and animation later in this chapter.

When you choose the GIF file format in the Optimize palette, you have the following settings (see Figure 6.20):

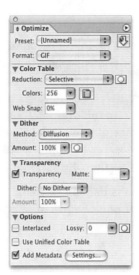

FIGURE 6.20
The available optimization settings for the GIF file format.

▶ **Color Table**—The Color Table settings allow you to specify exactly how many colors the GIF will contain. Lower numbers of colors will result in smaller file sizes, but may result in lower-quality images. Because a GIF can contain a maximum of 256 colors, you can choose from several color reduction algorithms, including the Restrictive option, which will choose only Web-safe colors.

▶ **Dither**—The Dither settings allow you to control what method of dithering (discussed earlier) will be used when the image is displayed on computers with different colors.

▶ **Transparency**—The Transparency settings allow you to define a single color that will display as transparent in a browser. For example, if you want to place a logo on a colored background, you can specify the background color of the GIF to be transparent, and the background color in the browser will show through those transparent areas. The edges where color meets the transparent edge will usually be white (or the background color you have chosen in your ImageReady document) when displayed in a browser, and specifying a matte color that matches the background will ensure that the art blends seamlessly with the background.

▶ **Options**—The Options settings allow you to specify some other settings for GIF files, such as adding metadata information, using a unified color table across multiple GIF files, and interlacing, which allows an image to load progressively in a Web browser.

JPEG

JPEG (pronounced *jay-peg*) stands for Joint Photographic Experts Group, and the file format was created to allow photographers to share images using a standard file format. JPEG files can contain millions of colors and use a *lossy* compression method, meaning that information is lost in the compression process. Digital images usually contain more color information than the human eye can see or detect, and by throwing out some of that extra information, JPEG images can achieve amazing file size savings. For example, a 10MB photograph can easily be compressed into a JPEG that's less than 1MB in size.

Because the JPEG format supports millions of colors (as opposed to 256 in a GIF), it's the perfect format to use for photographs or images with complex colors and gradient fills. JPEG files do not support animation as GIF files do.

When you choose the JPEG file format in the Optimize palette, you have the following settings (see Figure 6.21):

FIGURE 6.21
The available optimization settings for the JPEG file format.

▶ **Quality**—The Quality settings allow you to specify how much information is thrown out of a file when the file is compressed. A higher number means that less information will be thrown out, resulting in a larger file but a better-looking image. One of the most noticeable side effects of compression in a JPEG file is artifacts or stray pixels that appear in the image. Specifying a blur amount can help cover up those artifacts.

▶ **Transparency**—The Transparency setting allows you to specify a matte color for the edge of the graphic. JPEG files do not allow you to specify a single color to become transparent, however, as the GIF format does.

▶ **Options**—The Options settings for JPEG images include the capability to add ICC color profiles, and add metadata. The Progressive setting is similar to interlacing in that it allows the image to appear in low quality quickly in a browser and then, over time, brings the image up to full resolution.

PNG

The PNG (pronounced *ping*) format was developed mainly as an alternative to the GIF format. Shortly after the GIF format became popular on the Web, the Unisys corporation, which developed the compression algorithm used in the GIF format, tried to collect royalties on its technology from those who used the GIF format. To get around the legal issues, an open standard called PNG (Portable Network Graphic) was developed. The PNG format utilizes lossless compression and can support millions of colors. Instead of allowing you to specify a single color as being transparent, the PNG format supports 256 levels of transparency, similar to alpha channels inside Photoshop.

Older Web browsers require a special plug-in to view PNG files, although most newer browsers can display them natively. PNG files may also not be compatible with some PDA devices and cell phones. PNG files also come in two varieties, 8-bit and 24-bit.

The different optimization settings for PNG-8 (see Figure 6.22) are identical to those found for the GIF format, mentioned previously.

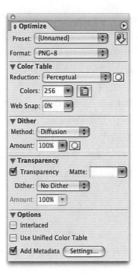

FIGURE 6.22
The available optimization settings for the PNG-8 file format.

WBMP

If you've been paying attention to the world lately, you're aware that it's now becoming possible to access the Internet on handheld PDA devices and also cell phones. These wireless technologies are slowly expanding in both capabilities and the number of people who use them. The WBMP file format, which stands for Wireless Bitmap, is a format that is optimized for wireless devices. These devices usually have slow connections (compared to desktop devices), and many have black-and-white screens. WBMP files are black-and-white images (color isn't supported) and are optimized via a dithering setting (see Figure 6.23).

FIGURE 6.23
The available optimization settings for the WBMP file format.

Adding Interactivity

Now we get to the fun part—making Web graphics interactive. One of the powers of the World Wide Web is the capability to create engaging Web sites that appeal to users. This not only makes surfing the Web fun, but also aids in creating Web sites that are more user-friendly, more useable, and help in selling products or services.

There are different levels of interactivity one can add to Web graphics using ImageReady CS. *Image maps* allow you to specify certain areas or *hotspots* in an image that allow users to click them to link to other pages or Web sites. Think of it almost as a button that you can place just about anywhere. For example, you might create an image map so that when a user clicks on the eye or nose of a portrait, different pages are loaded. *Animation* allows images to move, change color, or change appearance. Finally, *rollovers* have the capability to change graphics as a user interacts with them. An example of a rollover is a button that lights up when a user moves his mouse over it.

Image Maps

Creating an image map in ImageReady is easy. There are three kinds of image map shapes you can create, each with a different tool. The Rectangle Image Map tool draws image maps that are rectangular in shape. The Circle Image Map tool draws image maps that are circular in shape, and the Polygon Image Map tool creates image maps that are irregularly shaped. After you've selected an image map tool (see Figure 6.24), draw an area on your document. Choosing Window, Image Map opens the Image Map palette (see Figure 6.25), where you can specify a URL for the image map as well as other settings, such as alt text or specific size dimensions.

FIGURE 6.24
Choosing from the three types of image map tools.

FIGURE 6.25
The Image Map palette.

Animation

Animation in ImageReady is frame based, meaning that the illusion of movement is achieved by displaying image after image in succession. You have complete control in ImageReady over how many frames your animation will have, and you can also control timing, as to how long each frame is displayed in a browser. All the settings necessary to create animations are in the Animation palette (see Figure 6.26), accessed from the Window menu.

FIGURE 6.26
The Animation
palette.

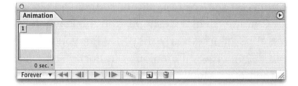

To add frames to a file, choose New Frame from the Animation palette flyout menu, or click on the Duplicates Current Frame button at the bottom of the palette. ImageReady also can help animate objects for you by using a process called tweening. The process of tweening, which comes from the word *between*, involves taking two frames in an animation and creating additional frames in between them, changing them slightly. For example, if you had some text at the top of your image in one frame (see Figure 6.27), and then created a new frame and moved the text to the bottom of your image (see Figure 6.28), tweening those two frames would produce an additional frame between the two, with the text in the middle of the image (see Figure 6.29).

FIGURE 6.27
The first frame in
an animation.

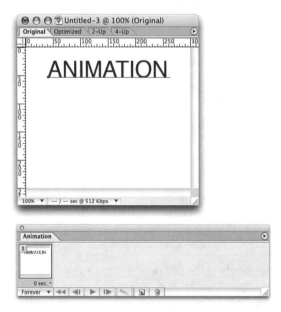

To tween frames in ImageReady CS, select a frame and choose Tween from the Animation palette flyout menu to get the Tween dialog box (see Figure 6.30). You can then specify to tween with the previous frame or first frame, as well as specify the number of frames you want to add to your animation. More frames will produce a smoother-looking animation but will result in a larger file size. You can also specify what parts of your image and what attributes should be tweened.

FIGURE 6.28
The second frame in an animation.

FIGURE 6.29
The tweened frame in the animation.

FIGURE 6.30
The Tween dialog
box.

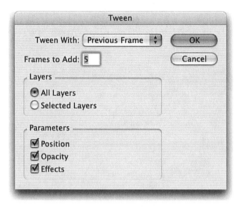

You can use the controls at the bottom of the Animation palette to play the animation to see how it looks (see Figure 6.31).

FIGURE 6.31
The playback controls at the bottom of the Animation palette.

Under each frame in the animation is a pop-up menu that allows you to specify the duration of that frame (see Figure 6.32). As an animation plays, you can specify pauses as desired to make the animation play as intended. To get a real good idea of how the timing will play back, preview your image in an actual Web browser by clicking on the Preview in Browser button on the toolbox.

FIGURE 6.32
Choosing a time duration for a frame in an animation.

Rollovers

If you've ever been to a Web site that had buttons that lit up when you ran your mouse over them, you know what a rollover is. To create a rollover in

ImageReady, you use the Layers palette in tandem with the Web Content palette (see Figure 6.33). First, select a slice from the list of slices in the Web Content palette. Then click on the Create Rollover State button at the bottom of the palette. This will add an Over state to your slice. You can then use the Layers palette to turn on a different layer, or to change the layer style for that new state.

FIGURE 6.33
The Web Content palette.

There are several different states you can specify for a slice. Each time you click on the Create Rollover State button, ImageReady adds a different kind of state for that slice:

- ▶ **Over**—The Over state appears when a user places the mouse cursor over the slice.

- ▶ **Out**—The Out state appears when the user moves the mouse cursor off of the slice.

- ▶ **Down**—The Down state appears when the user clicks and holds the mouse down on the slice.

- ▶ **Up**—The Up state appears when the user releases the mouse after clicking on the slice.

- ▶ **Click**—The Click state appears when the user has clicked once on the slice.

- ▶ **Selected**—The Selected state appears indicating that a user has clicked on a slice.

Automation

Everyone likes to save time, and nothing could be more true when working with Web graphics. The nature of optimized graphics for the Web usually results in many different images, each for different purposes. Having to manually work on each individual image can prove to be boring and nonproductive.

Luckily, the folks at Adobe have given plenty of power to ImageReady to do work on its own. Actions allow you to record a series of functions and then "play back" those functions whenever you want. These Actions can also be applied to an entire folder of images. Droplets are another form of Actions, except that they are drag-and-drop icons you can use to quickly optimize or modify a file with little thought required.

Actions

Actions are controlled via the Actions palette (see Figure 6.34), which you can find under the Window menu. ImageReady ships with 15 Actions you can use, and, of course, you can create your own. To define a new Action, click on the Create New Action button at the bottom of the Actions palette and give the new Action a name. You can also choose to assign a keyboard shortcut to the Action, for easier playback. Then click on the Record button.

FIGURE 6.34
The Actions
palette.

As you perform functions in your document, you'll notice entries being added to the Action. After you've completed the steps you want to record, click on the Stop Recording button at the bottom of the Actions palette. You can click on the disclosure triangle to view each individual step you recorded. Clicking the check mark to the far left of each entry will enable or disable that step in the process, and clicking on the box just to the right of the arrow will cause the Action to display a dialog box for that step during playback.

Additionally, you can add conditional logic to any step in your Action. Choose a step and then choose Insert Conditional from the Actions palette flyout menu. Choose a condition from the Conditional dialog box (see Figure 6.35) and click OK.

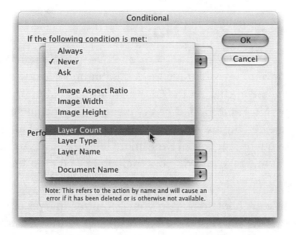

FIGURE 6.35
Specifying a condition for an Action.

To play back an Action, simply highlight the Action in the Actions palette and click on the Play button at the bottom of the palette.

Droplets

A droplet is similar to an Action, but it's a separate file you can place anywhere on your hard drive. You can then take any file on your computer and drag it on top of the droplet and release the mouse. The droplet will then process the file, as specified by the action it contains.

To create a droplet, highlight an Action in the Actions palette and choose Create Droplet from the Actions palette flyout menu. Additionally, you can click on the Create Droplet button in the Optimize palette (see Figure 6.36) to create a droplet that will automatically optimize a file to the settings you've specified in the Optimize palette.

FIGURE 6.36
The Create Droplet icon in the Optimize palette.

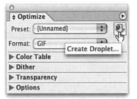

Saving and Exporting

After you've finalized your Web graphics, you have several options available. You can choose File, Save to save your file for editing in ImageReady or Photoshop on a future date, or you can click on the Edit in Photoshop button in the toolbox to bring your image into Photoshop. If you're going to be placing your Web images into a GoLive page layout, this would be the preferred method to use, and it will allow you to take advantage of GoLive's SmartObject feature. Any optimizations you've specified in ImageReady will pass through to GoLive in the process. Additionally, you'll be working with a single, editable file.

Alternatively, you can choose to export your optimized images as separate graphics files (in the formats you've specified for each slice in the Optimize palette). To do so, choose File, Save Optimized As, and you can choose to export both HTML and images, images only, or HTML only (see Figure 6.37).

FIGURE 6.37
Choosing to save an optimized file as HTML and Images.

Macromedia Flash (.SWF)

You can export files in the Macromedia Flash format (.SWF), and ImageReady will even export vector paths as vectors. Files with animation will also be exported as animated Flash files. To export a Flash file, choose File, Export, Macromedia Flash SWF. In the ensuing dialog, you can choose from several options (see Figure 6.38).

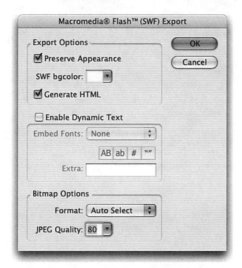

The Preserve Appearance option will flatten transparency where Flash won't support it and rasterize the result to allow the image to export with the correct appearance. You can also choose a background color for the SWF file, as well as export the HTML code that's required to load the SWF file.

You can also export text as dynamic text, and embed fonts into the SWF file, as well as specify how bitmap images are saved within the final SWF file.

Additional Export Options

ImageReady has the capability to export each layer of a file as a separate image, and also each animation frame as a separate file. Both of these options are available in the File, Export submenu. In either case, you can choose which layers or frames you want to export (see Figure 6.39), as well as choose an optimized image format for each of them.

FIGURE 6.39
The Export Layers
as Files dialog.

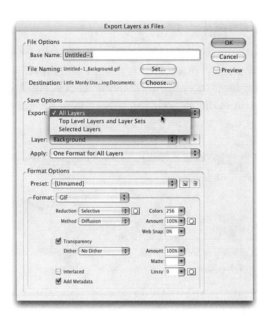

CHAPTER 7

Using Adobe Illustrator CS

Illustrator is one of those programs that seems to have an identity crisis. By that I mean it's a tool that can do many of the things that InDesign can (such as page layout), and it can also do many of the things that Photoshop can (such as Web design). Of course, there are also plenty of things that Illustrator alone can do (such as edit PDF files or create 3D graphics). As you'll see in this chapter, one thing is certain: Illustrator is a very deep program, with a wide range of features and uses.

What's New in Illustrator CS?

If you've used Illustrator before, here's a quick overview of what's new in the CS version of Illustrator: a new Unicode-based text engine that provides support for OpenType fonts, character styles, and paragraph styles; numerous other text enhancements, including optical kerning, optical margin alignment, and a paragraph composer; enhanced PDF file creation and support for the PDF 1.5 file format; faster performance; real 3D effects; an all-new Print dialog with print preview, color separations, and a fit-to-page option; an innovative Save for Microsoft Office command to easily export files to Word or PowerPoint; the capability to create template files; a huge selection of professionally designed content; and more than 100 OpenType fonts.

Introduction to Illustrator CS

When you first launch Illustrator, you're greeted with the new Illustrator CS welcome screen (see Figure 7.1). The welcome screen is split into two sections. The top half offers links to view a short video overview of new features (which plays online), tutorials that are geared for new users, and a PDF file which is a catalog of all the extra content that ships with Illustrator (we'll talk more about this later in the chapter). The lower half of the welcome screen is more functional in that it allows you to quickly create a new file, create a new file based on a template, or open an existing file.

FIGURE 7.1
The Illustrator CS
welcome screen.

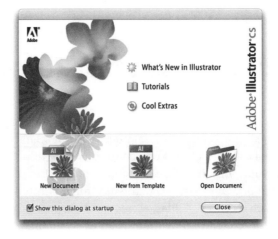

Unlike the Photoshop welcome screen, which is purely informational, the Illustrator welcome screen gives you quick shortcuts for creating and opening files (and it's pretty too). Even so, you can uncheck the Show This Dialog at Startup box to keep Illustrator from showing the screen automatically at launch time. You can always access the welcome screen from the Help menu.

Taking a look at the screen when you first start Illustrator (see Figure 7.2), you have the standard menu bar across the top of the screen. Along the left side of the screen is the toolbox, which contains all of Illustrator's tools, as well as several other functions. The color proxy indicates the fill and stroke colors (you can also choose colors by double-clicking on them), and the two icons surrounding the proxy allow you to set the colors to the default white fill and black stroke, and to swap the fill and stroke colors. Directly below the proxy icons are three buttons that can be used to quickly apply three kinds of colors: a white fill, a black-to-white gradient, and none. Under those are the different view modes, Standard, Full Screen with Menu Bar, and Full Screen (just as in Photoshop). You can toggle through the view modes by repeatedly pressing the F key on your keyboard (the letter F, not the Function key).

Some useful keyboard shortcuts to remember and get used to are the X key to toggle focus between the fill and the stroke, Shift-X to swap the two colors, and D to set the colors to their default settings.

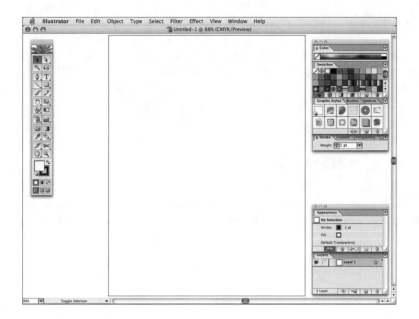

FIGURE 7.2
The Illustrator CS workspace.

Along the right side of your screen are some of Illustrator's palettes. We'll discuss what each of them does and how to use them as we go through this chapter.

Finally, the document window is where you work on your file. The black outline is your document size, or *artboard*. Illustrator lists the filename, the view percentage, and the color mode right in the title bar of each file. Along the bottom left of the window, you'll find a zoom indicator as well as the status bar.

By default, the status bar displays the tool you currently have selected. There are some other items you can display instead by clicking on the status bar. For something a little different, press and hold the (Option) [Alt] key when clicking on the status bar (see Figure 7.3).

Did you Know?

FIGURE 7.3
Yes, that's my home phone number listed in the status bar.

Creating and Opening Files

One of the things that has always been daunting about using Illustrator was starting with a blank page. In a program like Photoshop, you usually start with a scanned image or a digital photograph. With Illustrator, you'll most likely be creating new documents often, as well as creating new documents from predefined templates. Of course, Illustrator can also open existing documents.

Creating a New File

To start from scratch and create a new file, choose File, New or press (⌘-N) [Ctrl+N] to access the New Document dialog box (see Figure 7.4). Here you can give your file a name (you can do this later when you actually save the file too) and specify your artboard size. You can choose from any of Illustrator's supported measurement systems: points, picas, inches, millimeters, centimeters, ha, or pixels.

FIGURE 7.4
The New Document dialog box.

No it's not a joke. *Ha* is a real measurement system used in China, Japan, and Korea.

Color Modes

Illustrator lets you create files in one of two color modes, and it's important to know which one to choose. Although you can change color modes later, such changes will cause color shifts. Each color mode has a *gamut*, or range of colors that can be produced. Some gamuts are wider, or can contain more colors, than others. For example, certain colors can be displayed in RGB that simply can't be reproduced in CMYK (for example, bright greens or oranges or pastel colors). So converting an RGB file to CMYK might cause some colors to become dull or change color altogether because those colors don't exist in CMYK. Let's take a look at each of the supported color models:

▶ **RGB Color**—RGB (Red Green Blue) is a *subtractive* color method. Subtractive means that if you mix all the colors together, the result is white, and if none of the colors are present, the result is black. Televisions, computer monitors, and the like use the RGB color model (when your TV is turned off, the screen is black). When you're working on files that will be used in video, in broadcast, on the Web, or for onscreen presentations, RGB is the format you should use.

▶ **CMYK Color**—Unlike RGB, CMYK is an *additive* color method, which means that if you mix all the colors together, you get black, but if none of the colors are present, you get white. Anything you see in print uses CMYK (a blank piece of paper is white), so obviously when you're designing content that will be printed in color, CMYK is the color model of choice. CMYK stands for Cyan (a shade of blue), Magenta (a shade of red), Yellow, and Key (Black). The reason black is referred to as Key is that black is traditionally the key color because it reinforces and invigorates the other colors (or so a printer once told me).

> As I mentioned earlier, the CMYK gamut isn't nearly as wide as most designers would like, so designers use spot colors (for example, Pantone colors) that allow designers to pick a specific color ink (including metallic inks, bright colors, pastels, and so on). We'll cover spot colors in detail later in the chapter.

By the Way

After you've specified your new document settings, you can click the OK button to create a new Illustrator file.

Creating a New File from a Template

An Illustrator template file is a special kind of Illustrator file, sporting an .ait file extension instead of the usual .ai usually reserved for Illustrator files. Templates are used for designs that are used repeatedly, and they can contain anything a normal Illustrator file can contain, including layers, paragraph styles, symbols, page size—even artwork itself. When you open an Illustrator template, the file opens as an untitled document (as if you had created a new file). This prevents you from accidentally overwriting the template file.

Adobe ships with nearly 300 professionally designed royalty-free templates you can use. When you choose the File, New from Template command, Illustrator will automatically navigate to the folder where these templates are installed (see Figure 7.5). Unfortunately, there's no easy way to preview these templates to see what they look like before you open them.

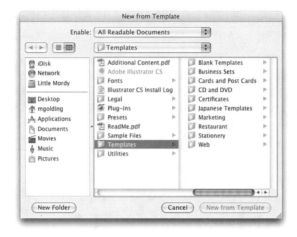

You can view a PDF catalog of the templates that Illustrator ships with by clicking on the "Cool Extras" button on the Illustrator welcome screen. Alternatively, you can open the `Additional Content.pdf` file that's in your Adobe Illustrator application folder.

For those who feel that using prerendered content is beneath them, Illustrator also ships with a full collection of blank templates. These can be quite useful for nearly any user. Of course, you can also create and save your own template files, and we'll discuss how to do that later in the chapter.

Illustrator installs all templates by default, and they can be found in the `Adobe Illustrator CS/Templates` folder.

The Open Dialog

As with just about any computer program, you can open a file by choosing File, Open or pressing (⌘-O) [Ctrl+O] to bring up the standard system Open dialog box. As you highlight files in the dialog, you may or may not see a low-resolution preview, depending on the file type and what your operating system supports. After you've located the file you want to open, click on the Open button to open the file.

If you want to choose a file from a Version Cue project, click on the Version Cue button at the lower left of the dialog. We'll talk more about Version Cue in Chapter 11, "Using Version Cue."

Illustrator does more than just open Illustrator files. You can open a wide range of files in Illustrator, including PDF, EPS, JPEG, PSD, GIF, PNG, and more (see Figure 7.6). Illustrator can also open native CorelDRAW and FreeHand files (versions 8, 9, and 10 officially, although other versions may work with varying success). In many ways, both Photoshop and Illustrator can be used as utilities to open just about any kind of graphics file.

FIGURE 7.6
A list of the file formats Illustrator CS can open.

If you need to edit PDF files, you can open them in Illustrator, but you'll have to remember a few limitations. Illustrator can open only one page of a PDF at a time (see Figure 7.7), spot colors may get converted to process colors, form data may be removed, and structured text (tagged text) will be lost.

By the Way

FIGURE 7.7
When you're attempting to open a multipage PDF file, Illustrator asks you which page you want to open.

Drawing Basic Vector Objects

Back in Chapter 2, "So Many Applications: Which One to Use?" we discussed the underlying basics of vector graphics. Now we'll learn how to draw them. We'll begin with drawing closed paths and then we'll move on to drawing open paths. Finally, we'll discuss how to edit existing vector paths and objects.

Drawing Closed Vectors: Shapes

Illustrator can draw primitive shapes quite easily, and there are several shape tools that allow you to create rectangles, ellipses (circles and ovals), polygons (multisided shapes) and stars. We'll go through each of these tools and how they are used, but, of course, the best way to get to know them is to launch Illustrator and try them out for yourself.

One thing you'll notice, though, as you read through the remainder of this chapter, is that there are usually several ways to accomplish the same task. This is true for most of the functionality you'll find in Illustrator. As you become more familiar with Illustrator, you'll get a better feel for which method makes the most sense for a specific purpose.

Finally, as you'll see, most of Illustrator's drawing tools are dynamic in that you can press certain keys on your keyboard to change certain aspects of the shape, as you are drawing it.

The Rectangle Tool

To draw a rectangle, choose the Rectangle tool (see Figure 7.8) and click and drag the mouse on the artboard. Before you release the mouse, you can utilize any of the following functions that will affect the shape you are drawing:

- ▶ Press the Shift key to constrain your shape to be a perfect square.
- ▶ Press the (Option) [Alt] key to draw your shape from the center outward.
- ▶ Press the spacebar to "freeze" your shape and position it elsewhere on your artboard.
- ▶ Press the tilde key to create numerous copies of your shape.

To draw a rectangle numerically, choose the Rectangle tool and click once on your artboard to get the Rectangle dialog box (see Figure 7.9). Enter a value for the Width and Height, and click OK. To draw a rectangle numerically from its center, press and hold the (Option) [Alt] key while you click once on the artboard.

FIGURE 7.8
Choosing the
Rectangle tool.

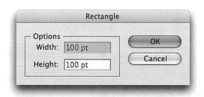

FIGURE 7.9
The Rectangle
dialog box.

The Rounded Rectangle Tool

To draw a rounded rectangle (in which the corners of the rectangle are rounded), choose the Rounded Rectangle tool (see Figure 7.10) and click and drag the mouse on the artboard. Before you release the mouse, you can utilize any of the following functions that will affect the shape you are drawing:

▶ Press the Shift key to constrain your shape to be a perfect square with rounded corners.

▶ Press the (Option) [Alt] key to draw your shape from the center outward.

▶ Press the spacebar to "freeze" your shape and position it elsewhere on your artboard.

▶ Press the tilde key to create numerous copies of your shape.

To draw a rounded rectangle numerically, choose the Rounded Rectangle tool and click once on your artboard to get the Rounded Rectangle dialog box (see Figure 7.11). Enter a value for the Width, Height, and Corner Radius, and click OK. To draw a rounded rectangle numerically from its center, press and hold the (Option) [Alt] key while you click once on the artboard.

FIGURE 7.10
Choosing the
Rounded
Rectangle tool.

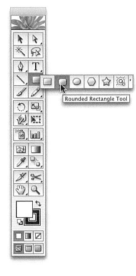

FIGURE 7.11
The Rounded
Rectangle dialog
box.

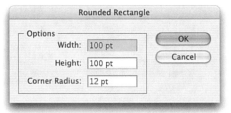

Did you Know?

> You can use the Rounded Corners live effect to apply rounded corners to any vector object, with an added benefit that you can make adjustments to the corner radius setting at any time. We'll cover this live effect later in the chapter.

The Ellipse Tool

To draw an ellipse (aka oval), choose the Ellipse tool (see Figure 7.12) and click and drag the mouse on the artboard. Before you release the mouse, you can utilize any of the following functions that will affect the shape you are drawing:

▶ Press the Shift key to constrain your shape to be a perfect circle.

▶ Press the (Option) [Alt] key to draw your shape from the center outward.

▶ Press the spacebar to "freeze" your shape and position it elsewhere on your artboard.

▶ Press the tilde key to create numerous copies of your shape.

FIGURE 7.12
Choosing the
Ellipse tool.

To draw an ellipse numerically, choose the Ellipse tool and click once on your artboard to get the Ellipse dialog box (see Figure 7.13). Enter a value for the Width and Height, and click OK. To draw an ellipse numerically from its center, press and hold the (Option) [Alt] key while you click once on the artboard.

FIGURE 7.13
The Ellipse dialog
box.

The Polygon Tool

The Polygon tool in Illustrator is a bit disconcerting. A real polygon is simply a closed shape with more than three sides. In Illustrator, the Polygon tool can create only closed shapes with three or more sides, but in which all the sides are equal in length.

To draw a polygon, choose the Polygon tool (see Figure 7.14) and click and drag the mouse on the artboard. A polygon is always drawn outward from its center. Before you release the mouse, you can utilize any of the following functions that will affect the shape you are drawing:

▶ Move your mouse in a circular motion to rotate the shape.

▶ Press the Shift key to constrain your shape straight to the baseline (or whatever your constrain angle is set to in General Preferences).

▶ Press the up-arrow key on your keyboard to add sides to your shape.

▶ Press the down-arrow key on your keyboard to remove sides from your shape.

▶ Press the spacebar to "freeze" your shape and position it elsewhere on your artboard.

▶ Press the tilde key to create numerous copies of your shape.

FIGURE 7.14
Choosing the Polygon tool.

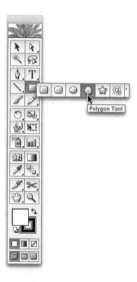

To draw a polygon numerically, choose the Polygon tool and click once on your artboard to get the Polygon dialog box (see Figure 7.15). Enter a value for the Radius and the number of Sides, and click OK.

FIGURE 7.15
The Polygon dialog box.

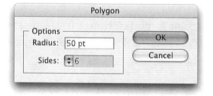

Did you Know?

Need to draw a quick triangle? You can use the Polygon tool to create an equilateral triangle in an instant.

The Star Tool

The Star tool in Illustrator can be quite useful for creating starbursts to call out specific items in a design.

To draw a star, choose the Star tool (see Figure 7.16) and click and drag the mouse on your artboard. A star is always drawn out from its center. Before you release the mouse, you can utilize any of the following functions that will affect the shape you are drawing:

▶ Move your mouse in a circular motion to rotate the shape.

▶ Press the Shift key to constrain your shape straight to the baseline (or whatever your constrain angle is set to in General Preferences).

▶ Press the up-arrow key on your keyboard to add points to your shape.

▶ Press the down-arrow key on your keyboard to remove points from your shape.

▶ Press the (Option) [Alt] key to align the shoulders of your star (forcing lines on opposite sides of the star to share the same baseline).

▶ Press the (⌘) [Ctrl] key to adjust the inner radius of the star. Dragging toward the center of the star will decrease the radius, and dragging away from the center of the star will increase it.

▶ Press the spacebar to "freeze" your shape and position it elsewhere on your artboard.

▶ Press the tilde key to create numerous copies of your shape.

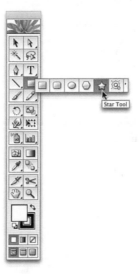

FIGURE 7.16
Choosing the Star tool.

To draw a star numerically, choose the Star tool and click once on your artboard to get the Star dialog box (see Figure 7.17). Enter a value for Radius 1 and Radius 2, enter the number of Points, and click OK.

FIGURE 7.17
The Star dialog
box.

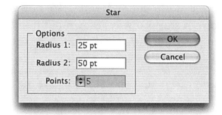

Drawing Open Vectors: Paths

Although drawing complete shapes is something just about everyone needs to do inside of Illustrator, it's equally important to create open-ended paths. Illustrator has several tools for creating these kinds of paths and, as you'll see, different ways to edit them as well.

The Line Tool

To draw a straight line, choose the Line Segment tool (see Figure 7.18) and click and drag the mouse on the artboard. Before you release the mouse, you can utilize any of the following functions that will affect the path you are drawing:

▶ Press the Shift key to constrain your path to increments of 45 degrees.

▶ Press the spacebar to "freeze" your path and position it elsewhere on your artboard.

▶ Press the tilde key to create numerous copies of your path.

To draw a line numerically, choose the Line tool and click once on your artboard to get the Line Segment Tool Options dialog box (see Figure 7.19). Enter a value for the Length and the Angle, and click OK.

FIGURE 7.18
Choosing the Line
tool.

FIGURE 7.19
The Line Segment
Tool Options dialog
box.

The Arc Tool

To draw an arc, choose the Arc tool (see Figure 7.20) and click and drag the
mouse on the artboard. Before you release the mouse, you can utilize any of the
following functions that will affect the path you are drawing:

▶ Press the Shift key to constrain your path so that the length of the X and Y
axes are the same (thus creating a perfect quarter-circle).

▶ Press the (Option) [Alt] key to draw your path from the center outward.

▶ Press the up-arrow key on your keyboard to make the slope of the path
more convex.

▶ Press the down-arrow key on your keyboard to make the slope of the path
more concave.

▶ Press the C key to draw the arc as a closed path shape.

> ▶ Press the F key to flip the path along its axis.
>
> ▶ Press the spacebar to "freeze" your path and position it elsewhere on your artboard.
>
> ▶ Press the tilde key to create numerous copies of your path.

To draw an arc numerically, choose the Arc tool and click once on your artboard to get the Arc Segment Tool Options dialog box (see Figure 7.21). Enter values for the length of the x-axis and the y-axis, and for the slope. Choose also to draw an open or closed path and an axis to base the path on. Click OK.

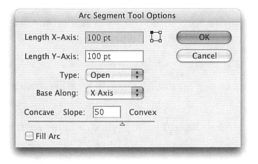

The Spiral Tool

Illustrator has a cool tool for drawing spirals, and the best part is that you don't get dizzy drawing them!

To draw a spiral, choose the Spiral tool (see Figure 7.22) and click and drag the mouse on the artboard. A spiral is always drawn outward from its center. Before you release the mouse, you can utilize any of the following functions that will affect the path you are drawing:

- ▶ Move your mouse in a circular motion to rotate the path.

- ▶ Press the Shift key to constrain the path to increments of 45 degrees.

- ▶ Press the up-arrow key on your keyboard to add segments (or winds) to your path.

- ▶ Press the down-arrow key on your keyboard to remove segments (or winds) from your path.

- ▶ Press the (Option) [Alt] key to adjust the length of the path.

- ▶ Press the (⌘) [Ctrl] key to adjust the decay of the path. The decay setting controls how close the winds of the spiral are to each other.

- ▶ Press the spacebar to "freeze" your path and position it elsewhere on your artboard.

- ▶ Press the tilde key to create numerous copies of your path.

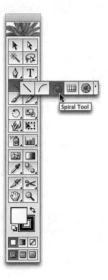

FIGURE 7.22
Choosing the Spiral tool.

To draw a spiral numerically, choose the Spiral tool and click once on your art-board to get the Spiral dialog box (see Figure 7.23). Enter values for the Radius, the Decay, and the number of Segments; choose a Style; and click OK.

FIGURE 7.23
The Spiral dialog box.

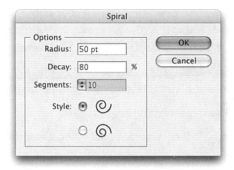

The Rectangular Grid Tool

Although it's not necessarily a path tool, the Rectangular Grid tool allows you to easily construct a grid using both paths and a single rectangle.

To draw a rectangular grid, choose the Rectangular Grid tool (see Figure 7.24) and click and drag the mouse on the artboard. Before you release the mouse, you can utilize any of the following functions that will affect the grid you are drawing:

▶ Press the Shift key to constrain your grid to a perfect square.

▶ Press the (Option) [Alt] key to draw your grid out from its center.

▶ Press the up-arrow key on your keyboard to add rows to your grid.

▶ Press the down-arrow key on your keyboard to remove rows from your grid.

▶ Press the right-arrow key on your keyboard to add columns to your grid.

▶ Press the left-arrow key on your keyboard to remove columns from your grid.

▶ Press the X and C keys to skew your columns to the left and right.

▶ Press the V and F keys to skew your rows to the top and bottom.

▶ Press the spacebar to "freeze" your grid and position it elsewhere on your artboard.

▶ Press the tilde key to create numerous copies of your grid.

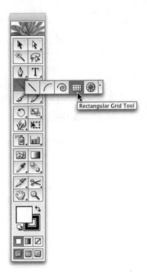

FIGURE 7.24
Choosing the Rectangular Grid tool.

To draw a rectangular grid numerically, choose the Rectangular Grid tool and click once on your artboard to get the Rectangular Grid Tool Options dialog box (see Figure 7.25). Enter the appropriate values and click OK.

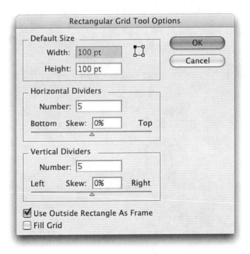

FIGURE 7.25
The Rectangular Grid Tool Options dialog.

The Polar Grid Tool

Similar to the Rectangular Grid tool, the Polar Grid tool creates grids that are circular in form.

To draw a polar grid, choose the Polar Grid tool (see Figure 7.26) and click and drag the mouse on the artboard. Before you release the mouse, you can utilize any of the following functions that will affect the grid you are drawing:

▶ Press the Shift key to constrain your grid to a perfect circle.

▶ Press the (Option) [Alt] key to draw your grid out from its center.

▶ Press the up-arrow key on your keyboard to add concentric dividers to your grid.

▶ Press the down-arrow key on your keyboard to remove concentric dividers from your grid.

▶ Press the right-arrow key on your keyboard to add radial dividers to your grid.

▶ Press the left-arrow key on your keyboard to remove radial dividers from your grid.

▶ Press the X and C keys to skew your concentric dividers closer to or farther from the center.

▶ Press the V and F keys to skew your radial dividers to the left and right.

▶ Press the spacebar to "freeze" your grid and position it elsewhere on your artboard.

▶ Press the tilde key to create numerous copies of your grid.

FIGURE 7.26
Choosing the Polar
Grid tool.

To draw a polar grid numerically, choose the Polar Grid tool and click once on your artboard to get the Polar Grid Tool Options dialog box (see Figure 7.27). Enter the appropriate values and click OK.

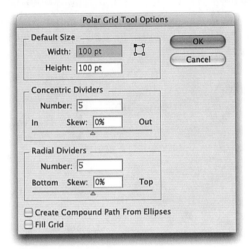

FIGURE 7.27
The Polar Grid Tool Options dialog box.

The Pencil Tool

For drawing freestyle on your artboard, use the Pencil tool (see Figure 7.28). This tool can be especially useful for sketching if you have a tablet. If you hold down the (Option) [Alt] key as you draw, Illustrator will close the path for you when you release the mouse.

FIGURE 7.28
Choosing the Pencil tool.

There are several settings for the Pencil tool, which you can access by double-clicking on the Pencil tool itself in the toolbox. The Pencil Tool Preferences dialog box (see Figure 7.29) allows you to edit the Fidelity and Smoothness settings, which affect how clean and smooth your drawn lines will be. The Keep Selected option keeps the last path you've drawn with the Pencil tool selected, and the Edit Selected Paths option allows you to simply draw over an existing path to adjust it.

FIGURE 7.29
The Pencil Tool
Preferences dialog
box.

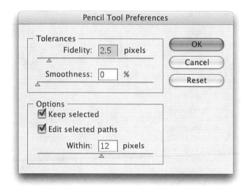

Béziers and the Pen Tool

Back in Chapter 2, we discussed briefly how Illustrator employs three kinds of "anchor points" to draw Bézier paths. We'll discuss these in further detail, as well as learn how paths work inside of Illustrator.

The first type of Bézier path is a straight line; it contains two anchor points with a straight line connecting them (see Figure 7.30). This type is the simplest Bézier path and requires the least amount of memory to store and print—you just need the coordinates of the first and second point.

FIGURE 7.30
A straight Bézier
path with the anchor
points visible.

The second type of Bézier path is the curve, and here the description gets complicated. A curve consists of two anchor points, with a curved line connecting them. The curve is determined by control handles, which are attached to each anchor point. The control handles define exactly how the curved line is drawn between the two anchor points (see Figure 7.31).

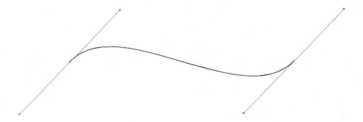

FIGURE 7.31
A curved Bézier path, with the anchor points and control handles visible.

Of course, when the paths print, you don't see the anchor points or the handles. They just appear onscreen so that you can edit the paths. When the paths print, all you see are the lines themselves.

Until now you've been creating Bézier paths without even knowing it. The shapes and paths you've created are all made up of Bézier paths. You were doing fine until now, so why bring up all of this complicated anchor-point and control-handle information? The answer is, sure, you could perform several tasks in Illustrator without knowing what Bézier paths are, but you lose out on all the power that Illustrator offers. Additionally, both Photoshop and InDesign have the Pen tool and allow you to draw and edit Bézier paths.

The Anchor Points

Illustrator has three kinds of anchor points: the straight corner point, the smooth point, and the combination point. Each kind of anchor point has its specific attributes, and each is used to create different types of paths. A Bézier object can be made up of any of the three kinds of anchor points and can contain any combination of them as well. For example, a square is made up of four straight corner anchor points, whereas a circle is made up of four smooth anchor points. A shape such as a pie wedge contains both straight corner and combination anchor points.

The Straight Corner Anchor Point

The straight corner is the simplest form of the anchor point, and it is primarily used to connect straight lines (see Figure 7.32). To draw straight lines, press "P" to switch to the Pen tool and click once on your screen to define the first point in your line. Now click where you want the second point to appear (don't drag from the first point, just click and release). Each time you click in a different place, Illustrator will draw a line connecting the anchor points. To create a closed shape, click on the first anchor point (the Pen tool icon will appear with a little "O" next to it when you're about to close a path).

FIGURE 7.32
The straight corner
anchor point.

The Smooth Anchor Point

The smooth anchor point contains two control handles (see Figure 7.33). By adjusting the control handles, you determine the slope and sharpness of the curve on either side of the point. Because the path continues through the point without a sharp change in direction, it is called a smooth anchor point.

FIGURE 7.33
The smooth anchor
point.

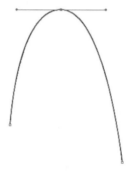

To draw curved lines, click and drag the mouse with the Pen tool to create your first point. Notice that as you drag, you're pulling control handles out from the point. Release the mouse button and then click and drag again at a different place on your artboard. As you drag, you'll see control handles being created for the second point, and a curved line will appear between the two points.

The Combination Anchor Point

The combination point is a combination of the straight anchor point and the smooth anchor point (see Figure 7.34), so using these types of points can get a bit confusing. To draw a path using a combination point, click and drag with the Pen tool to create a smooth point. Then just click elsewhere on the screen to create a corner point. Then click and drag again elsewhere to create yet another smooth point.

FIGURE 7.34
The combination
anchor point.

You'll notice that the point in the middle has no control handles, yet it has curved paths connected to it. In reality, the combination point has two sides to it: a straight side (from the single click) and a curved side (from the click and drag).

In its documentation, Adobe uses different terms for what I call control handles and control lines; it sometimes calls them direction points and direction lines. Also, you won't find a combination anchor point mentioned anywhere in the Adobe Illustrator manual. I use my own terms here because I feel my terminology is easier to understand. I wanted to bring this to your attention in case you reference the Illustrator manual and you happen upon those terms.

By the Way

Editing Shapes and Paths

After you draw a path, you might want to change the shape or style of the points, adjusting the curve of the path or making a corner point into a smooth point. Several tools enable you to modify a path by changing, adding, or deleting a point.

The Direct Selection Tool

Perhaps the simplest form of editing a path is to use the Direct Selection tool. By selecting only one anchor point, you can reposition it (see Figure 7.35). By selecting a path and then dragging on a control point, you can change the shape of the curve for that path.

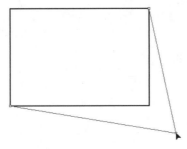

FIGURE 7.35
Repositioning a single point on a path with the Direct Selection tool.

The Add Anchor Point Tool

Simple in concept, the Add Anchor Point tool—which looks just like the Pen tool with a little + (plus sign) next to it—enables you to place additional anchor points on an existing path (see Figure 7.36). Each new point takes on the attributes of the path that you click on. If you add a point to a straight path, the new anchor point is a straight anchor point, and clicking a curved path results in a new smooth anchor point.

FIGURE 7.36
Before and after adding an anchor point to an existing path with the Add Anchor Point tool.

The Delete Anchor Point Tool

The Delete Anchor Point tool simply deletes existing anchor points. It also looks just like the Pen tool, except that it has a – (minus sign) next to it. If you click an anchor point with the Delete Anchor Point tool (see Figure 7.37), the point is removed, and Illustrator automatically joins the preceding anchor point with the next point on the path. If you were to select an anchor point and press the Delete key on your keyboard, the anchor point would be deleted, but the path would be broken at that point.

FIGURE 7.37
Before and after removing an anchor point from an existing path with the Delete Anchor Point tool.

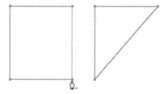

By the Way

Illustrator has a preference setting that will automatically cause the Pen tool to change to the Add Anchor Point tool anytime you mouse over an existing path. Likewise, the Pen tool will automatically change to the Delete Anchor Point tool when you mouse over an existing anchor point. This preference is turned on by default. Although this behavior is desirable at times, it can also get in the way. To turn it off, check the Disable Auto Add/Delete option in the General panel of the Preferences dialog (see Figure 7.38).

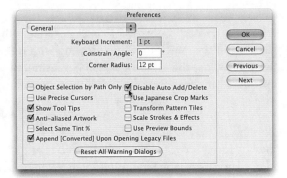

FIGURE 7.38
The Disable Auto Add/Delete option in the General panel of the Preferences dialog.

The Convert Anchor Point Tool

What do you do when you already have an anchor point, but you need to change it from one type of point to another? You use the Convert Anchor Point tool. You can easily access this, the last tool from the Pen tool quartet, by pressing (Option) [Alt] when any of the Pen tools is active. Notice that the cursor changes to an inverted "V" shape.

This tool works the same way as the Pen tool; clicking a point converts it to a straight anchor point. Clicking and dragging on a point makes that point a smooth anchor point. To make a smooth point into a combination point, click and drag on a control handle (see Figure 7.39).

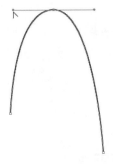

FIGURE 7.39
Converting a smooth anchor point into a combination anchor point, using the Convert Anchor Point tool.

If you want to convert a straight anchor point to a combination point, you must first make the point a smooth point, and then click and drag on the control handle.

Did you Know?

The Smooth Tool

When you create paths, they aren't always as clean or as smooth as you might like, especially when using the Pencil tool and drawing with a mouse. The Smooth tool allows you to "get the kinks out" and get a smooth vector path. Use the tool to draw over any part of a selected path to smooth out that section of the path.

Simplifying Paths

Sometimes a shape has many extra anchor points (as a result of autotracing, or an autotrace program such as Adobe Streamline). There are also times when entire paths need to be smoothed out. Although you can use the Smooth tool, as mentioned previously, for certain applications, there are times when you want to apply those effects on a larger scale.

With any path or object selected, you can choose Object, Path, Simplify (see Figure 7.40) to remove extra anchor points and smooth out vector paths. You can specify that only straight lines are used (no curves), and you can also choose to show a preview of the original path, to compare how close the new simplified path will be to the original (see Figure 7.41). Making adjustments to the Curve Precision and Angle Threshold sliders will control how many anchor points are removed and how smooth the result will be.

FIGURE 7.40
Choosing the Simplify command from the Object, Path menu.

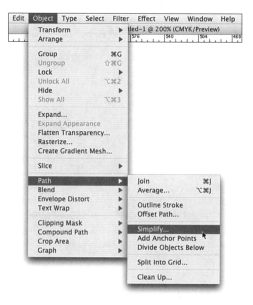

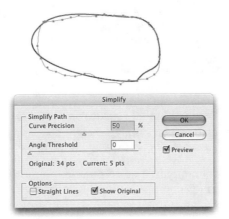

FIGURE 7.41
The Simplify feature gives you the option to compare the original path with the proposed simplified one.

The Erase Tool

The Erase tool doesn't erase the fill of an object, nor does it work the way the eraser tool does in Photoshop by erasing pixels. The Erase tool can be used only on a selected path. Any part of a path that you draw over with the Erase tool will be deleted from that path.

Using Simple Shapes to Create Complex Shapes

No doubt you had more fun drawing the simple shapes discussed earlier, than you did trying to make sense of the likes of the Pen tool. When it comes to creating more complex shapes, however, you can still use the primitive shape tools that are easy to use, along with a powerful collection of functions called Pathfinder. In fact, these functions are so useful that they have their own palette.

The idea behind the Pathfinder functions is that you can use several simple shapes to create a single, more complex shape. The Pathfinder palette is split into two rows of functions. The buttons on the top row are called shape modes, and they allow you to Add, Subtract, Intersect, and Exclude shapes. The buttons on the bottom row are referred to as Pathfinders, and they allow you to Divide, Trim, Merge, Crop, Outline, and apply a Minus Back function (see Figure 7.42).

FIGURE 7.42
The Pathfinder palette, with the shape mode functions on the top row and the Pathfinders on the bottom row.

> If you've used older versions of Illustrator, you might be wondering what happened to the Unite pathfinder command. That function has been replaced by the Add shape mode.

Shape Modes

The shape modes are used primarily to create complex shapes from two or more other paths. To use these functions, you simply select the shapes you want to affect, and click on the appropriate shape mode. There are four shape modes in Illustrator CS:

▶ **Add**—The most commonly used command, the Add shape mode takes all the selected objects and combines them into one object (see Figure 7.43).

FIGURE 7.43
Two objects, before and after the Add shape mode is applied.

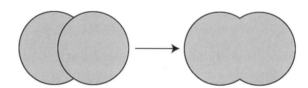

▶ **Subtract**—The Subtract shape mode takes the frontmost object in your selection and subtracts it from the shape behind it, leaving a hole cut out of it (see Figure 7.44).

FIGURE 7.44
Two objects, before and after the Subtract shape mode is applied.

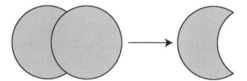

▶ **Intersect**—The Intersect shape mode is used on two or more objects that overlap each other, and when it's applied, only the area where the objects overlap remains. The other parts of the objects are not visible (see Figure 7.45).

FIGURE 7.45
Two objects, before and after the Intersect shape mode is applied.

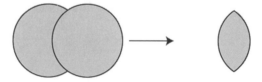

▶ **Exclude**—The Exclude shape mode is the exact opposite of the Intersect shape mode. When it's applied to overlapping objects, only the parts that don't overlap will remain visible (see Figure 7.46).

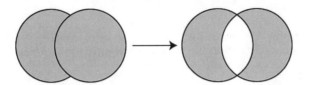

FIGURE 7.46
Two objects, before
and after the
Exclude shape
mode is applied.

Shape modes are nondestructive, meaning that you can continue to edit the primitive shapes after you've applied a shape mode. Objects that have shape modes applied to them are called compound shapes. You can use the Direct Selection tool to select parts of a compound shape to edit them (see Figure 7.47).

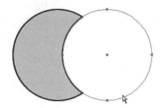

FIGURE 7.47
Editing individual
elements of a com-
pound shape after
the shapes have
been combined.

If at any time you want to "flatten" a compound shape so that the individual primitive shapes are no longer accessible, select the compound shape and click on the Expand button in the Pathfinder palette (see Figure 7.48). Alternatively, if you want to create a flattened object to begin with, you can press and hold the (Option) [Alt] key while applying any of the shape modes.

FIGURE 7.48
Expanding a com-
pound shape.

Illustrator's compound shapes are similar to Photoshop's shape layers (vector masks). In fact, you can copy an Illustrator compound shape and paste it into Photoshop as a vector shape layer. Likewise, you can copy a vector shape layer from Photoshop and paste it into Illustrator as a compound shape (see Figure 7.49).

Did you Know?

FIGURE 7.49
When you're pasting a
vector shape layer
from Photoshop,
Illustrator asks
whether you want to
paste the art as a
compound shape.

Pathfinders

The Pathfinder functions are primarily used for splitting objects into parts, or deleting unwanted parts of objects. There are several kinds, each with a different purpose:

▶ **Divide**—The Divide pathfinder takes any overlapping shapes and cuts them up into separate shapes wherever they overlap (see Figure 7.50). An invaluable tool, Divide enables you to split up objects quickly. Divide looks at each object and divides each overlap individually, so it makes no difference whether you're dividing compound paths, groups, or whatever—they all become individual shapes. After Divide is applied, all the resulting objects are grouped together. You have to ungroup them if you want to work with each piece separately (or use the Direct Selection tool).

FIGURE 7.50
Two objects, before and after the Divide pathfinder is applied.

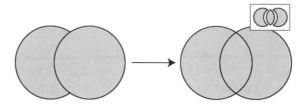

▶ **Trim**—The Trim function removes the parts of the back object that are behind front objects. It also removes the stroke (see Figure 7.51).

FIGURE 7.51
Two objects, before and after the Trim pathfinder is applied.

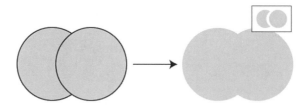

▶ **Merge**—The Merge function operates differently depending on the fills of the selected objects. If the fills are all the same, the result is similar to what's achieved with the Add shape mode, making the objects form one single (flattened) object. If the fills are all different, Merge works like the Trim function. If some of the objects are filled the same, the like objects are united, and the rest are trimmed (see Figure 7.52).

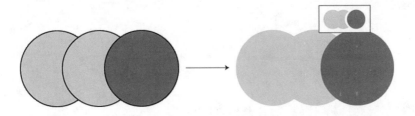

FIGURE 7.52
Three objects, two of
them with the same
fill, before and after
the Merge pathfinder
is applied.

▶ **Crop**—The Crop function removes any parts of selected objects that are
not directly under the frontmost object (see Figure 7.53). The final result of
the Crop function is similar to what you would see if you created a mask.
The only difference is that the Crop function actually deletes the art that
is not visible, unlike a mask, which just covers it up. Be careful before you
run this command because you cannot retrieve the artwork that is
cropped out.

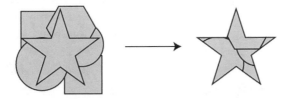

FIGURE 7.53
Two objects, before
and after the Crop
pathfinder is applied.

▶ **Outline**—Choosing the Outline function converts all shapes to outlines and
also divides the lines where they intersect, similar to a Divide function for
strokes (see Figure 7.54).

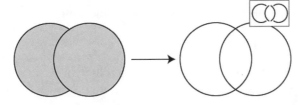

FIGURE 7.54
Two objects, before
and after the
Outline pathfinder
is applied.

▶ **Minus Back**—The reverse of the Subtract shape mode, Minus Back subtracts
a part of an object based on what's behind it (rather than what's in front
of it). This function is also not a shape mode, so the final result is a single
flattened object (see Figure 7.55).

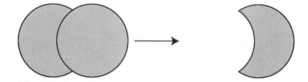

Working with Selections

Back in the Photoshop chapter, we spoke about the importance of making selections, and Illustrator is no different. In Photoshop we were selecting pixels, whereas here in Illustrator, we are going to be selecting objects instead. There are several selection tools and selection methods in Illustrator, so let's take a look at them.

The Selection Tool

The Selection tool (or the black arrow as I like to call it, because of its appearance) is used to select entire objects. You select an object simply by clicking on it (see the sidebar "Selecting Objects"). After an object is selected, you can move it by dragging the object (see Figure 7.56).

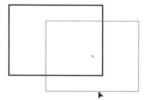

You can select multiple objects by holding down the Shift key as you click on other objects.

The Shift key technique can really save time when you're making certain selections, such as when you want to select all objects in your file except for one of them. In this case, you can simply select all and then Shift-click the one you want to deselect, and you're done.

Another method of selecting objects with the Selection tool is called marquee selecting, in which you click on a blank area and then drag the mouse while holding down the mouse button. As you drag the mouse, a box will appear. Any objects that fall within the marquee box will become selected when you release the mouse button (see Figure 7.57). It's almost like catching fish with a net.

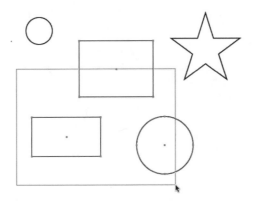

FIGURE 7.57
Selecting a range
of objects using the
marquee selection
method.

Selecting Objects

By default, you can click anywhere inside a filled object to select it. However, if you
turn on the option in General Preferences called Object Selection by Path Only (see
Figure 7.58), you will be able to select a path only by clicking on its path or outline. I
find it useful to turn this preference on when I'm working in very complex illustrations, because this option makes it more difficult to accidentally select unwanted
objects.

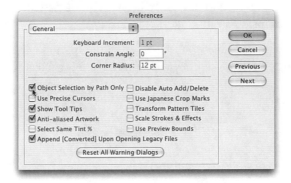

FIGURE 7.58
The Object
Selection by Path
Only preference in
the General panel
of the Preferences
dialog.

The Direct Selection Tool

The Direct Selection tool, or as I like to call it, the white arrow, is the selection tool
used the most in Illustrator. In a few moments, you will see why. As you just
learned, the Selection tool is used to select entire objects. The Direct Selection tool,
on the other hand, is used to select parts of an object. If you click on a path and
drag, only that path will move. The same applies when you click on an anchor
point—only that anchor point will move (see Figure 7.59).

FIGURE 7.59
Moving a single
anchor point using
the Direct Selection
tool.

FIGURE 7.59
Moving a single
anchor point using
the Direct Selection
tool.

You can use either the Shift-click method or the marquee method to select multiple anchor points and move them at the same time.

Grouping Objects

Illustrator allows you to group several objects to make it easier to organize your artwork. However, the benefits of grouping objects together go far beyond having art that is "neat" or organized. First, when you use the Selection tool to select one object in a group, the entire group is selected. This makes it easier to move objects around. Second, as you'll see later in the chapter, a group itself can have certain attributes or effects applied to it. Finally, groups can be nested. That means you can have a group inside another group (and so on).

To make a group, select the objects you want to group, and choose Object, Group (see Figure 7.60). To release a group, select it and choose Objects, Ungroup.

FIGURE 7.60
Choosing the Group
command.

Groups are extremely helpful when you are working in complex documents, and grouping items as you create them is always a good idea. After you create a logo, for instance, group it. This way, you can move it around easily and, more important, you won't accidentally lose parts by trying to select each and every piece, every time (inevitably, you'll miss one or two parts).

The Group Selection Tool

The Group Selection tool is a variation of the Direct Selection tool. You can find it by pressing and holding the mouse button on the Direct Selection tool in the toolbox (see Figure 7.61). In complex illustrations, you might have nested groups that contain many groups. The Group Selection tool makes working with these files easy.

FIGURE 7.61
Choosing the Group Selection tool.

Each time you click with the Group Selection tool, it selects the next higher group, giving you easy access to any group with a nested group.

As mentioned earlier, the Direct Selection tool is the most-used selection tool in Illustrator. If you switch back to the Direct Selection tool and press and hold the (Option) [Alt] key, you'll notice that the cursor for the Direct Selection tool on your screen turns into the Group Selection tool. Releasing the (Option) [Alt] key returns you to the Direct Selection tool.

Now, you have the power to select parts of an object, or, by simply holding down the (Option) [Alt] key, you can select an entire object or entire groups of objects. For 90% of your work, you never have to go back to the Selection tool (black arrow).

The Lasso Tool

Using the marquee method for making selections with the Selection and the Direction Selection tools can be useful, but only if you're okay with selecting objects that fall into a rectangular-shaped marquee area. The Lasso tool allows you to draw irregularly shaped marquees to select objects, or parts of objects.

The Lasso tool works much like the Direct Selection tool in that if an object falls completely within the boundaries of the marquee, the entire object will become selected. But if only a portion of the object falls into that marquee area, only that portion of the object becomes selected (see Figure 7.62).

FIGURE 7.62
Selecting only a portion of an object with the Lasso tool (left) will result in only those parts of the object falling within the marquee to become selected (right).

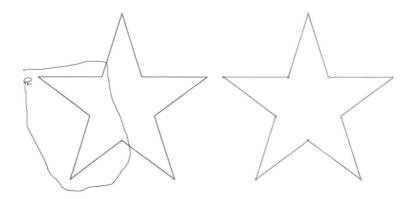

To use the Lasso tool, choose it from the toolbox and draw a marquee area. You don't have to complete the marquee by drawing back to the point you started from, because the Lasso tool will complete the marquee selection area after you release the mouse.

The Magic Wand Tool

Photoshop has a Magic Wand tool that's used to select pixels of similar color. Likewise, in Illustrator, the Magic Wand tool is used to select objects of similar attributes. Double-clicking on the Magic Wand tool in the toolbox opens the Magic Wand palette, where you can specify a Tolerance setting, as well as which attributes the Magic Wand is sensitive to (see Figure 7.63).

FIGURE 7.63
The Magic Wand palette, with all options displayed.

Fills and Strokes

Illustrator wouldn't be incredibly useful if it were able to create only shapes with white fills and black strokes. It's time to splash a bit of color on the topic of applying fills and strokes to objects in Illustrator.

You can specify colors for selected objects in Illustrator by using the Color palette. When expanded fully, the Color palette contains a fill and stroke indicator, color sliders, and a color ramp (see Figure 7.64). To specify a color for the fill of an object, you have to click on the fill indicator first. Likewise, to specify a color for the stroke of an object, click on the stroke indicator.

Fill indicator

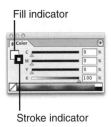

Stroke indicator

FIGURE 7.64
The fully expanded Color palette.

The keyboard shortcut to change the focus between the fill and the stroke is the X key. Learning this shortcut will save you many trips to the Color palette. A fill and stroke indicator also appears in the toolbox.

The Color palette can define colors in grayscale, RGB, HSB, CMYK, and Web-safe RGB colors modes. To switch between these color modes in the Color palette, choose from the list in the palette flyout menu (see Figure 7.65). Alternatively, you can Shift-click on the color ramp to cycle through the different supported color modes.

FIGURE 7.65
Switching between color modes in Illustrator.

Even though you can specify colors in any of several color modes, after those colors are applied to objects in your document, those colors are converted to the document-specified color space. So it usually makes sense to specify colors using the color space that your document is using.

You can store saved colors in the Swatches palette (see Figure 7.66). To create a swatch, simply drag a color from the stroke indicator or the fill indicator in the Color palette into the Swatches palette. Illustrator also ships with numerous swatch collections, which you can access by choosing Open Swatch Library from the Swatches palette flyout menu.

FIGURE 7.66
The Swatches palette.

There are basically three kinds of swatches you can create inside of Illustrator: solid colors, gradients, and patterns.

Solid Colors

Solid colors are simple and are really prerequisites for the other types of swatches. You can define a solid color just as mentioned previously, by specifying a color in the Color palette. However, there are really two *types* of solid colors you need to be aware of: process colors and spot colors.

Process Colors

A process color, by definition, is a color made up of a mix of colors. In the print world, a process color is one made up of different values of CMYK. In the Web arena, Illustrator would also consider an RGB color a process color.

You would specify a process color for jobs you'd be printing in four-color process, or publishing on the Web.

There is a variation of the process color, called a global process color (see Figure 7.67), that allows you to easily track and update colors throughout your document.

FIGURE 7.67
The Swatches palette with the Large Thumbnail View option chosen from the palette fly-out menu. Global process colors display with a white triangle in the corner of the swatch.

Spot Colors

A spot color is a predefined ink color you can either specify on your own, or choose from a list such as Pantone, Focoltone, or Toyo. Spot colors may also be referred to as *custom colors*. They are standard colors that have been designated to ensure color accuracy.

Spot colors have a single value, or a *tint value*, that determines the strength at which the ink will be printed. Spot colors are usually specified when you want to print a specialized ink (a metallic color, for example), or when you want to save money by printing a two- or three-color job (instead of having to print a full-process-color job).

Illustrator ships with many standard custom color libraries, all of which you can load by choosing Open Swatch Library from the Swatches palette flyout menu (see Figure 7.68).

FIGURE 7.68
Choosing from the list of swatch libraries that Illustrator CS ships with.

Gradients

Gradients are a powerful feature in Illustrator, enabling you to specify a fill of different colors blending with each other. Illustrator can create a gradient between just 2 colors or up to 32 colors. Gradients can be used to achieve cool shading effects or to add dimension to objects (see Figure 7.69).

FIGURE 7.69
Using gradient fills to achieve cool effects.

You can apply a gradient to a selected object simply by selecting a gradient swatch from the Swatches palette. To create or edit a gradient, however, you need to open the Gradient palette. With the palette expanded fully, you will find a gradient swatch, an option to make the gradient linear or radial, fields for Angle and Location, and a gradient slider (see Figure 7.70).

FIGURE 7.70
The fully expanded Gradient palette.

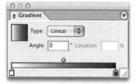

Defining a Gradient

You create a gradient in much the same way you create a color. First you define the gradient, and then you click the New Swatch icon in the Swatches palette. After you create the new swatch, you should double-click it and give it a name. Illustrator gives your creations the names New Gradient Swatch 1, New Gradient Swatch 2, and so on, which don't really offer any insight into what they are.

Click on the Gradient swatch in the Gradient palette. Notice that under the gradient slider are icons that look like little houses. They are *color stops*, indicating the points at which a color is used in the gradient (see Figure 7.71). To create a new color stop, click anywhere beneath the gradient slider. When a new color stop appears, you can drag it to the left or right. You can also drag any color from the Swatches or Color palette onto the gradient slider to create a color stop in that color. To change an existing color stop, either drag a new color directly on top of it, or click the color stop icon to select it and choose a new color in the Swatches or Color palette.

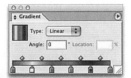

FIGURE 7.71
A gradient with its color stops visible.

To delete a color stop from a gradient, simply drag the color stop off the bottom of the Gradient palette and it will disappear.

Did you Know?

Notice also that little diamond-shaped icons appear on top of the gradient slider. These indicate the location of the midpoint of the gradation. In other words, wherever the icon is, that's the place where 50% of each color appears. You can drag the *midpoint indicator* left or right to adjust where the midpoint should be (see Figure 7.72).

FIGURE 7.72
Dragging the mid-point indicator of a gradient.

Using the Gradient Tool

The Gradient tool in Illustrator works identically to the Gradient tool in Photoshop. It's used to control the direction and placement of a gradient in an object, or over several objects. After you fill an object with a gradient, select the Gradient tool and, with the object still selected, click and drag across the object in the direction you want the gradient to go (see Figure 7.73). The place where you begin dragging is the position where the gradient starts, and the place where you let go is the position where the gradient ends. If you stop dragging before you get to the end of the object, Illustrator continues to fill the object with the color at the end of the gradient.

FIGURE 7.73
Using the Gradient tool to draw a single gradient across multiple objects.

Patterns

Patterns can be real time-savers. A pattern is a defined piece of art, or tile, created in Illustrator that, as a fill attribute, is repeated over and over again, much like wallpaper (see Figure 7.74).

FIGURE 7.74
An object filled with a pattern.

Defining a Pattern

Defining a pattern is a little different from defining gradients or colors. Instead of clicking the New Swatch icon, you drag your objects directly into the Swatches palette from the artboard. After you create a pattern swatch, remember to give it a unique name so that you can identify it quickly when you need it.

Did you Know?

> If you want to edit a pattern that is already defined, simply drag the swatch itself out from the Swatches palette into your artboard, and Illustrator will place the art that was used to create the pattern.

When you're creating a pattern design, remember that your object will be repeated over and over again, so be careful how you set it up. If you need extra space around your art (which is usually the case), create a box with a fill and stroke of none and send it to the back of your artwork. Then, select your art, along with the empty box in the background (see Figure 7.75) and define the pattern. Illustrator will treat a no-fill, no-stroke box that's at the bottom of the stacking order as a boundary for the repeat area of the pattern.

FIGURE 7.75
Selecting the art, along with a no-fill, no-stroke rectangle in the background, before dragging it into the Swatches palette to define a pattern.

In truth, you could probably write an entire book on creating patterns. Designing repeats is an art form in itself, and practicing how to define and apply patterns in Illustrator will certainly help over time.

By the Way

Strokes

A stroke is the line that's drawn around an object, and you can specify solid colors, gradients, or patterns to color a stroke. The Stroke palette is where you can control the actual settings for how a stroke appears (see Figure 7.76).

FIGURE 7.76
The fully expanded Stroke palette.

The most-used option in the Stroke palette is *Weight*. It determines how thick or thin the stroke is. Illustrator's default is 1-point. For hairline rules, most people use 0.25-point (anything thinner won't show up on an offset printing press).

The Miter Limit option determines how far the stroke protrudes on a sharp corner. A thick line, for example, needs more room to complete a sharp point than a thin one does (see Figure 7.77).

FIGURE 7.77
An acute angle combined with a thick stroke needs a higher miter limit to draw the complete point.

Line Caps and Joins

Line caps determine the appearance of the ends of a stroked path (see Figure 7.78). This setting in the stroke palette is used only for open-ended paths. By choosing different caps, you can make the ends either flat or rounded or have the stroke width enclose the end of the path as well.

FIGURE 7.78
The three types of line caps (left to right): Butt, Round, Projecting.

Line joins control how the stroke appears at each corner of the path (see Figure 7.79). You can choose from Mitered, Round, and Beveled options.

FIGURE 7.79
The three types of line joins (left to right): Mitered, Round, Beveled.

Dashed Strokes

The last option in the Stroke palette, Dashed Line, can be one of the most powerful. Here, you can specify dashed or dotted lines. Depending on what settings you have set for weight, line caps, and joins, you can create a stitched line, a skip line, or almost anything. You control the dash and gap (the space between each dash) by entering numbers into the Dash and Gap fields at the bottom of the palette. If you're using only one sequence, you can enter just the first two fields. Alternatively, you can enter up to three different Dash and Gap settings to achieve complex dash patterns (see Figure 7.80).

FIGURE 7.80
Several dash patterns, with their dash and gap settings.

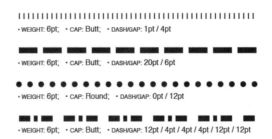

Offset Path and Outline Path

For outlining and special effects, Offset Path is a great function. Offset Path creates an object that perfectly outlines, or traces, a selected path at an offset that you specify. To use it, select one or more objects, and choose Object, Path, Offset Path (see Figure 7.81). The Offset Path dialog box then appears. Enter an amount for the offset (you can use positive or negative numbers) and click OK. Note that Offset Path always makes a copy of your selection and does not affect the original.

FIGURE 7.81
Choosing the Offset path command.

Outline Path is another great feature that converts strokes into filled objects. Found in the same location as the Offset Path command, the Outline Path works by taking the stroke width and creating a filled shape the size of the stroke width.

> The Outline Path command doesn't outline dash information. To outline a dashed stroke, choose Object, Flatten Transparency, and click OK.

Brushes

There are four kinds of brushes inside of Illustrator; however, they are all applied in the same way. The traditional way to apply a brush in Illustrator is to use the Paintbrush tool, which works similarly to the Pencil tool, although instead of just drawing a plain stroked path, the Paintbrush tool applies one of the four kinds of brushes.

Brushes are stored in the Brushes palette (see Figure 7.82), and the truth is that you don't need to use the Paintbrush tool to apply a brush at all. That's because you can select an existing object and click on any brush in the Brushes palette to apply that brush stroke to the selected path. Of course, the Brush tool makes it easier to create more artistic brush strokes, but as you'll soon see, certain kinds of brushes don't require that kind of artistic touch.

FIGURE 7.82
The Brushes palette.

Calligraphic Brushes

The first kind of brush is the Calligraphic brush. A calligraphy pen has an angled tip, or nib, which, when used to draw or write, creates a tapered line that gets thicker or thinner, depending on the angle and direction of the stroke. The Calligraphic brush simulates this effect (see Figure 7.83).

FIGURE 7.83
An example of the kind of art the Calligraphic brush can create.

To create a new Calligraphic brush, click on the New Brush icon in the Brushes palette and choose New Calligraphic Brush (see Figure 7.84) to get the Calligraphic Brush Options dialog box (see Figure 7.85).

FIGURE 7.84
Choosing to create a new Calligraphic brush.

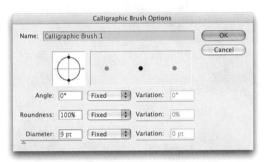

FIGURE 7.85
The Calligraphic Brush Options dialog.

In the Calligraphic Brush Options dialog box, you can specify the following settings:

- At the top of the box, you can specify a name for the brush.

- Directly under the name is a white box with a picture of an ellipse with an arrow going through it and two black dots on either side. This is the Brush Shape editor. Simply click and drag on the arrow to rotate the brush shape and adjust its angle. Click and drag inward on the black dots to adjust the roundness of the brush shape.

- To the immediate right of the Brush Shape Editor is an area that shows you a preview of your brush shape. Notice the three shapes, of which the outer two are grayed out and the center one is black. If you have variations set (see the next bullet item), the gray shapes illustrate the minimum and maximum values for the brush shape.

- You can also specify these values numerically at the bottom of the dialog. Each option can also have one of three attributes: Random, in which Illustrator randomly changes the setting; Pressure, which allows you to utilize how hard you press with a pressure-sensitive pen and tablet; and Fixed, which assigns a constant value that you define. Random and Pressure settings also allow for a variation setting.

Scatter Brushes

The Scatter brush takes predefined art and distributes it along the path you draw with the Paintbrush tool (see Figure 7.86). To define a new Scatter brush, you have to start with a piece of art. After you've created the art you want to use for the brush, select the art and drag it into the Brushes palette. When the New Brush dialog appears asking what kind of brush you want to create, choose New Scatter brush and click OK.

FIGURE 7.86
An example of the kind of art the Scatter brush can create.

Illustrator will then open the Scatter Brush Options dialog box, where you can specify the behavior of the new Scatter brush (see Figure 7.87).

FIGURE 7.87
The Scatter Brush Options dialog.

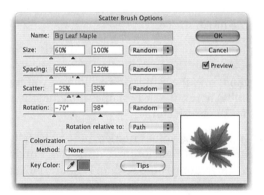

In the Scatter Brush Options dialog box, you can specify the following settings:

▶ At the top of the box, you can specify a name for the brush.

▶ Directly under the name are four options for which you can enter numerical values to specify the Size of the art when it's drawn on the path; the Spacing between the art as it appears on the path; the Scatter, which defines how far from the path the art can stray; and, finally, the Rotation, which specifies the rotation of each individual piece of art on the path. You can set the rotation to be relative to the page or to the actual path itself. For each of these four settings, you can specify Fixed, Random, or Pressure, just as you could for the Calligraphic brushes. The Pressure option works only if you are using a pressure-sensitive tablet, such as a Wacom tablet.

▶ The final option for the Scatter brush is Colorization. This option allows you to specify color changes to the art that appears on your painted strokes. Choosing None keeps the color consistent with the original color defined with the brush you have selected. To use the Hue Shift option, click the Eyedropper box, and click to choose a color from the art that appears in the box to the right. This procedure works on colored objects only, not black-and-white objects. Clicking the Tips button can help you see how the color changes are applied.

If you're thinking that the Scatter brush seems similar to the brushes we created in Photoshop, you're absolutely right. As you'll see later in this chapter, there's another feature in Illustrator, the Symbol Sprayer tool, that can create art that looks similar to the Scatter brush, only a lot more powerful.

Art Brushes

The Art brush differs from the Scatter brush in that the Art brush stretches a single piece of predefined art along a path (see Figure 7.88), whereas the Scatter brush litters the path with many copies of the art. To define a new Art brush, you have to start with a piece of art. After you've created the art you want to use for the brush, select the art and drag it into the Brushes palette. When the New Brush dialog appears asking what kind of brush you want to create, choose New Art Brush and click OK.

Illustrator will then open the Art Brush Options dialog box, where you can specify the behavior of the new Art brush (see Figure 7.89).

FIGURE 7.88
An example of the
kind of art the Art
brush can create.

FIGURE 7.89
The Art Brush
Options dialog.

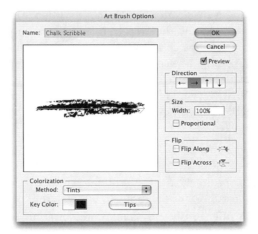

In the Art Brush Options dialog box, you can specify the following settings:

▶ At the top of the box, you can specify a name for the brush.

▶ Directly under the name is a white box with the art in it. Notice that an arrow goes through the art. This arrow indicates the direction the art is drawn on the path; you can edit it by clicking any of the arrows that appear to the right of the white box.

▶ Below the Direction option is the Size option, in which you can specify what size the art appears on the painted path. If you select the Proportional option, the artwork will retain is height-to-width relationship for the length of the stroke. You can also specify whether the art should be flipped along or across the painted path.

▶ The final option for the Art brush is Colorization, which functions exactly like the Scatter brush does, as described earlier.

Pattern Brushes

Apparently, three kinds of brushes in Illustrator just weren't enough for the engineers over at Adobe, so they added a fourth—arguably the most powerful of the bunch. The Pattern brush takes patterns and applies them across a painted path (see Figure 7.90). What makes this different from any brush until this point is that you can define patterns with different attributes for corners and ends. We covered how to create patterns earlier in the chapter, and after you have your patterns listed in your Swatches palette, you can define a Pattern brush by clicking on the New Brush icon in the Brushes palette and choosing New Pattern Brush.

FIGURE 7.90
An example of the kind of art the Pattern brush can create.

Illustrator will then open the Pattern Brush Options dialog box, where you can specify the behavior of the new Art brush (see Figure 7.91).

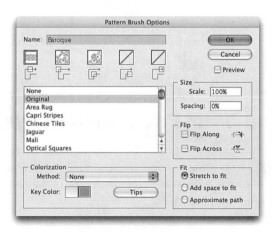

FIGURE 7.91
The Pattern Brush Options dialog.

In the Pattern Brush Options dialog box, you can specify the following settings:

▶ At the top of the box, you can specify a name for the brush.

▶ Directly under the name are five boxes, each representing a different tile of the pattern: Side, Outer Corner, Inner Corner, Start, and End. You do not need to define all five parts, and Illustrator uses the parts only when necessary. With a tile section selected, choose a pattern from the list that appears directly under the tiles.

▶ As with the previous brushes, you can specify Scale and Spacing, as well as specify whether the pattern should be flipped along or across the path.

▶ With the Pattern brush, you can decide how Illustrator fits the pattern to the path. Obviously, not every pattern will fit every path length perfectly. If you select Stretch to Fit, Illustrator stretches the pattern tiles to make the pattern fit seamlessly across the entire painted path. If you select Add Space to Fit, Illustrator does not adjust the size of the pattern tiles, but spaces them evenly across the painted stroke. Finally, the Approximate Path option adjusts the size of the path itself to fit the size of the pattern tiles.

▶ The final option for the Art brush is Colorization, which functions exactly like the Scatter and Art brushes do, as described earlier.

In closing, if you find it hard to tell what type each brush is just by looking at the Brushes palette, you can opt to view the brushes by name. Choose View by Name from the Brushes palette flyout menu, and you'll notice that on the far right of each brush listing, there's an icon that indicates what kind of brush each one is (see Figure 7.92).

FIGURE 7.92
Viewing the list of brushes by name. The icons on the far right of each listing indicate the brush type.

Organizing Your Files Using Layers

Using layers in Illustrator allows you to better organize the objects in your file. Although it may not make much sense to spend time creating and working with layers to work on a simple logo, it certainly makes sense for illustrations or designs that are more complex.

The Layers Palette

Illustrator's layers are specified in the Layers palette. When you start working in a new document, all artwork is automatically placed on a layer called Layer 1 (see Figure 7.93). To open the Layers palette, choose Show Layers from the Window menu. The order in which layers appear in the Layers palette is important: Layers that appear closer to the top of the palette will appear above (or in front of) other objects that might appear on layers that are closer to the bottom of the Layers palette.

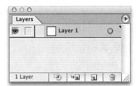

FIGURE 7.93
The Layers palette, with the default Layer 1 showing.

Editing Layers

Some artists prefer to create several layers before they begin working, adding art to each layer as they progress. Others prefer to add or delete layers as necessary as they work on a project. Still others like to create the entire piece and then chop it into different layers afterward. As you'll soon see, there are certainly some benefits to working with layers during the design process (rather than after the fact).

To create a new layer, click on the New Layer button at the bottom of the Layers palette. Illustrator creates the layer and assigns it a name. You can double-click on the layer to rename it, or instead you can (Option-click) [Alt-click] on the New Layers button to create a new layer and name it in one step. In either case, it's a good idea to name your layers, because trying to identify layers that are named Layer 1, Layer 2, Layer 3, and so on is going to be difficult (to say the least).

When you click the New Layer button, a new layer is added just above the currently selected layer. If you hold down the (⌘) [Ctrl] key while clicking the New Layer icon, a new layer will be added to the top of your Layers palette.

Did you Know?

To delete a layer, either click the layer in the Layers palette to highlight it and then click on the trash can icon at the bottom of the palette, or drag the layer itself into the trash icon. If you try to delete a layer that contains artwork on it, a warning dialog appears, alerting you about the situation (see Figure 7.94), and Illustrator proceeds to delete the layer and its contents only with your permission.

FIGURE 7.94
Illustrator warns
you if you try delet-
ing a layer with art
on it.

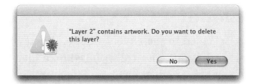

You can duplicate a layer—and all the contents of that layer along with it—by clicking and dragging an existing layer onto the New Layer icon in the Layers palette.

Using Layers in the Design Process

As I mentioned earlier, there are certainly benefits to working with the Layers palette as you design your art. Let's take a closer look at the Layers palette to better understand these benefits.

Each layer in the Layers palette has a several different icons, which allow you to perform certain functions (see Figure 7.95). We'll discuss these functions, beginning on the far left of a layer listing.

FIGURE 7.95
The different icons
within each layer in
the Layers palette.

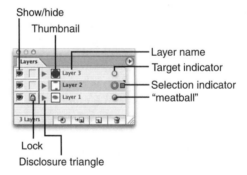

On the far left, each layer has an icon that looks like an eye. Clicking on the eye will toggle the visibility of that layer. Pressing the (Option) [Alt] key while clicking on the eye will hide/show all other layers at once.

The next icon to the right of the eye is a lock indicator. Click in the box to toggle the layer to be locked or unlocked. Pressing the (Option) [Alt] key while clicking on the lock will lock/unlock all other layers at once.

The next icon to the right of the lock is a disclosure triangle. Click on the triangle to reveal the content of the layer. If there isn't a triangle on a layer, there are no objects on that layer.

Take note that layers are shaded with a gray background. However, objects them-selves (which appear inside of layers) appear in the Layers palette with a white background (see Figure 7.96). People often get confused with Illustrator's behavior of "automatically creating all of these layers each time I create something," but in reality, each time you create a new object, Illustrator isn't creating a new layer at all.

By the Way

FIGURE 7.96
Layers and objects, displayed in the Layers palette. Objects are colored white.

To the right of the disclosure triangle is a thumbnail icon that gives a graphical preview of the objects on that layer. Be aware that for documents with many lay-ers, thumbnails can slow the performance of Illustrator, because it has to draw each and every thumbnail.

To the right of the thumbnail is the layer name.

To the right of the layer name is a little circle. This is the target icon. For an effect or attribute to be applied to an object in Illustrator, that object (or group, or layer) has to be targeted. Illustrator actually employs something called smart targeting that automatically does the targeting for you; however, there are times when you want to specifically target something yourself. To target a layer or an object, click once on the circle icon, which will then appear with a circle outlined around it. Layers or objects that have an appearance applied to them display the circle as a shaded 3D sphere (which the Adobe engineers refer to as the "meatball").

Finally, if you click on the far right of the layer, it will select all the objects in that layer. Selections are indicated by a colored square. This square can appear in two sizes. If all the objects on the layer are selected, you will see a large square, but if only some of the objects on a layer are selected, a smaller square will display instead. You can move artwork from one layer to another simply by dragging the colored square to a different layer. At the same time, you can press the (Option) [Alt] key while dragging the square to copy the selected art to a different layer.

Illustrator layers can be used for more than just organizing artwork inside Illustrator. When saving files for SVG or for certain Web applications, you can have Illustrator convert layers to CSS layers. You can also export an Illustrator file as a Photoshop file with layers intact. Finally, you can save a PDF file out of Illustrator CS that's compatible with Acrobat 6, allowing you to view Illustrator's layers in Adobe Reader and Acrobat 6.0 Professional.

The Appearance Palette

Ask me what I think the key is to getting a real grasp on using Illustrator, and I'll tell you it's the Appearance palette. That's because the Appearance palette gives you the information you need to know about your targeted selections. For example, if you select a rectangle, the Appearance palette will tell you that a path is targeted and will indicate what the fill and stroke of that object are. More important, the Appearance palette will tell you if transparency settings or live effects have been applied to the object (see Figure 7.97). Later in the chapter, we'll cover exactly what live effects are, but an example would be a soft drop shadow or a warp effect.

FIGURE 7.97
The Appearance palette helps identify the appearance of an object.

The Appearance palette also enables you to add multiple strokes or multiple fills to an object, a group, or a layer. To do so, simply choose Add New Fill or Add New Stroke from the Appearance palette flyout menu (see Figure 7.98).

FIGURE 7.98
Adding a new (additional) stroke to an object.

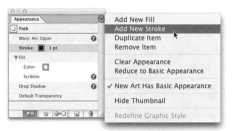

We're going to be looking at the Appearance palette a bit more closely later in the chapter while discussing live effects, but I wanted to point out that, just as with the Layers palette, items that appear in the Appearance palette represent the stacking order for those items. By default, an object's stroke appears above the fill, but you can actually change that in the Appearance palette by dragging the fill to appear at the top of the stacking order. Following the same line of thinking, you can also click on just the fill to highlight it, and then apply an opacity setting that will be applied only to the fill, and not to the stroke of that object (see Figure 7.99).

FIGURE 7.99
An opacity setting applied specifically to the fill of an object.

Masking Objects

A mask conceals, or covers, parts of an object behind the mask, yet it reveals parts of the object behind it as well. For example, a mask that you wear to a masquerade party might cover parts of your face, yet there are some parts that are not covered. A mask in Illustrator works in much the same way: You can take just about any shape or object in Illustrator and use it to mask other elements in your design. After a mask is applied, you can edit the art behind the mask or the mask itself, independently of each other.

There are basically three types of masks you can apply in Illustrator: a clipping mask, a layer clipping mask, and an opacity mask. Each of these masks has its own specific uses and capabilities.

Clipping Masks

The clipping mask, the simplest kind of mask in Illustrator, can be made of any vector shape. A clipping mask works in this way: You have a shape that sits on top of your objects. When the mask is created, any objects that fall within the boundary of the top shape (the mask) will be visible, but anything that falls outside that boundary will be hidden. It's important to realize that the hidden art is not deleted—rather, it's still there, just hidden from view.

To create a clipping mask, draw a shape for your mask and bring it to the front of the stacking order. Position your mask over the art you want the mask to affect and select both the art objects and the mask shape above it (see Figure 7.100). Then choose Object, Clipping Mask, Make to create the mask (see Figure 7.101). When the mask is applied, both the objects and the mask above it will become grouped together; however, you can use the Group Selection tool to select just the mask or just the objects to make edits. This is useful when you want to reposition the mask to reveal a different part of the objects below it.

FIGURE 7.100
The objects selected, with the object that will be the mask on top.

FIGURE 7.101
The masked art.

To release a mask (and have all the objects below the mask revealed again), select the group of the mask and objects, and choose Object, Clipping Mask, Release.

Layer Clipping Masks

Layer clipping masks are very similar in concept to clipping masks, except they are applied in the Layers palette and affect all items on a specific layer. To create a layer clipping mask, simply create a shape that's on the same layer as the art you want to mask, and click on the layer listing in the Layers palette to highlight it. Then click the Make/Release Clipping Mask button at the bottom of the Layers palette (see Figure 7.102).

FIGURE 7.102
Creating a layer clipping mask.

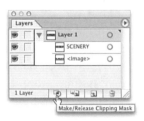

Any object you add to that layer will automatically become masked as well. Likewise, any object you pull out of that layer will no longer be masked. A mask object is indicated by a listing in the Layers palette with an underline (see Figure 7.103). To release a layer clipping mask, highlight the layer in the Layers palette and click the Make/Release Clipping Mask button.

FIGURE 7.103
An object with an underline in the Layers palette indi-cates that it's a clipping mask.

Opacity Masks

As Emeril Lagasse says, let's kick it up a notch! Opacity masks are like clipping masks on steroids. First of all, you can use just about anything as an opacity mask—even gradients and photographs. If you remember how we discussed creat-ing alpha channels and layer masks inside of Photoshop, you'll quickly see that opacity masks inside Illustrator are practically the same thing.

> Because opacity masks use the luminosity values of the mask itself, you can actual-ly create a photograph or a vector object that truly fades to transparent. Simply use a black-to-white gradient as your opacity mask.

Did you
Know?

The same basic rule applies to opacity masks in that you place the mask at the top of the stacking order and then select both the mask and objects under it before applying the mask.

After you have the objects selected, open the Transparency palette and expand the palette so that you can see all the options. You'll see a thumbnail of your selection on the left side of the palette (see Figure 7.104). From the Transparency palette flyout menu, choose Make Opacity Mask (see Figure 7.105). You'll now see that a second thumbnail appears in the Transparency palette beside the original one, which is the mask itself (see Figure 7.106).

FIGURE 7.104
The fully expanded Transparency palette with the thumbnail visible.

FIGURE 7.105
Creating an opacity
mask.

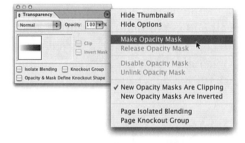

FIGURE 7.106
After the opacity
mask is created,
both thumbnails
are visible.

Did you Know?

The thumbnail icons in Illustrator's Transparency palette function exactly the same way layer mask icons work in Photoshop. For example, if you Shift-click on the mask thumbnail, the mask will be disabled.

After an opacity mask is applied, you have several options in the Transparency palette:

► To edit the art, click on the left thumbnail. You can tell that the thumbnail is highlighted if you see a black outline around it. Any edits you make on the artboard will affect the art objects themselves, and there's no way for you to access or edit the mask object itself.

► To edit the mask object itself, click on the right thumbnail. There are two ways you can tell that you're editing the mask itself and not the art under it. The mask thumbnail will be highlighted with a black outline, and the Layers palette will change to display only a single item—the opacity mask itself (see Figure 7.107). While you're editing an opacity mask, you will not be able to make any edits to other art in your file.

FIGURE 7.107
The Layers palette,
when an opacity
mask thumbnail is
highlighted.

▶ Between the two thumbnails, there is a link icon (on by default). When the art and the mask are linked, they will be transformed together. So if you move the art, the mask will move with it as well (so that the appearance will be the same). However, you can click on the link icon to disable the link, at which time you can move the mask and the art independently.

▶ The Clip option uses the shape of the mask to also clip the art under it (basically giving the same effect as a clipping mask in addition to the opacity levels).

▶ The Invert Mask option allows you to reverse the luminosity values of the mask object. In simple terms, when you toggle this option, anything that was previously visible through the mask becomes hidden, and everything that was hidden becomes visible.

An object with an opacity mask applied to it is indicated in the Layers palette with a dashed underline (see Figure 7.108). To release an opacity mask, select the masked object and choose Release Opacity Mask from the Transparency palette flyout menu.

FIGURE 7.108
An object with an opacity mask applied to it, as seen from the Layers palette.

Applying Transformations

Illustrator has five basic transformation functions: Move, Rotate, Scale, Reflect, and Shear. Illustrator also has a Free Transform tool and a feature called Transform Each that enables you to apply transformations to multiple objects with one click. You can also use the Transform palette, which makes for quick and precise transformations. I know it sounds confusing, but hang in there, because this will all be second nature before you know it.

Before we talk about transformations, I want to point out one particular keyboard shortcut that is a real time-saver. Holding down the (⌘) [Ctrl] key at any time activates the most recent arrow selection tool you've used. If, for example, you last used the Selection tool, pressing this keyboard shortcut while using any of Illustrator's other tools temporarily activates the Selection tool.

When it comes to transformations specifically, you are always selecting objects and making minor changes to the art. Having to switch back and forth between the transformation tools and the selection tools is a pain. With the (⌘) [Ctrl] key, the selection tool is always just a keystroke away.

Moving Objects

Although not necessarily a transformation in that the actual object is changed, moving an object is considered a transformation because the coordinates of the object are being changed (we'll talk more about coordinates shortly, when we discuss the Transform palette).

You already learned one way to move an object: by clicking and dragging a selection. Illustrator also lets you move things more precisely. If you click and drag a selection and then hold down the Shift key, you are able to drag your selection only along a constrained axis in increments of 45 degrees.

Want to get even more precise? After you make a selection, you can use your keyboard's arrow keys (up, down, left, and right) to "nudge" your selection incrementally. You can control how much each nudge is in the General preferences panel by pressing (⌘-K) [Ctrl+K] (see Figure 7.109).

FIGURE 7.109
Specifying the keyboard increment in the General preferences panel.

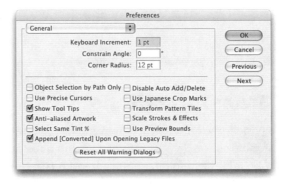

Still not precise enough for you? If you want to move objects numerically, make your selection and then double-click on the Selection tool in the toolbox (the black arrow). In the resulting dialog box, you can specify an exact amount to four decimal places (see Figure 7.110). Entering negative numbers will move the object down or to the left. In this dialog box, you can also choose to move a copy of your object—and there's a Preview button that enables you to view the results of the move before clicking OK.

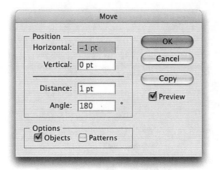

FIGURE 7.110
The Move dialog.

There's yet another way to move something: Illustrator's Transform palette, which we'll get to soon.

Rotate, Scale, Reflect, and Shear

The four transformation tools—Rotate, Scale, Reflect, and Shear—are very similar. As you should know by now, before making any transformations, you must first make a selection.

The Bounding Box

With Illustrator's default setting, when you make a selection, the object is highlighted with a rectangular shape that has hollow squares at the corners and the centers of each line (see Figure 7.111). This is called the *bounding box*, and it allows you to make certain transformations to the selection, without having to select a different tool.

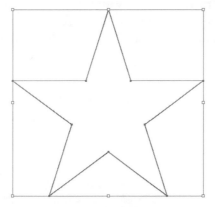

FIGURE 7.111
A selected object, with the bounding box shown.

You can turn off the bounding box by choosing View, Hide Bounding Box (see Figure 7.112), or you can use the keyboard shortcut, (⌘-Shift-B) [Ctrl+Shift+B].

Did you Know?

Clicking and dragging on any of the hollow squares allows you to scale the selection in that direction. Pressing the Shift key while dragging one of the hollow squares will constrain the proportions of your selection. Pressing the (Option) [Alt] key when dragging will scale the selection from its center.

If you position your cursor just outside any of the corner hollow squares, you'll notice that your cursor changes from a straight arrow to a bent arrow. If you click and drag outside of the object, while the bent-arrow cursor is showing, you can rotate your selection around its center (see Figure 7.113). Pressing the Shift key while dragging will constrain your rotations to increments of 45 degrees.

FIGURE 7.113
Rotating an object
using the bounding
box.

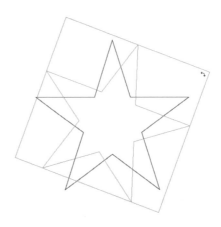

Using the Transformation Tools

I'm not a big fan of the bounding box myself. For one, it was added to Illustrator a few versions back to appeal to users who had used other illustration tools, like CorelDRAW, that featured this kind of functionality. Second, as you're about to find out, there are specific scale and rotate tools in Illustrator that offer more powerful options. Finally—and most important in my opinion—you can't perform certain transformations when the bounding box is turned on. For example, say you wanted to drag an object by its corner to move it (I'll explain in a moment why you would want to do that). With the bounding box turned on, if you drag from a corner, the object will scale, rather than move. Illustrator has a snap-to-point feature that allows you to easily align objects as you position them. So I might want to grab a rectangle by its corner and move it to the edge of the page where the corner would snap to the edge of the page, making it easy to move my objects with precision.

Anyway, I digress. The bottom line is that you're now going to learn the most powerful way to perform scale, rotate, reflect, and shear transformations in Illustrator. The bounding box was really created for anyone who doesn't plan on reading this book. Although you can certainly keep the bounding box option turned on when using the other transformation tools, I'm going to suggest that you turn it off for now, because it will be easier to learn the new tools that way. You can toggle the bounding box by pressing (⌘-Shift-B) [Ctrl+Shift+B].

Rotate

To apply a rotation, make a selection and press the R key on your keyboard. Right away, you'll notice a new icon appear in the center of your selection, which is called your *origin point* (see Figure 7.114). The origin point is the place from where your transformation begins. As you'll soon see, all the transformation tools use an origin point, but specifically with the Rotation tool, your origin point dictates the center of your rotation.

If you want to rotate your selection around a point other than its center, you can redefine the origin point simply by dragging it to a new location. In fact, you can set the origin point to just about any arbitrary point on your artboard. You'll see why this is so useful as we progress with the transformation tools.

To rotate a selection, position your cursor a fair distance away from the origin point and click and drag with the mouse (see Figure 7.115). You don't necessarily grab the object itself (although you can), but if you click too close to the origin point, it will be difficult to accurately apply your rotation.

FIGURE 7.114
The origin point of
a transformation.

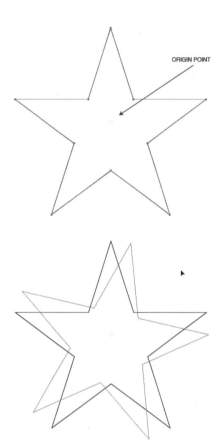

FIGURE 7.115
Rotating an object
using the Rotate
tool.

Pressing the Shift key while you drag will constrain the rotation to increments of 45 degrees. Pressing the (Option) [Alt] key while dragging will rotate a copy of your selection.

Scale

Probably the most frequently used transformation tool, the Scale tool (see Figure 7.116) allows you to change the size of your selected objects. You apply a scale transformation in much the same way as you do for rotate. Make a selection and press the "S" key on your keyboard. If you want, you can move the origin point to a location other than the center of the selected objects.

To scale a selection, position your cursor a fair distance away from the origin point and click and drag with the mouse. As you drag away from the origin point, your objects will scale larger. As you drag toward the origin point, your objects will scale smaller.

FIGURE 7.116
The Scale tool.

Pressing the Shift key while you drag will constrain your objects to scale proportionally. Pressing the (Option) [Alt] key while dragging will scale a copy of your selection.

Scale Stroke & Effects

Specifically with the Scale tool, Illustrator gives you the option to specify whether you want to scale any strokes or effects that are applied to your selection in addition to the object itself.

In a simple example, say you had a rectangle that had a 1pt stroke applied to it. By default, when you scale that rectangle, the stroke will remain at 1pt even though the rectangle is now a different size. If you double-click on the Scale tool in the toolbox, you'll be presented with the Scale dialog box, where you can check the Scale Strokes & Effects box to have the stroke setting change size as well (see Figure 7.117). In a more complex example, if you have an effect applied to your selection, such as a drop shadow, that effect's settings will change size only if this option is turned on.

Reflect

The Reflect tool (see Figure 7.118) allows you to flip or mirror your selected objects. This tool is most useful for creating symmetrical artwork. After you create one side of your art, simply flip a copy of it to complete the design (see Figure 7.119). Make a selection and press the "O" key on your keyboard. If you want, you can move the origin point to a location other than the center of the selected objects—which is common with the Reflect function because rarely will you reflect an object from its center.

FIGURE 7.117
The Scale Stroke &
Effects option in
the Scale dialog
box.

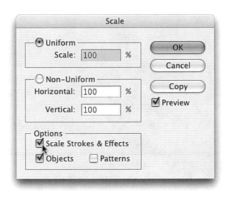

FIGURE 7.118
Choosing the
Reflect tool.

FIGURE 7.119
Creating a reflec-
tion of a design.

To reflect a selection, position your cursor a fair distance away from the origin point and click and drag with the mouse. As you drag, you will reflect your artwork.

Pressing the Shift key while you drag will constrain your objects to reflect in increments of 45 degrees. Pressing the (Option) [Alt] key while dragging will reflect a copy of your selection.

Shear

The Shear tool allows you to skew your selected objects. You apply a shear transformation in much the same way as you do for the other transform functions. Make a selection and switch to the Shear tool (it's found behind the Scale tool in the toolbox, as shown in Figure 7.120). There's no keyboard shortcut assigned to this tool (although if you find yourself using this tool often, you can assign one to it). If you want, you can move the origin point to a location other than the center of the selected objects.

FIGURE 7.120
Choosing the Shear tool.

To shear a selection, position your cursor a fair distance away from the origin point and click and drag with the mouse. As you drag away from the origin point, your selection will skew (see Figure 7.121).

FIGURE 7.121
Shearing a select-
ed object.

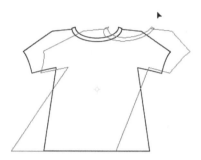

Pressing the Shift key while you drag will constrain your selection, and pressing
the (Option) [Alt] key while dragging will shear a copy of your selection.

Going by the Numbers

There are times when you need to make a precise transformation, such as rotating something 38 degrees, or scaling something 221%. In those cases, you can
apply transformations numerically by making your selection and then double-
clicking on the transformation tool you need to use. A dialog box will appear,
where you can enter specific values and choose to apply the transformation to
your selection, or to a copy of your selection (see Figure 7.122).

FIGURE 7.122
Rotating a selec-
tion numerically.

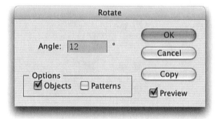

When you double-click on a tool to apply a transformation numerically, the origin
point for that transformation will always be the center of the selection. If you want
to apply a transformation numerically and you also want to specify an origin
point, make your selection, choose the appropriate transformation tool, and click
where you want the origin point to be while holding down the (Option) [Alt] key.

Do You See a Pattern Here?

If your selection has a pattern fill applied to it, you can choose to transform both
the object and the pattern, just the object, or just the pattern (see Figure 7.123).
By default, Illustrator scales just the object and not the fill pattern. When you're
applying transformations via any of the transform dialog boxes (see the preceding subsection, "Going by the Numbers"), there's a check box where you can
specify whether pattern fills are transformed. Alternatively, you can press and
hold the tilde key (that's the squiggly one usually near the Escape key) as you're

dragging with any of the transform tools. This works even when you're dragging with the Selection tool to move something.

FIGURE 7.123
An object that was rotated with the Pattern option turned on (left) and off (right).

The Free Transform Tool

Admittedly, I was a bit unkind to the bounding box feature in Illustrator earlier in this chapter. The truth is, there's a tool that offers similar functionality to the bounding box in Illustrator—yet is far more powerful—called the Free Transform tool (see Figure 7.124).

FIGURE 7.124
The Free Transform tool.

The Free Transform tool originally appeared in Photoshop. At that time, a simple transformation such as a rotate or a scale could take several minutes to calculate and apply, and if you had to apply both a scale and a rotate, it meant applying one transformation, waiting, and then applying the second one. The Free Transform tool allowed you to specify several kinds of transformations all in one step. The tool was added to Illustrator shortly thereafter, although the benefits aren't as revolutionary in Illustrator.

By the Way

To use the Free Transform tool, make a selection and press the "E" key on your keyboard, or choose the Free Transform tool from the toolbox. Unlike the other transformation tools, you can't change the origin point when using the Free Transform tool.

The Free Transform tool allows you to perform a plethora of functions, which I've conveniently listed for you here:

▶ Click inside the bounding box and drag to move the selection.

▶ Click outside the bounding box and drag to rotate the selection.

▶ Click and drag on any of the four corner handles to scale the selection. Press the Shift key to constrain proportion. Press the (Option) [Alt] key to simultaneously scale the opposite side of the selection.

▶ Click and drag on any of the middle four handles to scale horizontally or vertically. Press the Shift key to constrain proportion. Press the (Option) [Alt] key to simultaneously scale the opposite side of the selection.

▶ Click and drag on any of the four corner handles and press the (⌘) [Ctrl] key to distort your selection (see Figure 7.125). Press the (Option) [Alt] key to simultaneously distort the opposite side of the selection. Make sure you click on the handle first and then press the (⌘) [Ctrl] key.

FIGURE 7.125
Using the Free Transform tool to distort a selection.

▶ Click and drag on any of the four middle handles, and press the (⌘) [Ctrl] key to skew your selection. Press the (Option) [Alt] key to simultaneously skew the opposite side of the selection. Make sure you click on the handle first and then press the (⌘) [Ctrl] key.

Unlike with Photoshop, you don't have to press Enter to apply a transformation with the Free Transform tool. Simply deselect your objects and you're done.

Transform Each

The Transform Each function offers two excellent benefits: the capability to perform scale, move, rotate, and reflect transformations simultaneously, and the capability to transform each object in a selection independently of the others. Let's take a closer look.

First, making multiple transformations is a snap when you use Transform Each. Make a selection and choose Object, Transform, Transform Each to bring up the Transform Each dialog box (see Figure 7.126). Here, you can specify measurements for scaling, moving, rotating, and reflecting your selection. A Preview box enables you to view your transformation in real-time. You'll see in a minute how the Transform Each feature is more powerful than you might think.

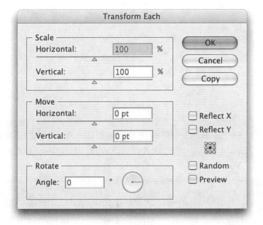

FIGURE 7.126
The Transform Each dialog.

The second benefit I mentioned was the capability to transform multiple objects individually. To demonstrate, I've created a grid of squares (see Figure 7.127). If I select all the squares and use the Rotate tool to rotate my selection 45 degrees, my entire selection rotates as one—sharing a single origin point (see Figure 7.128). However, if I apply the Transform Each function to the same selection and specify a 45-degree rotation, each square rotates individually—each with its own origin point (see Figure 7.129).

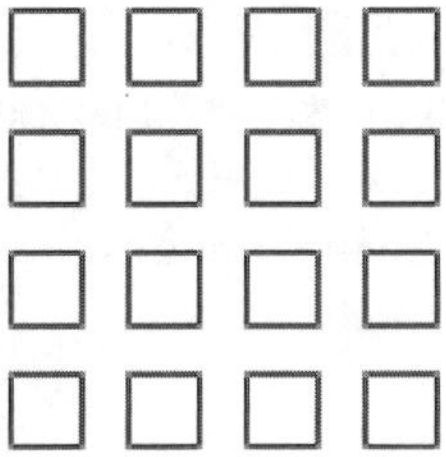

FIGURE 7.127
A grid of squares.

FIGURE 7.128
The grid of
squares, rotated 45
degrees with the
Rotate tool.

FIGURE 7.129
The grid of squares,
rotated 45 degrees
with the Transform
Each command.

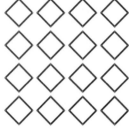

*By the
Way*

> Although you can't set an exact origin point with the Transform Each function, you
> can use the proxy inside the dialog box to choose from one of nine origin-point loca-
> tions (the default is set to center).

The Random button in the Transform Each dialog box transforms each object a
little differently, making for an irregular, almost hand-drawn look. If you have
the Preview box checked, you can see how the objects will be affected. Unchecking
and then checking the Random option gives different results each time (it truly is
random!).

The Transform Palette

Simply because there aren't already enough palettes in Illustrator, you can also
apply transformations via the Transform palette (see Figure 7.130). In truth, this
palette is quite valuable because it allows you to precisely position artwork on
your page, using X and Y coordinates. No other transform function in Illustrator
offers that capability. On the left side of the palette is a proxy you can use to
specify an origin point, and to the left, there's a lock icon that allows you to automatically scale objects proportionally.

FIGURE 7.130
The Transform palette.

Transform Again

Arguably the most powerful transform feature in Illustrator, the Transform Again command allows you to repeat the last-applied transformation. I'll illustrate how this feature works by creating the tick marks for a clock:

1. I'll begin by drawing a single tick mark.

2. I'll press the "R" key to choose the Rotate tool, and I'll (Option-click) [Alt-click] below the mark to specify a numeric rotation while setting a custom origin point (see Figure 7.131).

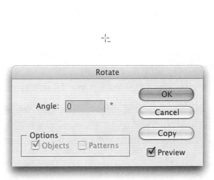

FIGURE 7.131
Positioning the cursor to (Option-click) [Alt-click] to define a custom origin point and bring up the Rotate dialog, all in one step.

3. I'll enter a value of 30 degrees for my rotation and I'll click the Copy button.

4. I'll press (⌘-D) [Ctrl+D] repeatedly until all 12 tick marks have been created (see Figure 7.132).

FIGURE 7.132
The completed illustration.

Take what you've learned until now about transformations and you'll quickly see how powerful this feature can be. You can use Transform Again after you've applied a transformation using the Transform Each command, so you can even use this command to repeat multiple transformations at once. We'll use this exact technique later, in Chapter 12, "Creating a Corporate Identity."

Aligning Objects

While we're talking about moving artwork around, I should mention that there are plenty of times when you need to align objects—either to each other or to the artboard itself. The Align palette (see Figure 7.133) is perfect for this task, and for distributing objects as well. You can find the Align palette in the Window menu (by default, it's clustered with the Pathfinder and Transform palettes).

FIGURE 7.133
The Align palette.

The icons in the top row in the palette are alignment functions. Simply select multiple objects and click on the icons to align them as specified. If you're trying to align an object to the artboard (for example, centering an item on the page), you can choose the Align to Artboard option in the Align palette flyout menu. This function is actually a toggle, so your objects will align to the artboard until you go back to the palette flyout menu and disable the feature.

The Align palette recognizes groups, which makes it easier to align art made up of several objects. When you align a grouped item, the Align palette treats that group as a single object.

The icons in the bottom row in the palette are distribution functions. After you select a range of objects, clicking on these buttons will evenly distribute them, using the objects on the extreme ends as anchors. The objects that fall in the middle will magically spread evenly between the two anchors (see Figure 7.134). By choosing Show Options from the Align palette flyout menu, you can also specify to distribute objects a set distance from one another.

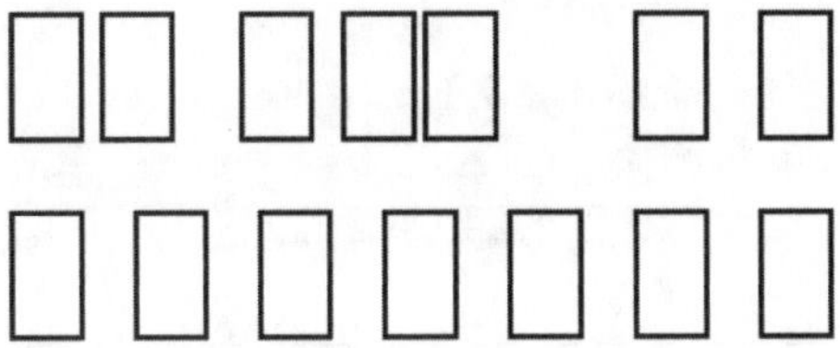

FIGURE 7.134
Several objects, before and after the distribute commands have been applied.

Defining a Key Object

You'll notice that when you're aligning several objects, they all shift when they are aligned. However, at times you might want to align several objects to a specific object. In other words, you want to have one object remain stationary, and all other objects align to that one object.

You can accomplish this task in Illustrator by defining a *key object*. After you've selected all the objects you want to align, click on the object you want all the other objects to align to. Then align your objects as you would normally with the buttons on the Align palette. After you've defined a key object, you can choose a different one simply by clicking on a different object. You can also choose Clear Key Object from the Align palette flyout menu.

Using Symbols

One of the most powerful features added to Illustrator over the years is symbols. A symbol is a saved set of objects that can be referenced within a document. That probably sounds vague, so I'll give you an example. Say you create a company logo, which is made up of several objects. You can take that completed logo and define it as a symbol, which you can then reuse as many times as your heart desires within your document. Each *instance* of the symbol is a reference or alias of the original art that you defined. Should you ever update or modify the symbol, all the instances would automatically update as well.

> Illustrator also uses symbols for the artwork mapping 3D feature, which is covered later in this chapter.

Did you Know?

Defining a symbol is easy. Simply create your art and then drag it into the Symbols palette (which you can find in the Windows menu). After you've defined a symbol (see Figure 7.135), you can delete the art you created because you can always access that art again later. Double-click on a symbol in the Symbols palette to rename it.

FIGURE 7.135
The Symbols palette, with several symbols defined.

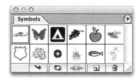

To place a symbol instance, drag it from the Symbols palette onto your artboard. You can apply any transformation to a symbol instance, and you can also apply settings from the Transparency palette. You'll always be able to tell a symbol instance from actual art because an instance has a square bounding box when you select it with the Direct Selection tool (see Figure 7.136).

FIGURE 7.136
A symbol instance appears with a square bounding box when selected (right).

If you want to edit a symbol, you can drag it onto your artboard and then click on the Break Link to Symbol button at the bottom of the Symbols palette (see Figure 7.137). Doing so will disassociate the art from the symbol, and you'll have access to the art objects themselves. You can then make any changes or modifications to the art.

FIGURE 7.137
Breaking the link to
a symbol.

If you want to redefine a symbol, you can first edit it, as mentioned previously, and then select the art. Then, in the Symbols palette, click on the symbol you want to redefine. You'll know that the symbol is selected when you see a black outline around it. Then choose Redefine Symbol from the Symbols palette flyout menu (see Figure 7.138).

FIGURE 7.138
Redefining a
symbol.

> Symbols save file size space. PDF, SVG, and SWF are three formats that can take advantage of symbols to save precious disk space (and file download time from the Web).

Did you Know?

To save your own library of symbols, create a document and define a collection of symbols. When you're done, choose Save Symbol Library from the Symbols palette flyout menu and give your collection a name. The next time you launch Illustrator CS, your symbol library will appear in the list of libraries you can access from the Open Symbol Library option in the Symbols palette flyout menu.

The Symbolism Tools

Before we learn about this next feature, I just want to say that this feature comes with a disclaimer attached to it. It's *extremely* fun and addictive. If you were intrigued by the use of symbols, this will blow your socks off. Okay, enough talking the talk—let's get to walking the walk.

The Symbolism tools are a collection of tools that allow you to exploit the power of symbols in a very graphical and natural way. There are eight Symbolism tools in all (see Figure 7.139). The first one, the Symbol Sprayer tool, allows you to add symbols to your page, and the remaining seven tools are used to adjust symbols that are already placed on your page.

FIGURE 7.139
The Symbolism tools.

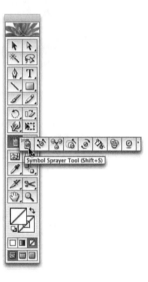

Did you Know?

The Symbolism tools are pressure-sensitive, so if you have a graphics tablet, you'll want to be sure to give it a try.

To use the Symbol Sprayer tool, select the tool from the toolbox and then open your Symbols palette. Select a symbol (which will be indicated by an outline), and then click and drag your mouse on the artboard to start flooding your screen with symbols (see Figure 7.140). Notice that when you're using the Symbol Sprayer tool, rather than having multiple instances of symbols placed on your page, a single *symbol set* is created. A symbol set acts as one single object (which you can clearly see if you change your view to Outline mode). If you click and drag the mouse again, with the symbol set selected, more symbols will be added to your symbol set. Press and hold the (Option) [Alt] key while dragging to remove symbols, if you've added too many.

FIGURE 7.140
Creating a symbol set by spraying symbols onto the artboard.

The remaining seven Symbolism tools will allow you to adjust and edit the symbols inside a symbol set:

▶ **Symbol Shifter**—This tool allows you to move symbols in a very organic fashion. It's almost like your cursor is a magnet, and as you click and drag, you can push symbols in a specified direction (see Figure 7.141). Pressing and holding the Shift key while using this tool will change the stacking order of the symbols.

FIGURE 7.141
Moving symbols with the Symbol Shifter tool.

▶ **Symbol Scruncher**—This tool allows you to make the symbols sit closer to each other, making the overall result more dense. Pressing and holding the (Option) [Alt] key while using this tool will reverse the effect and push symbols farther away from each other.

▶ **Symbol Sizer**—This tool allows you to enlarge the symbols as you click and drag over them (see Figure 7.142). Pressing and holding the (Option) [Alt] key while using this tool will reverse the effect and scale symbols to be smaller.

FIGURE 7.142
Scaling symbols
with the Symbol
Sizer tool.

▶ **Symbol Spinner**—This tool allows you to rotate the symbols as you click and drag over them. As you drag, you'll see arrows appear indicating the direction the symbols will spin (see Figure 7.143).

FIGURE 7.143
Rotating symbols
with the Symbol
Spinner tool.

▶ **Symbol Stainer**—This tool allows you to colorize the symbols as you click and drag over them. With the Symbol Stainer tool selection, choose a color from the Color palette or the Swatches palette. Then click and drag within your symbol set. You can change colors as often as you like.

▶ **Symbol Screener**—This tool allows you to reduce the opacity level of the symbols as you click and drag over them (making them transparent). Pressing and holding the (Option) [Alt] key while using this tool will reverse the effect and increase the opacity level of the symbols.

▶ **Symbol Styler**—This tool allows you to apply graphic styles to symbols as you click and drag over them. It works similarly to the Symbol Stainer tool. With the Symbol Styler tool selected, choose a style from the Graphic Styles palette and then click and drag within your symbol set.

When you're continually switching between the different Symbolism tools, it can be tiring traveling back to the toolbox each time just to select a different tool. With any of the Symbolism tools already selected, try this instead: If you're on a Mac, press Ctrl-Option and click; if you're using Windows, press the Alt key and right-click with the mouse. When the circle of tools appears (see Figure 7.144), simply move your mouse over the tool you want to switch to and let go.

Did you Know?

FIGURE 7.144
A special contextual menu allows you to switch among the different Symbolism tools.

As you can see, these tools are not only easy and fun to use, but quite useful as well. Try using a range of different symbols to achieve natural and organic effects. The Hair and Fur and the Nature symbol libraries that Illustrator ships with contain some great symbols to use.

It's no coincidence that each of the Symbolism tools begins with the letter s. Chalk that up to good old-fashioned "attention to detail" on Adobe's part.

By the Way

Working with Type

Illustrator CS has a brand-new text engine that gives it many of the features you will find in InDesign. Illustrator can create two kinds of text objects. The first is called *point text*, which is the simpler of the two. You create point text by selecting the Type tool (see Figure 7.145) and clicking on a blank area on your artboard. You'll be presented with a blinking cursor and you can begin to enter text immediately. Illustrator calls this point text because your text is aligned by the point that was created when you clicked with the Type tool (see Figure 7.146). Point text does not reflow, meaning that as you continue to enter text, the line will grow longer and longer, and won't break to a second line (unless you press Return or Enter).

FIGURE 7.145
Choosing the Type
tool.

FIGURE 7.146
A sample of point
text in Illustrator.

Point Text

The second kind of type object that Illustrator can create is called *area text*. There are two basic ways to create area text in Illustrator: either select the Type tool and click and drag with the tool to draw a box, or select the Type tool and click inside any existing closed vector path. Again, you'll be presented with a blinking cursor, where you can begin entering text. The difference here is that when your text gets to the boundary of the shape, the text will flow to the next line automatically (see Figure 7.147). Area text also has specific functionality that point text does not, and you can access some of those functions by selecting a text area object and choosing Type, Area Type Options to bring up the dialog (see Figure 7.148).

FIGURE 7.147
Text flows from
line to line in an
area text box.

Do you look at the clock at 4:00 PM and realize that you haven't eaten lunch yet? Are you the type of person who always comes 10 minutes late to a meeting — even when it seemed you left a few minutes early just to be on time? When was the last time you ate dinner with the family? Do you feel your business owns you rather than the other way around? And when you finally manage to get away for a few days, are you on the cell phone and checking email constantly? If this sounds like you, you're not alone... Like just about anything else, your time can be managed to take the most advantage of the things you need to do. Never miss appointments. Never miss a train. Or a plane. Even have some time to go over your note and grab a glass of water before a meeting. Your family might actually get to know you again and your blood pressure will finally make your doctor happy.

The key is prioritization. At Time Management we know how to manage time to help you prioritize the things in your life. Learn what's really important and what isn't. We'll teach you the difference between the things you want to do and the things you have to do. But that's not all. We offer more.

We are so confident in our techniques that we guarantee our work. That's right — if you don't see a marked improvement in your schedule (and stress level), we'll give you your money back — and an additional 10%. So call Time Management today!

Area Type Options
Width: 4.987 in
Height: 5.278 in
OK
Cancel
Preview
Rows
Number: 1
Span: 5.278 in
Fixed
Gutter: 0.25 in
Columns
Number: 1
Span: 4.987 in
Fixed
Gutter: 0.25 in
Offset
Inset Spacing: 0 in
First Baseline: Ascent
Min: 0 in
Options
Text Flow:

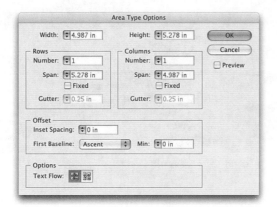

FIGURE 7.148
The Area Type Options dialog.

Area text can also be *threaded*, meaning that you can link several area text objects together so that the text flows from one to the next. Every area text object has an "in" link box and an "out" link box. Just as in InDesign, if your area text object isn't large enough to display all of your text, the out link box will display colored red with a plus sign, indicating that there's more text (see Figure 7.149). You can either enlarge the area text object or use the selection tool to click on the out link box and then click on another object, to make the overflow text continue into that object.

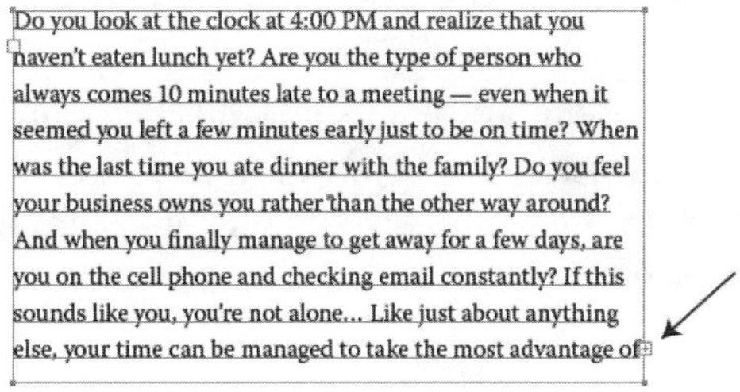

Do you look at the clock at 4:00 PM and realize that you haven't eaten lunch yet? Are you the type of person who always comes 10 minutes late to a meeting — even when it seemed you left a few minutes early just to be on time? When was the last time you ate dinner with the family? Do you feel your business owns you rather than the other way around? And when you finally manage to get away for a few days, are you on the cell phone and checking email constantly? If this sounds like you, you're not alone... Like just about anything else, your time can be managed to take the most advantage of

FIGURE 7.149
The overflow indicator, alerting you that there's more text.

> To see how text threading links between multiple area text objects, choose View, Show Text Threads.

Did you Know?

Text on a Path

There's a third kind of text object in Illustrator—type on a path—although in reality, it's a kind of area type object. To create text that follows along the outline of a vector path, select the Type on a Path tool (see Figure 7.150) and click on any path (it can be open or closed). You'll get a blinking cursor, where you can begin typing.

There are three distinct functions you can adjust when setting type on a path (see Figure 7.151):

▶ **In and Out link boxes**—As with Area Text, Type on a Path objects can also flow from one path to the next.

▶ **Start and End points**—You can determine where text begins and ends on a path by dragging these vertical bars with the Direct Selection tool.

▶ **Center point**—Type can flow along either side of a path, and you can choose which side by using this point. Click and drag the point to the side of the path you want the text to flow along. This point also allows you to position the center of the text.

FIGURE 7.151
The different func-
tions for a type on
a path object.

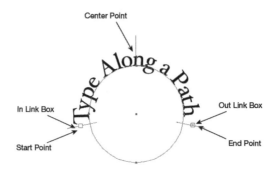

Formatting Text

Of course, it wouldn't be much fun if you were forced to use 12pt Myriad Regular for every text object in your document, so it's nice to know that Illustrator's text formatting capabilities are on par with those found in InDesign. Because much of the functionality between Illustrator CS and InDesign CS is consistent, I will discuss these features briefly here, and you can refer to Chapter 8, "Using Adobe InDesign CS," for more detailed information.

The Character Palette

Open the Character palette by choosing Window, Type, Character. Here you can specify font information (see Figure 7.152), type size, leading (pronounced *ledding*, which is the amount of space between lines), kerning, and more.

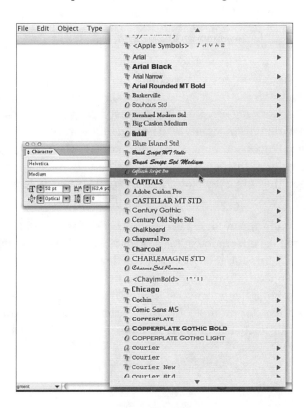

FIGURE 7.152
Illustrator CS has a "what you see is what you get" (WYSIWYG) font menu.

The Paragraph Palette

Open the Paragraph palette (see Figure 7.153) by choosing Window, Type, Paragraph. Here you can specify paragraph information such as alignment, justification, composition method, indents, spacing, and more.

FIGURE 7.153
The fully expanded
Paragraph palette.

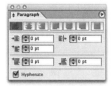

The OpenType Palette

OpenType is a new font standard that really takes typography to a whole new level. Illustrator CS ships with more than 100 OpenType fonts, so you have a head start on getting to use them. Type 1 fonts (PostScript) have a limit of 256 glyphs per font. This is why Type 1 fonts always had these Expert font collections—there was simply no way to store all of those extra glyphs in a single font file. OpenType fonts, on the other hand, have a limit of 65,000 glyphs per font file (yes—65,000—that's not a typo). This gives type designers the freedom to add all of these cool variations of letters, swashes, ligatures, fractions, and the like to their type designs. Probably the most important aspects of OpenType fonts are that they are stored in a single file (instead of separate files for screen fonts and printer fonts), and they are cross-platform compatible (so a single file can be used for either Mac or Windows).

Illustrator CS has full support for OpenType fonts and also has added functionality that allows you to take advantage of the special features OpenType offers. You can access these features through the OpenType palette (which you can find in the Windows, Type submenu). To use it, simply select a range of text and click on the buttons at the bottom of the palette (see Figure 7.154). If the font you're using contains swash characters, for example, those characters will automatically appear. The same applies for fractions, ordinals, and other special type treatments.

FIGURE 7.154
The OpenType palette
lets you easily access
standard ligatures,
contextual alternates,
discretionary ligatures,
swash, stylistic alter-
nates, titling alter-
nates, ordinals, and
fractions.

Finding Special Characters

If you want to find a specific glyph character in a font, you don't have to try pressing every character combination on your keyboard to find it. Choose Type, Glyphs to open the Glyphs palette (see Figure 7.155). From the pop-up menu at the bottom of the palette, choose a typeface, and every glyph present in that font will display in the palette's window. If you have a blinking text cursor anywhere in your document, double-clicking on any glyph in the Glyphs palette will place that glyph in your text string.

FIGURE 7.155
The Glyphs palette
in Illustrator CS.

Paragraph and Character Styles

Paragraph and character styles allow you to easily style and format type. It's also a way to consistently manage and update text formatting across your entire document. You can find the Paragraph Styles palette by choosing Window, Type, Paragraph Styles. The Character Styles palette appears in the same submenu. Refer to Chapter 8 for information on how to define and use paragraph and character styles.

Converting Text into Vector Shapes

At times you might want to edit actual character shapes in Illustrator. For example, you may start off designing a logo with some text, and then you might want to make adjustments or modifications to the shapes of the letters themselves. To convert text to editable vector paths, select your type with the Selection tool (not the Type tool), and choose Type, Create Outlines (see Figure 7.156). You can convert only an entire point text object or an entire area text object to outlines—there's no way to convert just a few characters in a text string.

FIGURE 7.156
Text that is convert-
ed to outlines can
be modified and
edited as Bézier
paths.

Live Effects

With Illustrator 9, Adobe added a new menu item called Effects, which have since changed the face of Illustrator. Effects are a wide range of options you can apply to your objects. For example, you can apply soft drop shadows, 3D extrudes, warping, Gaussian blurs, feathering, and more. What makes these effects so unique is the way they are applied in Illustrator. Effects are applied to objects as *appearances*, leaving the original objects intact. For example, you might draw a plain rectangle and apply a warp effect to it. The rectangle will appear as being warped, but behind the scenes, it's still a rectangle (see Figure 7.157). If you edit the rectangle, the effect that was applied to it simply updates to reflect the change. This also means that at any time, you can remove the effect completely and be left with the rectangle you created. For this reason, effects in Illustrator are referred to as live effects.

FIGURE 7.157
A rectangle with a
Warp effect applied
to it. Although you
can see that the
rectangle is select-
ed, its appearance
is quite different.

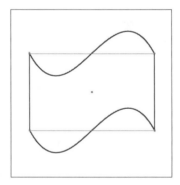

You may wonder why many of the items listed in the Effect menu are also present in the Filter menu. Items that appear in the Filter menu are applied to an object and then cannot be reversed. They are sometimes referred to as "dead effects" for this reason. I imagine that one day, Adobe will remove the Filter menu from Illustrator altogether.

As mentioned before, effects are applied as appearances, so when you apply an effect to an object, that effect will show up in the Appearance palette when that object is selected (see Figure 7.158). As you'll soon see, you will be applying a new effect to an object by choosing it from the Effect menu. However, when you want to edit an effect that you've already applied, you have to double-click on the effect item that appears in the Appearance palette.

FIGURE 7.158
After an effect is applied to an object, you can see the effect listed in the Appearance palette.

Live effects can be applied to objects, but they can also be applied to groups or layers. To apply an effect to a group or a layer, you have to specifically target the group or layer in the Layers palette, which we discussed earlier in the chapter. If a layer has an effect applied to it, for example, any object you add to that layer will automatically take on that effect attribute.

There's a wide variety of effects in Illustrator, and some of them (Gaussian Blur, for example) are raster effects. Some effects can also be applied to placed images (like Drop Shadow). In fact, effects can also be applied to text—without having to convert the text to outlines. Let's take a look at some of the more popular live effects found in Illustrator CS.

The 3D Effects

A feature completely new in Illustrator CS, the capability to create 3D graphics is not only exciting, but fun (and extremely addictive). I should emphasize that the 3D you're about to learn isn't just some cute effect, but real 3D rendering, including extrusions, bevels, revolves, and something called artwork mapping. If these terms sound foreign to you, don't worry—you've been doing great so far and I'm sure you'll catch on to this as well.

To start off, 2D graphics have two coordinates, referred to as X and Y values, usually indicating Width and Height. In addition to the X and Y coordinates, 3D graphics have a third, referred to as the Z value, which indicates Depth. When describing 3D graphics, the X, Y and Z values are usually referred to as axes, rather than values. From now on, when talking about 3D, we'll refer to these settings as the *x-axis*, the *y-axis,* and the *z-axis*.

> Because Illustrator is rendering real 3D, performance is something to keep in mind. Complex art can take time to render, especially on an older or less capable machine. For those lucky enough to have a Macintosh G5 on hand, you might like to know that the 3D feature inside Illustrator CS has specific optimizations that take advantage of the G5 processor (I'm accepting donations for the *Mordy Golding Needs A G5 Fund*).

3D Extrude & Bevel

The 3D Extrude effect adds dimension to your selected object. To apply the effect, make a selection and choose Effect, 3D, Extrude & Bevel. In the 3D Extrude & Bevel Options dialog, click on the Preview button so that you can see what your selected art will look like with the effect applied (see Figure 7.159).

FIGURE 7.159
The 3D Extrude & Bevel Options dialog.

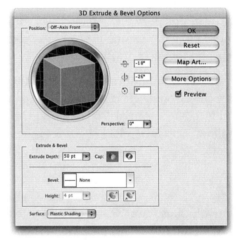

> The 3D effect in Illustrator is very deep, meaning that there are many different settings, but don't get frustrated with all the settings. You don't have to know what every setting is in order to produce great 3D art. Familiarity with all the functions will come over time.

At the top of the dialog is the *track cube*, which you can use to rotate your object in 3D space. To use it, click and drag anywhere on the cube, and you'll see a wireframe (outline) of your object on your screen update as you drag with the mouse. If you move your mouse over any of the edges of the track cube, you'll notice that the edges highlight in red, green, or blue (see Figure 7.160). Clicking and dragging on these highlighted lines will constrain the track cube to rotate the shape only along the x-, y-, or z-axis. Right above the track cube is a pop-up menu that contains several predefined views for your object.

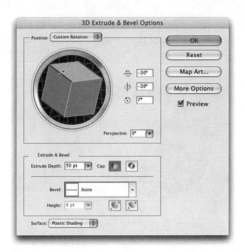

FIGURE 7.160
Clicking on a high-lighted edge will allow the object to rotate on a single axis only.

The Perspective slider controls lens distortion. If you press and hold the Shift key while you drag the slider, you will see your art update in real-time.

The Extrude Depth setting determines how far back in space your object will extend. Here also, you can press the Shift key while adjusting the slider to see real-time feedback.

Illustrator draws 3D graphics differently based on whether an object has a stroke applied to it. If an object has a fill and a stroke applied, the fill color will be used for the face of the object, and the stroke color will be used for the extruded part of the object. If no fill is specified on the object, the extrude color will be the same as the fill color (see Figure 7.161).

Did you **Know?**

FIGURE 7.161
The object on the left has a stroke applied. The object on the right does not.

A bevel is a chiseled edge you can apply to your 3D object. Bevels are added only to the front surface and the back surface. To apply a bevel, choose one from the Bevel pop-up menu (see Figure 7.162). Illustrator ships with several predefined bevels, although you can create your own if you dare (instructions for how to do so can be found in the `Bevels.ai` file found in the Illustrator `Plugins` folder). After you've applied a bevel from the pop-up menu, you can specify a height for the bevel as well. To remove a bevel that you've already applied, choose None from the Bevel pop-up menu.

FIGURE 7.162
Choosing from a list of bevels.

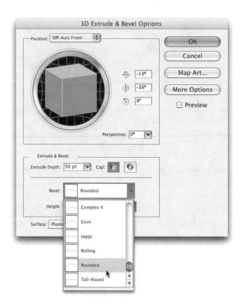

Illustrator's 3D effect also lets you choose a surface type for your object from the Surface pop-up list (see Figure 7.163). By default, the Plastic Shading option is chosen, which gives your shape a glossy, reflective look. Choose Diffuse Shading for a surface that is matte in appearance. You can also choose to not shade your object at all by choosing No Shading. Finally, you can also specify to have your 3D object display as a wireframe.

Did you Know?

Remember that if you want to edit a 3D effect after it has been applied, don't choose 3D from the Effect menu, but double-click on the 3D effect in the Appearance palette.

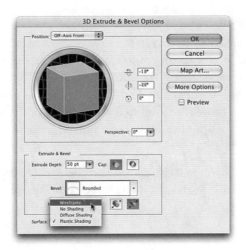

FIGURE 7.163
Choosing a surface
property for your
object.

Extended 3D Functionality

In an effort to make the 3D feature as easy to use as possible, Adobe created the
3D Options dialog in two parts. If you click on the button marked More Options,
you'll see some additional 3D features to choose from (see Figure 7.164).

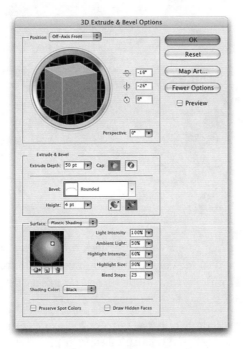

FIGURE 7.164
The additional fea-
tures in the expand-
ed 3D dialog.

To create realistic shading and highlights on a 3D object, Illustrator utilizes lighting effects. The sphere that appears in the lower left of the dialog is a representation of your graphic, and you can position a light to shine and illuminate your object from any direction. Making adjustments to the lighting of your object can change its appearance dramatically. To adjust the position of the light, click and drag on the light and move it around to different parts of the sphere. Pressing and holding the Shift key while you drag the light will allow you to see a preview of the result in real-time.

You can also add multiple lights by clicking on the Add Light button under the sphere (see Figure 7.165). To delete a light, select it on the sphere and click on the Trash button.

FIGURE 7.165
Adding and positioning multiple lights.

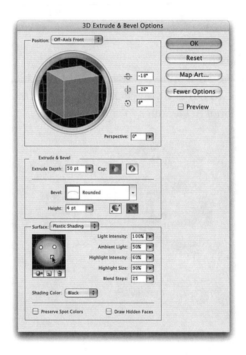

If you're working with spot colors, you can check the Preserve Spot Colors option, which will use black as a shade color and set that black color to overprint. You'll have to have the Overprint Preview mode turned on to see the correct results on your screen.

Ordinarily, Illustrator will draw only the parts of a 3D object that are visible to you. For example, if the back of a box isn't visible in the view you've specified with the track cube, it won't be drawn (unless you change the view again, of course).

Illustrator does this to save render time. However, you can force Illustrator to draw these hidden sides by checking the Draw Hidden Faces option. This option is useful when you're creating 3D objects that are transparent (and you want to see through the front of the object to the back). It's also useful when you want to break apart the different sides of the object after you've applied the effect (something called Expand Appearance, which we'll cover later in the chapter).

A very important setting is the Blend Steps setting, which is set to 25 by default. Illustrator creates the shading of 3D objects by drawing blends. For printing high-quality jobs, you may want to use a value of 100 blend steps, or even higher. Note that higher numbers will slow performance, so you may want to leave it at a low setting when working on concepts and proofs, but change it to a higher setting when sending out the final job (see Figure 7.166).

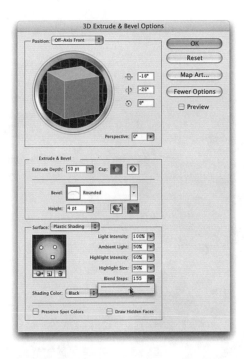

FIGURE 7.166
Changing the number of blend steps for the shading of the 3D object.

3D Revolve

The 3D Revolve feature takes the profile of an object you draw in Illustrator, and then revolves that profile around an axis to produce a 3D shape. For example, you might draw the profile of a vase (see Figure 7.167) and then use the 3D Revolve effect to create a realistic vase (see Figure 7.168). To apply this effect, select the profile you've drawn, and then choose Effect, 3D, Revolve. When the 3D Revolve Options dialog appears, check the Preview button so that you can see how your object will look with the Revolve effect applied (see Figure 7.169).

FIGURE 7.167
The profile of a vase.

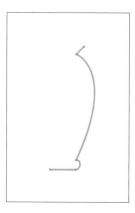

FIGURE 7.168
The revolved profile results in a 3D vase.

FIGURE 7.169
The 3D Revolve Options dialog.

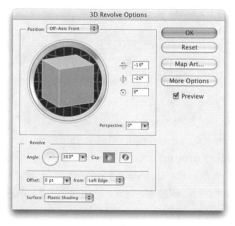

You can rotate your object in 3D space the same way as we discussed when talking about the 3D Extrude effect. Use the track cube to position your artwork to your liking, and use the Perspective setting to apply lens distortion.

The Angle setting determines how far Illustrator will apply the Revolve effect around the axis. By default, this is set to 360 degrees (a full, complete revolve); however, you can adjust this number to be lower, in which case you'll see a part of your shape removed, or "cut out" (see Figure 7.170).

FIGURE 7.170
The same vase as before, except this one has an angle setting of 300 instead of 360.

We've mentioned that the Revolve effect uses an axis, almost as an origin point, which the profile is revolved around. By default, the axis is set to the leftmost part of the object. However, you can choose to specify the rightmost part of the object as your axis. Additionally, you can specify an offset, meaning you can choose to move the axis a specified amount from the edge of your object. This is useful if you want to create a hole that goes through the center of your object (see Figure 7.171).

FIGURE 7.171
The vase, with an offset value applied, resulting in a visible hole in the center of the vase.

At any time, either in the 3D Revolve Options dialog or the 3D Extrude & Bevel Options dialog, you can press the (Option) [Alt] button and the Cancel button will change to the Reset button, which will reset all the settings of the dialog to the way they were when you first opened it.

3D Rotate

The 3D Rotate effect allows you to rotate your object in a 3D space, but without adding any depth (extrusion) to it. You can apply this effect by making a selection and choosing Effect, 3D, Rotate. The settings in the 3D Rotate Options dialog are a subset of what appears in the 3D Extrude & Bevel Options dialog.

Artwork Mapping

What sets Illustrator's 3D feature apart from any of its competitors is something called *artwork mapping*, which is the capability to take 2D art and place it, or wrap it around, a 3D object. For example, you might want to use the 3D Revolve effect to create a vase, and with artwork mapping, you could also place a label onto the surface of that vase (see Figure 7.172).

FIGURE 7.172
A 3D object with artwork mapped onto its surface.

The first step in using the artwork mapping feature in Illustrator is to define a symbol. Illustrator uses symbols to map art onto a 3D surface, so in the case we mentioned previously, if you want to place a label onto a 3D rendering of a bottle, you first have to define your label as a symbol. Earlier in the chapter, we discussed how to define and modify symbols.

When you're creating 3D art that will have artwork mapping applied, it's best to use shapes that are not stroked. This is because Illustrator will see each stroke as a side that can contain a mapped symbol and may result in a 3D shape with many more sides than necessary.

After you've defined a symbol, create your 3D object by using either the 3D Extrude & Bevel effect or the 3D Revolve effect. In the 3D options dialog, click on the Map Art button (it's right under the Cancel button), and you'll be presented with the Map Art dialog (see Figure 7.173). Check the Preview button to see the results onscreen as you apply effects.

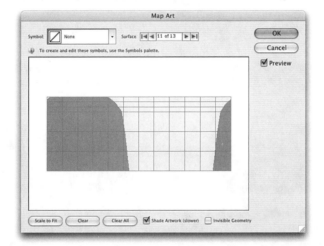

FIGURE 7.173
The Map Art dialog.

When you create a 3D object, there are several sides to the object (for example, a cube has six sides). When you want to map art in Illustrator, you first have to indicate which side of the object you want the art to appear on. Use the arrows at the top of the dialog to cycle among the different sides of an object. In the window area of the dialog, you'll see the shapes of the different sides. Shaded areas (see Figure 7.174) indicate the parts of the objects that are hidden from view (for example, the back side of a cube). Illustrator will also draw a red outline on the artboard to indicate the side of the object that is chosen.

FIGURE 7.174
The shaded areas indicate the parts of the object that are hidden from view.

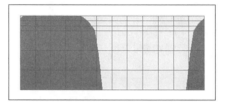

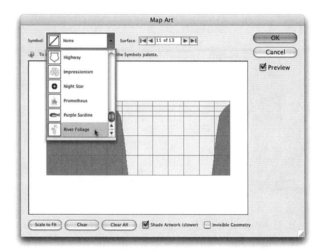

By the
Way

If you see a large number of sides on your shape, you most likely have a stroke on your object, or you've applied a bevel to an extruded object.

When you've found the side of the object you want, choose a symbol from the Symbol pop-up menu (see Figure 7.175). If you defined a symbol earlier, it will appear in this list.

FIGURE 7.175
Choosing a symbol to apply to the selected side.

You can then position the art by dragging it, or by using the bounding box handles to scale or rotate it. The Scale to Fit button will reduce or enlarge the symbol to fit the entire surface that is selected. A single symbol cannot be wrapped around multiple surfaces—each surface is basically on its own. You can then switch to another surface and apply a symbol, and so forth.

The Shade Artwork option will also apply lighting and shading effects to your artwork. The Invisible Geometry option will actually hide the 3D shape itself, showing only the mapped art, which can be used to create some interesting effects.

After you're happy with the settings, click OK to apply the Map Art settings, and then click OK to apply the 3D settings. Because Illustrator uses symbols for artwork mapping, if you were to modify the symbol that you used, it would automatically update on the 3D object (you don't have to reapply the mapped art).

The Rasterize Effect

The Rasterize effect (see Figure 7.176) allows you to convert a vector into a raster as an effect, which is pretty cool when you think about it. The underlying shape is still a vector shape, but the result is a raster. You can specify the resolution for the raster as well as other settings, such as anti-aliasing. Later in the chapter when you read about Web graphics, you'll see why this feature is important.

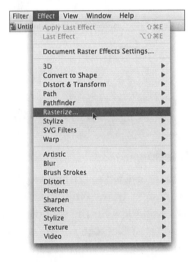

FIGURE 7.176
Applying the Rasterize effect.

The Rasterize effect is also very useful for rasterizing rasters. By that, I mean you can place a full-color photo but apply a rasterize effect and change the color mode to grayscale. The original image is still intact, but it appears in grayscale.

Did you Know?

The Stylize Effects

The live effects you will utilize most often are found in the Effect, Stylize submenu. Things such as adding arrowheads, soft drop shadows, or rounded corners are all found here.

Adding Arrowheads

To add arrowheads at the ends of a selected path, choose Effect, Stylize, Add Arrowheads. In the resulting dialog (see Figure 7.177), you can specify a wide variety of arrowheads to appear at the start, the end, or both parts of a vector path. You can also choose to scale the arrowhead to be bigger or smaller, to your preference, by using the Scale value.

FIGURE 7.177
The Add
Arrowheads dialog.

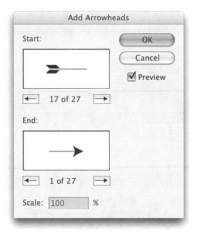

Adding a Soft Drop Shadow

To add a soft drop shadow to a targeted selection (text and images included), choose Effect, Stylize, Drop Shadow. In the dialog (see Figure 7.178), choose an X Offset value and a Y Offset value (how far the shadow falls from the object) and a Blur value (how soft the shadow is). You can choose a color for the drop shadow as well, although there's no way to specify a spot color.

FIGURE 7.178
The Drop Shadow
dialog.

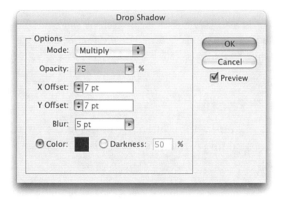

Feathering Vector Objects

To apply a feathered edge to a selected vector object (see Figure 7.179), choose Effect, Stylize, Feather and specify a value for the feather (higher numbers result in softer edges). Remember that to edit a feather, you double-click on the feather item in the Appearance palette.

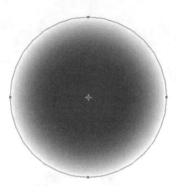

FIGURE 7.179
A vector object with a feathered edge applied.

Applying Rounded Corners

If you want to round off the corners of a selected vector shape, choose Effect, Stylize, Rounded Corners and specify a radius value. This effect works on any vector shape that has a corner anchor point in it.

Using the Scribble Effect

The Scribble effect is one of those effects that look straightforward, but after you take a closer look, you begin to realize that it's far more powerful than you originally imagined. On a very basic level, the effect gives a hand-drawn appearance to your selection (see Figure 7.180). However, if you think about how effects can be used, and how multiple effects can be applied to a single selection, you can easily create interesting hatch effects and textures.

FIGURE 7.180
A simple Scribble effect applied.

To apply this effect, make a selection and choose Effect, Stylize, Scribble. It might be easier to grasp the plethora of settings if you understand what Illustrator is really doing with the Scribble effect, which is basically converting the fill (or stroke) of the object into one long stroke. Let's start simple by taking a look at the Scribble Options dialog (see Figure 7.181).

FIGURE 7.181
The Scribble
Options dialog.

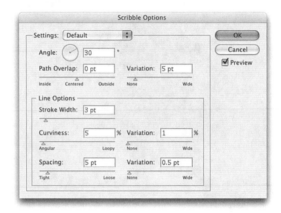

In the Scribble Options dialog box, you can specify the following settings:

▶ The **Settings** pop-up menu allows you to choose from several presets that Adobe ships with. Unfortunately, you can't save your own presets here (although you can always save a graphic style after you've applied the effect). Adobe included these presets to quickly show how you can achieve very different results by adjusting the settings of this effect.

▶ The **Angle** setting determines the angle at which the scribble is drawn.

▶ The **Path Overlap** determines how far the scribble draws "out of the lines." A setting of zero will cause the scribble to come just to the edge of the boundaries of the objects. A positive setting will make the scribble extend past the boundaries of the object, whereas a negative value will force the scribble to stay farther inside the boundaries of the shape. This setting also has a Variation slider, which will vary the length of each scribble to make the effect look more random and hand-drawn.

▶ The **Stroke Width** setting allows you to specify how thick or thin your scribble stroke will be.

▶ The **Curviness** setting controls how straight or curved the scribble path will be. This setting also has a Variation slider, which will vary the Curviness setting to make the effect look more random and hand-drawn.

▶ The **Spacing** setting controls how much spacing there will be between the strokes as they are drawn across the entire shape. A low setting will result in very tight lines with little whitespace between them, whereas a higher setting will produce more whitespace in the scribble. This setting also has a Variation slider, which will vary the spacing to make the effect look more random and hand-drawn.

The Scribble effect can be applied to vector objects and to text. It can't be applied to a raster image, but it can certainly be used as an opacity mask for a photograph. You can also specify several different fills for a single object, each with a different scribble setting, to achieve spectacular effects, such as hatching (see Figure 7.182).

FIGURE 7.182
An object with several fills applied to it, each with a different Scribble effect setting, results in a hatch-like effect.

Warp

At times you want to stretch or distort a graphic, and the Warp effect is perfect for those kinds of tasks. To apply a warp to a selected object, choose Effect, Warp, and pick one of the 16 kinds of warps Illustrator supports. Note that it really isn't important which one you choose because in the Warp dialog box that will appear, you can switch among the warps easily (see Figure 7.183).

In the Warp Options dialog, specify settings for how much bend you want to apply and whether you want distortion applied as well. Check the Preview box to see your effect before it's applied.

FIGURE 7.183
Choosing a warp
type from the Warp
Options dialog.

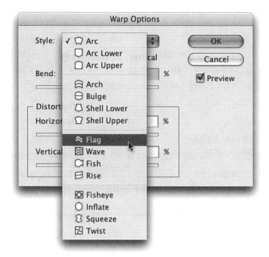

Global Live Effects Settings

It's important to realize that some effects employ techniques that involve raster data. For example, the soft drop shadow effect draws its drop shadows as a raster image. The 3D effect rasterizes gradients and images that are used for artwork mapping.

By default, all the effects in Illustrator are set to rasterize art at 72dpi. This was done for performance reasons. *However, if you're creating art that will be used for high-quality printing, you'll want to set your effects to render at a higher resolution (like 300dpi).*

You can adjust this setting by choosing Effect, Document Raster Effects Settings (see Figure 7.184). Note that the settings in this dialog apply to all live effects in your document, so you can't have some live effects using one resolution setting and some using another.

The thing to watch out for is that some effects, mainly the ones that fall in the lower half of the menu (what I call "below the line"), base their appearance on the resolution chosen. For example, the Pixelate effect bases its results on how many pixels there are. In that case, changing the Document Raster Effects Settings could change the appearance of any objects which have that effect applied. So it's important to make any necessary adjustments to the Document Raster Effects Settings dialog *before* you begin working on your design.

FIGURE 7.184
Choosing to edit
the Document
Raster Effects
Settings.

Expanding an Appearance

When you apply an effect, you can't physically select it or work with it because it's
simply an appearance that's applied to your object. However, there may be times
when you want to "break apart" an appearance so that you can make adjustments
or edits that the effect itself might not support. To do so, select the object with the
effect applied to it, and choose Object, Expand Appearance (see Figure 7.185).

FIGURE 7.185
Choosing Expand
Appearance from
the Object menu.

After this function is applied, the effect will no longer be live, and you'll be able to edit the actual final appearance of the object. If the object had several different effects applied, or had multiple fills or strokes, the Expand Appearance function may create several overlapping objects.

Distortion with Envelopes

At times you might want to distort an object using a specific shape. For example, you might want to squeeze some art into the shape of a circle. Although the Warp effect provides some simple distortion tools, it's limited in that you can't customize the distortions themselves. That's where envelope distortion comes in. Almost similar to the way a mask works, you create a vector shape that will be the envelope. Then you place your art inside the envelope, but the result is that the art stretches or squeezes itself to conform to the shape (see Figure 7.186).

FIGURE 7.186
An envelope in Illustrator.

Illustrator can place any kind of art into an envelope, even raster image files. There are three ways to create envelopes in Illustrator:

▶ **Make with Warp**—Select the object you want to distort and choose Object, Envelope Distort, Make with Warp. You'll be presented with a dialog that looks similar in functionality to the Warp effect, except that when you click OK, you'll notice that an envelope shape was created for you in the shape of the warp you specified (see Figure 7.187). You can use the Direct Selection tool to move each of those points individually, and you can also use the Mesh tool to add more points for better control.

FIGURE 7.187
The envelope shape, created in the shape of the warp specified.

▶ **Make with Mesh**—Select the object you want to distort and choose Object, Envelope Distort, Make with Mesh. Specify how many Rows and Columns you want for your mesh (although you can always add more later with the Mesh tool) and click OK. Again, you can use the Direct Selection tool to move the mesh points around, which will distort the art inside the envelope.

▶ **Make with Top Object**—Draw or select a shape you'd like to use as the envelope. Bring the shape to the front of the stacking order. Then add the art you want to distort to your selection as well, and choose Object, Envelope Distort, Make with Top Object.

As mentioned before, working with envelopes is similar in many ways to working with opacity masks. After you apply an envelope, you can access only the envelope itself, not the art that's inside of it. If you need to make a change to the art inside of the envelope, select the envelope and choose Object, Envelope Distort, Edit Contents (see Figure 7.188). You will then be able to make changes to the art itself. When you're done, remember to choose Object, Envelope Distort, Edit Envelope so that you can work with the envelope again.

FIGURE 7.188
Choosing to edit the contents of a selected envelope.

Blends

Illustrator has the capability to take two vector objects and create a blend between them. If the shapes are different, Illustrator will morph one shape into the other, which can produce some cool effects (see Figure 7.189). Blending can be used to create airbrush-like effects. Blends can also be used to help create steps or frames for animations, which we'll discuss later, when we talk about the Flash file format.

FIGURE 7.189
A blend between two vector objects.

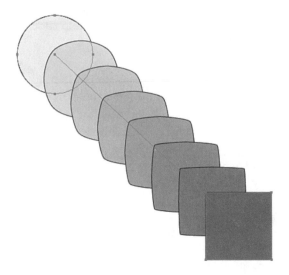

To create a blend, select two vector shapes and choose Object, Blend, Make. To change the options of a blend, select the blend and choose Object, Blend, Blend Options. You can specify a smooth colored blend, which will automatically calculate how many *steps* will be created in the blend, or you can choose to specify the exact number of steps you want to create (see Figure 7.190).

FIGURE 7.190
The Blend Options dialog.

A blend follows along a straight path that is automatically drawn between the two objects (it doesn't print), which is called the spine of the blend. If you want the blend to follow a specific curve (see Figure 7.191), select both the blend and the curve and choose Object, Blend, Replace Spine.

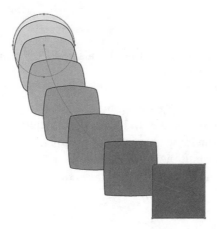

FIGURE 7.191
Replacing the straight spine with a curved one.

A blend in Illustrator is live, meaning that if you make changes to the two outer shapes, the blend will update accordingly. If you want to break a blend into its individual parts, choose Object, Blend, Expand.

Working with Raster Images

You can place raster images into Illustrator to perform various tasks, including applying transformations (rotating, scaling, and so on), as well as using images in a mask.

Images in Illustrator can be either linked or embedded. Linking a file involves placing a reference to that file into your Illustrator file, but the image remains a separate file. If you want to make an edit to that image, you open the original file and change it. Upon saving the file, you return to using Illustrator. Because Illustrator maintains a link to that image, Illustrator will know that you've updated the image and ask whether you want the image to be updated in your layout. However, if you were to delete that linked image from your computer, Illustrator would not be able to print the file correctly.

Embedding an image is the process of permanently adding the image to the Illustrator file. Any changes you make to the original image will not be updated in your Illustrator layout. Embedding a file will also increase the file size of your Illustrator document—significantly, if you're embedding large high-resolution images.

You can choose to either link or embed your placed image at the time you place it. The Place dialog box contains a check box marked Link (which is on by default).

Did you Know?

When you're placing PDF or EPS duotone images in Illustrator, always use the Link option. If you embed a duotone image, the image will be converted to the document color space (CMYK or RGB).

You can track and manage the use of linked images in your Illustrator documents by using the Links palette (found in he Window menu). If you want to edit a linked image, select the image in the Links palette (see Figure 7.192), and click on the Edit Original button at the lower right of the palette. Additionally, you can double-click on any of the items in the Links palette to get more information about that link (see Figure 7.193).

FIGURE 7.192
The Links palette.

FIGURE 7.193
Seeing more information about a linked image.

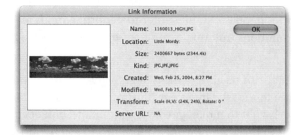

Charts and Graphs

The advantage of using Illustrator to create graphs over a dedicated graph program is that when you create a graph in Illustrator, it is made up of vector objects. Therefore, you can edit the graph just as you would any illustration, giving you complete control over the appearance of your graph or chart. If necessary, you can also export the graph in any of Illustrator's many export formats, including the Save for Microsoft Office feature.

Illustrator can draw any of nine types of graphs: Column, Stacked Column, Bar, Stacked Bar, Line, Area, Scatter, Pie, and Radar.

Creating a Graph

To create a graph, choose one of the graph tools from the toolbox (see Figure 7.194). You start by first defining the area or size for your graph, and you specify this in much same way that you do to create a rectangle. Either click and drag with the mouse, or click once on the artboard to enter a numeric value.

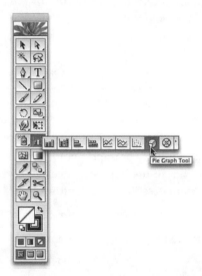

FIGURE 7.194
Choosing from one of Illustrator's nine graph tools.

The next step is to give Illustrator the facts—the actual values that will be used to make the graph mean something. After it creates the bounding box for your graph, Illustrator presents you with the Graph Data palette. If you've ever used Microsoft Excel, this palette will look familiar to you. It is filled with rows and columns in which you enter the graph data (see Figure 7.195).

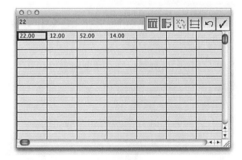

FIGURE 7.195
The Graph Data palette.

> In reality, the Graph Data palette acts more like a dialog than a palette. For one, you have to click the Apply button to update values. Second, there are certain functions you can't perform until you close the window. Finally, there's no collapsible palette tab that palettes usually exhibit. Kinda makes you want to sing that classic Sesame Street song, "One of these things is not like the others...."

Adding Graph Data

Across the top of the Graph Data palette are several items. The first is an area where you input your values. Select a cell (cells are the boxes that actually contain the data), and then type your value. Pressing Tab takes you to the next column; pressing Enter takes you to the next row.

> Cells can also be navigated using the arrow keys. Additionally, unlike with most data entry programs, Shift-Tab does not move to the previous cell; rather, it is used to select multiple cells. Both Shift-Tab and (Shift-Return) [Shift+Enter] can be used to highlight multiple contiguous cells for such purposes as copy and pasting.

You can either enter data manually or import data from Excel or any tab-delimited text file. Notice that in the upper-right corner of the Graph Data palette are six buttons. The following describes these buttons from left to right:

- ▶ **Import Data**—Imports data from an external file.

- ▶ **Transpose**—Switches columns and rows of data, no matter what the graph type is.

- ▶ **Switch X/Y**—Swaps the values of the x- and y-axes on a scatter graph only.

- ▶ **Cell Style**—Sets the parameters for a selected cell. You can set the number of decimal places as well as the column width.

> You can also change the column width manually by grabbing a vertical line and dragging it to the left or right.

- ▶ **Revert**—Sets the data in the graph back to the way it was before you last clicked the Apply button.

- ▶ **Apply**—Accepts and applies your changes to the graph.

Editing Graph Data

What makes the graph function in Illustrator even more powerful is the capability to update the data in your graph. At any time, you can select the graph and choose Object, Graph, Data (see Figure 7.196). You are presented with the Graph Data palette again, where you can update the numbers. When you click the Apply button in the Graph Data palette, the graph is automatically updated with the new information.

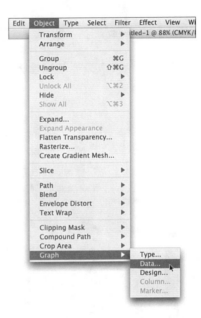

FIGURE 7.196
Choosing to open the Graph Data palette to edit an existing graph.

Graph Options

After you create your graph, you can edit it to perfection. Choose Object, Graphs, Type, and you are presented with the Graph Type dialog box (see Figure 7.197). You are first presented with Graph Options. Here you can change the type of graph, even though you selected another type from the toolbox. You can also choose where you place the value axis.

In addition to the options to add drop shadows or add a legend across the top, you can set the column width and cluster width here. These settings control the width and spacing of the bars or columns in a graph. Specifying a value greater than 100% causes the columns to overlap and may produce very interesting results (see Figure 7.198).

FIGURE 7.197
The Graph Type
dialog.

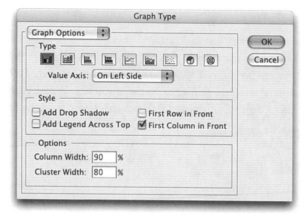

FIGURE 7.198
Some different col-
umn settings.

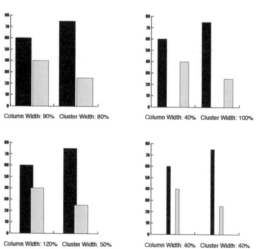

In the Graph Type dialog box, you can also specify settings for the Value Axis
and Category Axis. Select them from the pop-up menu at the top of the dialog
box. In the Value Axis screen, you can set the length of tick marks, which are the
lines along the side of the graph that help indicate the position of data.

Setting tick marks at full length causes them to be drawn as lines throughout the
entire graph (see Figure 7.199). You can also specify tick marks for the Category
Axis.

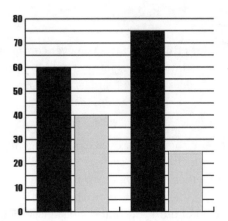

FIGURE 7.199
Tick marks set to
full length.

Ungrouping Your Graph

A graph is actually a special kind of group. You can ungroup a graph at any time; but be aware that when you do, the art loses its reference as a graph, and you can no longer make changes to it through the Graph Data palette and Graph Type dialog box. This process is similar to converting text to outlines: After you change it, it becomes a different kind of object. If you need to ungroup a graph, save a copy of the original grouped graph so that you can go back to that stage if needed.

For some interesting graph ideas, try applying a 3D Extrude effect to a pie chart, or a Scribble effect to a bar graph. Because they are live effects, you can still update the data of the graph at any time.

*Did you
Know?*

Web Graphics

Illustrator is a great tool for designing Web graphics. Be it an entire site design, a navigation design, or a single graphic, the object-based properties of Illustrator graphics make it easy to create, design, and edit them. Additionally, because the graphics in Illustrator are resolution independent, if you ever need to use the graphics for print purposes, you won't need to re-create them at a higher resolution (something you may need to do if you use Photoshop).

Pixel Preview

When you're designing for print, rarely are you ever concerned about pixels themselves. This is because imagesetters print at very high resolutions, such as 2400dpi or 3600dpi, and edges are always razor sharp. Even when you're printing to lower resolution devices, such as a 600dpi laser printer, the dots themselves are barely noticeable.

Web graphics are different, though, because images are rendered at the resolution of a computer monitor, which in most cases is 72 pixels per inch. To make graphics look prettier and smoother onscreen, a computer uses a method called *antialiasing* to slightly blur the edges of color. The result is an image that looks clean and smooth instead of hard-edged and jagged (see Figure 7.200).

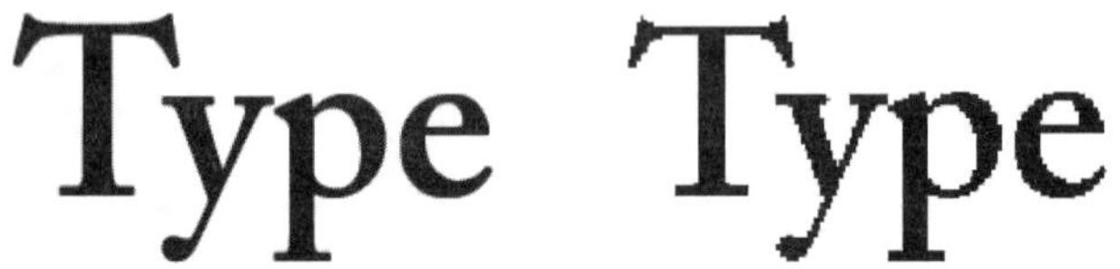

FIGURE 7.200
The image on the left is antialiased.

When you save or convert your graphic in a raster format, you can specify that Illustrator should apply antialiasing. However, when you're viewing your graphic in Illustrator on the artboard, you also want to see what your graphic will look like with antialiasing applied. For that reason, Illustrator has a special preview mode called *Pixel Preview*, which you can find under the View menu (see Figure 7.201). In Pixel Preview mode, your graphics display on your artboard as they would when viewed in a Web browser. You can work and edit graphics in Pixel Preview mode and should do so when designing graphics for the Web.

Now I know you're probably thinking, *Why should I care what my image looks like when it's antialiased?* The answer is that although antialiasing is generally a good thing, at times it can work against you. The side effect of blurring edges of color is that it sometimes makes your graphics illegible. This is especially true when your design contains small text or thin lines (see Figure 7.202). Using Pixel Preview will help you see these issues before you export these graphics.

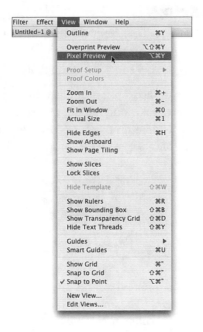

FIGURE 7.201
Turning on Pixel
Preview mode.

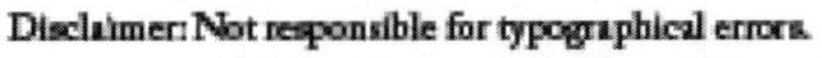

Disclaimer: Not responsible for typographical errors.

FIGURE 7.202
Small text becomes
unreadable when
antialiasing is applied.

Disabling Antialiasing on a Per-Object Basis

If you want to disable antialiasing for a single object, you can use the Rasterize
live effect to do so. Make your selection and choose Effect, Rasterize. Choose 72ppi
for the Resolution setting, choose None for the Anti-aliasing setting, and click OK
(see Figure 7.203). With Pixel Preview turned on, you can clearly see the difference.

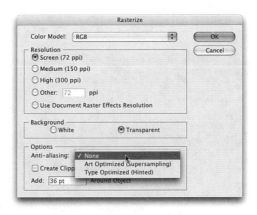

FIGURE 7.203
Choosing None for
Anti-aliasing in the
Rasterize effect
dialog.

Object-Based Slicing

In Chapter 6, "Using Adobe ImageReady CS," we talked about image slicing for Web graphics. Illustrator has a Slice tool and a Slice Select tool for creating and selecting Web slices, as Photoshop and ImageReady do, although it's a bit different in Illustrator.

When you draw a slice with the Slice tool, what Illustrator is really doing is drawing a rectangle with no fill and no stroke, and making it a slice. You can actually see the slice show up in the Layers palette as an object (see Figure 7.204). When you want to edit the slice, you can use the Slice Select tool to change the boundaries of the slice.

FIGURE 7.204
Slices are visible in the Layers palette.

However, Illustrator also has a different kind of slice. Rather than creating graphics and drawing slices over them, you can apply a slice as an attribute to a selection—something that Illustrator calls an *object-based slice*. To apply this kind of slice, make a selection and then choose Object, Slice, Make (see Figure 7.205). Using this method, if you make an edit to your graphic, the slice will update automatically along with it.

FIGURE 7.205
Specifying an object-based slice.

If you want to hide all the little squares and numbers that indicate slices on your screen, you can do so by choosing View, Hide Slices.

After a slice is applied, you can choose Object, Slice, Slice Options to specify settings such as URL, and ALT text. When you specify text as an object-based slice, you can also set the slice to be an HTML slice (rather than an image slice). In that case, Illustrator will export the text as editable HTML text instead of a graphic.

HTML text slices may not format exactly as you see them in Illustrator. Although bold or character attributes will be preserved, exact fonts and sizing will depend on the browser used. Other text features such as kerning or baseline shift will be ignored.

Save for Web

In Chapter 5, "Using Adobe Photoshop CS," we discussed a feature called Save for Web that allows you to preview and export graphics for use on the Web. Illustrator's Save for Web feature is nearly identical. Like Photoshop, Illustrator's Save for Web feature is powered by Adobe ImageReady.

You can use Illustrator's Save for Web feature to preview up to four optimized settings at once to help you choose the perfect Web image (see Figure 7.206). You can also set different optimizations for your Web slices and export graphics in GIF, JPEG, PNG, and WBMP formats.

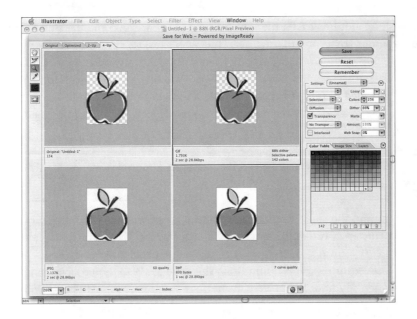

FIGURE 7.206
Illustrator's Save for Web feature allows you to view up to four optimizations at once.

Illustrator's Save for Web feature does have two additional capabilities you won't find in Photoshop, however: the capability to save in Web vector formats and support for CSS layers.

Vector Formats Support

Illustrator is a vector graphics application, so it only makes sense that Illustrator would support the vector graphics formats that are supported on the Web. Although the most popular graphics formats for Web use are raster-based (GIF, JPEG, PNG), there are two formats that have become the standard on the Web for displaying vector-based graphics (see Figure 7.207). These two formats are the Macromedia Flash format (SWF), and the Scalable Vector Graphics format (SVG).

FIGURE 7.207
Choosing a vector Web format from the file format pop-up in the Save for Web dialog.

Macromedia Flash (SWF)

The Flash format has taken the Web by storm and has become the standard for creating interactive content, and even full Web sites, for the Web. The benefits of Flash are that you can animate content, add interactivity, add sound, and even script it with logic. To view SWF files in your Web browser, you need to have a plug-in installed (a free download from Macromedia's Web site). Just about every Web browser these days already comes with the Flash plug-in pre-installed.

Before it became Flash, the technology was known as FutureSplash. Macromedia acquired the technology and defined the format as SWF, which stands for Shockwave Flash.

For animation, the Flash format uses a frame-based model. Much like movies are made, each step of the animation is a separate frame. As each frame plays back, it gives the appearance of motion. For Illustrator specifically, you can use top-level layers as frames of an animation. The Save for Web dialog gives you two options when saving a file in SWF format (see Figure 7.208): AI File to SWF File, which saves your art as one static SWF file; or Layers to SWF Frames, in which your layers will be converted to frames at export time and your SWF will play as an animation in a Web browser or any Flash-capable browser.

FIGURE 7.208
Choosing to save a static SWF file or an animated one.

You can also choose a frame rate (higher numbers make your animation play back faster; lower numbers make your animation play back slower). Setting your animation to loop will make it replay over and over again in your browser. Otherwise, it will play once and then stop.

If you have repeating objects in your design, you should define and use symbols because the Flash format supports the use of symbols to save file size. Remember that you can blend between symbols in Illustrator as well. Illustrations that are drawn using the Symbolism tools are also exported to SWF as symbols. In fact, if you save your file in the SWF file format and then open that file in Macromedia Flash (the Macromedia application), any symbols in your file will become editable symbols in Flash as well.

Flash doesn't support slicing, but you can use the Attributes palette in Illustrator to apply image maps to objects, and those URLs will export correctly to SWF.

Scalable Vector Graphics (SVG)

The SVG format isn't as widely used as the Flash format, but it has specific features that make it a better choice for certain kinds of graphics. Many people look at SVG and SWF as being competing formats, mainly because Macromedia has always been pushing SWF and Adobe has been pushing SVG. In truth, the formats are built for different purposes. As you read on about what SVG is and what it supports, you'll get a clearer understanding of the roles of each of these formats.

SVG is an open standard file format based on XML and JavaScript. It supports animation, interactivity, and scripting. There's no direct support for sound inside SVG, but you can use the SMIL standard to add sound to SVG graphics.

Because SVG is based on XML, which is also an open standard, SVG files are really just text files—meaning they can be edited or changed very easily, and at any time. That opens SVG up to a high level of customization functionality, including interaction with a database. It's for this reason that back-end developers and programmers lean toward SVG, because it empowers them to use quality graphics, but control and customize those graphics very easily. Many of the new cell phones that are available on the market today use SVG to display their graphics onscreen.

By the Way

In contrast, the Flash format is a binary file, and it can't be opened or edited other than in the Macromedia Flash application itself.

Animation in SVG is timeline-based. That means you specify an object to travel a set distance over a set amount of time (most video-based applications such as Adobe's Premiere and After Effects and Apple's Final Cut Pro use this method). Illustrator itself does not have a timeline, and there's no way to specify SVG animation from within Illustrator. Most people who use Illustrator to create SVG graphics hand-code animation into their files manually after they've exported the file from Illustrator as an SVG file.

By the Way

Adobe LiveMotion was a product that used a timeline-based animation interface to create animated SWF files. Unfortunately, Adobe cancelled the product shortly after shipping LiveMotion 2.0. You still might find a copy of it on eBay, though.

SVG does support image slicing, as well as image maps that you can define using the Attributes palette. Any URLs you specify for an object inside Illustrator will export correctly in an SVG file.

Finally, Illustrator also provides variable support inside of SVG files. We mentioned earlier how SVG is an open text-based file, allowing SVG to update graphics on-the-fly. Illustrator's Variables palette (see Figure 7.209) allows you to define XML-based variables for text, linked images, and graphs, and to control visibility.

FIGURE 7.209
The Variables palette in Illustrator.

CSS Layer Support

More and more, Web designers and developers are seeing the benefits of using CSS layers in their Web designs. CSS (Cascading Style Sheets) is a way to define how objects lay out on a Web page. Using CSS allows designers to position graphics precisely, as well as overlap graphics. Developers also like CSS because of how efficient it can be when they're creating large sites with many pages; it's easy to make global changes using cascading style sheets.

In Illustrator, you can export graphics from the Save for Web dialog with CSS layers by clicking on the Layers tab and specifying which top-level layers you want to export (see Figure 7.210). You can also choose to export a layer as visible or hidden.

FIGURE 7.210
Choosing to export CSS layers from the Save for Web dialog.

Saving/Exporting Files

Illustrator can save files in various formats, each suited for different uses. Illustrator can also export files in a wide range of formats, which is one of the reasons some people consider Illustrator a valuable utility—even if they never actually draw anything with it.

Save

Generally, Illustrator uses the Save command to save files that are "round-trippable," meaning that those files can be reopened in Illustrator with no loss of editability. To save a file, choose File, Save, and then from the pop-up menu choose a format to save your file in (see Figure 7.211). If you want to save an existing file with different options, choose File, Save As.

FIGURE 7.211
Choosing a format
to save your file in.

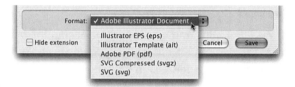

Adobe Illustrator Document (.ai)

In reality, Illustrator's native file format is PDF—when you save a file as a native Illustrator file, you can open and view that file in Adobe Acrobat or in the Adobe Reader. This is also how InDesign is able to place native Illustrator files—because it reads the file as a PDF file.

There are several options you can choose from when saving an Illustrator file (see Figure 7.212):

FIGURE 7.212
The Illustrator
Options dialog.

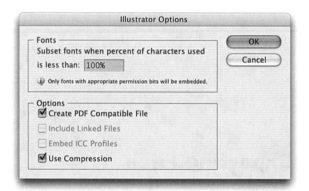

▶ **Create PDF Compatible File**—As I mentioned earlier, you can view a native Illustrator file in Adobe Acrobat because the Illustrator file is really a PDF. However, this is true only when the Create PDF Compatible File option is checked when you save your file (it's on by default). To significantly save file size, you could turn this option off, but beware that other applications won't be able to open the file correctly. For example, you won't be able to place the file into InDesign. Uncheck this option only if you know that you will be opening the file again in (and printing it from) Illustrator CS only (the file won't open in older versions of Illustrator either).

▶ **Include Linked Files**—Check this option to include linked images inside the Illustrator file itself. This will add to your final file size, but may allow Illustrator to print linked images if the link is broken or lost. To reopen the file in Illustrator, you'll still need the linked images, though. If you have no linked images in your document, this option will be grayed out.

▶ **Embed ICC Profiles**—If you have placed images into Illustrator that contain ICC color profiles, you can choose to embed those profiles using this option. If you have no images with ICC profiles in your document, this option will be grayed out.

▶ **Use Compression**—Check this option (it's on by default) to allow compression in the file to create a smaller file size.

You should save in the Illustrator format for the following:

▶ Files that will be opened again in Illustrator CS

▶ Files that will be placed into InDesign 2.0 or later

▶ Files that will be imported into an After Effects composition

Illustrator EPS (.eps)

EPS, which stands for Encapsulated PostScript, has been an industry-standard format since the industry of desktop publishing was created. The printing of EPS files requires a PostScript printer (or one that has a PostScript emulator). Because the EPS format has been around for so long, most applications that allow you to place art support the popular file format.

There are several options you can choose from when saving an Illustrator file (see Figure 7.213):

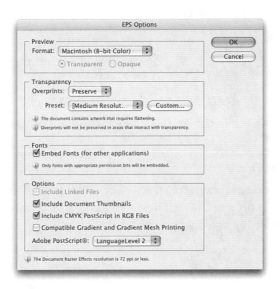

FIGURE 7.213
The Illustrator EPS Options dialog.

▶ **Preview**—A PostScript file itself can't be displayed on your screen (unless your computer screen understands PostScript), so a raster preview is included in the file as well. Macintosh previews (PICT files) won't show up on a Windows computer, so if you're planning to use your EPS on a Windows machine, choose a TIFF preview instead.

▶ **Transparency**—You have the option to either preserve or discard your overprint settings when saving an EPS file (some RIPs or trapping software prefer to handle overprint settings themselves). Additionally, if your document contains transparency, it requires flattening (PostScript doesn't support transparency), and you can choose a transparency flattener style to use for that process.

▶ **Adobe PostScript**—If you're printing to a PostScript Language Level 2 or 3 device, you can specify that here. By default, Language Level 2 is chosen, but you can change that to Language Level 3, if you have a printer that supports it, to take advantage of such things as smooth shading (which prevents banding in gradients).

You should save in the EPS format for the following:

▶ Files that will be placed into QuarkXPress

▶ Files that will be placed into various other applications that support the EPS format (video applications, 3D rendering programs, and so on)

Illustrator Template (.ait)

Saving a file as an Illustrator template allows you to use that file as a document template to base other files on. We discussed templates back in the beginning of this chapter. There are no specific settings for saving a template file.

You should save in the Illustrator template format for the following:

▶ Files that you want to use as a template for future Illustrator documents.

Adobe PDF (.pdf)

One of the most popular formats chosen for saving files out of Illustrator is PDF. The PDF format has become universally accepted around the world for viewing high-quality graphically rich documents.

There are many different settings you can specify when saving a PDF file (see Figure 7.214):

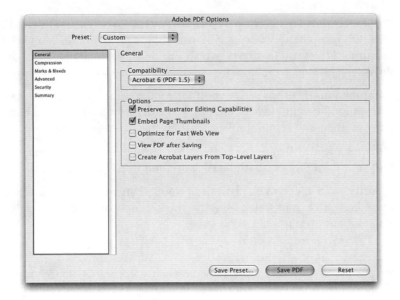

FIGURE 7.214
The PDF Options
dialog.

▶ **Compatibility**—There are three versions of PDF to choose from in
   Illustrator. PDF 1.3 is the version of PDF that Acrobat 4 uses, and it does not
   support transparency (and requires flattening). PDF 1.4 is the version of PDF
   that Acrobat 5 uses, and it does support transparency (no flattening is
   required). PDF 1.5 is the version of PDF that Acrobat 6 uses, and it supports
   both transparency features and PDF layers.

▶ **Preserve Illustrator Editing Capabilities**—This option (on by default) will
   include extra information in the file that will allow Illustrator CS to reopen
   the PDF file and retain full editability. Turning this option off will result in a
   significantly smaller PDF file, but may result in lost information when the
   file is reopened in Illustrator. If you're going to turn this option off, I suggest
   keeping a copy of your original file for future editing.

▶ **Embed Page Thumbnails**—On by default, this option embeds raster thumbnails into the file, which some programs use to display PDF page previews.

▶ **Optimize for Fast Web View**—This options allows the PDF to start loading
   in a Web browser as soon as it begins downloading, allowing viewers to see
   some contents of the PDF as they load, rather than having to wait until the
   entire PDF is downloaded. This is similar in concept to interlacing.

▶ **View PDF After Saving**—If you're sending your file off to a client or a printer, you might want to open the file in Acrobat just to review it and make
   sure that it's correct. Checking this option will automatically open the newly
   created PDF file in Acrobat as soon as you save it.

▶ **Create Acrobat Layers from Top-Level Layers**—When using the Acrobat 6 (PDF 1.5) compatibility setting, you can choose to export your top-level Illustrator layers as PDF layers (which can be viewed in either Acrobat 6 or the Adobe Reader).

▶ **Compression**—PDF has full support for compression, and you can specify settings for different kinds of images. You can also specify the downsampling of images to create smaller PDF files (for onscreen viewing).

▶ **Marks & Bleeds**—If your file is going to a printer, you want to make sure that your final PDF has both bleed space and trim marks specified.

▶ **Security**—PDF files can be password-protected on two levels. You can choose from these settings as well as specify whether files can be printed at high-resolution or even printed at all.

Did you
Know?

> You can use the Save Preset button at the bottom the Adobe PDF Options dialog to save frequently used settings for PDF files. Saved PDF presets will show up in the Preset pop-up menu at the top of the Adobe PDF Options dialog box.

More detailed information on specific PDF settings can be found in Chapter 10, "Using Adobe Acrobat 6.0 Professional." You should save in the PDF format for the following:

▶ Files that will be opened in Adobe Acrobat or Adobe Reader

▶ Files that will be sent to a client for review

▶ Files that will be submitted to a printer for final processing

▶ Files that will be submitted as ads for publications

SVG (.svg)

As discussed earlier, SVG files are XML-based graphics files. Although you can export SVG files from the Save for Web feature, you can also save SVG files, which by default contain round-trip information to allow the files to be reopened in Illustrator CS with no loss in editability.

There are several settings you can specify when saving an SVG file (see Figure 7.215), including these:

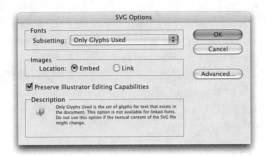

FIGURE 7.215
The SVG Options
dialog.

▶ **Preserve Illustrator Editing Capabilities**—This option (on by default) will
include extra information in the file that will allow Illustrator CS to reopen
the SVG file and retain full editability. Turning this option off will result in a
significantly smaller SVG file, but may result in lost information when the
file is reopened in Illustrator. If you're going to turn this option off, I would
suggest keeping a copy of your original file for future editing.

▶ **Include Extended Syntax for Variable Data**—If you've defined variables in
your Illustrator file, make sure that this option is checked (on by default),
which includes variable information in the file. This setting is available in
the Advanced options dialog.

SVGZ is a compressed SVG format that exhibits the same settings as SVG. You
should save in the SVG format for the following:

▶ Files that will be uploaded to a Web page

▶ Files with variables that will be dropped into GoLive as SmartObjects

▶ Files that will be used as templates for the Adobe Graphics Server

▶ Files that will be sent to a Web or back-end developer

Export

When you export a file from Illustrator, you can expect to lose some editability
should you want to reopen that exported file in Illustrator. To export a file, choose
File, Export, and then choose a format to save your file in from the pop-up menu.

Whenever you are exporting files from Illustrator, you always should save and keep a ver-
sion of your file in case you need to make edits later.

Illustrator Legacy (.ai)

The Illustrator Legacy export option is used when you want to save art from Illustrator CS to open in older versions of Illustrator (see Figure 7.216). The settings are similar to those found when saving native Illustrator files, but you have the option to choose which version of Illustrator you want to save back to (10, 9, 8, or 3). Versions 8 and 3 don't support transparency, and exporting in those formats will require flattening.

FIGURE 7.216
The Illustrator
Legacy Options
dialog.

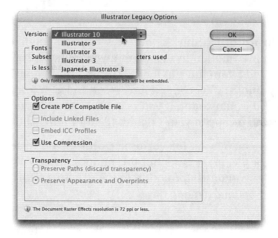

Be aware that any text in your file will be broken up into individual letters or converted to outlines upon export. This is because older versions of Illustrator won't understand text from the new text engine that's in Illustrator CS.

By the Way

You can specify how text is exported to older versions of Illustrator by opening the Document Setup dialog and choosing Type from the pop-up menu. The Export menu setting Preserve Text Editability will retain the type as text characters (see Figure 7.217), but the text strings themselves will be broken up into individual type characters. Preserve Text Appearance will guarantee the same appearance of the text by converting all type to vector outlines.

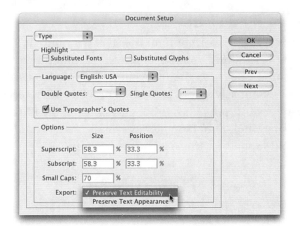

FIGURE 7.217
Choosing how text
should be exported
to legacy versions.

Illustrator Legacy EPS (.eps)

Similar to exporting legacy Illustrator files, the Illustrator Legacy EPS option allows you to export EPS files that are compatible with earlier versions of Illustrator (see Figure 7.218). The same issue with text being broken up also applies here (unfortunately, there's not much you can do about it).

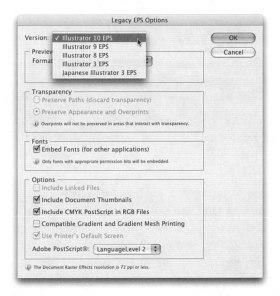

FIGURE 7.218
The Illustrator EPS
Legacy dialog.

PNG (.png) and JPEG (.jpg)

The .png (pronounced *ping*) format is a raster-based format, and you may remember that we mentioned you can export this format from the *Save for Web* function in Illustrator. However, the .png format can also be used for non-Web applications. For example, you can place PNG files into Microsoft Word (which is what the Export for Microsoft Office feature uses). Using the PNG export feature allows you to export high-resolution files as well as specify certain features such as interlacing and support for transparency (see Figure 7.219).

FIGURE 7.219
The PNG Options dialog.

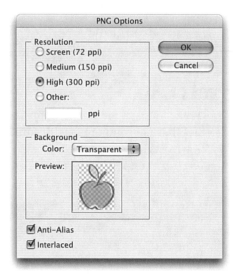

By the same token, you can also save high-resolution JPEG images in RGB, CMYK, or Grayscale color modes via the Export feature in Illustrator.

Photoshop (.psd)

Most people aren't aware that you can actually save a Photoshop file from Illustrator. Instead of copying and pasting data from Illustrator to Photoshop, you can retain a lot more information by writing a Photoshop (.psd) file right from Illustrator (see Figure 7.220). Features that are retained using this method are layers, layer names, nested layers, transparency blending modes, opacity levels, clipping masks, opacity masks, compound shapes, text, Web slices, slice optimization settings, and image maps. We'll actually see how this works later, in Chapter 15, "Creating a Web Banner."

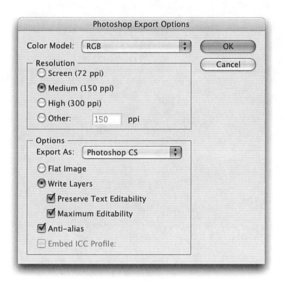

FIGURE 7.220
The Photoshop Export Options dialog.

TIFF

For times when you simply want to rasterize your entire Illustrator file, you can export a TIFF file using the TIFF export option.

Save for Microsoft Office

One of the challenges a designer faces is when a client asks for an image that he or she can place into a Microsoft Office application. With Illustrator CS, you can use a new feature called Save for Microsoft Office that will create a PNG file with one click of a button. Although PNG files are raster-based images, they are saved with high enough resolution to look great both onscreen and on a printout.

If you require specific PNG settings, you can always use the PNG export option mentioned earlier.

To save a file for use in Microsoft Word, Excel, or PowerPoint, choose File, Save for Microsoft Office (see Figure 7.221). After the file is created, you should use the Insert from File command in the Office application of choice to place the file.

FIGURE 7.221
Choosing the Save for Microsoft Office command.

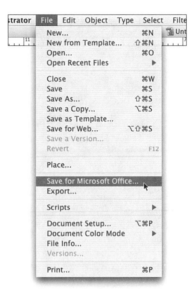

Printing

Illustrator CS received a long-awaited overhaul of its print engine and Print dialog box. Just about all the options you need to specify for printing are encompassed in a spectacular Print dialog box that was based on the user-friendly InDesign print dialog box.

To print a file, choose File, Print and you'll be presented with the Print dialog box (see Figure 7.222). Along the left side of the dialog is a list of different groups of options. The dialog was designed so that most users wouldn't really have to go beyond the first group of options, though. Near the bottom of the dialog is a Fit to Page option, which allows you to automatically enlarge or reduce your art to fill the paper size that's chosen.

The lower left of the dialog also contains a print preview window, which gives you a real-time representation of what your file will look like when it's printed. You can click on the preview and drag it to reposition the art on the page if you like.

Illustrator also lets you save all the Print dialog's settings as a print preset, which will then appear for reuse in the Preset pop-up menu at the top of the dialog.

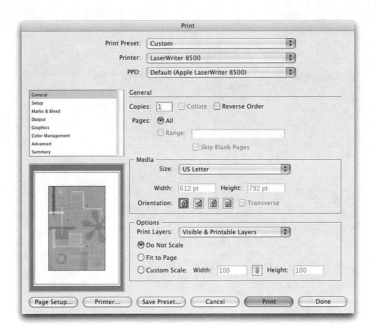

FIGURE 7.222
The new Illustrator
CS Print dialog.

CHAPTER 8

Using Adobe InDesign CS

Read a magazine lately? How about a newsletter? Up until a few years ago, such publications were produced using either Adobe PageMaker or QuarkXPress, software specifically designed for producing multipage documents for professionals. A few years ago Adobe introduced InDesign, its successor to PageMaker and a program hailed by many as the new standard in professional page layout. InDesign hasn't quite earned that title yet, but with each new version it gains more and more momentum. InDesign is already as good as any page layout software has ever been, and its underlying technology will allow it to continue to make strides that no other page layout contender can hope to match in the foreseeable future. However, you don't need a title like Senior Art Director to use InDesign; with a little bit of guidance (provided in this chapter) and a little bit of time on your part (as you read this chapter), you'll be creating art-director-worthy documents in no time.

What's New in InDesign CS

For those who have used InDesign before, here's a quick overview of what's new in InDesign CS:

- ▶ The Story Editor, a fully integrated and customizable word processing environment
- ▶ Flattener and Separations preview palettes that let print professionals prevent potential printing problems (how's that for some alliteration!)
- ▶ Enhanced performance when zooming, scrolling, wrapping text, or importing Photoshop, Word, or Excel files
- ▶ Capability to specify document-specific bleed and slug areas and set bleed and slug print options
- ▶ Option to save page size, columns, margins, and other document settings as presets that you can apply to any new document you create
- ▶ Character styles nested within paragraph styles; enhanced text import options; a new Info palette that displays text statistics, image resolution, color space, and file type
- ▶ XML validation through DTD (Document Type Definition) support
- ▶ Mapping character styles to XML tags
- ▶ A new Measure tool

- ▶ A context-sensitive, dockable Control palette that lets you format text and edit objects easier than ever
- ▶ Collapsible, dockable palettes to keep your monitor as clutter-free as possible
- ▶ The capability to create saved, customized Workspaces for different documents or different phases of the design and production process
- ▶ A Pathfinder palette to combine individual shapes into compound shapes
- ▶ Usability enhancements (tool functionality and keyboard shortcuts) for manipulating text and graphics
- ▶ Running headers and footers for tables that span multiple text frames
- ▶ Enhanced text wrap
- ▶ A strokes style editor
- ▶ Mixed ink support
- ▶ Color swatch enhancements
- ▶ User-specified glyph (font symbol) sets
- ▶ Enhanced PDF authoring including interactive features such as movies, sounds, and buttons, as well as direct PDF export
- ▶ Enhanced support for XMP (extensible metadata platform) and Photoshop files
- ▶ A Package for GoLive feature to export InDesign pages for easy integration into GoLive layouts
- ▶ The ability to use Adobe Version Cue features to increase productivity when working with other Adobe Creative Suites products or when collaborating with other Adobe Creative Suites users

Introduction to InDesign CS

InDesign CS is the latest incarnation of Adobe InDesign (the previous version was version 2.0), with new functionality specifically designed so that it works better than ever before with all the Adobe Creative Suite products.

The Toolbox

Just as in Photoshop and Illustrator, the various tools you work with in InDesign are contained in a toolbox (see Figure 8.1) on the left side of the InDesign application window (although you can move it anywhere you want by dragging the title bar at the top of the Toolbox). Most of these tools will already be familiar to you from other Adobe Creative Suites applications, but a few of them may be new to you.

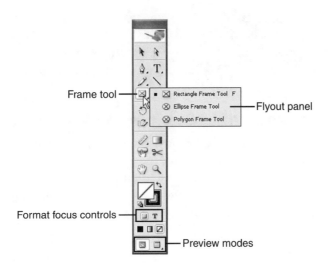

Frame tool

Flyout panel

Format focus controls

Preview modes

FIGURE 8.1
The Rectangle, Ellipse, and Polygon Frame tools, the Button tool, the Format focus controls, and the Preview modes.

The Frame tool creates frames within which you can place text or graphics. The default Frame tool is the Rectangle Frame, but you can also choose Ellipse Frame or Polygon Frame from the Frame tool flyout menu.

The Button tool is used to add interactivity to an InDesign document. A button can be used to allow the viewer to go to a different part of the document, open a new document, display an image, play a sound or movie, or do much more.

Below the color controls are two buttons that change the focus of any formatting commands you give from the text box itself to the actual text inside the text box.

Finally, the last two buttons on the Toolbox let you change from the normal viewing mode to one of three other viewing modes: Preview mode (the default), Bleed mode, and Slug mode. We'll be discussing the Bleed and Slug modes a little later in the appropriately named "Bleeds and Slugs" section.

The Control Palette

New to InDesign CS is the Control palette (see Figure 8.2), located just below the menu bar in the InDesign application window. It is used to control the appearance of selected objects. The Control palette is context-sensitive, meaning that the options within it change based on the type of object you have selected. For example, the Control palette options for text (font, font size, paragraph alignment) are far different from those that appear if you have an object selected (position, scale, rotation angle).

FIGURE 8.2
The Control palette
with text selected
(top) and with an
object selected
(bottom).

Palette Management (Custom Workspaces)

As with all the applications in the Adobe Creative Suite, InDesign is prone to palette clutter. Palettes in InDesign can be moved, combined, docked, and saved as workspaces to make the time you spend in InDesign as uncluttered and productive as possible. Working with palettes is covered in detail in Chapter 4, "The Key That Makes It All Work: Integration."

Viewing Your Work

InDesign has an incredibly powerful display engine, capable of displaying full-resolution imagery as well as vector artwork and fonts at up to 6400% (that's 64 times actual size to you and me) without losing one iota (or pixel) of detail. However, all that power can slow down even the mightiest of computers when you're viewing a complex document, so InDesign provides the capability to customize exactly how detailed (and thus how memory- and performance-hungry) your document will display. You can quickly pick from various viewing performance settings from the View, Display Performance submenu. In case you feel even more tweak-happy, there's a whole pane in the Preferences dialog box dedicated to customizing your viewing options.

Rulers

Knowing where you are on a page is extremely useful when you're doing page layout, so you will probably want to have your rulers showing when working in InDesign (View, Show Rulers to show the rulers or View, Hide Rulers to hide them). You can change the ruler *zero point* (the point from which distances are measured) by dragging the intersection of the horizontal and vertical rulers to any location within your document window (see Figure 8.3). This is helpful when you're positioning objects relative to other objects or to a spot other than the upper-left corner of the page (the default zero point).

Ruler zero point

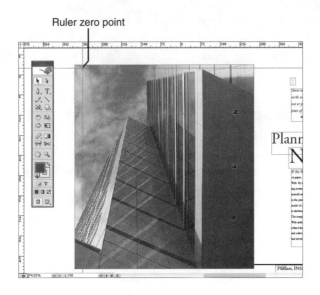

FIGURE 8.3
Setting a new zero point.

Guides

InDesign has three primary types of guides: margin guides, column guides, and ruler guides (see Figure 8.4). Margin guides indicate the document margins, and column guides indicate column and gutter settings for a page or master page.

Column guides

Margin guides

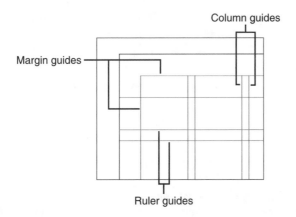

Ruler guides

FIGURE 8.4
Margin, column, and ruler guides.

To set margin and column guides for a specific page, go to that page and then set up your guides using Layout, Margins and Columns. To set margin and column guides for a master page, double-click on the desired master page in the Pages palette, and then choose Layout, Margins and Columns.

Ruler guides help you precisely position objects. To create a ruler guide, click either the vertical or the horizontal ruler, drag the guide to the desired location, and release the mouse button. Drag the guide back up into the ruler to remove it.

Making Selections

As mentioned in Chapter 4, InDesign is primarily an object-oriented application, like Illustrator, and similar selection tools are used. The two primary selection tools are the Selection tool (which has a black-arrow Toolbox icon and cursor) and the Direct Selection tool (which has a white-arrow Toolbox icon and cursor).

Selection Tool

Use the Selection tool to select objects or groups of objects. For the most part, this is the tool you will do 90% of your nontext selecting with. You can Shift-click to add additional objects to your selection or remove objects from an existing selection. (⌘-clicking) [Ctrl-clicking] allows you to select objects hidden under other objects, which is an invaluable technique when you're working with crowded layouts.

Direct Selection Tool

The Direct Selection tool is used to select single objects out of a group (several individual objects grouped together with the Object, Group command) or to select one or more points on a path of a single object.

Selecting Text

Text selection in InDesign works just like text selection in virtually every application on the planet. Just click and drag across text to select it, or click and then Shift-click to conveniently select larger blocks of text. After the text is selected, a mind-boggling variety of formatting commands can be applied to the text, as described later in the "Character Formatting" and "Paragraph Formatting" sections.

> If you double-click on a text frame with either the Selection tool or the Direct Selection tool, you get an insertion point inside the text frame and the Text tool becomes active.
>
> You can double-click with the Text tool to quickly select a word, triple-click to select a line, quadruple-click to select a paragraph, and quintuple-click to select an entire story.

Creating New Files

Creating a new InDesign file is pretty much the same as creating a new file in any of the Adobe CS applications: Start with File, New, select document sizes and other options, click OK, and you're good to go. For InDesign these options include whether your document will have facing pages, the number of pages in your document, the page size, the number of columns per page, and the page margins.

Document Presets

If you commonly work with custom page sizes or unusual document settings, consider saving your document settings as a preset by clicking the Save Preset button in the New Document dialog box. After the preset is saved, your custom settings will be available from the Document Preset pop-up menu at the top of the New Document dialog box (see Figure 8.5).

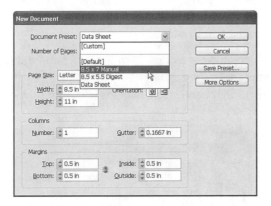

FIGURE 8.5
Document presets in the New Document dialog box.

Bleeds and Slugs (eeeew!)

Clicking the More Options button in the New Document dialog box gives you two additional settings to specify: bleed and slug. The *bleed* is the portion of a document outside the page boundaries that gets printed but trimmed off (most often used for borders and large graphics). The *slug* is an area outside both the page and the bleed that contains notes or other information about the document.

The Pages Palette

The Pages palette is used to navigate within your document, rearrange pages, insert pages, duplicate or delete spreads, create master pages, and apply master pages to document pages.

You can jump to a page simply by double-clicking it, rearrange pages by dragging them within the Pages palette, and insert new pages by clicking the Create New Page button at the bottom of the Pages palette.

Spreads

A spread is a collection of pages designed to be viewed together. The simplest type of spread is a two-page spread, such as the one that you are viewing right now as you read this book.

To duplicate or delete a spread, select the spread in the Pages palette and choose Duplicate Spread or Delete Spread from the palette flyout menu.

Master Pages

Master pages serve as templates for the pages within your document. If a master page has two text boxes and a placeholder for a page number in one corner and you apply that master page to a regular page in your document, that regular page will have two text boxes and the correct page number in the corner. Master pages help ensure consistency from page to page.

To create a new master page, select the New Master command from the Pages palette flyout menu (see Figure 8.6). Double-click on the new master page to view it and then just create elements on the page as you normally would.

FIGURE 8.6
Creating a master page.

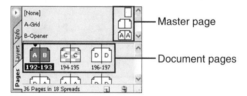

To apply a master page to a document page, simply drag the master page icon onto the desired document page.

To rename a master page or change other options, select the master page and then choose the Master Options command from the Pages palette flyout menu.

Margins

The margin is the area of the page between your text and the edge of the page. InDesign lets you specify margins when you create a document in the New Document dialog box, or you can change them later using the Layout, Margins and Columns command.

Layers

Like Photoshop and Illustrator, InDesign supports document layers. In InDesign the best use of these layers is to separate different elements of your layout, such as text from graphics, or background objects from foreground objects, or different versions of a layout (say, for client approval). All documents have a default layer (labeled *Layer 1* in the Layers palette; see Figure 8.7) that contains everything unless you create your own layers.

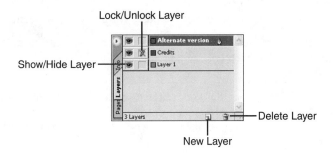

FIGURE 8.7
The Layers palette.

The three most common layer-related actions are adding layers, rearranging layers, and deleting layers: .

▶ To add a layer to a document, click the New Layer button at the bottom of the Layers palette.

▶ To rearrange layers (moving one above or below another), simply drag the layer up or down in the list of layers.

▶ To delete a layer (which deletes everything on the layer), drag it to the Trash button at the bottom of the Layers palette.

Double-clicking a layer lets you rename it or set layer options, and the two boxes to the left of the layer name let you set layer visibility (the eye icon) and lock a layer to prevent any changes to it (the null-pencil icon).

Drawing

InDesign CS's drawing tools provide quick access to the most commonly used drawing tools. Although they're not a replacement for Adobe Illustrator CS, you'll find that the similarities between the two programs allow you to quickly achieve many basic illustration functions without ever having to leave InDesign. Even better, many of the InDesign drawing tools can be used on artwork that was originally created in Illustrator, so you don't have to continually jump between programs.

The Pen Tool

The Pen tool is the standard drawing tool from which you can create virtually any artwork. The Pen tool provides a superior level of control relative to any other drawing tool, enabling precise positioning of lines and curves. Although it can be somewhat intimidating at first, adhering to a few basic rules will make this tool indispensable. Even better, after you learn how to use the Pen tool in InDesign, you'll be able to use it in Illustrator and Photoshop (where the tools are virtually identical). Chapter 7, "Using Adobe Illustrator CS," contains more detailed information on the Pen tool, but here are some basic rules to get you started:

► **Click for straight lines**—When you want to make straight lines (like those in a starburst), click each corner—*do not drag.*

> Press the Shift key while using the Pen tool and you'll be constraining point placement (and dragging; see the next bulleted entry) to 45-degree angles. This is great for drawing objects with 90-degree angles, or when you want curves to be very precise.

► **Drag for curved lines**—Click and drag about one-third of the distance of the intended curve in the direction of the "bump" on the curve. On the next click *do not click where you released the mouse button,* but instead click at the intended end of the curve.

► **Finish what you're drawing before you start to edit**—If the shape (especially if you're using curves) isn't looking exactly as you'd like it, *don't stop and edit in the middle of the drawing process.* Instead, finish what you're drawing and then go back and edit the path with the Direct Selection and Pen tools.

The Pencil Tool

The Pencil tool is used for freeform drawing of virtually any shape, except those shapes that have straight edges—use the Pen tool for all straight edges. The Pencil tool is perfect for sketching and drawing amorphous blobs such as putting greens, puddles, and wavy lines. To use the Pencil tool, click and drag on any page; release the mouse button when you're done drawing.

If you click and hold on the Pencil tool in the toolbox, you'll see two Pencil tool "helpers," the Smooth tool and the Erase tool. The Smooth tool is used to make bumpy, jagged lines much smoother and rounded-looking, and the Erase tool erases any portions of the path that you drag it across.

Before you start drawing with the Pencil tool, double-click on it to display the Pencil Tool Preferences dialog box (see Figure 8.8). Here you can set the following options:

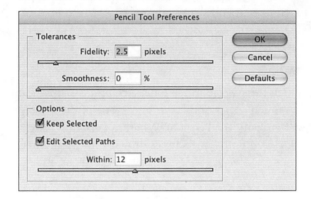

FIGURE 8.8
The Pencil Tool
Preferences dialog
box, where you can
change how paths
will appear before
you draw them.

▶ Fidelity controls how closely the path you end up with is to the exact place-ment of the mouse as you drag. Because the mouse is quite hard to control (even for seasoned computer users and graphic artists), you'll find that slid-ing this to the right makes your lines look less jerky and much smoother.

▶ Smoothness controls how "smooth" your curves are. The farther you drag this to the right, the bigger and wider your curves, and the less detail you'll see. You'll need this set to the left when drawing detailed edges such as a coastline, but toward the right when drawing the aforementioned putting greens.

▶ Keep Selected keeps the path selected (points visible) when you release the mouse button. You'll be able to delete (by pressing the Delete key) the path if you don't like it after you've drawn it, or edit it immediately using the Direct Selection or Pencil tools if you keep this option on.

▶ Edit Selected Paths lets you edit any paths (even those drawn with other tools such as the Rectangle or Pen tools) by simply dragging over the select-ed paths with the Pencil tool.

You'll find a similar set of options in the Smooth Tool Preferences dialog box (accessed by double-clicking on the Smooth tool).

The Line Tool

The Line tool draws single line segments quickly. Press the Shift key to constrain the angle of these line segments to 45 degrees. The Line tool is great for making arrows, using the Start and End stroke options (see "Fills and Strokes," a little later in the chapter).

Vector Shapes

InDesign comes with three basic shape tools: Rectangle, Ellipse, and Polygon. In all three cases, it's much easier and faster to use one of these tools than to attempt to draw them with the Pen tool. Whereas Pen- and Pencil-drawn paths are either open or closed paths, the shapes drawn with these three tools are always closed.

You can edit vector shapes using the Pencil tool, because those shapes are made of paths.

Rectangles

The Rectangle tool draws both rectangles and squares. To draw a rectangle, click and drag. To constrain that rectangle to a square, press the Shift key while dragging (be sure to keep it pressed until you release the mouse button).

Normally, as you click and drag with any of the vector shape tools, you'll be drawing from a corner. To draw from the center of any shape, press the (Option) [Alt] key (and keep it pressed until you release the mouse button).

Ellipses

The Ellipse tool draws ovals and circles. To draw an oval, click and drag. To draw a circle, press the Shift key while dragging.

Polygons

The Polygon tool allows you to draw polygons (a shape with any number of sides, in which all the sides are of equal length, using all obtuse angles) and stars (any number of "points" with all the points of equal length).

By default, the Polygon tool draws a hexagon. You can change the number of sides of that polygon while you're drawing by pressing the up or down arrow on your keyboard to increase or decrease the number of sides to the shape.

You can also double-click the Polygon tool (displaying the Polygon Settings dialog box, as shown in Figure 8.9) before drawing to set the number of sides, or to change the polygon into a star (increase the Star Inset % to make the points of the star longer).

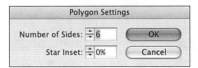

FIGURE 8.9
The Polygon Settings dialog box, which is most useful for its capability to change mild-mannered polygons into super-powered stars.

Pathfinder Palette

The Pathfinder palette is used to control the way shapes interact with each other. For instance, you can use the Pathfinder Add button to merge three circles together to form a snowman (see Figure 8.10). Access the Pathfinder palette from the Window menu.

FIGURE 8.10
Three circles (at left) overlap each other, giving the appearance of a CAD-based snowman. On the right, the Add button from the Pathfinder palette was used on the circles, making the snowman much more handsome.

The Pathfinder functions in InDesign aren't "live" the way they are in Illustrator, so the original objects are gone after you click the button, leaving the resulting shape(s) only.

To use any of the Pathfinder functions, select the paths you want to affect, and then click the button. Here are the different buttons and what they do:

▶ Add merges two or more paths into a single path.

▶ Subtract removes the area of the frontmost objects from the backmost object.

- ▶ Intersect leaves only the overlapping area of the selected objects.

- ▶ Exclude Overlap removes the overlapping area of the selected objects.

- ▶ Minus Back removes the area of the backmost object from the frontmost objects (pretty much the opposite of Subtract).

Grouping Objects

Any objects you create (paths, text objects, images) can be grouped together so that they stay with each other when they're moved or otherwise manipulated. You can even group groups to keep things more organized.

To group objects, select the objects and choose Object, Group. When objects are grouped, clicking on any one of the objects in a group selects the entire group. You can still use the Direct Selection tool to select a single object or point, however.

Corner Effects

Corner Effects can be used on any corner of any path (the corners on a rectangle, a star, or any path you've drawn with the Pen tool) to give the corners a little more visual interest than a standard corner. Figure 8.11 shows the different Corner Effects applied to a 90-degree angle.

FIGURE 8.11
Different effects applied to corners.

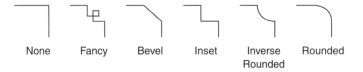

None   Fancy   Bevel   Inset   Inverse   Rounded
                                   Rounded

Coloring Objects

You can change the color of any selected object by either choosing a color from the Color palette or clicking on a swatch in the Swatches palette.

Fills and Strokes

Most objects in InDesign can have both their fill (the color, gradient, or pattern inside an object) and their stroke (the actual lines or borders that define the object) changed. The fill/stroke proxy in the toolbox, the Color palette, and the Swatch palette controls what is being changed. The solid square represents fill, whereas the hollow square represents stroke. Whichever of these is in front controls what is being changed. To make the stroke active when the fill is in front, click the stroke proxy. To make the fill active when the stroke is in front, click the fill proxy.

Stroke Styles

The Stroke palette (shown in Figure 8.12) lets you change the weight (thickness), corner, and ends of a stroke (if the selected path is closed and has no ends, the start and end options do nothing).

FIGURE 8.12
The Stroke palette provides detailed control over how strokes are displayed.

Choosing Colors

The Color palette (Window, Color; shown in Figure 8.13) provides a quick mechanism for selecting colors to apply to your text and objects. You can either click in the color ramp at the bottom of the palette, or manipulate the sliders in order to "tune in" the color you'd like to use. If you have an object selected, you'll change the color of it instantly.

FIGURE 8.13
The Color palette.

Gradients

Gradients (shown in Figure 8.14) are smooth, continuous tones between different colors. All the gradients in the document are stored in the Swatches palette, and can be applied the same way colors are (see the next section, "Working with Swatches").

FIGURE 8.14
These objects have
different gradients
applied to them.

Working with Swatches

Swatches are a way for you to keep track of which colors are being used in your document. They also help you keep those colors consistent so that all your light blues match each other (because they're applied to your objects with the same swatch).

To create a new swatch, click the New Swatch button at the bottom of the Swatches palette (see Figure 8.15). Adjust the sliders until the color looks just right, and then click the OK button. A new swatch will be created.

FIGURE 8.15
The InDesign CS
Swatches palette
stores colors and
provides an easy
mechanism for
applying them to
objects and text in
your document.

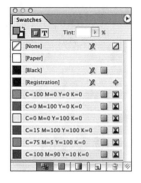

To apply a color to an object, select the object and click on the swatch.

Spot Colors

There are two types of colors when it comes to printing: process colors and spot colors. Process colors are made by combining various percentages of cyan, magenta, yellow, and black (the four standard colors used in color printing).

Spot colors are made by using a single ink that is a specific color. If you're creating a design that is black and green, you'll probably want to use a spot color for the green. If you're using several colors or color photographs, you'll want to use process colors.

Although you *can* use any number of spot colors in a document, doing so will result in your printer having to use a different ink for each color, which can cost significantly more than using process colors.

You can change between spot and process colors in the Swatch Options dialog box (shown in Figure 8.16; accessed by double-clicking on a swatch in the Swatches palette). You can also set certain spot colors to print as process (turning them from a single ink into a combination of cyan, magenta, yellow, and black) in the Print dialog box, but you'll need to remember to do so at print time.

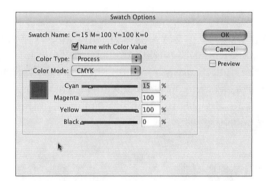

FIGURE 8.16
The Swatch Options dialog box.

The World of Transparency

Most objects in InDesign can be made "transparent," which is really to say that you can make them less opaque so that objects below can be viewed through them. Of course, InDesign provides more than just basic opacity controls, but that's what you'll be using the most.

To see transparency on objects more clearly, choose View, Show Document Grid. This will put the grid behind all objects in the document, and will show you the difference between tinted objects and partially opaque ones.

Opacity and Blending Modes

In the Transparency palette (shown in Figure 8.17), you control both opacity (via the Opacity slider) and blending mode (via the pop-up menu). Slide the Opacity slider to the left (toward 0%) to make the selected object more transparent. Experiment with the different blending modes to see the results.

FIGURE 8.17
The Transparency palette controls object opacity.

Soft Drop Shadows

You can apply drop shadows to any object (though this is done most often with type). To do so, select the object (or text), and choose Object, Drop Shadow. Although most of the options are self-explanatory, one isn't: The Blur field controls how fuzzy the edges of the drop shadow are. Increase Blur to make the shadow edges fuzzier (the fuzziness is transparent). Figure 8.18 shows text with a nice soft drop shadow applied.

FIGURE 8.18
This text has a soft-edged drop shadow applied to it.

Feather

Feathering makes the edges of an object gradually fade transparently into the background. Figure 8.19 shows text with feathering applied to it. To feather an object, select it and choose Object, Feather.

FIGURE 8.19
This text has feathering applied to the edges.

Native Photoshop and Illustrator Transparency Support

If you place (using the Place command only, not copy and paste or drag and drop) Photoshop or Illustrator native files into InDesign, any transparency in those files is retained for InDesign.

Transformations

There are several ways to transform objects in InDesign: rotating, scaling, and shearing (see Figure 8.20). These transformations can be done with their respective tools or by menu commands found in the Object, Transform submenu.

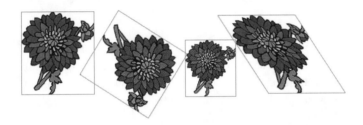

FIGURE 8.20
The original object (left) has been rotated, scaled, and sheared, from left to right.

You can also align and distribute objects through the Align palette.

Rotate

To rotate any object, select that object and then choose Object, Transform, Rotate. Enter the number of degrees you want to rotate the object, and click the OK button.

> Rotation works counterclockwise, so if you enter 90 degrees, what was on the top of the object will be on the left after you rotate it.

Did you Know?

You can also use the Rotate tool to rotate objects. To use the Rotate tool on a selected object, click and drag with the Rotate tool, and the object will rotate around the upper-left corner. If you'd like the object to rotate around a different *origin point*, click (but do not drag) with the Rotate tool to set the origin point to a different spot, and then click and drag to rotate.

Did you
Know?
Pressing the Shift key constrains rotation to 45-degree increments, which is quite useful for 90-degree rotations.

Scale

To scale an object, select that object and then choose Object, Transform, Scale. Enter the % size you want to scale the object, and click the OK button.

You can also scale objects by using the Scale tool. Click and drag on a selected object, and the object will be scaled up or down depending on which way you drag. Press the Shift key to constrain the proportions of the scale (so that the object doesn't become distorted).

Shear

Shearing is the process of slanting an object sideways. To shear an object, select that object and then choose Object, Transform, Shear. Enter the number of degrees you want to shear the object, and click the OK button. You can also use the Shear tool to shear objects, but it's easy to lose control of the shear, making your object shear off into infinity.

Free Transform

The Free Transform tool combines scaling and rotating into one tool. By clicking on the edge points that appear when the tool is selected, you can quickly scale the selected object easily. Clicking just outside the corners allows for quick rotation of your objects.

Aligning and Distributing Objects

InDesign has the capability to quickly align and distribute several objects at once. This is done through the Align palette (shown in Figure 8.21), accessed by choosing Window, Align.

FIGURE 8.21
The Align palette has controls for both aligning and distributing objects.

To align objects, select them and click any of the align buttons. The graphics on the buttons show the type of alignment that will occur when you click the buttons. Figure 8.22 shows several objects aligned to the right.

FIGURE 8.22
These objects have all been aligned to the right.

To distribute objects, select them and click any of the distribute buttons. Objects will be evenly distributed in accordance with the graphics on each of the buttons. Figure 8.23 shows several objects that have been distributed horizontally on center.

FIGURE 8.23
These objects have all been distributed horizontally on center.

Working with Text

Back in the heyday of desktop publishing (the early 1990s for you youngins out there), font and type control was incredibly important to designers. Fifteen years later, nothing has changed; type and text manipulation is at the top of the list for designers. The more control and precision, the better. If you want to know why InDesign is on its way to being the leading page layout application, type is the answer.

Placing Text

InDesign is a software program specifically designed to allow you to combine text and graphics on a page. Obviously, the first step is getting your source text into your document. InDesign supports every major text format (and most minor ones), so whatever application you use to compose your text, it should import with no problems. Placing text is a simple matter of loading the text and then either creating a new text frame or placing the text into an existing text frame.

Follow these steps to place text into a document:

1. Choose File, Place.

2. Locate the text file you want to place, select it and click the Open button on the right side of the Place dialog box.

3. Your cursor changes to the loaded text cursor, indicating that the text is ready to be placed into your document.

4. Either click to place the text (filling the current column from the point at which you clicked to the end of the page) or click and drag to create a new text frame.

5. If a text frame cannot contain all the text placed within it, a red plus-sign overflow symbol appears on the lower-right border of the text frame. Clicking this overflow symbol loads the remaining text into your cursor for placement in an additional text frame. To place this text, just click or click and drag to create a new text frame with the additional text. This new text frame is linked to the previous text frame. When linked, text flows freely between the two frames if you change the size of the frames or the formatting of the text (see Figure 8.24).

FIGURE 8.24
A text frame and loaded text cursor.

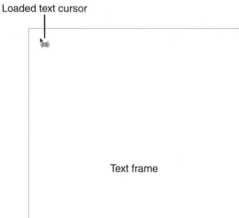

Loaded text cursor

Text frame

You can save a lot of time when placing text by either Shift-clicking or (Option-clicking) [Alt-clicking]. Shift-clicking places all incoming text at once, flowing from one column or page to the next until all the text is placed. If necessary, InDesign will even add pages to your document to make room for all the text. (Option-clicking) [Alt-clicking] places the text into the current column (just like clicking without a modifier key held down), but it loads any overflow text back into the cursor for further placement, saving you the step of clicking on the overflow indicator.

Text Frame Options

Each text frame has several options for displaying the text within it. These include multiple columns within a single frame, inset spacing (similar to page margins, but applied to the frame), baseline offset (the vertical distance above or below the imaginary line the text sits on), and vertical justification (the vertical placement of the text in its text box). To change any of these options, select a text frame and choose Object, Text Frame Options.

Character Formatting

InDesign has a full range of character formatting capabilities, from simple stuff such as font and size to very precise control over kerning (space between pairs of characters), tracking (space between a range of characters), scaling (resizing), and baseline shift (vertical position of characters relative to the rest of the line).

Character formatting can be accomplished using either the Control palette (at the top of the screen on a Macintosh or the document window on a Windows PC) or the Character palette (Window, Type & Tables, Character). The Control palette actually has more functionality than the Character palette because it also includes controls for applying character styles. Two very useful but often-missed dialog boxes can be found in the flyout menu (for both the Control and the Character palettes): Underline Options and Strikethrough Options, which give you total control of your underlines and strikethroughs (see Figure 8.25).

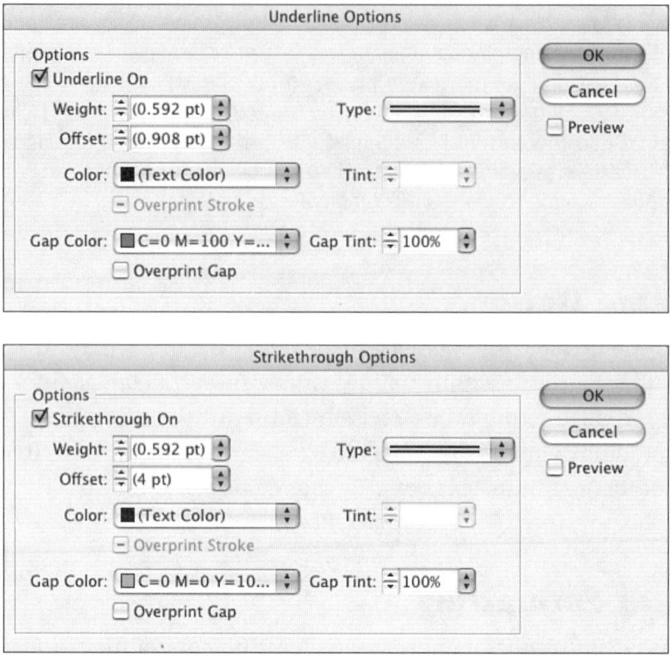

FIGURE 8.25
The Underline
Options and
Strikethrough
Options dialog
boxes.

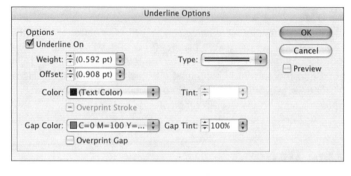

Kerning and Tracking

InDesign's kerning and tracking controls are particularly useful for making head-lines and body text look good and fit the way you want them to. Both kerning and tracking work very subtly but can have a profound effect on the overall aesthetic of the page.

To kern a letter pair, position the insertion point between the two letters and use the kerning controls in the Character palette until the two letters are positioned as desired (see Figure 8.26). Kerning is usually used to reduce whitespace between letter pairs, but it can be used to increase it as well.

FIGURE 8.26
Headlines with no kerning (top), stan-dard kerning (mid-dle), and optical kerning (bottom).

Creative Suite!

Creative Suite!

Creative Suite!

To change the tracking for a block of text, start by selecting the entire block. Use the tracking controls in the Character palette to adjust the spacing of the text. If your text flows into other text frames or pages, be sure to check these from time to time as you work.

Virtually all fonts have instructions (called *metrics*) that specify adjustments to kerning for certain letter pairs. InDesign, however, has a really slick feature called *optical kerning* that adjusts the space between letters based on what the letters actually look like together. It's a subtle difference, but I'd always recommend checking out optical kerning (the first option in the Kerning pop-up menu) anytime you are adjusting letter pairs.

OpenType Support

InDesign boasts full support for the OpenType font format. (As well it should, because OpenType was developed by Adobe and Microsoft.) OpenType fonts are completely platform-independent (so there are no reflow problems when switching platforms) and have hundreds of additional glyphs per typeface.

Glyphs Palette

The Glyphs palette lets you view all characters in a typeface, including characters that require special keystrokes (which is a pain on a Windows computer, and not too much fun on a Macintosh, either).

To view the Glyphs palette, select Window, Type & Tables, Glyphs. To insert a glyph into your text, just double-click the desired glyph.

Paragraph Formatting

The difference between character and paragraph formatting is subtle yet significant: Whereas character formatting affects as little as a single character at a time, paragraph formatting automatically affects the entire paragraph. Keeping this in mind makes it simple to remember what type of formatting category a certain control falls into. For instance, alignment (flush left, center, justified, and so on) is paragraph-based because you'll always affect an entire paragraph with a change to that option.

Paragraph formatting controls are located primarily in the Paragraph palette, accessed by choosing Window, Type & Tables, Paragraph. Other paragraph-specific options are Paragraph Styles and Paragraph Rules (see the following text for more details on each).

Adobe Paragraph Composer

One incredibly useful but totally invisible technology in InDesign is the Adobe Paragraph Composer, the type engine that controls character placement within InDesign. The Adobe Paragraph Composer is on all the time, so all you have to do is set your type to Justified (in the Paragraph palette) and let InDesign do its magic for you.

Drop Caps

The term *drop cap* refers to the first character of a paragraph that has been enlarged downward to span more than one line (think books of fairy tales and nursery rhymes). Creating drop caps (see Figure 8.27) is almost ridiculously easy in InDesign. All you have to do is click in the desired paragraph and then use the Drop Cap controls in the Paragraph palette to set the height of the drop cap.

FIGURE 8.27
A paragraph with a drop cap.

> Your job, as a rising star/henchman/consigliore-in-training in your Family, is to find a suitable suburb and add it to the Family's cache of assets by taking over at least one of each of the basic location types: Office, Government, Restaurant, Store, Residential and Public. To do this, you'll need to recruit soldiers, shore up your locations with defenses, assemble an impressive cache of weapons, and attempt to control as many locations as you can.

Paragraph Rules

A rule is a horizontal line above or below a paragraph of text. It looks like an object but acts like text, and moves with the paragraph if text reflow causes the paragraph to move. Although usually simple lines, InDesign rules can be one of 17 distinct types and can be any color or width.

To create a rule, select a paragraph and then access the Paragraph Rules command from the flyout palette menu on the Paragraph palette or Control palette (in paragraph mode). Select Rule Above or Rule Below from the pop-up menu at the top of the dialog box, and click the Rule On check box.

To create rules both above and below a paragraph, select Rule Above or Rule Below, click Rule On, choose your desired rule formatting options, repeat the process to create the other rule, and then exit the dialog box.

Styles

Styles are, without a doubt, the most powerful and flexible formatting feature of InDesign. A style is a collection of formatting instructions that can be applied to paragraphs or to characters. With styles you can ensure consistent formatting of all text in your document and you can reformat vast amounts of text in just a few seconds. Both paragraph styles and character styles can be accessed in the same palette group (choose Window, Type & Tables, Character Styles or Window, Type & Tables, Paragraph Styles).

Paragraph Styles

Paragraph styles are styles that are applied to entire paragraphs. Paragraph styles contain both paragraph-level formatting, such as alignment, line spacing, and tab stops, and character-level formatting, such as font and font size.

To create a paragraph style, select a paragraph of text and format it as desired. With the paragraph still selected, click the Create New Style button at the bottom of the Paragraph Styles palette. A new paragraph style (titled "Paragraph Style 1") appears in the list of styles. Double-click this new style to open the Paragraph Style Options dialog box (see Figure 8.28). From here you can type in a new name for the style and set additional formatting options, if desired.

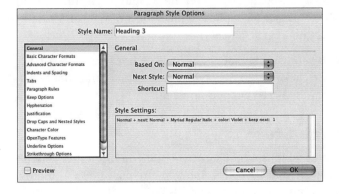

FIGURE 8.28
The Paragraph Style Options dialog box.

To apply a paragraph style to text, select the desired text and click on the name of the style you want to apply to that text. The paragraph will be reformatted to match the selected style.

If you change a style (by changing any of the formatting settings within the Paragraph Style Options dialog box), all paragraphs which have that style applied to them will be instantly updated to reflect the changes. This is a huge timesaver and ensures a consistency that you could never achieve if you had to go back and reformat the text manually.

Character Styles

As you might suspect, character styles are styles that are applied to characters, not full paragraphs. Character styles are created, applied, and modified exactly the same way paragraph styles are, but to smaller blocks of text.

Nested Styles

The term *"nested styles"* refers to styles that are based on other styles. Basing one style on another tells InDesign that the secondary style should be formatted just like the primary style, with specific exceptions (such as a different size). For example, you might have a Heading style that is 18-point, boldface, red Arial, and a Subhead style that is 14-point, boldface, red Arial. If the Subhead style is based on the Heading style, then the actual formatting instructions for the Subhead style would be *[Heading] + 14 point*. Any change to the Heading style other than size (such as a different font or color) would also be applied to the Subhead style. If the Subhead style were not based on the Heading style, then changes to the Heading style would not be applied to the Subhead style, and your headings and subheads would no longer match.

To base one style on another, open the Style Options dialog box for the secondary style (by double-clicking it in the Style palette listing) and choose the desired primary style from the Based On pop-up menu.

Setting Tab Stops

Tabs are variable-width spacer characters that you insert into your text by pressing the Tab key on your keyboard. *Tab stops* are paragraph formatting instructions that determine how far a tab travels before it stops. Tab stops are created, modified, and deleted in the Tabs palette (see Figure 8.29), which can be displayed by choosing Window, Type & Tables, Tabs.

To set a tab stop, click on the type of tab stop you want (left-aligned, centered, right-aligned, or character-aligned), and then either click in the narrow strip above the dialog box ruler at the desired location or simply enter a location measurement in the X field.

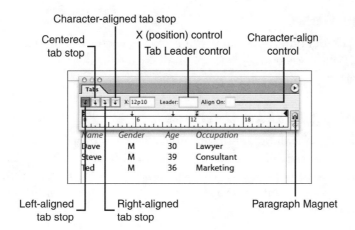

Character-aligned tab stop

Centered tab stop

X (position) control

Tab Leader control

Character-align control

Left-aligned tab stop

Right-aligned tab stop

Paragraph Magnet

FIGURE 8.29
A tabbed list with the tab stops used to create it.

If you want this tab stop to have a tab leader (a set of characters leading up to the tab stop), enter the character in the Leader field. If you are creating a character-aligned tab stop, the Align On field becomes active and you can enter a character other than a decimal point (the default) into this field.

To move an existing tab stop, just drag it to a new location. To delete a tab stop, drag it down off the tab ruler.

It is easiest to set up tab stops when the Tabs dialog box is positioned directly over the selected paragraph(s). Click the Position Palette Above Text Frame button in the lower-right corner of the Tabs dialog box to snap it over the selected paragraph(s).

Did you Know?

Find Font

The Find Font command lets you make global font changes to your document. This is especially useful if you open a document for which you don't have the correct fonts.

To replace fonts in your document, choose Type, Find Font. This displays the Find Font dialog box with a list of all fonts used in the document. Select a font from the list and then choose a replacement font from the pop-up menus at the bottom of the dialog box. After you have specified the source and replacement fonts, you can either find and replace specific instances of a font with the Find and Change buttons or do a global replacement with the Change All button.

Change Case

InDesign has four handy commands for changing text case: Uppercase, Lowercase, Title Case, and Sentence case. All are available from the Type, Change Case submenu.

Converting Text to Outlines

Converting text to outlines transforms normal text to drawn objects (see Figure 8.30). After it's converted, text can no longer be edited as text, but it can be manipulated as a graphic object. This is perfect for creating logos, labels, or other textual graphic treatments. It also lets you use text as a frame within which you can place other graphics.

FIGURE 8.30
Text before and after being converted to outlines.

To convert text to outlines, select the desired text and choose Type, Create Outlines.

The Story Editor

The story editor is the name of InDesign's built-in text editor. It has all the basic functionality you'll need to edit your text. It also shows you the paragraph styles that are applied to your text in a resizable frame along the left side of the screen. Note that formatting other than character emphasis (bold, italic, and underline) is not displayed in the Story Editor—all you see is the text itself and what paragraph styles are applied (see Figure 8.31).

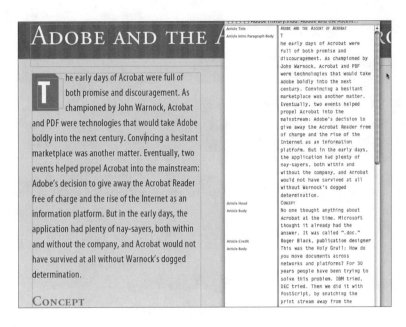

FIGURE 8.31
A page in Layout mode (left) and Story Editor mode (right).

To activate the Story Editor, select a text frame and choose Edit, Edit in Story Editor. Choose Edit, Edit in Layout to return to the normal view.

Checking Spelling

InDesign has the capability to check the accuracy of your spelling in your document. Because the spell-checking isn't live (that is, you get no cute red squigglies under misspelled words like you see in a certain popular word processing application), it makes sense to wait until you've entered all of your text before doing a spell-check.

To perform a spell-check, choose Edit, Check Spelling. The Check Spelling dialog box will appear; just click the Start button and InDesign will find all the words that aren't in the InDesign dictionary (it's interesting to note that "InDesign" is in the dictionary, but "QuarkXPress" is not). You can customize a few options for which words get flagged in the Spelling pane of the Preferences dialog box (and no, there's no option for "don't flag competing products").

Dictionary

As you're checking your spelling, you might run across a word that you know is spelled right that InDesign doesn't recognize, such as *"qoph"* (a favorite "legal" word of Scrabble players everywhere). Click the Add button in the Check Spelling dialog box to add the word to your custom dictionary. From that point on, *"qoph"* won't be flagged as being spelled incorrectly (which is nice, because it wasn't spelled wrong in the first place).

Search and Replace

InDesign's search and replace feature is deceptively powerful. In addition to the standard options for finding and changing text, pop-up menus to the right of the Find and Change fields in the Find/Change dialog box contain a very thorough list of special characters that you can search for and replace. You can also search for and replace text or special characters in all open documents with a single command!

The Find/Change dialog box can be accessed by choosing Edit, Find/Change.

Creating and Using Tables

One very useful feature of InDesign CS is how easy it is to create attractive and functional tables. InDesign tables support borders, fill colors, paragraph formatting, and table headers and footers. Tables also flow between text frames just like regular text.

To create a table, place the insertion point inside a text frame and choose Table, Insert Table. In the Insert Table dialog box (see Figure 8.32), specify how many rows and columns you want. You can also specify header and footer rows (see "Table Headers and Footers," a little later in the chapter). Click OK when done.

FIGURE 8.32
The Insert Table dialog box.

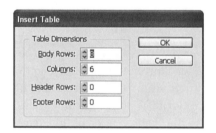

To convert tabbed text to a table, select the text and choose Table, Convert Text to Table. In the Convert Text to Table dialog box, specify which characters to use as column separators (usually tabs) and row separators (usually paragraphs). Click OK when done.

After your table is created, you can enter data into it by clicking in a cell, typing your data, and pressing the Tab key to move to the next cell (or Shift-Tab to move to the previous cell). A tab character can be inserted into a cell with (Option-Tab) [Alt+Tab].

Modifying Tables

After tables are created, they can be easily modified. Typical changes include adding or deleting rows or columns, changing row height or column width, and merging cells.

Basic table modification in InDesign is a simple matter of adding, deleting, and adjusting rows and columns and merging cells:

▶ To add rows or columns, select the same number of rows or columns that you want to add at the location where you want the new rows or columns inserted, and then choose Table, Insert, Row or Table, Insert, Column.

▶ To delete rows or columns, select the rows or columns you want to remove, and choose Table, Delete, Row or Table, Delete, Column.

▶ To adjust row height or column width, drag the bottom edge of the row or the right edge of the column. Hold down the Shift key while dragging to prevent rows below or columns to the right from moving.

▶ Shift-drag the bottom or right edge of the entire table to change the height of all rows or the width of all columns.

▶ To merge cells, select the desired cells and choose Table, Merge Cells.

Styling Tables

InDesign has a wide variety of formatting options to make your tables attractive and easy to read. The most common options are column/row strokes (cell borders), table borders, and fills. Before applying any formatting, though, you will need to select exactly the columns, rows, or individual cells you want to work with.

Use the following techniques to quickly select the areas of your table that you want to work with:

▶ To select multiple cells, drag across them with the text cursor.

▶ To select entire rows, position the cursor on the left side of the table until the cursor changes to a right-pointing arrow, and then click or click and drag.

▶ To select entire columns, position the cursor at the top of the table until the cursor changes to a down-pointing arrow, and then click or click and drag.

After cells are selected, you can format them by choosing Table, Cell Options, Strokes and Fills (choose Table, Table Options, Table Setup for stroke and fill options for the entire table). This dialog box contains controls for changing the weight, color, and type of stroke, as well as the fill color. The only tricky thing about this dialog box is the cell border proxy. This is a fake cell (or group of cells if you have multiple cells selected) with blue borders (see Figure 8.33). Any border that is blue will be affected by your changes. Clicking a proxy toggles it between blue (selected) and gray (unselected).

FIGURE 8.33
The Strokes and Fills tab of the Cell Options dialog box.

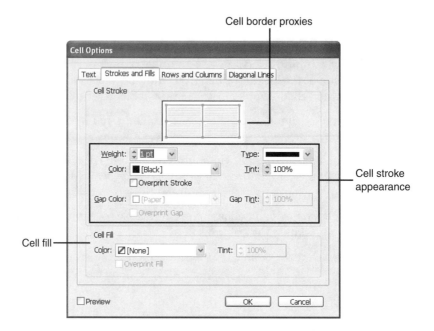

Using the Table Palette

After your table is created, the Table palette can be a quick way to perform such common table functions as changing the number of rows and columns, changing row height or column width, changing the vertical text alignment or the text rotation, or changing the text inset. The Table palette cannot be used to insert rows or columns, merge cells, or add borders and shading.

Table Headers and Footers

Conceptually, table headers and footers are very similar to traditional document headers and footers. The main difference is that with document headers and footers you have no control over the "units" of document data that they enclose—they always appear at the top and bottom of the page. With InDesign's table headers and footers, though, you can have them appear once per page, once per frame, or every text column. Table headers and footers can also consist of as many rows as you want.

To set up table headers and footers, follow these steps:

1. Choose Table, Table Options, Headers & Footers.

2. Specify how many rows to use for your header and footer.

3. Specify how often your table header will appear and how often your table footer will appear.

4. You can also choose to skip the first or last appearance of your table header or footer.

Working with Images

As I mentioned earlier, InDesign and other print publishing applications are all about combining text and images together on a page. You've already learned how to add text to your InDesign documents, and now it's time to learn about adding images.

Placing Images

Virtually all the images you add to your InDesign documents will come from an outside source. The most common sources are Photoshop and Illustrator files, PDF files, or raw scanned images. Regardless of the source, all of these images are placed into your document the same way.

To place an image, follow these steps:

1. Choose File, Place.

2. Locate the file you want to place, select it, and click the Open button on the right side of the Place dialog box.

   Your cursor changes to the loaded image cursor, indicating that the image is ready to be placed into your document (see Figure 8.34).

3. Click anywhere to place the image.

Loaded image
cursor

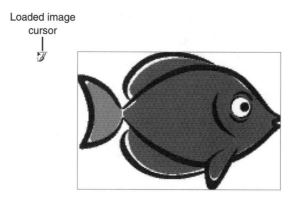

FIGURE 8.34
An image loaded
into the cursor
and placed on
the page.

To place a framed image, do this:

1. Create a frame using the Rectangular Frame, Ellipse Frame, or Polygon Frame tool, or select an existing shape.

2. Choose File, Place.

3. Locate the desired image, select it, and click the Open button.

   The image appears within the previously selected frame or shape.

Frames containing images can be moved or resized like any other object. To move the image within the frame, select it with the Direct Selection tool and click and drag the image.

| If you click and hold for a few seconds before dragging, you'll be able to see the entire image as you drag. This makes repositioning much easier. |

The Links Palette

When you place an image in your document, you don't actually add the image (that would make your InDesign files incredibly huge and incredibly slow). Instead, InDesign places a low-resolution screen version of the image in the document so that you can see what it looks like, and makes a note of the location of the actual file. You'll need the actual file in order to print, but while you are working it's enough to just know that it's linked to your document.

The Links palette lists all linked images, along with their current status (normal, modified, or missing; see Figure 8.35). If you are notified that a link is missing, you can simply browse to the correct file and relink it.

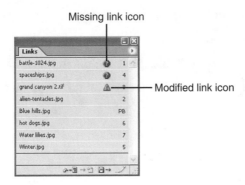

Missing link icon

Modified link icon

FIGURE 8.35
The Links palette.
Note the missing
and modified links.

Edit Original

Occasionally you'll place an image and realize that there is something about it that needs to be changed. The Edit Original button in the Links palette opens the selected image in the application that created it—or you can just (Option-double-click) [Alt-double-click] on the image to do the same thing.

Creating a Text Wrap

One of the coolest things you can do with publishing software is to wrap text around an image (see Figure 8.36). This is accomplished quite easily in InDesign with the Text Wrap palette.

FIGURE 8.36
Two text wraps.
Text jumps over the
first image and
wraps around the
second.

To apply text wrap to an image, follow these steps:

1. Select the image you want to work with.

2. Choose Window, Type & Tables, Text Wrap to display the Text Wrap palette.

3. In the Text Wrap palette, select the type of text wrap and the offset between the text and the object.

Adding Interactivity

InDesign has many of the same interactivity features you will find in Acrobat, such as hyperlinks, bookmarks, buttons, and embedded sound and movie files. These features let a viewer of a PDF version of your document click on things to jump to new locations or otherwise interact with the document. Obviously, if you are not going to be creating a PDF version of your document, you won't be using any of these features. This section focuses on the two most common interactivity features, hyperlinks and bookmarks. Although you can add other types of interactivity in InDesign, it is much easier to open the PDF file in Acrobat and add the features there (especially because interactivity features cannot be previewed in InDesign anyway).

Hyperlinks

A hyperlink is a section of text that, when clicked, sends the viewer to a new location. This location can be either a page in another document or a URL that points to a Web page or a file. All hyperlinks have two parts: source and destination. The source is the text that sends the viewer to a new location, and the destination is the location itself.

Although InDesign can be used to create all types of hyperlinks, the process for creating anything but URL hyperlinks is extremely convoluted and counter-intuitive. I highly recommend creating document hyperlinks in Acrobat, as discussed in Chapter 10, "Using Adobe Acrobat 6.0 Professional." Actually, you'll be better off creating *all* of your hyperlinks in Acrobat, but if all you need is a quick link to your Web site, InDesign can handle that easily enough.

To create a hyperlink to a Web page, do the following:

1. Select the text you want to use as the source.

2. Choose Windows, Interactive, Hyperlinks.

3. Click the Create New Hyperlink button at the bottom of the Hyperlinks palette.

4. In the New Hyperlink dialog box (see Figure 8.37), select URL from the Type pop-up menu.

5. Enter the full URL in the URL field.

6. Click the OK button.

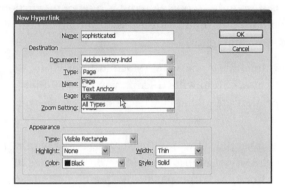

FIGURE 8.37
The New Hyperlink
dialog box.

You can set the appearance of the link here as well; but you won't be able to see what it looks like until you export the file to PDF, and none of the options create an acceptable appearance. I'd recommend instead that you choose the Invisible Rectangle option and format the text yourself in a way that lets the viewer know that it is a clickable item (such as blue underlined text).

Bookmarks

Bookmarks are a feature of Acrobat that let you create a navigational structure for the viewer which they can use to quickly move between pages or entire sections of a document. Unlike hyperlinks, bookmarks don't appear within the document itself, but rather as a separate pane within the PDF document window.

Using and editing bookmarks is covered in detail in Chapter 10, but basically there are two types of bookmarks: page and text. Page bookmarks take you to a specific page, whereas text bookmarks take you to a specific block of text. Creating bookmarks can be done just as easily in InDesign as in Acrobat.

To create a bookmark, follow these steps:

1. Choose Window, Interactive, Bookmark.

2. Either navigate to the page that you want the bookmark to point to (for a page bookmark) or select a block of text (for a text bookmark).

3. Click the New Bookmark button at the bottom of the Bookmarks palette.

4. Rename the bookmark, if necessary.

Scripting Support

One of the most powerful and flexible features of InDesign (or any of the Creative Suites products) is support for scripts. A script is a set of instructions that an application can run without user input. This lets you automate most of your most repetitive or time-consuming tasks.

Scripts are created in either AppleScript (Macintosh) or Visual Basic (Windows). Even if you don't know how to write a script, you can still make use of the hundreds of free scripts that are available (check out www.adobestudioexchange.com for some).

To use scripts, you must place them in the Scripts folder within the Presets folder, which is in the InDesign application folder. You can access all scripts placed in the Scripts folder from the Scripts palette by choosing Window, Scripting, Scripts.

Working with Large Documents

The longer your document, the more structure and navigational aids you need to give your reader. InDesign makes it easy to add page numbers, tables of contents, and indexes. It also lets you group document files into books to keep them organized.

Page Numbering

One universal requirement of both large and small documents is page numbers. InDesign makes it very easy to add page numbers to your documents. You can also easily change the format or starting number for the page numbers in different sections of your document.

To add page numbers, carry out these steps:

1. Double-click on the master page icon in the Pages palette.

2. Create a text frame on the master page where you want the page number to appear.

3. Choose Type, Insert Special Character, Auto Page Number.

   If your document layout includes facing pages, repeat this process for the second master page.

Creating a Book

A book in real life is a collection of related pages, all bound together. A book in InDesign is a collection of related documents, also bound together (see Figure 8.38). Collecting document files into a book makes it easier to access and organize documents, sequentially number chapters, and create tables of contents and indexes that span multiple documents.

FIGURE 8.38
The single book file provides a way to easily access all of these document files.

To create a book, follow these steps:

1. Choose File, New, Book.

2. Click the Add Documents button at the bottom of the Books palette.

3. Browse to the document you want to add and click the Open button.

    Continue adding files until the book is complete. Drag filenames up or down in the list to change the order in which the documents appear in the book.

Table of Contents

The TOC (Table of Contents) feature in InDesign is very deep and powerful, allowing you to create any variation of TOC imaginable. To start creating a TOC, you must first define TOC styles (Layout, Table of Contents Styles). Create a new style (click the New button), and choose which paragraph style is associated with that style. Repeat for each level of heading that you want to appear in the TOC.

To generate the Table of Contents, choose Layout, Table of Contents; click OK; and then place the TOC in your document. You'll need to replace the TOC each time you make an update to your document that might affect the TOC.

Indexing

InDesign takes all the pain out of indexing: The process of tracking words and what pages they occur on is automatic and straightforward. All you have to do is provide the entries for the index, set up the basic structure, and apply any formatting to the index. In many ways indexes and TOCs are alike—they track where certain words (indexes) or styles (TOCs) are located within your document.

To create an index, start by selecting an entry (any word in your document), and then display the Index palette (Window, Type & Tables, Index). Click the Create a New Index Entry button (at the bottom of the palette), and then click OK in the dialog box that follows. You've created your first entry!

After you've created all your index entries, you'll notice that the Index palette is giving you a preview of your index. To create the real thing, choose Generate Index from the Index palette submenu, and place the text as you would any story. The Index text is *not* live or linked to the index palette, so if you make changes to your document, you'll need to generate a new index and place it again.

Saving and Printing

Save your work often. You've heard it ad nauseam, but it bears repeating here. Although InDesign CS is relatively stable, it's easy to get lost in the realm of all those different pages (not to mention jumping back and forth between the other Creative Suite applications), and before you know it you may lose something you don't want to have to re-create.

To save your InDesign file, choose File, Save. It's that easy. No wacky options, and (some would say regrettably) no way to save backward to a previous version of InDesign.

Exporting Files

InDesign files can be exported to a few different file types. In some cases, such as PDF, the result matches (at least visually) exactly what was in the original document. However, in all cases, the native InDesign information is lost, meaning that InDesign functionality tied to the document such as layers and object definitions is gone when the file is exported. For that reason, be sure to always save a copy of the original InDesign file in addition to the exported version.

Exporting PDF

To export to PDF directly from InDesign, choose File, Export, and then choose Adobe PDF. However, you'll get better results (smaller file size, better clarity) by using Acrobat Distiller (with a PostScript file generated from the Print dialog box), even though it takes a few extra steps.

Exporting EPS

If you need to export single pages in the EPS format (this can be useful for opening InDesign files in Adobe Illustrator or Photoshop), you can do so through the Export dialog box (File, Export). Choose EPS as your file type (which will change the extension to .eps), and click the Save button.

The Export EPS dialog box will appear with a myriad of options. If you'll be exporting for use in Photoshop or Illustrator, there's no need to mess with most of the options unless you have placed images in your document; then you should review and adjust options as appropriate in the Advanced panel of the Export EPS dialog box.

Separation Preview

You can view individual spot or process color plates onscreen live in your document at any time. This is accomplished through the Separations Preview Palette (accessed by choosing Window, Output Preview, Separations). In this palette (see Figure 8.39), you can view each of the colors individually, or in any combination with other colors, by clicking the eyeballs on the left. Note that when you are down to any one color, it will always appear onscreen as black.

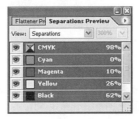

FIGURE 8.39
The Separations Preview palette.

Preflight

Preflighting in InDesign is the process of ensuring that all files and fonts are intact and current, and that all colors and print settings are correct. InDesign makes this process straightforward by providing a Preflight dialog box, accessed by choosing File, Preflight. Clicking on each of the items in the list on the left of the box (Summary, Fonts, Links and Images, Color and Inks, Print Settings, External Plug-ins) displays detailed information about those areas.

PDF/X-1a

PDF/X-1a is a version of the Portable Document Format Exchange specifically tailored for CMYK and spot-color printing workflows. The most important thing to know about using PDF/X-1a is that color management is *not* allowed within the original file.

Package

The Package command (File, Package) provides a quick method for placing your InDesign file, all linked files, and any fonts used in the document into a single location (the same lists you saw when you chose File, Preflight, as described previously). You can then easily drag these files into an e-mail or burn them onto a CD, confident that the recipient will have all the files needed to open, edit, and print your document.

Package for GoLive

The Package for GoLive command (File, Package for GoLive) takes the components of your document (text blocks, imagery, and so on) and packages it all up into a form that GoLive (the Web authoring package in the Adobe Creative Suite) can use to create a Web page (or series of pages) from your InDesign document content. This function does *not* create an HTML Web page; you'll still need to assemble the content in GoLive.

Printing

Because InDesign is an aggregation application, you'll find yourself needing to print from it more than all the other applications in the Adobe Creative Suite combined. To that end, the printing capabilities in InDesign (most of which are mimicked in Illustrator CS) are phenomenal. The following sections talk about some of the more commonly used functions in the Print dialog box (see Figure 8.40).

FIGURE 8.40
The InDesign Print
dialog box.

Print Dialog Options

Although there are all sorts of detailed options that InDesign supplies at print time, only a handful are used by most people, such as copies and page ranges.

Change the number of Copies to match the number of copies you'd like; check the Collate button if (when printing more than one copy) you'd like the pages to come out in sets in order, as 1/2/3, 1/2/3, 1/2/3, instead of 1/1/1, 2/2/2, 3/3/3.

To print a subset of the pages in your document, choose the Range radio button and type in the pages you want to print. For contiguous pages, use a hyphen (for example, 2-4). For individual pages, use commas (for example, 1, 4, 7).

Print Presets

If you're a tweaker when it comes to the Print dialog box, you'll find the Print Presets invaluable. They allow you to store *all* the Print dialog box settings (save them by clicking the "Save Preset" button at the bottom of the dialog box) and retrieve them simply by choosing them from the Print Preset pop-up menu at the top of the Print dialog box.

Marks and Bleed Settings

If you click the Marks and Bleed item in the list at the left in the Print dialog box, you'll be presented with an array of options for how various printer's marks appear and how to handle bleeding (which is how far past the edge of the defined page ink should appear).

Clicking the All Printers Marks check box and then printing a test document is a great way to see what all these things look like and where they will appear on your document.

Printing Separations

Separations are necessary for printing presses to reproduce color documents. Instead one sheet being printed with all the colors on it, a separate sheet is printed for each color. Typically, you won't be choosing this option unless you're printing directly to plate or negatives (which are used to make plates for a printing press). To print separations, choose Output from the list on the left, and then choose Separations from the Color pop-up menu.

CHAPTER 9

Using Adobe GoLive CS

Adobe InDesign CS and Adobe GoLive CS are kindred spirits. Both of these applications are what I call "aggregators," meaning you use them to bring together text, images, and multimedia elements created elsewhere. Yes, you can do some drawing in InDesign, and yes, you can do image compression, cropping, and animation in GoLive; but the heavy lifting in terms of creating image assets is done in Adobe Photoshop, ImageReady, and Illustrator.

None of the graphics tools in the Creative Suite, however, have anything remotely like GoLive's incredibly powerful site management capabilities for links. Web sites can have dozens, hundreds, even thousands of pages, each including multiple links to additional pages, images, and more. Long, long ago (like 1992), most people kept track of URLs by keeping copious notes and by testing, testing, testing. These days, though, you leave that stupefying job to GoLive.

What's New in GoLive CS?

New features in GoLive CS are support for CSS Level 2, Syntax hinting, and code-completion. Package for GoLive is an innovative new way of reusing print assets on the Web. Queries for finding site elements and Collections for grouping pages together are two more unique GoLive CS tools. We'll cover these new features as well as the basics of Web site creation as we continue through this chapter.

Introduction to GoLive CS

Like the other applications in the Creative Suite, GoLive helps you out when you first open the application by greeting you with a few basic choices in the Welcome dialog box: New Page, New Site, and Open. If you prefer not to have this dialog salute you every time you open the application, you can disable it by unchecking Show This Dialog at Startup in the lower-left corner (see Figure 9.1). No worries; if you change your mind, you can turn it back on again in the GoLive preferences. Our suggestion? Turn it off. Anything you can do there you can also do after the application has launched, thank you very much.

What do the choices in the Welcome screen do? If you choose New Page, you'll get a new blank generic HTML page, called untitled.html. If you choose New Site, you'll invoke the GoLive Site Wizard, which steps you through the creation of a site. We'll go over the steps in the wizard shortly, but for now you need to know only this: To take advantage of GoLive's incredibly powerful site management and link tracking tools, you always need to work from within a site window, and that is exactly what the Site Wizard creates. So forego the single new page in favor of a new site and you'll be on the right track. You will, of course, be able to create new pages from within your site.

Let's define "site" at this point. A site, in GoLive-speak, consists of the following things: a site file, a web-content folder, a web-data folder, and a web-settings folder. These four items are automatically created on your hard drive whenever you create a new GoLive site or import an existing site into GoLive, and they are neatly tucked into an umbrella folder that keeps them all together. Double-clicking on a site file opens it up in a site window. The site file is the shepherd that keeps track of the sheep, the sheep being the other three folders and any items included in them.

By the Way

Using GoLive, you can create as many sites as you want. You can have more than one site window at a time, and you can even drag and drop from one to another. Use caution when working with more than one site window at a time, though. It's very easy to inadvertently save work into the wrong one, and it can be a real pain to put things right again. If you are a novice at GoLive, you are better off opening only one site file at a time.

Creating a Project

Let's begin. Open GoLive, say hello to the Welcome screen, and then dismiss it so that we can find out where those same options are when you are in GoLive proper.

The New Page and New Site commands are conveniently found in the File menu, but look closely at what else is hiding there. Under New Special are a host of additional document types you can create—everything from XHTML pages to plain old text (TXT) files (see Figure 9.2). XML, CSS, SMIL, JavaScript, QuickTime, Perl, PHP, MMS, and other Web-related file formats are documents GoLive CS can handle with ease. In this chapter we'll cover only the basic file types, but be aware that GoLive CS has a depth and breadth beyond what is discussed here.

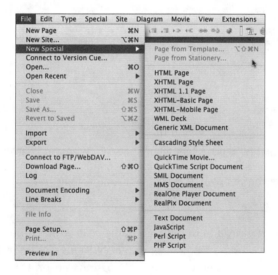

FIGURE 9.2
GoLive can create various documents suitable for the Web via the New Special command in the File menu.

Also located in the File menu are the Open and Open Recent commands. The Open Recent submenu is especially helpful because it lists not only recently opened sites, but also individual HTML pages and other types of documents you may have opened recently. At the very bottom of the Open Recent submenu is the option Clear Entries, which will delete everything in the list and begin building the recent files list all over again.

Creating a Site

Before anything can be listed in the Open Recent submenu, though, it must be created. Press (⌘-Option-N) [Ctrl+Alt+N] to invoke the GoLive Site Wizard (see Figure 9.3).

FIGURE 9.3
The GoLive Site Wizard steps you through the creation or importation of a site.

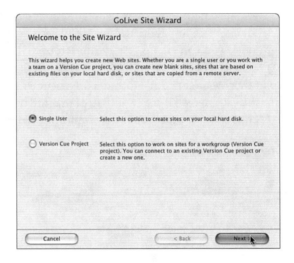

> **By the Way**
>
> Here's a suggestion for proceeding through the Site Wizard successfully: Read the instructions on each screen before clicking any buttons. No one likes to read dialog text, but because you've opted to purchase this hefty tome, we'll assume you are up to the task.

The first question you need to answer is whether you want a Single User site or a Version Cue Project. Choose Single User and click Next. (For information on creating Version Cue projects, refer to Chapter 11, "Using Version Cue.")

In the next screen you'll have several options. Choose Blank Site if you are starting from scratch. If you need to bring an existing site into GoLive that has been designed by someone else or in another Web authoring application, choose Import from Folder. If the existing site you want to work on is already online, then Import from Server is what you need. Finally, you can create a site from a template if you have previously placed sites into GoLive's Site Templates folder.

> **By the Way**
>
> Import from Folder is what you should opt for if you want to import a site that was created in an older version of GoLive. GoLive CS can directly open GoLive 6 site files, but sites created before GoLive 6 should be imported.

Creating a Blank Site

The simplest of the New Site options is Blank Site. Click the radio button for Blank Site, click Next, and you'll be asked to name your site. Give the site a name and click Next again, and you'll be asked to designate a location for your site. Browse to the location of your choice, click Choose, and click Finish. GoLive creates the site and opens it.

Importing a Site from a Folder

If you select Import from Folder and click Next, you'll be asked to locate the existing site you want to import. There are two Browse buttons in this screen. The top Browse button is for locating the root folder of the site you want to import; the bottom one is for locating the home page of that site. Although you can use either button, it's easiest to use the bottom one. Click it and navigate to the home page (often called index.html or index.htm) of the existing site. After doing so, you'll notice that the path to the site you are about to import is shown in the Site Wizard (see Figure 9.4).

FIGURE 9.4
The path to the folder you are going to import is shown in the Site Wizard.

Using the Site Wizard's Browse button to navigate to the home page of an existing site works nicely, but you can also drag and drop the index page of an existing site right onto the Site Wizard's screen to achieve the same results.

Did you *Know?*

The last step is to find a home for the Site File that GoLive will create for the imported site. Name the new site file, keeping its .site extension; browse to a suitable location for it; click Save. GoLive imports the site and opens it.

> Do *not* put the site file inside the site's root folder. It's fine to put it on the same level as that folder, but not inside. The site's root folder is the one that holds the home page.

Importing a Site from a Server

Sometimes you need to import a site that is already online. GoLive CS handles this task with ease. You have your choice of importing from either an FTP or an HTTP server. In the case of an FTP server, you'll need the FTP address, login name, and password; for an HTTP server you'll simply need the URL (see Figure 9.5).

FIGURE 9.5
Depending on whether you choose FTP or HTTP, you'll be required to enter certain information.

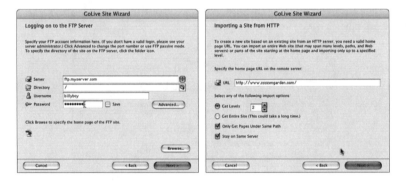

Begin by selecting Import from Server, click Next, choose FTP or HTTP, fill out the appropriate information, and click Next again. Select a name for the folder that will hold the new site file and its accompanying web-content, web-data, and web-settings folders, and click Next. Use the Browse button to select the location where the site will be placed, and click Finish. GoLive downloads the site and opens it.

> If you are unsure of the FTP address, login name, and password you need to use, contact your Web hosting service.

Using the Objects Palette and Toolbar

Like other applications in the Creative Suite, GoLive has an impressive array of palettes and tools accessible from the Window menu. You can, of course, configure the palettes however you'd like, but for now let's explore the default configuration. Choose Window, Workspace, Default Workspace to return the palettes to their default locations. For more information on using palettes, workspaces, and keyboard shortcuts, refer to Chapter 4, "The Key That Makes It All Work: Integration."

The Objects Palette

On the left side of the screen is what appears to be a toolbox similar to that found in Photoshop, ImageReady, Illustrator, and InDesign. Looks, in this case, are deceiving, because in GoLive it is called the Objects palette, and it functions differently than the toolbox in the sibling apps. The Objects palette has a series of square buttons at the top. Clicking a button opens a set of objects in the lower portion of the palette. Hover your mouse over a button, and a ToolTip with the name of that set of objects will pop up. You can also select a set of objects by clicking the Palette Options button at the lower-right corner of the Objects palette and choosing the name of the set from the list. To limit the available objects shown to only those that conform to a specific Document Type Definition (DTD), choose Configure from the Palette Options and select the DTD of your choice.

Although the name of this palette is not Toolbox, you will find that you need to access it just as often as you use the tools in the graphics applications.

Those of you familiar with previous versions of GoLive might want to revert the Objects palette to its old look. You can easily do that by clicking the Toggle Orientation button at the lower left of the Object palette.

Did you Know?

You can use all the objects in the Objects palette (see Figure 9.6) by dragging and dropping them into place. You can also place many of them by double-clicking on them.

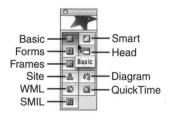

Basic — Smart
Forms — Head
Frames — Basic
Site — Diagram
WML — QuickTime
SMIL

FIGURE 9.6
The default configuration of the Objects palette includes the following sets of objects: Basic, Smart, Forms, Head, Frames, Site, Diagram, QuickTime, and SMIL.

The Inspector Palette

Objects are configured via the context-sensitive Inspector palette. For example, you could drag and drop a Table object from the Basic set of the Objects palette onto a page, and then set its attributes, such as the number of rows and columns or its width and height, via the Inspector palette. The Inspector palette will change according to whatever object is currently selected so that you can set the attributes for that particular object (see Figures 9.7 through 9.9). You can tell which object is selected by reading the label in the lower-left corner of the Inspector palette.

FIGURE 9.7
The Inspector palette offers attributes for the currently selected object. This figure shows a Table object selected.

FIGURE 9.8
The Inspector palette attributes with a Smart Object selected.

FIGURE 9.9
The Inspector palette attributes with a file selected.

The Toolbar

If GoLive has an Object palette where the sibling application's toolbox resides, does it mean that GoLive is toolbox-less? *Au contraire, mon ami!* If you look closely at the toolbar at the top of your screen, you'll see that what initially appears to be one toolbar is actually three toolbars docked together: the Main toolbar, the Document toolbar, and the Version Cue toolbar. You can turn one or all of the toolbars off via the Window menu, but you need to separate them first. Put your cursor over one of the dividers and it will turn into a white hand icon; now click and drag to detach a toolbar from its neighbors.

The Main toolbar is context-sensitive like the Inspector palette. It will contain a different set of tools depending on whether you are working on a page, a site, a layout grid, and so on (see Figure 9.10).

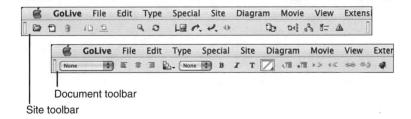

Document toolbar

Site toolbar

As we go through this chapter, we'll learn how to use the Objects palette, the toolbars, and the Inspector palette together to easily create pages, place images and text on those pages, link them together to build a Web site, and upload the whole caboodle to the Web server.

Understanding the Site Window

The site window is your best friend. Never work on individual pages without first opening the site window if you want your site to be trouble free. GoLive depends on the site window to do its heavy-duty link checking and site management; so heed this simple rule of thumb and your job will be significantly easier. Open a site now. Notice that the site window is split into two panes, and that each pane has a series of tabs across the top. There's a good reason for that...keep reading.

The Files Tab

Click the Files tab on the left side of the site window. Any item that will ultimately end up on the Web server, such as HTML pages, images, QuickTime movies, PDFs, or external CSS or JavaScript files, will be listed in the Files tab. This tab is a reflection of the items that physically exist in the web-content folder of the site.

From within the site window you can create new pages or folders, rename pages or folders, or move any of them around just as you would in the Mac's Finder or in Windows Explorer. The difference between doing those things on your desktop and doing them in the Site window is that when you use the Site window all your links and references remain intact. Promise me now that you will always work with your site window opened!

The Extras Tab

Now click the Extras tab on the right side of the site window. The Extras tab displays additional folders that were automatically created when you created a site or imported a site into GoLive. The purpose of those folders is to help you organize your project. The items housed here, such as templates, components, and Smart Objects, are used during the creation process, but because there is no need to upload them to the Web server, they are kept separate from the items shown in the Files tab. They physically exist in the folder called web-data.

Did you Know?

> Just as you can with palettes, you can tear off tabs in the site window and rearrange them as you like.

To close the right pane of the site window, click the Toggle Split View button in the lower-right corner (see Figure 9.11).

Contents of the web-content folder are listed in the Files tab
Contents of the web-data folder are listed in the Extras tab

FIGURE 9.11
The site window opens into two panes by default. You can close the right pane by clicking the button with a double arrow in the lower-right corner.

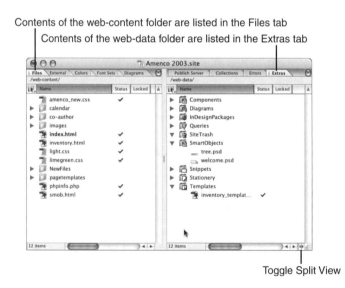

Toggle Split View

Did you Know?

> The web-content folder is the one that holds your home page, which is the default page that loads into a browser when someone visits your site. The web-content folder is also referred to as the root folder of your site.

The nine folders automatically created and displayed in the Extras tab are Components, Diagrams, InDesignPackages, Queries, SiteTrash, Smart Objects, Snippets, Stationery, and Templates. Let's define what is stored in these folders:

- ▶ **Components**—Components are pieces of a page that are reuseable. You may, for example, create a navigation bar and save it as a component. Then you simply drop the component onto a page and have all the links intact. Later, if you want to change a link on the navigation bar, you simply need to make the change to the component and GoLive will update all the pages on which you have used that component.

- ▶ **Diagrams**—Diagrams are a method of mapping out the architecture of your site before actually building it. You can create a hierarchy of folders and pages, show links between pages, add annotations, and more. Although diagrams are stored here, you open a diagram from the Diagram menu.

- ▶ **InDesignPackages**—If you havecreated a document in Adobe InDesign and want to reuse its elements in your Web site, you would invoke the Package for GoLive command in InDesign. Packages imported into GoLive are placed in the InDesignPackages folder.

- ▶ **Queries**—Queries are a powerful way to search for items in your site using multiple criteria. After you have created a query, you can save it. Saved queries are stored in the Queries folder.

- ▶ **SiteTrash**—The SiteTrash folder is a holding area for files you have removed from your site. They remain in the SiteTrash folder until you put them into your system trash.

- ▶ **SmartObjects**—This folder is where you can place native Photoshop, Illustrator, and Acrobat PDF files that you intend to use in your site. GoLive's Smart Object technology allows you to create Web-ready versions of these files while retaining a link to the original. Thus, if you update the original file, your Web version will update as well. More information on Smart Objects follows later in this chapter.

- ▶ **Snippets**—Pieces of HTML, images, text, or just about anything you might like to have handy to use throughout your site are stored in the Snippets folder.

- ▶ **Stationery**—You can design a page the way you like it, and save it into the Stationery folder. Later you can use the stationery to create a new page that is a duplicate of the original.

- ▶ **Templates**—Template pages work similarly to stationery, but are even more powerful. If you update a template page, all the pages that are based on that page will be updated, too.

Although all these items are stored in the web-data folder, which causes them to appear in the Extras tab of the Site window, the easiest way to use many of them is by dragging and dropping them from the Library palette, where they will also be listed.

To save a page as a component, stationery, or template, set up the page as necessary, choose Save As from the page's flyout menu, and select an option from the list. GoLive's Save dialog will open and take you directly to the appropriate folder on your hard drive. Give the file a descriptive name and save it. From then on the file will appear both in the corresponding folder in the Extras tab and in the Library palette.

Library Items

GoLive's Library palette is a repository for various reuseable items, each of which can be made accessible on an application-wide level or on a per-site level. Access the Library palette from the Window menu and look at the buttons across its top. Hovering your mouse pointer over a button for a second will produce a ToolTip with the button's label on it. (On a Mac, making the Library palette wider causes the buttons to expand and actually display the label names on the buttons, though this didn't appear to work on the Windows version.)

As with the Objects palette, each button in the Library reveals a different set of library objects. From left to right the buttons represent Snippets, Smart Objects, Components, Stationery, and Templates (see Figure 9.12). A definition of each of these items can be found in the preceding section.

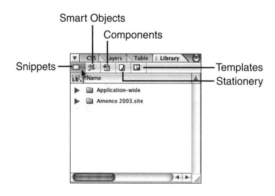

FIGURE 9.12
Use the buttons in the Library palette to access the various sets of library items.

Click the Snippets button and notice the folders listed there. The Application-wide folder will always be in the list, and any item inside that folder can be accessed at any time, no matter which site you are working on. The Library items from individual sites are available only when that site is opened (see Figure 9.13). You can drag an item from a site folder to the `Application-wide` folder to make it available application-wide. Likewise, you can add an item from the `Application-wide` folder to a particular site by dragging the file into the site folder.

FIGURE 9.13
Opened site's library items as well as the application-wide library items can be found in these folders.

To create a snippet, select anything on your page and drag it into one of the folders in the Snippets set of the Library palette. To use a snippet, drag it out of the folder and drop it onto a page. Snippets can contain any portion of a page including, but not limited to, tables, text, images, or links. You can also store source code in the snippets area.

Any file stored in the `SmartObject` folder of your site window will be listed in the Smart Objects portion of the Library palette. Add additional Smart Objects by dragging them into a folder. Use one by dragging it onto a page.

Components, like snippets, can be created from any part of a page. They are especially useful for elements that may change at times, such as a copyright notice. You use a regular blank page to set up the component as you'd like it; choose Save As, Save as Component from the page's flyout menu at the upper-right corner of the page; and then save it into the site's component folder. (For more information on how to modify a page, refer to the section "Using Basic Objects," later in this chapter.) The component will appear in the `Components` folder of the Extras tab and in the Components section of the Library palette. To use the Component, drag and drop it onto another page. To modify the component, double-click it. When you close or save the file, GoLive will prompt you to update any other files dependent on the component.

You can usestationery pages instead of opening a page and choosing Save As from the File menu. A page created from a stationery file looks exactly like the original; however, if the original is changed, that does not affect the look of the pages that have been created from it. To create a page based on the stationery, double-click it. In the dialog that appears, choose whether to create a new page or modify the existing stationery (see Figure 9.14).

FIGURE 9.14
Clicking Modify
allows you to edit
the Stationery
page, whereas
clicking Create cre-
ates a new page
based on the
Stationery page.

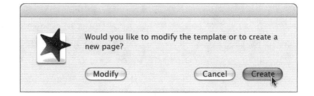

Create a template page by setting up the page and then opening the Template Regions palette from the Window menu. (You can find information on how to build pages later in this chapter, in the "Using Basic Objects" section.) For the page to be defined as a template, it needs to have at least one editable region. Regions that are not specified as editable cannot be modified in the pages made from the template. To define an editable region, select an area on the page and click the Create New Editable Region button in the lower right of the Template Regions palette (see Figure 9.15). You can rename the region if you'd like. When you are done assigning editable regions, choose Save As, Save as Template from the page's flyout menu. To create a page based on the template, double-click the template's name in the Library palette's Templates tab. In the dialog that appears, choose whether to create a new page or modify the existing template.

FIGURE 9.15
Only the designated
editable regions in
a template page
can be altered in
the pages subse-
quently created
from the template.

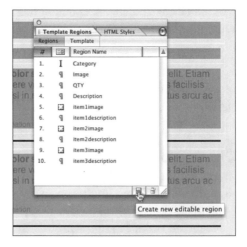

Adding Assets to the Site

Although it's obvious that there are lots of places to store things in your site win-dow, it's not quite as clear how you actually get items in there. GoLive, like the other CS apps, usually gives you several ways to approach a task. Let's explore those now. Make sure that your site window, not a document window, is in front.

Adding New Pages

To add a blank new page to your site, do any of the following:

- ▶ Choose File, New Page from the main menu bar.

- ▶ Control-click or right-click in the site window and choose New, New Page.

- ▶ Click the Site set of tools in the Objects palette, and then drag a generic page icon into the site window.

- ▶ Click the Site set of tools in the Objects palette, and then double-click the generic page icon.

The first option opens a new page with the generic filename untitled.html. GoLive appends a number to that name if you create more than one new page. After the page has opened, you must save it into your Files list for it to become part of the site. Choose File, Save As, and give the page an appropriate name.

In the Save dialog box is a handy-dandy button at the lower left that is a real time-saver. It's called the Site Folder button, and clicking on it reveals a direct shortcut to your root folder, as well as your Stationery, Components, and Templates folders (see Figure 9.16).

Did you Know?

FIGURE 9.16
The Site Folder button saves you time by bringing you directly to your root folder or other frequently accessed folders in your site.

The other three options in the list put the new page directly into the Files tab of the Site window and highlight the portion of the name that comes before the file extension. This makes it very easy to create a new page, and then immediately give it an appropriate name (see Figure 9.17). After the page has been named, you would simply double-click on it to open it.

By the
Way

When adding a new file by double-clicking from the Objects palette, you'll need to focus the pane and/or folder in which you want it to land. For example, if you want to create a new blank page inside the `Templates` folder in the Extras Tab, select the folder and then do the double-click trick.

Using the contextual menu method or dragging from the Site objects puts a new file into your site and immediately lets you name it.

If you need to create a file type other than a "generic" HTML page, you would choose File, New Special, and then the file type from the menu, or use your contextual menu and select one of the choices in the New menu.

Did you
Know?

If you save a file from an external source, for example, from Photoshop, into your site at the Finder or Explorer level, you'll need to click the Refresh View button in the Main toolbar to update your Files list.

Adding Folders

You'll want to organize your site in a logical way, and the easiest way to accomplish that task is by creating folders for the various sections of your site. To add a folder, click the Create New Folder button at the right end of the Main toolbar, or use the contextual menu by [Control-clicking] (right-clicking) in the site window and then selecting New, New Folder. You can also choose Site, New, URL from the menu. When the new folder is created, you can give it a name and then drag pages, images, multimedia files, and so forth into or out of the folder to create an easy-to-maintain structure.

A gray triangle on a Mac to the left of a folder name, or a plus sign on Windows, indicates that the folder has contents (see Figure 9.18). To reveal the contents of the folder, click on the triangle or the plus sign.

To open a folder, double-click on the folder icon. Instead of the folder merely opening to show the list of contents, this actually brings you down one level into the folder itself, which means you no longer see the items at the same level as the folder, but only the items inside the folder. To move back up a level, click the Upwards button found in the upper-left corner of both the left and right panes of the Site window.

FIGURE 9.18
A marking to the left of a folder indicates that the folder has contents.

Clicking the Upwards button when you are already at the root level of your site will open a Local File Browser that allows you to navigate through your hard drive.

Did you Know?

Deleting Files or Folders

To delete a file or folder, select it, and then click the Trash button on the Main Toolbar. This moves the item (and its contents if it's a folder) into the `SiteTrash` folder on the right side of the Site window. A dialog appears asking you to confirm the move. The great thing about the Site Trash is that if you've deleted an item in error, you can simply drag it back into the site at any time. To permanently delete a file or folder from your site, select it in the Site Trash and click the Trash button a second time. This moves the item into your Finder trash or Explorer Recycle Bin (see Figure 9.19).

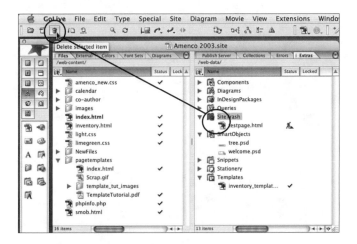

FIGURE 9.19
The `SiteTrash` folder is a built-in escape route should you need to recover a file you inadvertently deleted.

Adding Existing Files

Suppose you need to add files that already exist to your site? For example, you may have images, QuickTime movies, PDFs, Photoshop files, Illustrator files, JavaScript files, CSS files, or any number of other documents that you want to incorporate into your site. No problem. To add files to your site window, do one of the following:

▶ From the menu choose File, Import, Files to Site. When the dialog box opens, navigate through your drives and select the files that are to be added.

▶ Drag and drop a file or files from your drive directly into the Site window.

You can target a specific folder into which you want the files placed by first selecting it in the Files or Extras tab and then importing. When the importation is complete, the items will be inside the selected folder.

Site Window View Options

New in GoLive CS is the capability to view items in the Files, Extras, or Collections tab in various ways. GoLive's default view is List, but other options include Icons, Thumbnails, and Tiles. To change the view, (Control-click) [right-click] in the Site window, choose View, and then select your view option (see Figure 9.20).

FIGURE 9.20
You can view your Files list as Icons, List, Thumbnails, or Tiles. This shows both how to select the Tiles view and the Files tab of the site window in Tiles view.

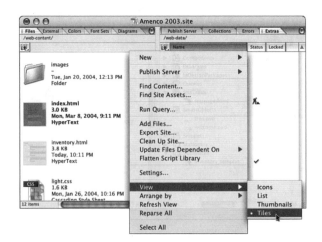

The External Tab

The External tab of the site window is an area to store external Uniform Resource Locators (URLs), which are unique addresses to any file on the Internet. External URLs specifically link to a location outside of your Web site. For example, if your site resides at www.mysite.com, a link to www.someothersite.com would be an external URL.

To create an external URL, click the External tab of the Site window, and then do one of the following:

▶ Click the Site set of Objects in the Objects palette, and then drag and drop a URL icon into the External tab.

▶ Click the Site set of Objects in the Objects palette, and then double-click the URL icon.

▶ (Control-click) [right-click] and select New URL from the menu.

▶ Choose Site, New, URL from the main menu bar.

Select an external URL in the External tab and use the Inspector palette to set up the link's name and URL (see Figure 9.21). Later, when you drag the External URL icon onto a page, a link will automatically be made using the text from the Name field and the URL from the URL field.

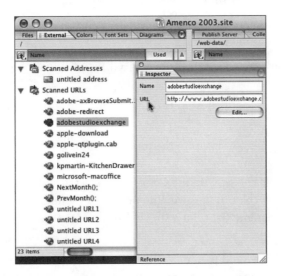

FIGURE 9.21
Set an external URL's name and URL in the Inspector palette.

You can also link to an external URL using the Fetch URL tool as described later in this chapter, in the section "Creating Hyperlinks."

> If you want to link to an external URL, but don't have the External tab selected, simply employ the Fetch URL tool; point and shoot at the External tab, which will pop it to the front; and then select the URL from the list.

If you have pages in your site that already contain external URLs, you can add those URLs to the list in your External tab by selecting Site, Get References Used from the main menu bar. Likewise, you can remove unused URLs by choosing Site, Remove Unused References. You can check the validity of external URLs by choosing Site, Check External Links. Finally, you can delete an external URL by selecting it and pressing Delete on your keyboard.

E-mail addresses can also be stored in the External tab, and then dragged onto a page to automatically create a link that opens the visitor's e-mail application.

The Colors Tab

The Colors tab of the site window is a special place for you to designate the color scheme of your sites. You create colors there that you can then reuse throughout your site to color text, tables, and more. To create a site color, click the Colors tab of the site window, and then do one of the following:

- ▶ Click the Site set of Objects in the Objects palette, and then drag and drop a Color icon into the External tab.

- ▶ Click the Site set of Objects in the Objects palette, and then double-click the Color icon.

- ▶ (Control-click) [right-click] in the Colors tab, and select New Color from the menu.

- ▶ Choose Site, New, Color from the main menu bar.

After placing a color object into the Colors tab, select it and assign it a color, either by clicking a color in the Swatches palette or by mixing a color in the Color palette. You can rename the color either in the Colors tab or via the Inspector palette.

To add colors already used in your site to the list in the Color tab, choose Site, Get Colors Used. Similarly, you can remove unused colors from the list in the tab by choosing Site, Remove Unused Colors. To delete a color from the list, select it and click the Trash button in the Main toolbar, or invoke the contextual menu for the selected color and choose Delete.

Colors listed in the Colors tab also make an appearance in the Swatches palette. Put a few colors into the Colors tab, then Choose Window, Swatches to open the Swatches palette. Click the palette menu button (the right-facing arrow in a circle at the upper right of the palette) and choose Site Colors (see Figure 9.22). Notice that the colors are the same as those in the Colors tab.

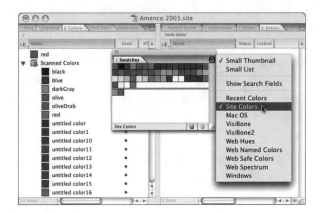

FIGURE 9.22
Colors assigned in the Colors tab will also appear in the Site Colors section of the Swatches palette.

The Font Sets Tab

Fonts on the Web are an interesting thing because no matter which font you assign to text on a page, the visitor must have the same font on his computer for the text to look the same way in his browser as it does in yours. Font sets are listings of fonts assigned to text that help get around this limitation somewhat. The font that is listed first is the one the browser will attempt to load first. If it does not find the font on the visitor's computer, it looks for the second font in the list and so on.

> Although font sets, which write <font> tags into the HTML, are still valid today, it is highly recommended that you use Cascading Style Sheets to format your text instead. CSS gives you more flexibility and allows you to make quick updates simply by editing the style sheet. You'll find more information in the section "Using Cascading Style Sheets," later in this chapter.

By the Way

To create a font set, click the Font Sets tab of the Site window, and then do one of the following:

▶ Click the Site set of Objects in the Objects palette, and then drag and drop a Font Set icon into the Font Sets tab.

▶ Click the Site set of Objects in the Objects palette, and then double-click the Font Set icon.

▶ (Control-click) [right-click] in the Font Sets tab, and select New Font Set from the menu.

▶ Choose Site, New, Font Set from the main menu bar.

Next, use the Inspector palette to set the attributes of the font set (see Figure 9.23). Select a name for the Font set and type it into the Name field. Click the Create New Font Family button at the bottom of the Inspector palette to add a prede-fined font set, or the New Font button to add individual fonts to a font set. Move fonts up or down in the font set list using the arrows in the Inspector palette. Delete a font from a set by selecting it in the list in the Inspector palette and click-ing the Trash button. Delete an entire font set by selecting it in the Font set tab and pressing the Delete key on your keyboard.

FIGURE 9.23
Define a font set in the Inspector palette.

To assign a font set to text, first select the text on the page. Then from the menu bar choose Type, Font, and select the name of the set from the list.

Did you Know?

> To remove font tags from text, use this handy method. Choose Window, HTML Styles from the menu bar. Select the text, and then from the palette flyout menu choose Clear Inline Styles and Clear Paragraph Styles. This should remove any font format-ting previously applied.

Queries and Collections

Queries and collections, though two different features, are very powerful when used in combination. Use queries to define complex searches that you can run on a page, on a range of pages, on a site, or application-wide. You can even run queries on the results of other queries to get really granular. Queries differ from the normal Find dialog because via a query you can search on much more than text. For example, you can run a query to find a set of files that were modified on a certain day, or all pages that contain a table. The options for creating queries are vast, and you'll quickly see how useful they are for managing large sites.

Collections are any particular set of files that you define. For example, if you had a Web site with pages nested several directories down that often need updating, you could create a collection of those pages. Then, instead of having to navigate through multiple directories to reach those files, you'd simply double-click the name of the collection in the Collections tab and those pages would be listed at the top level.

The results of a query can be saved as a collection, and a query can be attached to a collection so that it can be updated as necessary.

Running Queries

To run a query, choose Edit, Run Query from the menu bar. Select a query from the list and click Start, or click the New Query button to create a new query. Select a query from the list and click Edit Query if you want to change a query that already exists. Give your query a description, and then choose an option from the Find What pop-up menu. After you've made your selection, you can add criteria by clicking the little circle with the right-facing arrow in it and choosing an And, Or, or Not item. An And item means that both the first and second criteria must be met, an Or item means that one or the other must be met, and a Not item means that the first item must be met while the second must not be met. You can continue to add criteria to your heart's content (see Figure 9.24).

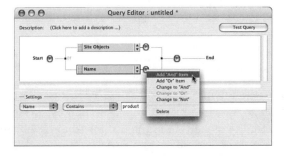

FIGURE 9.24
Create very specific searches in the Queries dialog box.

Click the Test Query button to test the query. You can remove items from the results by selecting them and clicking the Remove button, save the results as a collection by clicking the Save Collection button, or click the Use Results button to run another query on the results of the first query (see Figure 9.25). If you think you'll reuse the query, you should save it.

FIGURE 9.25
By clicking Use Results to run additional queries on the results of the first query, you can get searches that are incredibly granular!

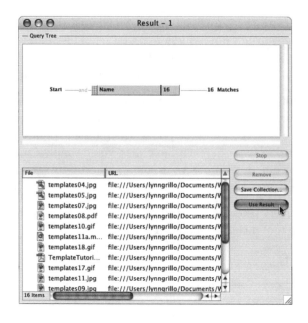

Creating Collections

To create a collection, click the Collections tab of the Site window, and then do one of the following:

▶ Click the Site set of Objects in the Objects palette, and then drag and drop a Collections icon into the Collections tab.

▶ Click the Site set of Objects in the Objects palette, and then double-click the Collections icon.

▶ (Control-click) [right-click] in the Collections tab, and select New Collection from the menu.

▶ Choose Site, New, Collection from the main menu bar.

Drag files from the Files tab into your collection. With the collection selected, use the Inspector palette to attach a query to the collection by clicking the Attach button and then selecting a query from the list (see Figure 9.26). You can also use the buttons in the Inspector palette to run or edit the query.

FIGURE 9.26
Use the Collection Inspector to permanently attach a query to a collection.

Designing Pages

When you make a new page, Adobe GoLive automatically puts the words *Untitled Page* in the Title field. Remember to change these words to something that better indicates the content of your page. Keep in mind that search engines use the title of a page to determine whether it is relevant to a search, so choose your title carefully. Click into the Title field at the top of the page to select the default title, and then simply type in the new title (see Figure 9.27).

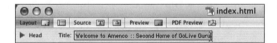

FIGURE 9.27
Search engines rely on descriptive titles. Don't forget to add one to your pages.

With your title in place, you're ready to begin building your page. You'll have your choice of several editing modes. Let's take a look at the editing modes and how they are used.

Page Editing Modes

Not everyone approaches building a Web page the same way. Some people have creative minds and like to work as they would in a page layout application. Other folks prefer to hand-code their HTML. Fortunately, GoLive CS has a set of tools to satisfy everyone.

When you open an HTML page in GoLive, you'll notice a set of buttons across the top. Those buttons represent the various page editing modes (see Figure 9.28). Each mode has unique features, so you will probably find yourself using a combination of editing modes as you become more familiar with GoLive.

The Layout Editor

You may have heard the acronym WYSIWYG (pronounced whizzy-wig), which stands for "what you see is what you get." WYSIWYG Web editors provide a visual process for designing pages, rather than requiring the developer to write HTML syntax. The Layout editor is the visual mode that works like a page layout program. You can drag images onto the page, type text, and use GoLive layout grids, tables, and layers to position elements just the way you like them, all without writing a line of HTML code.

The Layout Editor has two sections, the head section and the body section. When you first open a new page, the blank area that takes up most of the space is the body section. If you click the gray arrow at the upper left of the page next to the word *Head*, you'll toggle open the head portion of the page (see Figure 9.29). The difference between these two areas is that the body portion is what loads into the browser window, whereas the head portion is used to give directions to the browser. The head section is where you put meta tags, such as the keywords or description meta tags that are used by search engines to index your site, links to external CSS and JavaScript pages, and more. There is a whole set of objects in the Objects palette devoted to the head portion of the page. You can drag any head object and drop it onto a page and then configure it using the Inspector palette.

Next to the Head toggle is the page's title. By default, a new page uses the title Untitled Page, so remember to change it. You can do so by clicking in the Title field here and typing a new title.

At the upper right of the page are four buttons. The first, called Properties, opens the Page Properties Inspector when clicked. Use the Inspector as an alternative way of setting the page's title, or to select text and background colors other than the default (see Figure 9.30).

FIGURE 9.30
The Page
Properties
Inspector.

You can also use the Page Properties Inspector to designate a background image for a page. Images used in the background of HTML pages tile when they are displayed, meaning that they repeat. Small images are usually designed to tile seamlessly, giving the appearance of one large image, similar to the way wallpaper looks. If you prefer to use a large image that you don't want to repeat, you should consider using CSS to define the background image for the page. For more about CSS, refer to the section "Using Cascading Style Sheets," later in this chapter.

At the bottom of the page are more tools. On the left is the markup tree. Click anywhere in your document and the markup tree will indicate where you are in the hierarchy of the tag structure. You can select elements on your page by clicking a tag in the markup tree. If you click and hold on a tag in the markup tree, a list of elements contained within that tag will appear. You can navigate to a particular element by selecting it from the list (see Figure 9.31).

At the lower right of the Layout editor are the zoom tools and the layout dimensions. Use the plus and minus buttons to zoom in and out of your page as shown in Figure 9.32, or choose a percentage of zoom from the Zoom Value pop-up. The Layout Dimensions menu lets you choose the page size for your design. For example, if you needed to create a design that fits into a 720-pixel-wide page, you would select that size from the Layout Dimensions pop-up.

FIGURE 9.31
The markup tree is
a very convenient
way to select ele-
ments on a page.

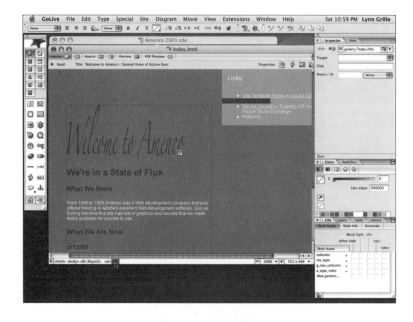

FIGURE 9.32
Zoom in and out of
your page, or
choose a size into
which you'd like to
fit your design.

The Frame Editor

Frames are a method of splitting up a browser window into sections so that you
can load different pages into each section. A common example of this is to have
a navigation frame that does not change containing links to other pages. When
clicked, the links load the other pages into a separate frame in the browser window. Frames mode allows you to drag and drop ready-made framesets from the
Frames tab of the Object palette into the Frame Editor. After you've added a
frameset, use the Inspector palette to edit the properties for both the frameset and
the individual frames contained within it.

When you drag a frameset object into the Frame Editor, GoLive may prompt you
to change the doctype (Document Type Declaration). The doctype specifies which
Document Type Definition (DTD) the browser should use when rendering the
page. Specifically, it states which version of HTML the page is using, and in the
case of frameset page a specific DTD is required. GoLive makes this easy for you
by checking to see whether the correct doctype is in place and by prompting you
if it is not. In most cases you should accept GoLive's recommendation if you get a
dialog box asking whether you'd like to change the doctype.

After a frameset has been placed into the Frame Editor, click in any frame and take a look at the Inspector palette. You'll notice two buttons, one for setting the frame attributes and one for setting the frameset attributes (see Figure 9.33).

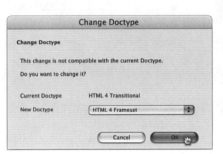

FIGURE 9.33
GoLive helpfully reminds you to change to the appropriate doctype for frames, and then lets you set frameset and frame attributes in the Inspector palette.

The Frame and the Frameset buttons in the Inspector palette offer various attributes you can edit:

▶ **Frame**—This button allows you to set the width and height of a frame, give the frame a name and an ID, link the frame to the page it will load, and choose the scrolling method. You can also create a new frame by clicking the appropriate button in the Inspector to add a frame before or after the currently selected frame, or to split the selected frame into two.

▶ **FrameSet**—This button allows you to set the orientation of the frames and set border attributes such as color and size.

Remember, a frameset is only part of the equation. You need to fill the individual frames with content, which means you must assign an HTML page to each frame. If a frameset has two frames, you must create two HTML pages to fill them, one for each frame. To assign a page to a frame, select the frame by clicking on it, and then use the Inspector palette to link to the page.

The Source Code Editor

Source mode is where the HTML code is actually generated. This mode is fully editable, and changes made here are reflected in the other modes. GoLive's Source Code Editor is very, very powerful, with new features such as themes, code markers, and code completion (see Figure 9.34).

FIGURE 9.34
The Source Code Editor.

Across the top of the page in Source mode are the following tools:

▶ **Check Syntax**—The lightning-bolt icon at the upper left of the page opens and runs the Syntax Checker.

▶ **Themes**—The Theme pop-up allows you to choose a color theme in which to view your syntax. Several themes are loaded by default, but you can edit themes and create custom themes in the Source section of GoLive's preferences.

▶ **Colorize Code**—To toggle the code colorization on and off, click the Colorize Code button.

▶ **Word Wrap**—Word Wrap wraps the code so that it is all viewable within the document window.

▶ **Display Line Numbers**—To turn the line numbers on and off, click the Display Line Numbers button.

▶ **Navigate Through Code**—New in GoLive CS is the capability to set markers in your source code.

Navigate Through Code comes in handy when you have specific areas of a page that you edit often. By placing a marker at that spot, you can jump directly to it. To create a marker in your code, place your cursor where you want the marker to go; then click and hold the Navigate Through Code button and select New Marker. When the dialog appears, give your marker a name. Now, when you want to jump to that marker, click and hold down the Navigate Through Code button and select the marker name from the list.

The Outline Editor

A unique and powerful way to edit your page, Outline mode allows you to work quickly by grouping tags together and offering pop-up menus of the attributes available for those tags. This is especially helpful to more advanced users who are familiar with HTML (see Figure 9.35).

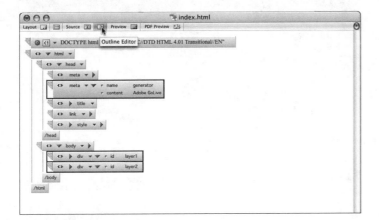

FIGURE 9.35
The Outline Editor shows your tags in pairs.

Split Source View

In the lower-left corner of the Layout, Frame, or Outline Editor is a small button with a double arrow on it called Show/Hide Split Source (see Figure 9.36). Clicking this button toggles the split source open and closed. This allows you to have two modes open at the same time—for example, you can have the Layout Editor on the top and the Source Code Editor on the bottom. (Option-click) [Alt-click] on the Split Source button to switch between orientations. One click moves the source code to the right, the next click puts it at the top, and one more click puts it on the left. When you toggle the split source off, it remains in the last orientation you used.

Preview Mode

The Preview tab lets you see what your page will look like in a real browser. On the Mac the Preview mode is rendered via the embedded Opera browser, whereas on Windows it is via Internet Explorer. Although having built-in previews is extremely helpful, as a Web designer you still need to preview and test your work in multiple browsers to be certain that your pages look and function in the manner you intended. Because the way a page behaves can vary greatly among browser types and versions, the only way to be certain your site will work as intended is to test across multiple browsers.

FIGURE 9.36
Work in Layout
mode and see the
source code at the
same time by using
Split Source.

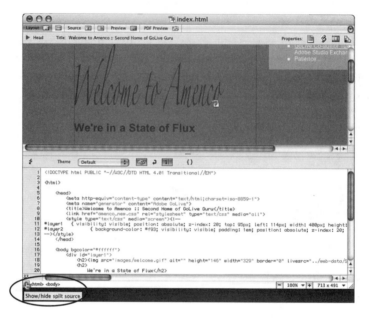

FIGURE 9.36
Work in Layout mode and see the source code at the same time by using Split Source.

PDF Preview

PDF Preview is an easy way to preview how the page will look as a PDF and to export to PDF. While in the PDF Preview mode, use the Creation, Page, and Description sections of the Inspector palette to set attributes, such as the version of PDF you'd like to use, whether to embed fonts and multimedia, the page margins and orientation, and the addition of metadata. When you've made your selections, use the buttons on the Main toolbar to export to PDF or to print (see Figure 9.37).

Using Live Rendering or Preview in Browser

Besides the Preview tab found in the document window, there are two additional ways to preview your pages. You can use the new Live Rendering window or use an actual browser. The Live Rendering window is really an embedded browser, and with this window opened, you can work in the Layout, Frames, Source, or Outline editing modes and see how your pages render as you make your edits.

To open the Live Rendering window, choose File, Preview In, Live Rendering. The Live Rendering window will preview the frontmost page you have opened. If you switch to another page, that page will load into the Live Rendering window.

To keep a particular page loaded in the Live Rendering window, you can choose Bound from the Live Rendering flyout menu (see Figure 9.38).

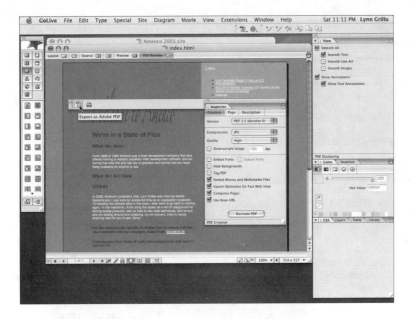

FIGURE 9.37
The PDF Preview mode, PDF Inspector, and tools.

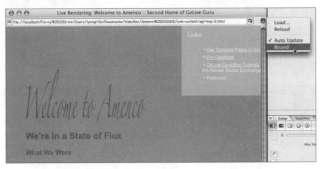

FIGURE 9.38
Use the Live Rendering window to preview pages and test links.

You can also bind the Live Rendering window to a specific file by using the Fetch URL button at the upper left of the window. Click on the little coil button and drag to a file in your Files tab. The selected file will load into the Live Rendering window and stay loaded no matter which file you are working on. Choosing Load from the Live Rendering window's flyout menu brings up a Choose window that allows you to navigate through your hard drive to load a particular file into the Live Rendering window. Reload refreshes the current window so that any changes made are updated. Finally, you can have more than one Live Rendering window opened at once.

If you have a live connection to the Internet, you can type a URL into the Live Rendering window's location bar, and the page from the Internet will load.

Besides the Live Rendering window, there is also a very easy way to preview pages in any browser that you currently have installed. Follow these steps to select the browsers for previewing:

1. Open the preferences panel by selecting (GoLive, Preferences) [Edit, Preferences].

2. Select Browsers on the left site of the Preferences window.

3. Click Find All at the lower left of the window, or click Add to navigate to a specific Browser, select it, and then click Open to add it to the list.

When you select Find All, GoLive will search through your hard drive, locate any installed browsers, and list them in the right pane (see Figure 9.39).

FIGURE 9.39
Browser
Preferences with
Safari chosen as
the default.

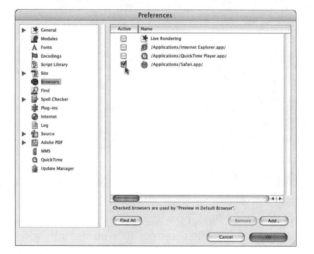

These browsers will be available to you from the Show in Browser button in the Main toolbar. To the left of each browser in the list is a check box. Select the browser you would like to have as your default for previewing your work by clicking the check box next to it. If you check off more than one browser in your list, then when you click the Preview in Browser button on the toolbar, the page you are previewing will open simultaneously in all the checked browsers.

After you have designated the browser(s) you would like to use for previewing, open a document and take a look at the Document toolbar. There is an icon on the right that looks like a browser icon. To the right of it is a small black triangle. That little arrow displays a pop-up menu when you hold down your mouse on it. To preview a page, click the Show in Browser button on the toolbar or select the browser of your choice from the pop-up menu.

Using Basic Objects

The Basic set of the Objects palette has objects that are frequently used during the building of pages. In this section we'll discuss the most used objects of the Basic set (see Figure 9.40).

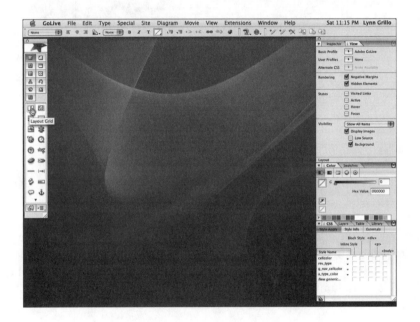

FIGURE 9.40
The Basic set of the Objects palette.

> To identify an object in the Objects palette, hold your cursor over the icon for a few seconds, which will cause a ToolTip to appear with the name of the object. For more information on that object, go to GoLive's Help menu and choose Help, GoLive Help, and then run a search on the object's name.

Using the Layout Grid

What the heck is a layout grid? In essence, GoLive's layout grids are nothing more than elaborate tables. Grids are an excellent tool for novice designers to use, offering a flexibility and precision that is difficult to achieve using regular tables.

A GoLive layout grid resembles a piece of graph paper (see Figure 9.41). It is divided into vertical and horizontal gridlines, which aid you in placing objects on your page with pixel precision. By default, the dimensions of a new grid are 200 by 200 pixels. To put a layout grid on a page, either drag and drop from the Objects palette, double-click the Layout Grid icon, or (Control-click) [right-click] and choose Insert Object, Basic, Layout Grid.

FIGURE 9.41
A standard layout grid.

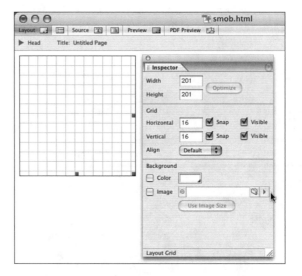

You can resize the grid by dragging its lower-right corner or by typing the dimensions in pixels into the Width and Height fields of the Inspector palette. A default grid has gridlines every 16 pixels both horizontally and vertically. To alter the gridlines, type a number into the Horizontal and Vertical fields in the Inspector palette.

If you'd like an object placed on the grid to snap into position, leave Snap turned on in the Inspector palette. You can turn the visibility of the gridlines on or off by checking Visible in the Inspector palette, but they work the same whether or not they are visible.

New in GoLive CS is a very cool feature called Smart Guides. Borrowed from Illustrator, where they first made an appearance, Smart Guides allow you to drag objects around on the grid, and whenever an object lines up with the edge of another object, a guide will appear, allowing you to precisely align the two. Smart Guides also appear when you're working with layers so that layers can easily be aligned to one another.

You can set the background color of a layout grid by clicking the rectangular color well in the Inspector palette, and then clicking a color in the Swatches or Color palette. Alternatively, you may want to have an image in the background of a grid. You can accomplish that task by enabling the check mark next to Image in the Inspector, and then using the Fetch URL tool to point and shoot to an image in your site window. The image will be placed into the background of the grid (see Figure 9.42). If the grid is smaller than the image, only the portion of the image covered by the grid will be shown. To fit the grid to the image size, click the Use Image Size button. If the image is smaller than the grid, it will tile. Again, you can click the Use Image Size button to fit the grid to the size of the background image.

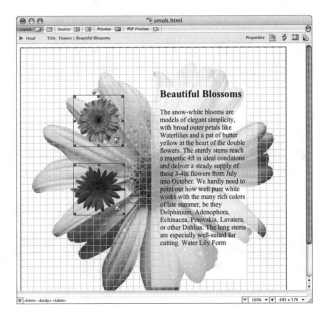

FIGURE 9.42
Images can be placed onto a grid, and even used as a background.

A layout grid can be placed directly onto a page, inside a table, on top of another grid, or inside a layer, and nearly everything that can be placed onto a page can also be placed onto a layout grid. For instance, you can drag and drop images onto a grid, and then align them using the Align palette (Window, Align). You can put a layout text box, found in the Basics set of the Objects palette, onto a grid, and then put text into it.

Using the arrow keys on your keyboard, you can move objects on the grid. Select an object and press an arrow key, and the object moves to the next gridline. To move the object one pixel at a time, hold down the (Option) [Ctrl] key and then use the arrow keys. This little trick comes in handy if you want to snuggle sliced graphics up against one another.

> A neat trick is to target the grid. Click on the grid at any point where two gridlines intersect, and then look closely. You see that the corner you clicked has a little blinking marker on it. Now, if you double-click an object in the Objects palette, the object will land exactly at the point you targeted.

With an object on a layout grid active (selected), the Main toolbar offers a special set of controls for positioning objects on the grid (see Figure 9.43).

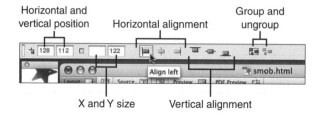

FIGURE 9.43
With a layout grid ʋe,ʿcted, the Main toc.bar displays these settings.

Here's a rundown on what each tool does:

- ▶ **Horizontal and Vertical Position**—These boxes allow you to type in numerically the position of the object on the grid relative to the left and top margins of the page.

- ▶ **X and Y Size**—You can designate the size of an object by typing the desired dimensions into the X and Y boxes.

- ▶ **Horizontal Alignment**—This aligns an object relative to the grid itself. You can align an object to the left, center, or right of the grid.

- ▶ **Vertical Alignment**—Similar to Horizontal, except that this aligns object to the top, middle, or bottom of the grid.

- ▶ **Group and Ungroup**—With several objects selected, clicking the Group button locks them in place relative to one another.

Grouping is useful, for example, when you want to move a whole set of buttons to another place on the grid without affecting the spacing between them. Ungrouping returns grouped items to individual objects once again.

If you'd like to convert a layout grid into a regular table, you can do so by choosing Layout Grid to Table, from the Special menu.

Using Tables

By default, GoLive creates a table that is 180 pixels in width, consisting of three rows and three columns. It has a border of 1 pixel, cell padding of 0 pixels, and cell spacing of 2 pixels (see Figure 9.44). Let's learn what all that means, and how you can alter those settings to create the kind of table you want.

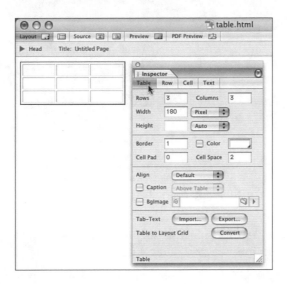

FIGURE 9.44
A default three-row by three-column table and the Table Inspector.

To put a table on a page, you can drag and drop from the Objects palette, double-click the Table icon in the Objects palette, or (Control-click) [right-click] and choose Insert Object, Basic, Table. Click once on the left or top border of the table to select it.

> If you hold down the (⌘) [Ctrl] key while you click the Table object in the Objects palette, you can drag out a table to the specific number of rows and columns you need. Let go of the modifier key when you've got the table the way you want it, and then continue to drag the table and drop it on your page.

Did you Know?

With the table selected, the context-sensitive Inspector becomes the Table Inspector. There are four tabs in the Table Inspector: Table, Row, Cell, and Text. All four tabs are visible, and selectable, when you're working on a table, but only the attributes that can be applied to the portion you are working on will be available for use. Those that are unavailable will be grayed out. GoLive helps you work efficiently by switching to the correct tab based on your selection. For example, if you select a cell within the table, the Inspector reacts by bringing the Cell tab to the front (see Figure 9.45).

FIGURE 9.45
The Table Inspector
with a cell
selected.

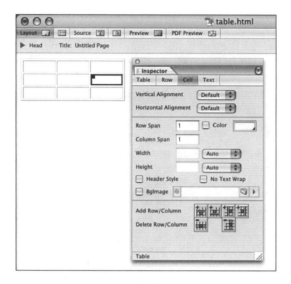

Let's take a look at the Table tab of the Inspector, where you can set the dimensions of your table:

- ▶ **Rows and Columns**—Type a number into the Rows and Columns fields to indicate the number of rows and columns you want.

- ▶ **Width**—Set the width of your entire table in pixels, by percentage, or to Auto. Choosing Pixels sets your table at a fixed width. Percentage allows your table to expand or contract according to the width of the page. For example, if you set the percentage at 50, the table will always be half of the width of the browser window, no matter how large or small that may be. Auto means that the table will expand to accommodate whatever elements you put into it.

- ▶ **Height**—As with the width, you can set the height of your table in pixels, by percentage, or to Auto.

- ▶ **Border**—This attribute draws a border around the table that by default has a 3D appearance. Set the size of the border in pixels by typing a number into the Border field.

- ▶ **Cell Pad**—Cell padding is the space between an element in a cell and the edge of the cell. For instance, if you place a graphic inside a cell, and set the cell padding at 5 pixels, GoLive will add a 5-pixel space between the edge of the graphic and the edge of the cell.

- ▶ **Cell Space**—Cell spacing is the amount of space between adjacent cells.

▶ **Color**—You can set the background color of your table by clicking inside the color well (the rectangle next to Color), and then clicking a color in the Swatches or Color palette.

▶ **Align**—This pop-up menu gives you the option of aligning your table to the right, left or center of other objects or text on the page.

▶ **Caption**—Check the box next to the word *Caption* and choose Above Table or Below Table from the pop-up menu to create a space above or below the table in which you can type a caption.

▶ **Import**—Use the Import button if you want to bring tab-, comma-, space-, or semicolon-delimited data into a table document. To do so, place a Table object onto your page. With the table selected, click the Browse button in the Inspector and navigate through your hard drive to the file containing the data you want to import. Choose the delimiter type from the pop-up menu in the dialog and click Open.

▶ **Export**—Use the Export button if you want to take data from a table and export it as a delimited text file.

▶ **Convert**—Use the Convert button to change your table to a layout grid.

There is a difference between selecting a cell and selecting the contents of a cell. They are two entirely different animals. If you see a blinking cursor inside the cell, it is in Text Edit mode, meaning you can type or drag items into the cell. To apply attributes to a cell, though, you need to select the cell itself. You will know that a cell has been selected when there is a black line around the inside of it with a small black square in the upper-left corner. To select a cell, click once on the bottom or right border of the cell. If you are in Text Edit mode within a cell, you can press (Control-Return) [Ctrl+Enter] to select the cell. To return to Text Edit mode, press Enter.

Selecting Table Rows and Columns

To select an entire row, place your cursor over the left border of the row until you see a right-facing arrow, and then click. Use the same technique to select a column, but place the cursor over the top border of the column. You can also drag across an entire range of cells to select them, or use Shift-click to select cells in different areas of the table.

Adding Table Rows and Columns

Flexibility is the name of the game in GoLive. So there are several ways to add rows and columns to your table:

▶ Select a cell, and then click the Add Row or Add Column button in the Cell tab of the Table Inspector.

▶ Change the number in the Rows or Columns field in the Table tab of the Inspector.

▶ To add a column before another column, select a cell in the column to the right of the spot where you want to add the column and type the + sign on your numeric keypad.

▶ To add rows at the bottom of the table, select a bottom cell, hold down the (⌘ key) [Ctrl+Shift keys] and drag the bottom border of the table.

▶ To add columns to the right side of a table, select a right cell, hold down (⌘) [Ctrl+Shift] and drag the right border of the table.

Deleting Table Rows and Columns

What if you decide to remove a row or column? You can do so in the following ways:

▶ Select a cell, and then click the Delete Row or Delete Column button in the Cell tab of the Table Inspector.

▶ Change the number in the Rows or Columns field in the Table tab of the Inspector.

▶ To delete a column or row, select the column or row and press the Delete key on your keyboard.

Spanning Table Cells

You may find that you want to create a layout that requires a long open column at the left of the table, and small multicell columns on the right. One way to approach this would be to span cells. You can do so in either of two ways:

▶ Select a cell, and then type a number into either the Span Row or the Span Column field found in the Cell tab of the Table Inspector.

▶ Select a cell, and then press Shift-right arrow to span across rows, or Shift-down arrow to span across columns. Use Shift-up arrow or Shift-left arrow to decrease the span.

By the Way

Be aware that when you're spanning cells, content in the selected cell remains intact, but content in the cells added to the right or bottom is lost.

You might find it more convenient to use the Table palette to navigate through and make selections in tables. Open the Table palette from the Window menu and notice that all the selection techniques mentioned for tables work just as nicely, if not more easily, in the Table palette. Additionally, if you have nested tables, you can move up one level by clicking the Select Parent table button, or down one level by clicking into a cell that contains the nested table. The Table palette also gives you access to sorting tools and table styles (see Figure 9.46).

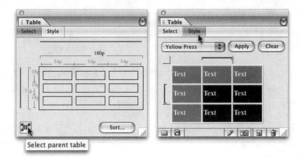

FIGURE 9.46
The Table palette's Select and Style modes.

Using Layers

Layers, formerly referred to as floating boxes in GoLive 5 and 6, are rendered via the use of DHTML, or Dynamic Hypertext Markup Language. Layers can be positioned anywhere on your page and can contain any other element, such as text or images. You can stack layers on top of one another, make a layer visible or invisible, and animate a layer.

When working with layers, you'll use both the Inspector palette and the Layers palette. The Inspector palette is where you'll set the attributes for a layer, and the Layers palette is where you'll see a list of the layers on your page. You may also use the DHTML Timeline Editor to animate layers, but let's not get ahead of ourselves! Begin by opening the Layers palette from the Window menu.

To put a layer on a page, do one of the following:

▶ Drag and drop from the Objects palette onto the page.

▶ Double-click the Layer icon in the Objects palette.

▶ (Control-click) [right-click] and choose Insert Object, Basic, Layer.

▶ Click the New Layer button in the Layers palette.

To select a layer, place your cursor over one of its edges until you see the sideways hand icon, and then click. Notice that when a layer is selected, the Inspector palette shows three buttons across the top. By default, the Layer area is selected (see Figure 9.47). It offers the following options:

- **Name**—It's important to name each layer. By default, GoLive names your layers incrementally—layer1, layer2, and so on. However, giving a layer a name that describes its contents is a better choice.

- **Top, Right, Bottom, Left**—These options are for positioning. By default, layers are positioned from the upper-left corner of the page.

- **Width, Height**—These attributes designate the size of the layer.

- **Z-index**—Z-index is the stacking order of layers. A higher number is higher in the stacking order. The stacking order is important if you intend to overlap layers in a particular way, or for animating layers.

- **Visible**—Turns off the visibility of a layer in the browser. This differs from the visibility choice in the Layers palette, which merely hides or shows a layer while you are working, but which has no bearing on whether a layer appears in the browser.

FIGURE 9.47
The Layer
Inspector.

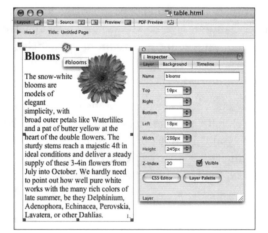

> **Did you Know?**
>
> When assigning a Z-index to your layers, you may want to use increments of 10. That way, if you need to insert a new layer between two existing layers, you can do so without having to reorder all the layers.

Click the Background button and you'll see options for giving your layer a background color or image. To give the layer a color, click the color well, and then click a color in the Swatches palette. To use a background image, click the check box next to Image and use the Fetch URL tool to point and shoot to an image in your Web site. Buttons to open both the CSS Editor and the Layers palette are conveniently located in both the Layer and the Background portions of the Layer Inspector.

The Timeline button offers options for animating layers. To do a simple animation, select a layer and then click the Record button. Move the selected layer around the page. Notice that a line with tiny squares on it is drawn on the page. That line is the path of the animation, and the squares are keyframes in the animation. Switch over to the Preview tab of the document to see the animation play. (Remember, the layer needs to have something in it, or you won't see a thing!) To do more complex animations, click the Open Timeline Editor button to access the Timeline Editor (see Figure 9.48).

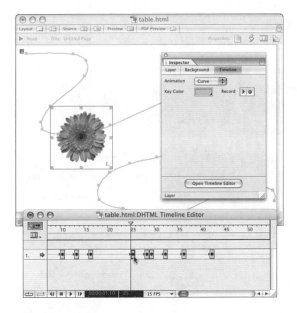

FIGURE 9.48
When you animate a layer, a path including keyframes is drawn. Edit the keyframes in the DHTML Timeline Editor.

To move a layer, simply select it and drag it into position on your page. You'll notice that if you have more than one layer on a page, as one layer lines up with the edge of another a guide will appear, allowing you to perfectly align the two layers. This is called Smart Guides and is a new feature of GoLive CS.

When you have multiple layers on a page, it's helpful to use the Layers palette to select them. You can also use the Layers palette to create a new layer, delete a layer, lock a layer to keep it from accidentally being moved, or hide a layer so that it's out of the way while you are working on parts of your page (see Figure 9.49). Remember, turning a layer off in the Layers palette turns it off only in the Layout Editor. That layer, if set to visible in the Inspector palette, will still show in the browser. The following options will help you create, delete, reorder, and manage layers:

▶ To add a new layer, click the Create New Layer button at the bottom of the Layers palette.

▶ To delete a layer, select one or more layers in the list, and then click the Trash button at the bottom of the Layers palette.

▶ To rename a layer, select it in the list and then click a second time to go into edit mode. Type the new name over the old name.

▶ To turn off a layer, click the eye icon next to its name.

▶ To lock a layer, click the lock icon next to its name.

▶ To edit a layer's Z-index, select it in the list, and then click its Z-index number to go into edit mode. Type the new Z-index over the old one.

▶ To reorder layers in the Layers palette, choose Hierarchic from the Layers palette flyout menu, and then drag layer names up or down in the list.

FIGURE 9.49
The Layers palette.

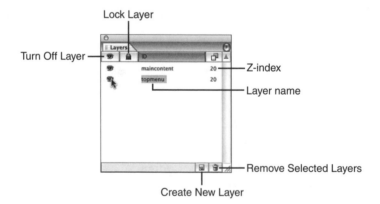

A couple of additional options in the Layers palette flyout menu are of interest. One of them enables you to convert your layers to a layout grid. This comes in handy if you need to create a version of your page viewable by older browsers that do not support layers. Note that this option should not be used if layers are overlapping.

The other option, Layer Grid Settings, when turned on, gives you an underlying grid to which you can align layers. This feature was implemented in GoLive 6, but with the new Smart Guides feature in GoLive CS, there is little need to turn on the Layer Grid Settings.

Converting Photoshop Layers to GoLive Layers

A very nice, but often unmentioned, integration feature between GoLive CS and Photoshop or ImageReady CS is GoLive's capability to import a layered Photoshop-format file. From the File menu choose Import, Photoshop Layers. An Open dialog will appear, allowing you to navigate to the file you want to import. After it's selected, GoLive will ask for a save location; because GoLive will be creating Web versions of the layers, they'll need to be saved. Choose your site's root folder (or a folder inside it) as the save location. Next, GoLive opens its Save for Web window and begins importing the layers one at a time.

As each layer loads into the Save for Web window, you can choose the file format that is best suited to the content of the layer. You can also select the amount of compression on JPEG files, the number of colors on GIFs, and the size you want the layer to be. If there is a layer in the Photoshop file you do not want to import, click Cancel when that layer loads into the Save for Web window, and GoLive will proceed to load the next layer until it has imported all the layers.

Each layer from the source Photoshop file is automatically placed into a GoLive layer. You can select a GoLive layer from the Layers palette and move, adjust the visibility of, or animate the layer as you would any other GoLive layer (see Figure 9.50).

Using the Color Palette

The GoLive CS Color palette is used to create color swatches that can then be added to your Swatches palette for use at any time during your design process. To open the Color palette, choose Window, Color from the menu bar.

There are five buttons across the top of the Color palette, each representing a color model. You can mix colors in any of the color models by using the sliders or typing in values. Notice that when colored text or a color object is selected on your page, the Color palette displays the color of that text or object.

A very powerful tool in the Color palette is the Eyedropper. Click the Eyedropper and click anywhere on your screen to pick up a color. This really comes in handy if you have a color in an image that you'd like to apply to text. Simply sample the color with the Eyedropper and then apply it to the text.

FIGURE 9.50
An imported lay-
ered Photoshop
file.

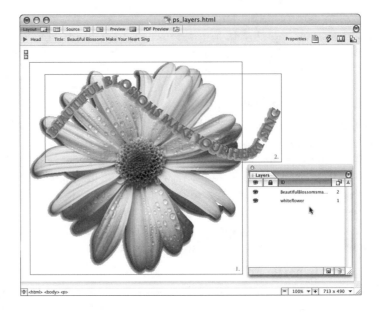

From the Color palette flyout menu, you can enable the Recent Colors list (see Figure 9.51). This will display the recently used colors along the bottom of the Color palette.

FIGURE 9.51
The Color palette.

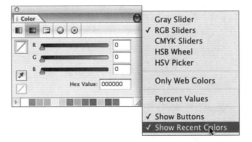

Using the Swatches Palette

The Color palette's alter-ego is the Swatches palette. After you have mixed a color in the Color palette, you can switch to the Swatches palette to add that color as a swatch which you can access at any time. To open the Swatches palette, choose Window, Swatches from the menu bar. Add a color by clicking the Create New Swatch button at the lower right of the Color palette. Delete a swatch by selecting it and clicking the Delete Swatch button.

GoLive CS offers several swatch sets to choose from, and they are accessible via the Swatches flyout menu. This author's favorite is VisiBone2, which displays

Web-safe colors in a very orderly way. The flyout menu also allows you to choose between a thumbnail view and a list view, and offers a neat feature called Search Fields. By enabling the search fields, you can search for a color by Value (hex number) or Name. Enter the number or name into the appropriate field and press Enter. The corresponding color will become selected in the Swatches palette (see Figure 9.52).

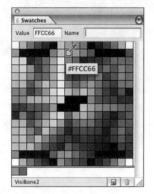

FIGURE 9.52
The Swatches palette.

Working with Text

As with most tasks in GoLive, placing text onto a page can be accomplished several ways. You can open your text document in the application in which it was created, and then use copy and paste to bring it into GoLive. You can also open a text document right in GoLive. From there you can also copy and paste, or simply drag the text directly to your page.

The simplest, most direct way of getting text onto your page is to put the cursor on the page and begin typing. But to have more control over the placement of text on your pages, you can elect to use a layout grid, table, or layer as described earlier. Text boxes are placed on top of layout grids and can be moved around the page for a more precise layout.

When you are working with text, you can use the tools in the Main toolbar to align or color text, change the base size or header type, add a bulleted or numbered list, add a bold or italic style, or even apply a CSS style if any styles have been defined.

To apply any of the options from the toolbar, select the text and then click the appropriate button. To apply color to text, select the text and then click a color in the Swatches or Color palette. Alternatively, you could select the text and click the lower-right corner of the color well in the Toolbar. This will open a temporary swatches palette from which you can choose a color (see Figure 9.53).

FIGURE 9.53
A temporary
swatches palette
drops open when
you click the color
well in the Main
toolbar.

Those preferring to use Cascading Style Sheets rather than font tags will want to use the handy-dandy Apply CSS Style button in the toolbar. To apply a style to text, select the text, click the Apply CSS Style button on the toolbar, and then put a check mark next to the style you want to apply. More information on creating and using Cascading Style Sheets can be found later in this chapter, in the section "Using Cascading Style Sheets."

Creating Hyperlinks

The Web is all about hyperlinks. When clicked, a link takes you from one page to the next or from one part of a page to another. Hyperlinks can be attached to text or images and are very easy to create in GoLive.

To create a text link, select the text and then do one of the following:

▶ Use the Fetch URL tool in the Inspector palette to point and shoot to a page in your Files list (see Figure 9.54).

▶ Type the URL into the Link field of the Inspector (see Figure 9.55).

▶ Click the Browse button at the right end of the Link field (see Figure 9.56), and browse to the file to which you want to link.

▶ Click the arrow at the right end of the Link field and choose a filename from the list (see Figure 9.57).

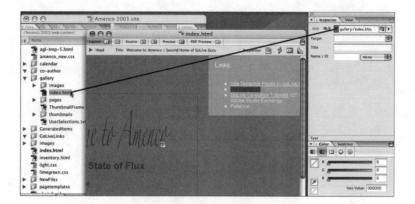

FIGURE 9.54
The world-famous Fetch URL tool has also been called the point and shoot tool, or the pick-whip, and is known for the way it squiggles back if let go without hitting its mark.

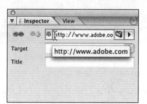

FIGURE 9.55
If you know the URL, you can type it into the URL input field.

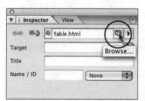

FIGURE 9.56
The Browse button looks like a folder.

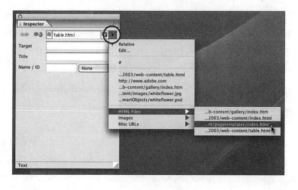

FIGURE 9.57
Recently used files are listed here.

▶ Press the (⌘) [Alt] key and drag from the selected text to the file to which you are linking (see Figure 9.58).

FIGURE 9.58
My favorite method,
dragging directly
from the selection
to make a link.

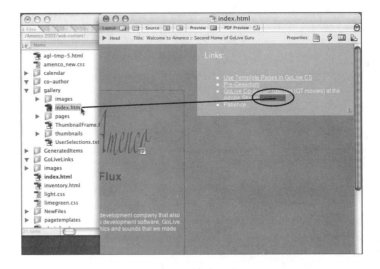

Creating a hyperlink on an image follows nearly the same process. The difference is that after you have your image on the page and selected, you must first click the Link button in the Image Inspector, and then proceed to create the link.

After a link is created, you'll notice additional options in the Inspector palette. Target refers to the window in which you want the link to open. If you are using frames and want the link to open a page in a different frame, you must specify a target. You can choose a frame name from the list (the frameset must be open for the frame names to appear), or choose from one of the default options:

_top opens the link in the full browser window, replacing the current frameset entirely.

_parent opens the link in the parent of the current page. For example, a link in a frameset that has a target of _parent will open the link in the frameset page.

_self opens the link in the window or frame containing the link.

_blank opens the link in a new window.

You can type a description into the Title field if you'd like. Internet Explorer will pop up the title when a visitor hovers her mouse over the link. Those concerned with meeting accessibility standards will want to give their links a name and an ID. Choose Name & ID from the pop-up list and type a name into the Name/ID field.

Using the Find Window

Unless you are the one and only person in the universe who never makes a mistake, at some point you will need to find or change text in your documents. GoLive has a very powerful Find Content window that lets you search one document, several documents, or a whole site. Open the Find window by choosing Edit, Find, Find Content from the menu bar. Notice that the Find window has two buttons at the top, one to find content In Current Document, and one to find content In Multiple Files.

In Current Document works only if you have a page opened, and will search only within the active editing mode. If you have the Layout Editor opened, you can search only for text, but if you have the Source Editor opened, you can search for text or HTML.

Additionally, you can choose from the following options:

- ▶ **Match Case**—Matches uppercase or lowercase letters exactly as you have specified. For example, if you search for Web, then web with a lowercase w would be ignored.

- ▶ **Entire Word**—Finds only a word that is not a part of another word. For example, a search for other will not also return another.

- ▶ **Regular Expression**—Allows you to run a search using regular expressions, which are special combinations of symbols and/or syntax used to match various patterns of text.

- ▶ **From Top**—Starts the search from the beginning of the page.

- ▶ **Wrap Around**—Begins the search at the cursor insertion point, goes to the end, then goes back to the top, and returns to the cursor insertion point again.

- ▶ **In Selection**—Searches only within the current selection.

If you simply want to find text on a page, type the word or phrase you are looking for into the Find field and click Find. If a match is found, it will be highlighted on the page. Click Find Next to move to the next match.

Typing a word or phrase into the Replace field and clicking Replace will replace the found text with the new text. You can choose to replace one instance at a time, or all instances in one pass.

Using Find in Multiple Documents works regardless of whether the pages are opened or closed. You can choose from three options when running the search:

Text in Layout Mode, Text in Source Mode, and Code Elements. All the options available in the single document search are also available in a multiple document search. To add files to the list of documents to be searched, select Files from the Search In pop-up, and then click the Add Files button and select the files, or simply drag files into the Search In field (see Figure 9.59).

FIGURE 9.59
Drag the files that
you want to search
right into the
Search In field.

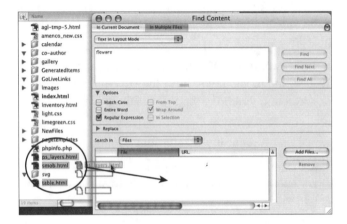

Using the Check Spelling Feature

Last but not least, you'll want to run a spell-check on your pages to tidy them up. You can check a single page or your entire site. To open the Check Spelling window, choose Check Spelling from the Edit menu.

If a page is opened, the spell-check will be run on that page, and if your cursor is in the middle of the page, the spell-checker runs from that position. To run the spell-check from the top of the page, click the From Top check box. You can also select a portion of the text to spell-check that piece only.

If you need to perform the check on multiple files or on a whole site, enable the Check in Files check box near the bottom of the Check Spelling window, and click the gray arrow to open the bottom portion of the dialog box. You can then choose your site's name from the pop-up list (see Figure 9.60), or drag files from the Files list of your site window directly into the Files field in the Check Spelling window.

Choose the language you prefer from the pop-up menu, and choose whatever options are appropriate for your check. Click Start to begin the spell-check. As the spell-check proceeds, you'll choose from the following options:

▶ Delete removes the word.

▶ Change replaces the suspect word with the first one in the Suggestions field. You can also choose a word from the suggestion list, or correct the suspect word by editing it yourself.

▶ Ignore skips over the suspect word with no correction.

▶ Ignore All skips all occurrences of that word with no correction.

▶ Learn adds the word to your personal dictionary so that it won't be flagged as an error any more.

▶ Next File takes you to the next document in your site if you are spell-checking the whole site.

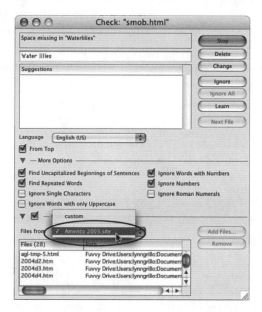

FIGURE 9.60
Check the spelling in your entire site by selecting the appropriate option from the Files From pop-up.

Working with Images

Because you've got the Adobe Creative Suite in your hot little hands, you've got the most powerful set of tools on the planet to create images of any type. A picture is worth a thousand words, but when it comes to the Web, it had better not be worth a thousand kilobytes. Not to worry, the CS tools offer various ways to prepare images for the Web, and you can find these tools in Photoshop, ImageReady, and Illustrator. So go crazy and design like a maniac; but when you are done, compress those little beauties into an appropriate Web format. (And be sure to read the upcoming section "Integration Using Photoshop CS, ImageReady CS, Illustrator CS, or Acrobat PDF Files," which will make the process quick and painless!)

The three most common image types for the Web are GIF, PNG, and JPEG. In general, you will want to use GIF or PNG for graphic images, especially those containing just a few colors, such as logos, while reserving JPEG for photographs.

Methods for Placing Images

To put an image on a page, you can simply select the image from the Files list in your site window and drag it directly onto the page. Images can be dragged onto a page or into a table cell, a layout grid, or a layer.

Another method of putting an image on a page is to use the Image object, which acts as a placeholder until you link it to the desired image. To put an image placeholder on the page, either drag and drop the Image object from the Objects palette, double-click the Image object in the Objects palette, or (control-click) [right-click] and choose Insert Object, Basic, Image. After the Image placeholder is on the page, your next step is to link it up to the image file. You can do so by using the Fetch URL tool to point and shoot at the image file in your Files list, or by clicking the Browse button at the right end of the Source field in the Image Inspector, or by choosing a filename from the Recently Used pop-up list at the far-right end of the Source field.

Let's take a look at the Image Inspector. Place an image onto a page and select it. Notice that the Inspector palette now has four buttons across the top, called Basic, More, Link, and Color Profile:

- ▶ **Basic**—The Basic area is where you reference the source file, set its size in width and height, choose an alignment, define the Alt text, and assign a name and an ID.

- ▶ **More**—Go to the More area to assign a low-source image, which is a low-resolution version of an image that the browser displays while a higher-resolution version is loading. You can have GoLive automatically generate the low-source version of your image by clicking the Generate button in the Inspector. In the More tab you can also choose horizontal or vertical spacing around the image (HSpace and VSpace), select a border size, designate whether the image is to be used as an image map, or define whether the image is to be used as a submit button for a form.

- ▶ **Link**—Select the Link area to create a hyperlink on the image and to set the link's target, title, name, and ID.

- ▶ **Color Profile**—Use the Color Profile area to select a color profile for the image.

A great way to bring images into GoLive is by using the operating system's internal clipboard. You can copy an image, including screenshots, to your internal clipboard, and then switch over to a GoLive page and paste. GoLive fires up the Save for Web window, which will allow you to compress the image to an appropriate Web format and save it into your site.

Image Maps

Image mapping, once a tedious and frustrating process done by hand, is now as easy and fun as using a drawing program. Using the drawing tools in GoLive, you can create hotspots on your image. The hotspots can be square, round, or other shapes. Each hotspot you draw can then be assigned a link. In this way, you can have one image that links to many places.

Select an image, and then click the More button in the Image Inspector. Click the check box next to the words Use Map. Doing so enables the hotspot drawing tools in the Main toolbar. Select the Rectangular, Circular, or Polygonal Map-area tool. Click and drag to draw with the Rectangular or Circular Map-area tool; click multiple times to draw a shape with the Polygonal Map-area tool (see Figure 9.61).

FIGURE 9.61
This image contains a rectangular, a circular, and a polygonal hotspot.

When you are done drawing hotspots, you can click the Select Map-area tool to move them around or resize them by dragging a corner point. Select each hotspot you have drawn, and create a hyperlink for it using any of the linking techniques we learned earlier in this chapter.

Rollovers

If you've ever visited a Web site and put your cursor over an image only to have it change color, you've likely encountered a rollover. A rollover is an image whose appearance changes as the user rolls her mouse over it. Combined with hyperlinks, rollovers give the user a clear visual clue as to which item she is about to click. Rollovers are created by using a different image for each state of the mouse. For example, you could assign a blue button image when the mouse is not on the button, and a yellow button image when the mouse is over the button.

GoLive CS includes a nifty feature called automatic rollover detection, and it is a real time-saver. Simply by naming your images in a particular way, you can enable GoLive to recognize them as rollovers and automatically write and implement the necessary JavaScript to make the rollovers function. To access settings that make this detection possible, open the Rollovers & Actions palette from the Window menu, and then choose Rollover Detection Settings from the palette's fly-out menu (see Figure 9.62).

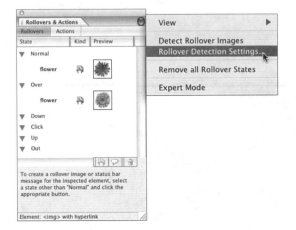

By default, three sets of naming conventions are already included in the list, but you can easily edit any of the defaults, or add your own set. How does it work? It's simple. If you place an image onto a page that is named house.jpg, and there is another image in your Files list called house_Over.jpg, GoLive automatically detects this pair and creates the JavaScript rollover. As you can see from the detection settings, you can have multiple states for an image, though Normal and Over are the most widely used (see Figure 9.63).

If you prefer, you can create rollovers manually in the Rollovers & Actions palette. Select an image on the page, and then choose a State in the list. Next, click the Create New Rollover Image button and link to the image you want to use for that state.

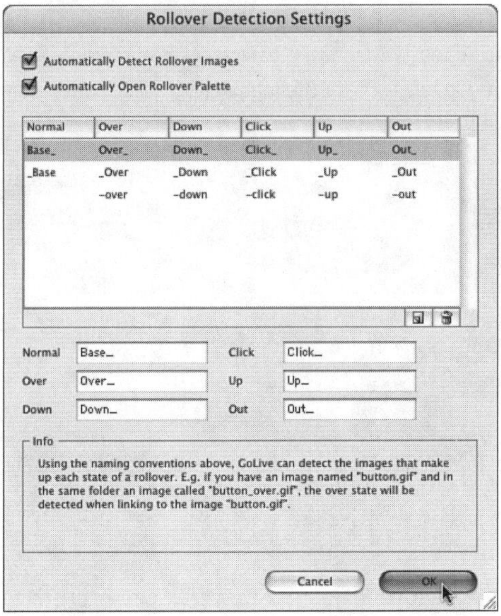

FIGURE 9.63
You can apply as many as six different states to a rollover automatically, simply by naming the images a certain way!

Integration Using Photoshop CS, ImageReady CS, Illustrator CS, or Acrobat PDF Files

One of the most compelling features (and definitely the coolest feature) of GoLive is its integration with the other applications in the Creative Suite. Through the use of Smart Object technology, it is possible to use your native Photoshop, ImageReady, Illustrator, and PDF documents in your Web pages. You read that correctly! GoLive accepts the native Photoshop, Illustrator, or PDF file and compresses it to an appropriate Web format. But the magic begins when the source file is edited, because those edits are automatically reflected in the Web-ready version of the image.

Take a native Photoshop (.psd), Illustrator (.ai), or Acrobat PDF document (.pdf), and drag it into an open GoLive HTML page. GoLive immediately recognizes the .psd, .ai, or .pdf filename extension as a friendly file type, one to embrace and care for. GoLive's first step toward accommodating the source document is to bring up the Save for Web dialog box, which will allow you to determine an appropriate Web file format for the image, adjust compression settings, resize the image if necessary, and then save the resulting GIF, JPEG, or PNG file into your Web site (see Figure 9.64). During the Save process, GoLive helpfully assigns the Web-friendly version of the image a filename based on the source file.

FIGURE 9.64
The Save for Web dialog box is built right into GoLive CS, allowing you to easily prepare images for the Web.

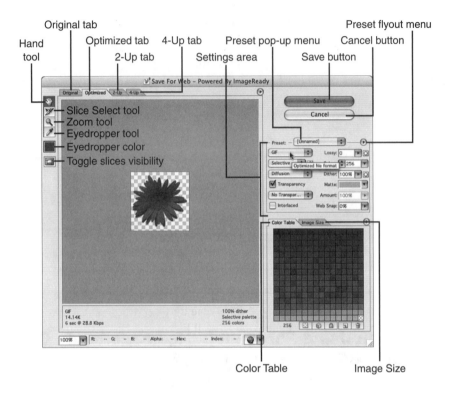

The Save for Web dialog box offers a wide variety of views and tools:

- ▶ **Original tab**—Shows the image in its original form.

- ▶ **Optimized tab**—Shows the image after optimization has been applied.

- ▶ **2-Up tab**—Shows original and optimized versions next to each other. Click one to edit its settings.

- ▶ **4-Up tab**—Shows original and three variations of the optimized image. Click one to edit its settings.

- ▶ **Hand tool**—Use to move the image in the window.

- ▶ **Slice Select tool**—Use to select a slice when optimizing a sliced image from Photoshop, ImageReady, or Illustrator. Click the slice to edit its settings.

- ▶ **Zoom tool**—Zooms in when you click on the image. Press the (Option) [Alt] key to zoom out.

- ▶ **Eyedropper tool**—Click on the image with the Eyedropper to select a color.

- ▶ **Eyedropper color**—Shows the currently selected color.

- ▶ **Toggle slices visibility**—Makes the borders of slices visible or invisible.

- ▶ **Settings area**—Choose the optimized file type, compression levels, transparency and dither types, and matte settings.

- ▶ **Preset pop-up menu**—Shows a list of preconfigured compression settings. Choosing one alters settings in the Preset area.

- ▶ **Preset flyout menu**—Save, edit, or delete settings from the list in the pop-up.

- ▶ **Color Table**—Shows colors used when GIF or PNG-8 is selected as the file type.

- ▶ **Image Size**—Adjust the image size, and then click Apply.

- ▶ **Cancel button**—Closes the Save for Web window without applying the settings.

- ▶ **Save button**—Closes the Save for Web window and opens the Save dialog.

When created, the Smart Object, called the target file, retains a link back to the original document, and it will be updated if the original is changed. The original document is referred to as the source file. You'll know it's a Smart Object and not a plain old GIF or JPEG because of the small icon in the lower-right corner (see Figure 9.65).

FIGURE 9.65
Smart Object target files are indicated by an icon in the lower-right corner.

To reopen the source file in Photoshop or Illustrator, just double-click on the target file. Edit the source file in its originating application, save it, and then flip back to GoLive. The target image will automatically update without asking you to recompress it, resize it, rename it, or anything!

Select the target version of the file on your page and look at the Inspector palette (see Figure 9.66). There are a few more options than those that were available when you placed a normal GIF or JPEG file. The first field indicates the location of the source file, and the second shows the path to the target file. Next are two important buttons called Settings and Variables. The Settings button opens the Save for Web dialog box so that you can edit your compression settings. The Variables button opens the Variable Settings dialog box, where you can assign a value to a variable, which is discussed in greater detail in the next section. Below those two buttons are some very nifty tools called Matte, Crop, and Scale, whose usage is also discussed in the next section.

FIGURE 9.66
The Smart Object Inspector.

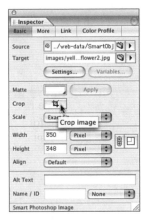

In the next section we'll take a look at what special integration features may exist between the various apps.

Did you Know?

> In the Extras Tab of the site window is a folder called SmartObjects. This is a convenient place to house your native Photoshop, Illustrator, and PDF files; however, it's not mandatory that they be placed there. You can add a Smart Object to your Web page from anywhere. As long as the original document does not move to a different location, GoLive will keep the connection between the Web version of the image and its original.

There are several ways to place a Smart Object onto a GoLive page:

▶ Drag and drop the source file from your drive onto the GoLive page.

▶ Drag and drop the source file from the SmartObjects folder onto the GoLive page.

▶ Drag and drop a Smart Object placeholder from the Smart set of the Objects palette onto the page, and then use the Inspector palette to link to the source file.

▶ Place your mouse pointer on the page where you want the Smart Object placeholder to go, and then double-click the Smart Object placeholder in the Smart set of the Objects palette. Use the Inspector palette to link to the source file.

Note that there are several Smart Object types in the Smart set of the Objects palette: Smart Photoshop, Smart Illustrator, Smart PDF, and one named Smart Generic. In my experience any one of them will do. I've used the Smart Photoshop object to load an Illustrator document, and the Smart Illustrator object to load a PDF. You get the idea. Mainly I prefer to drag a Photoshop, Illustrator, or PDF file right onto the GoLive page and forgo placing the Smart Object placeholder altogether.

Did you
Know?

There is one instance in which it is necessary to first place the Smart Object placeholder on the page, and then link to the source file—and that is when you want to use a file type besides the native Adobe file formats. The supported file types are BMP, PCX, Pixar, Amiga IFF, TIFF, TARGA, PDF, EPS, JPEG, JPEG 2000, PNG, and PICT (Mac OS only).

To resize a target file, simply select one of its corner handles and drag. To size proportionately, hold down the Shift key as you drag. When you release the mouse, GoLive will re-render the target file for you.

Photoshop transparency is recognized by GoLive CS as well, so if you create a Photoshop file with a transparent background and save it as a GIF with transparency, the transparent areas will be retained. If the matte color, which is the color on which the image was created, of the Photoshop image does not match the color of your GoLive page, you can re-matte the target file using the tools in the Inspector palette. This feature comes in handy, for example, when an image using transparency was matted on a white background, but the GoLive page color is blue. In such an instance the image would have a white halo around its edges. Re-matting the image on a blue background allows it to seamlessly blend in with the GoLive page.

To change the matte color of the target image, select the image on the page, click the Matte color well in the Inspector, either click a color in the Color or Swatches palette, or use the Eyedropper tool in the Color palette to pick up the background color on the page, and then click Apply in the Inspector palette. GoLive re-renders the target file with the new Matte color. Alternatively, you could click the Settings button in the Inspector palette and use the Matte color options in the Save for Web dialog box.

See Figure 9.67 for examples of how a source Photoshop file with a transparent background layer will appear as a target file.

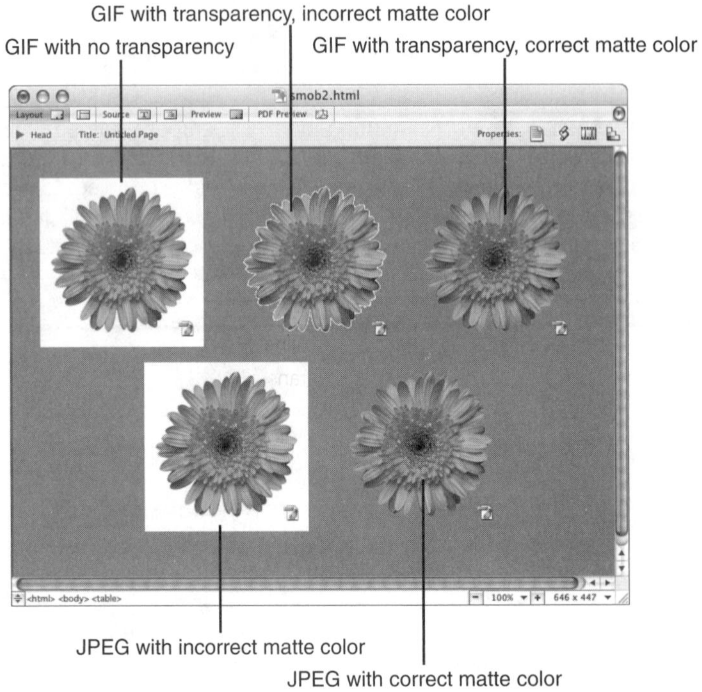

FIGURE 9.67
Smart Objects with various transparency and matte settings.

GIF with transparency, incorrect matte color
GIF with no transparency   GIF with transparency, correct matte color

JPEG with incorrect matte color
JPEG with correct matte color

Finally, you can crop a Smart Object using the new Crop tool in the Inspector palette. Select the target file on your page, and then click the Crop tool. Drag over the image to select the portion you want to keep, and the part that will be cropped becomes dimmed. If your selection is not quite right, you can move it around, or drag a corner point to resize it. To accept the crop, either double-click inside the crop marks or click the Crop Image button in the toolbar.

There are additional crop options in the toolbar (see Figure 9.68) that allow you to crop the transparent pixels at the top, bottom, right, or left side of the image. Also in the Main toolbar when the Crop tool is active is a pop-up menu called Scaling, which offers the following options:

▶ **Keep Scaling**—Crops the image to the size of the crop marks.

▶ **Keep Object Size**—Crops the image, but fills the space used by the original image. This works when you're cropping an image larger or smaller than the original.

▶ **Scale to Source File**—Crops the image to the size of the original file.

If, after all that cropping, you'd like to return the target image to its first incarnation, select it on the page, click the Crop tool in the Inspector palette, and then click the Use Original Image button in the Main toolbar.

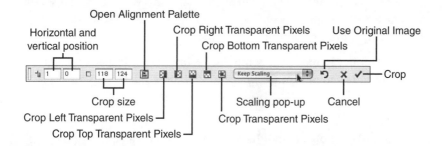

FIGURE 9.68
The cropping tools.

Photoshop Integration

If you are a Photoshop aficionado, you'll already be familiar with Photoshop layers. If you're new to Photoshop, take a look at Chapter 5, "Using Adobe Photoshop CS," to understand this wonderful feature. When you're using a Smart Photoshop object in GoLive, the layers feature works in a special way. Any Photoshop file that includes a top layer containing text can be used as a variable in GoLive. In case you are not familiar with the term *variable*, it simply means "something that varies." In the case of a Photoshop text layer, it's the text that can vary. To illustrate this point, let's do a very quick exercise.

In Photoshop CS create a new document. Select the Text tool and click on the page, and then type the words `Placeholder Text`. Format the text any way you'd like using your favorite font, color, and effect. Then save the file as a native Photoshop document.

Next, open a GoLive page, and drag and drop the new Photoshop document onto the page. A dialog box called Variable Settings will appear. Click the check box next to Topmost Text layer to enable it and an input field will open. In the input field type `Adobe GoLive CS`, and then click OK (see Figure 9.69).

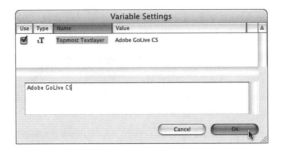

The Save for Web dialog box will open, and you'll see the image you just created in Photoshop, except that the text you entered into the Variable Settings dialog box will have replaced the placeholder text in the source file. Choose the file format GIF and click the Save button to save the GIF file.

Now, select your newly made GIF on the page, and in the Inspector palette click the Variables button to reopen the Variable Settings window. This time type **Very, very cool!** and then click OK. GoLive re-renders the target object using the settings you specified originally.

By now you are probably getting the idea, but just in case you've missed the point, let me be specific. You can use one source file to create multiple variations of the target file for use on different pages. If you update the original source artwork, the target files can be updated as well. The update happens automatically when you open a page using a target file, or you can force the update by selecting the source file in the SmartObjects folder and then choosing Site, Update Files Dependent On, Selection.

After having initially created a target file, you can place it on as many pages as you would like. However, if you want to be able to resize the image differently on various pages, then you need to create a unique target file with its own name for each instance in which it is used. You can manage this task by copying and pasting the target file to another page, and then, in the Inspector palette, click the folder icon at the right end of the target input field. You'll be able to re-optimize and/or resize the image, rename it, and save the new version of the target file into your site.

ImageReady and Illustrator Integration

If you think the text variables feature between Photoshop and GoLive is sweet, hold on to your hats, because it gets even better when you bring ImageReady CS or Illustrator CS into the picture. Using ImageReady or Illustrator, not only can the topmost text layer act as a variable, but *any* text layer can be designated as a variable. Additionally, you can add a visibility variable to any image layer, meaning that in GoLive you can specify whether an image layer is turned on or off. For instructions on how to set up variables in ImageReady CS, refer to Chapter 6, "Using Adobe ImageReady CS." For instructions on how to set up variables in Illustrator CS, refer to Chapter 7, "Using Adobe Illustrator CS."

When you drag and drop an ImageReady CS Photoshop-format document or an Illustrator SVG file that contains variables into a GoLive page, the Variable Settings dialog box opens and allows you to choose which layers to make visible or invisible and which text strings to change. To enable a variable, check the Use box next to the variable's name. For image layers choose Visible or Invisible from the pop-up menu; for text layers type the desired text string into the input field (see Figure 9.70).

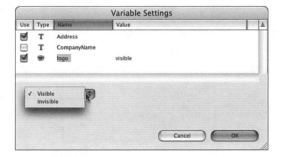

FIGURE 9.70
When you're using an ImageReady Photoshop-format file or an Illustrator SVG file, the Variable Settings dialog box lets you select the variables to use and which options to assign to each.

PDF Integration

In addition to GoLive's capability to generate PDF files from HTML pages, GoLive also tracks links in PDFs and allows you to create or edit links in PDFs. Double-click a PDF file in your Files list to preview the PDF, and then click the Link Editing button at the top of the window to enter the editing mode. Choose the New Link tool from the toolbar to draw links onto the PDF, or the Edit Links tool to edit existing links, and then set the link's attributes in the Inspector palette (see Figure 9.71).

Additionally, you can use a PDF as a Smart Object. This is especially useful if you'd like to create a thumbnail image of a PDF to use as a link to the full version. Drag and drop a PDF onto your GoLive page, and the PDF Options dialog box will appear, where you can select which page of the PDF you'd like to use for your target file (see Figure 9.72). Select the page and the orientation in the dialog box, and then click OK. When the Save for Web window opens, proceed as described in the "Photoshop Integration" section earlier in this chapter.

InDesign Integration

New in the Adobe Creative Suite Premium is the integration between InDesign CS and GoLive CS. This innovative feature allows for the intelligent repurposing of elements from print to Web. From InDesign's File menu you choose Package for GoLive, which creates a package (a folder, really) containing all the elements from the print project. When opened in GoLive, those elements appear as drag-gable objects that can be placed into your HTML pages. Let's take a look at how to view, access, and use those elements.

There is a folder in the Extras tab of the site window called InDesign Packages. Adobe recommends that you save your InDesign package into that folder using InDesign's Package for GoLive command. If you have done so already, you will see the little package icon (see Figure 9.73). To open the package, double-click on the package icon.

FIGURE 9.73
The package icon looks like, well, a package.

> Although there is an indicator to the left of the package icon that makes it appear as though you can toggle open its contents, you can't. If you want to see the contents of the package, you'll need to (Control-click) [right-click] and select (Open, Reveal in Finder) [Open, Reveal in Explorer].

By the Way

If you have created a package for GoLive but it isn't in the correct place, you can import it into GoLive by choosing File, Import, From InDesign. When the Select InDesign Package Folder dialog box appears, navigate to the folder containing the package, select it, and then click Choose. GoLive will ask whether you want to add the package to your site (provided you have a site opened at that time, which you should). Unless you have some compelling reason not to do so, go ahead and let GoLive import the package into the site by clicking Yes (see Figure 9.74).

The package opens into a little window containing two buttons at the top called Page Items and Assets (see Figure 9.75). The Page Items button reveals an exact replica of the InDesign document, which is accomplished via the magic of PDF technology. The Assets button displays an orderly view of the assets contained within the package, separated into four folders—Stories, Images, Movies, and

Sounds. If the InDesign file did not contain any movies or sounds, those folders will be empty. Likewise, if the file contained no stories or images, those folders will also be empty, although we can't imagine an InDesign document that doesn't contain at least *one* of these things.

FIGURE 9.74
Do the right thing and let GoLive import the package from InDesign.

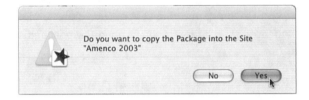

FIGURE 9.75
The Page Items and Assets views of the Package window.

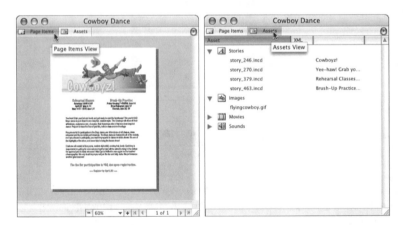

Click the Page Items view and click through the pages using the navigation buttons at the bottom of the package window. If you'd like, you can zoom up or down to see more or less of the preview. If you run your mouse over the page, various elements will be highlighted. The highlight indicates that your mouse is hovering above an asset that can be reused on your Web site (see Figure 9.76). To use an asset, drag and drop it from the package window onto your GoLive page.

Using Images from the InDesign Package

To use items from the package on your GoLive page, just drag and drop. Images from the package are treated as Smart Objects, meaning that when they are dropped onto the page in GoLive, the Save for Web dialog box is invoked. You can proceed to use the compression settings of your choice and save the target image into your site as described earlier in this chapter.

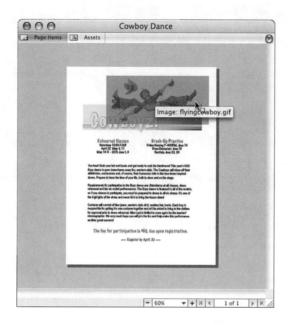

FIGURE 9.76
Assets in the package window are highlighted as you cursor over them.

Using Stories from the InDesign Package

Stories from the package are treated as components (you can find more info on components earlier in this chapter, in the section "The Extras Tab"), meaning that they retain a link back to the original InDesign document. If the data in a story changes in InDesign, you can update the component in GoLive. To do so, repackage the InDesign file and, when asked whether you want to update the package, choose Yes. Back in GoLive click once on the component to select it, and then in the Inspector palette choose InCopy from the Generator pop-up (see Figure 9.77). This causes the story to update.

If you don't need the story to remain connected to the InDesign document and would rather edit the text in GoLive, you have two choices. Either place the story and then release it from its component, or before placing the story, change its settings. To release a story from its component, (Control-click) [right-click] on the text and choose Components, Detach Selected Component. To change the settings before placing the story, select the story in the package window, and then click the Settings button in the Main toolbar. From the Content Usage pop-up, choose Direct.

If you have trouble selecting an asset because it is obscured by another asset, you can (Control-click) [right-click] and choose Select, and then select the asset name from the list (see Figure 9.78). The selected asset becomes highlighted so that you can easily drag and drop it onto a page.

FIGURE 9.77
If a story has been edited and repackaged from InDesign, you can update it in the Inspector palette.

FIGURE 9.78
An alternate method for selecting page assets is via the contextual menu.

Another method for selecting and using assets is to switch to the Assets view and drag and drop an item from its folder to your page. If you are not certain which asset is which, double-click a name in the Assets list and the asset will show in the Inspector palette. You could also drag the asset from the Inspector palette to your page.

And if those choices aren't enough, yet another way (options are a good thing, right?) of placing image assets would be to first place a Smart Object placeholder on your page, and then, using the Inspector palette's Fetch URL tool, point and shoot at the asset of your choice in the Page Items view of the package window.

Generating CSS Automatically from the Package

An amazing feature is the capability of GoLive to automatically translate the character and paragraph styles from the InDesign document into Cascading Style Sheets. The best method for doing this is to use the package window's flyout menu and choose CSS Styles, Save to Site. This will open the Save dialog and allow you to name and save the file as an external style sheet in your site. You can then open the CSS file and edit it as you see fit.

Using Cascading Style Sheets

GoLive CS's support for Cascading Style Sheets has been dramatically updated and now complies with the CSS2 specification. Not only does the Layout mode do a better job of rendering CSS designs, but the Style Sheet Editor itself has been redesigned to make it more efficient and easier to use.

Those of you familiar with paragraph and character styles in page layout applications will probably grasp the basics of CSS readily, but the scope of the CSS spec falls well beyond altering font faces, sizes, and colors. CSS can be used to position elements, not merely text, on a page. In fact, if you have played with layers in GoLive, you were working with CSS, because a layer actually writes a <DIV> tag which defines an area, and that area is positioned (and can be styled) with CSS.

Internal Versus External

Ever wonder why they're called Cascading Style Sheets instead of simply style sheets? It's because you can define styles in several ways, which at times could result in conflicting styles. The method of resolving this conflict is called precedence. For example, you can define a style internally, meaning that it's written into a page, or externally, meaning that the style is defined in a separate document and linked to the page. In such a case, any conflicting styles in the internally defined styles take precedence over those defined in the external styles. Likewise, a style can be written inline, which means that it is applied to only one element on a page rather than the whole page like an internal style. In this case, the inline style would take precedence over the internal style.

So if I have an external style sheet that defines a piece of text as red, and no internal or inline style on that text, it appears red. If I also have an internal style declaring that text to be blue, the internal would win and the text would be blue. But if I also had an inline style defining the text as green, the inline style would triumph over the others and the text would appear green.

Creating an Element Style

Let's start by creating an internal CSS. Open a blank GoLive page, and then click the CSS icon at the upper right (looks like steps) to access the page's internal CSS Editor. The editor employs two buttons at the top, CSS Definitions and Source. The CSS Definitions window gives you a visual way to create styles, and the Source window shows you the source code (see Figure 9.79).

FIGURE 9.79
The Definitions window and the Source window of the CSS Editor.

To define a style, you need to determine whether it will be an element style, a class style, or an ID style. Let's concentrate on element styles first. Element, in this case, refers to an HTML tag, which is a markup element. Say, for example, you wanted to create a style that would make all your hyperlinks appear with no underline, but you want the underline to show up when the visitor puts his mouse over the link. You'd need to define a style for the <a> tag, which is the tag used to make a link, and you'd need to define two variations of the tag, one for each mouse state, off the link and over the link.

In the CSS Editor, click and hold the Create New Element Style button, either at the right side of the CSS editor in its default view or at the bottom of the window, until a list of tags pops up (see Figure 9.80). Choose "a" from the list.

Next, "a" appears in the CSS Definitions list, and the right half of the editor changes to display tools with which you can define the style's attributes. Across the top right half of the CSS Editor is a series of buttons. Each button represents a unique set of properties that can be applied to a style (see Figure 9.81).

Click the Font Properties button and choose a color for your link. Then in the Decoration area, click the No Text Decoration button (see Figure 9.82). This removes the underline from the link in its normal state. Now we need to define the over state of a link that is called a:hover. Click into the whitespace of the CSS Definitions pane to go back to the editor's default state. Choose a:hover from the Markup Elements list. Choose a color for the mouse over state of your link, and then click the Text Decoration Underline button. It's that simple!

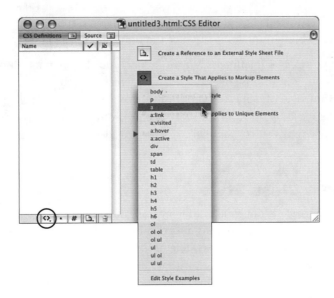

FIGURE 9.80
Clicking the button adds an untitled element, but clicking and holding reveals a list of markup elements from which to choose.

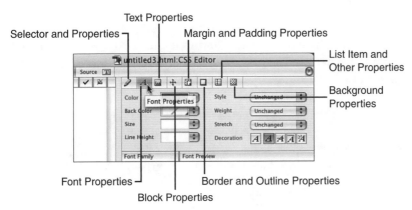

FIGURE 9.81
The buttons in the CSS Editor represent various sets of properties that can be added to your style definition.

FIGURE 9.82
Use the Text Decoration buttons to apply or remove an underline, strikethrough, overline, or blink.

Notice that in the lower-right portion of the CSS Editor a preview of the style appears and continues to update as you add attributes to a style. To preview all the styles in your definitions list, select one and then use the arrow keys to move up or down the list. The preview updates as each new definition is selected. It's also helpful that the label of an attribute that has been applied to the selected style appears in blue in the top section of the right half of the pane.

To test out the styles you defined, create a link on your HTML page, choose Preview, and put your mouse over the link. Remember, when you create an element style, that style attaches to every instance of that element in the page, or in all pages referenced by an external style sheet. In some instances you may want to define a style that you can apply only where needed. In that case, you need a class style.

Creating a Class Style

Defining a class style is not much different from defining an element style, but unlike an element style, which automatically adheres to every occurrence of a specific HTML tag in a page, a class style needs to be manually applied wherever it is desired. Class style names begin with a . and won't work properly without it. Let's try one. Click the New Class button at the bottom of the CSS Editor and change the name of the style to .bodyclass.

In the Font Properties area, choose White for the Color and Navy for the Back Color and 16px for the type Size. Hold down the Create New Font Family button and choose Trebuchet Set. The preview gives you a very clear idea of how this style will look (see Figure 9.83).

FIGURE 9.83
The New Font Family pop-up menu. Notice how the CSS Editor gives you a preview of your style as you edit properties.

> Whereas clicking the pop-up next to a color well provides a list from which to choose, clicking into the color well opens the Color palette, and clicking on the black triangle in the lower-right corner of the color well opens a temporary Swatches palette.

By the Way

Now click the Margin and Padding Properties button, and under Padding type **5** into the All field. When you click out of the input field, the attribute will automatically fill in for all four sides (see Figure 9.84).

> The CSS Editor uses pixels by default in all the input fields. If you'd like to change to points, picas, inches, ems, percentage, or another unit, click the pop-up next to the field and make your selection.

By the Way

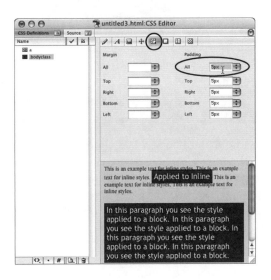

FIGURE 9.84
You can define Margin and Padding values for any side, or for all of them. If all sides are to use the same setting, you need to define only the All field and the others will be filled in automatically.

Click the Border and Outline Properties button and make sure that Border is active. Type **2** into the All input field, and choose Lime from the color list and Solid from the border type pop-up (see Figure 9.85). Save your changes and go over to your HTML page. Type the words **try it!** and select them. In the toolbar, click the Apply CSS Style button. Holding your mouse over the check boxes invokes a style preview.

Moving the mouse across the check boxes allows you to see how the style will look applied as an inline style, a block style, a paragraph style, and so on. Click the inline style box to both apply the style and dismiss the Apply CSS Style window simultaneously, and then preview your page.

FIGURE 9.85
Add a border to finish off your style.

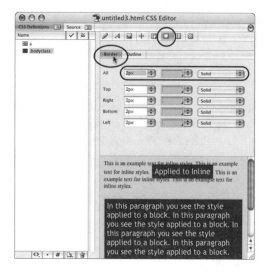

External CSS

Although internal style sheets are useful, it's the external version that has the real power. When you reference an external style sheet from multiple pages in a site, all it takes is an edit to that one CSS document to make a quick site-wide change.

You can create a new external style sheet by choosing New Special, Cascading Style Sheet from the File menu, or by (Control-clicking) [right-clicking] in the site window and choosing New, Cascading Style Sheet. After the CSS Editor for your external style sheet opens, create your definitions in exactly the same manner as you did for internal styles. When you are finished, save and name the file, but be sure to keep the .css extension.

At times you might want to define an internal style sheet for a page and also link to an external style sheet. You can do this several ways. From an internal CSS Editor window, click Create a Reference to an External Style Sheet, and in the next window use the Fetch URL tool to link to the CSS document in your site window (see Figure 9.86).

Another method is to drag a CSS file from the Files tab of the site window and drop it onto the Page Properties button at the upper right of the page (see Figure 9.87).

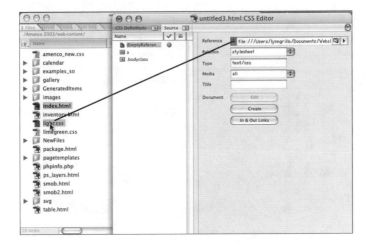

FIGURE 9.86
You can link directly from the page's internal CSS Editor to an external CSS file.

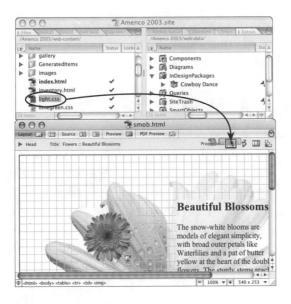

FIGURE 9.87
Drag and drop a CSS file onto the Page Properties button to create a link.

A third way is to use the CSS palette. First select the page or pages in the Files list of the site window, and then click and hold the mouse on the Create Link to External CSS button and choose the name of the CSS file to which you want to link (see Figure 9.88). Alternatively, you could select the pages in the Files list and use the Fetch URL tool or browser button in the CSS palette.

FIGURE 9.88
Use the CSS
palette to link mul-
tiple pages to an
external CSS file.

FIGURE 9.88
Use the CSS palette to link multiple pages to an external CSS file.

There are entire books devoted to CSS, but hopefully this section will get you started. CSS is somewhat addicting. After you realize its incredible power, you'll never want to go back to the old way of styling your pages again!

JavaScript Actions

JavaScript is a language especially for browsers that allows for interactivity beyond the scope of plain HTML. GoLive CS comes with a whole bunch of prewritten JavaScripts called Actions. Using the Rollovers and Actions palette, you can set up an Action to perform a whole range of tasks and never write one word of JavaScript.

Actions must be triggered somehow, either by a move the visitor makes, such as clicking a link or submitting a form, or by something the browser does, such as loading a page. Although there isn't space in this book to show how to use each and every GoLive Action, we will look at the basics of how to set them up.

Open the Rollovers & Actions palette from the Window menu, and then click the Actions button. We'll create a very simple action to get your started. Follow these steps:

1. From the File menu choose New Page.

2. Type **Please choose a size** on the page.

3. Select the text, and in the Inspector palette type a pound sign (#) into the URL field to create a dummy link.

4. In the Actions palette, click Mouse Click.

5. Click the Create New Action button.

6. From the Actions pop-up list choose Link, Open Window Prompt.

That's it! Now, preview the page in a browser and click the link. You'll be asked to enter a width and then a height, and then the page will reload itself into a browser window at the size you just requested.

That is one small example of what you can do, but there are many more tricks easily accomplished with GoLive Actions. For specific instructions on setting up a particular Action, check GoLive's help files, accessible from the Help menu. Remember, too, that the Actions that ship with GoLive are only a few of the many available. A quick search on Google for GoLive Actions should turn up a list of both free and commercial varieties.

Link Warnings

At times you'll notice a little bug icon next to a page or folder in the Status column of the Site window. This is an indication that there is a broken link on the page, or in the case of a folder the broken link is on a page inside the folder.

To troubleshoot the broken link, open the page and then click the Show Link Warnings button on the Main toolbar (the bug). Errors on the page will be highlighted in red (see Figure 9.89), making it easy to identify the trouble spot and then correct it by relinking it in the Inspector palette.

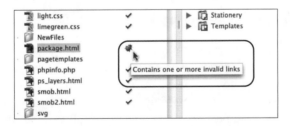

FIGURE 9.89
A bug icon indicates an error on the page.

In the event you do not immediately see the highlighted error, take a look at the arrow that opens the head section. If that is highlighted, it means that the error is contained in the head portion of the page. You can toggle open the head portion, select the highlighted icon, and make your correction.

Link warnings show not only in Layout mode, but also in Outline mode, which is often the simplest avenue toward finding and fixing the error.

In & Out Links Palette

The In & Out Links palette has got to be one of the most powerful Web maintenance tools ever developed. When a page has a bug in the status bar, use the In & Out Links palette to help correct the error. Select the page in the Files list of the site window, and then click the In & Out Links button on the Main toolbar.

The In & Out Links palette opens and displays a diagram of all the links going into and out of the selected page. Look carefully at the icons and you'll likely find one with a question mark on it. Click the icon with the question mark, which will cause the In & Out Links palette to display all links coming into and out of the file in question. Then, fix the link by grabbing the Fetch URL tool next to the file in error and pointing and shooting at the correct file in your site window (see Figure 9.90). When you let go, the reference will update the path and correct the reference.

FIGURE 9.90
The In & Out Links palette makes short work of fixing broken links.

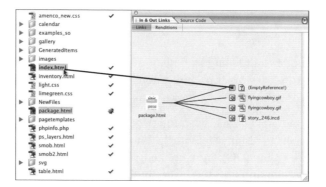

Publishing the Site

When your site is ready to go, chances are you will want to publish it to a Web server and make it available to the world. Again, GoLive gives you an easy way to accomplish the task and even keeps track of the work you have done during each work session and prompts you to upload the files that have changed. Before publishing, however, you need to enter some information about the server so that GoLive knows where to put the files.

Publishing via FTP or HTTP

To set up GoLive for publishing via FTP or HTTP, you need to be connected to the Internet. Choose Server from the (GoLive) [Edit] menu. Click New to create a new entry. Give the server a nickname, and select a protocol from the pop-up list. Enter the server IP address, username, and password, and then click the Browse button (looks like a folder) at the right end of the Directory field. Browse to the directory to which you will be publishing, and select it (see Figure 9.91).

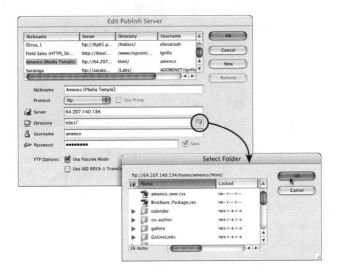

FIGURE 9.91
Set up the location of a Publish Server before uploading the site.

If you do not know the server IP and other necessary information, you need to contact your Web hosting service.

By the Way

Publishing to a Local Folder

New in GoLive CS is the capability to publish to a local folder. In the Server settings window choose File from the Protocol pop-up. Click the Browse button (looks like a folder), browse to the local or network folder of your choice, and select it.

Designating a Server Location for the Site

You can have more than one location set up in the Publish Server settings, so you'll need to tell GoLive which one to use for the site you are working on. To do so, click the Site Settings button on the Main toolbar, and when the settings dialog box opens choose Publish Server on the left. Click the radio button next to the server of your choice and close the settings window.

Uploading the Site

Now that your server settings are ready to go, you can publish the site. To do so, make sure that your site window is in front of all other windows, and click the Connect/Disconnect button on the Main toolbar (see Figure 9.92). GoLive will connect to the server, bring the Publish tab of the site window forward, and display a list of any files that may already reside on the server.

FIGURE 9.92
You can easily connect and upload using the buttons on the Main toolbar.

Next, click and hold the Upload button on the Main toolbar and choose from one of the options in the list. You can also select your default option by using the Change Button To menu item (see Figure 9.93). For example, if you change the button's default to Upload Modified (my personal favorite), then, instead of having to click and hold the Upload button and choose an upload method each time, you can simply click on the button to begin the upload process.

FIGURE 9.93
Select a default upload method.

After clicking Upload, GoLive will do a check on the files, comparing them to those on the server, and will open a window showing you what files will be uploaded. You can make changes in this window by selecting a filename and then clicking one of the four buttons at the bottom that designates the action you would like to be taken on the file. You can choose Skip, Upload, Download, or Delete. Under each section of the Upload window is information that clearly shows what will happen to a file both in the site and on the server.

When you are all ready, click OK. You'll receive a confirmation message, and when you click OK a second time, the files will be transferred. During the upload process you'll get an indicator, and when the process is complete you are returned to the site window.

Begin Creating

In this chapter we touched on the basics needed to begin working with GoLive CS. There are many additional tools in GoLive, and you will probably discover new features every time you work with it. Although it's true that the application is incredibly deep and very powerful, you don't need to know it all to begin creating your Web site. Just jump on in and get started. With the Adobe Creative Suite's incredibly powerful toolset, your ideas can spring to life both in print and on the Web more easily than ever before.

GoLive Extensions

Another terrific feature of GoLive is that it is extensible. Using the included Software Development Kit (SDK), you can extend GoLive's capabilities in countless ways. There are various samples inside the `Adobe GoLive SDK` folder, which is inside the `Adobe GoLive CS` application folder. Using the SDK, one can develop customized palettes, menu items, and objects for use inside of GoLive. One example of an amazing GoLive extension is Big Bang's MenuMachine, which allows Web designers to create complex pop-up menu systems in a beautiful interface right inside of GoLive. For more info visit their Web site at `www.menumachine.com`.

To install an extension from the `Samples` folder in the SDK, copy the folder to `Adobe GoLive CS/Modules/Extend Scripts`, and then restart Go Live. To use an extension, read the documentation for that particular extension.

Co-Author

Included with GoLive CS is an application called GoLive Co-Author. Using Co-Author, you, the designer, can set up pages that your client, the co-author, can update on his own. Every box of GoLive CS and every copy of the Adobe Creative Suite Premium comes with one free license of the standalone Co-Author client application for you to try. The Co-Author client is the part you give to your client.

The process goes like this: You design and set up the pages in GoLive CS and upload any necessary files to the server. Next you export the Site Locator file from the File menu in GoLive CS, which you can e-mail to your client. The client loads the site locator file into his Co-Author application, which loads the site's publish settings for him. Using the very simple interface in Co-Author, which is similar to using a Web form, the client can update pages or create new pages. Those pages will then be uploaded automatically when he clicks the Publish button in Co-Author.

The entire Co-Author application is built into GoLive CS, so it is not necessary to install the standalone client version for testing. In fact, you cannot install both GoLive CS and GoLive Co-Author on the same computer, because one will over-write the other!

If you try Co-Author and decide you like it, additional copies can be purchased from Adobe's online store. At the time of this book's printing, the price for one copy of Co-Author was $89. For more information on using Co-Author, visit the Adobe Studio Exchange and check the tutorials in the GoLive section at www.adobestudioexchange.com.

CHAPTER 10

Using Adobe Acrobat 6.0 Professional

Adobe has taken Acrobat to the next level. Dividing the program into two versions, Standard and Professional, allows the user to choose between basic editing and advanced editing features with Acrobat 6. PDF (Portable Document Format) or `.pdf` is a file type you see almost anywhere on the Web. This fabulous format is easily read by any computer system. If you don't have Reader, you can download it *free*! Many Web designers use Acrobat 6.0 to create their PDF files, add forms to their Web sites, and add a reviewing/commenting system to multiple-page documents.

What's New in Acrobat 6.0 Professional?

If you have used Acrobat before, here is a quick overview of what is new in Acrobat 6.0 Professional: one-click PDF creation from various applications, merging of multiple documents into one file, review managing, layers and large format support, ability to print high-quality files, preflight included, easy form creation, advanced commenting and drawing tools, improved viewing and navigation, accessibility enhancements, and integrated standards such as JavaScript and XML form data.

Introduction to Acrobat

PDF, or Portable Document Format, is a wonderful file format that is used universally as a standard for file transmission. PDF is perfect for use across multiple platforms as well. Adobe PDF files retain all the original file information, such as fonts, graphics, and text formatting. The files are small and easily transferred anywhere to anyone with Internet access. Many companies today use PDF files for enabling Web surfers to send in applications or order stuff online, and for passing documents for review between departments and to other divisions within a company.

Viewing PDF Files

Viewing a PDF file in Acrobat starts with opening a PDF file. To open a PDF file, you can choose File, Open; double-click on a PDF file; or drag the PDF file icon to the Acrobat program icon. After you have a file open, you have some viewing options. In Full Screen mode you see only the document—no menus, toolbars, or windows.

By the Way

> To view a PDF file in Full Screen mode, choose Full Screen View from the Window menu, or press (⌘-L) [Ctrl+L]. See Figure 10.1. Pressing the key command a second time toggles between Full Screen mode and default mode. You can also press the Esc key in Full Screen mode to return to default mode.

FIGURE 10.1
A PDF file in Full
Screen mode.

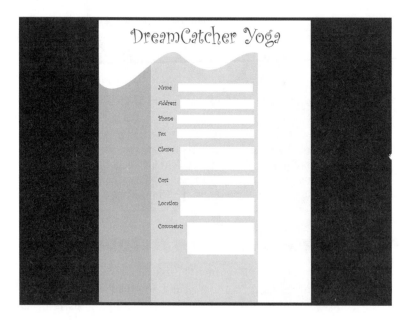

Another option is to view a single page or continuous pages of a PFD file. One nice advantage to viewing continuous pages is you can set it up to view facing pages to read your documents as you would a book. This is a perfect setting for reading eBooks with Acrobat. More on eBooks later in this chapter.

By the Way

To view a PDF in continuous facing pages, choose Continuous–Facing from the Page Layout submenu of the View menu. To go back to Single Page view, you can choose from the Page Layout submenu, or click on the Single Page button in the status bar (see Figure 10.2).

FIGURE 10.2
The Single Page button in the status bar.

Navigating Pages

Now that you have opened a PDF and set how you want to look at it, navigating the document is the next step. Getting around the page quickly and efficiently is easy using the status bar, the Navigation bar, and the various tools.

Zoom Tools

Acrobat offers various tools to zoom in, zoom out, and move around your PDF file. The Zoom toolbar houses the Zoom In tool, the Zoom Out tool, the Dynamic Zoom tool, the Loupe tool, and the Pan and Zoom Window commands; Zoom In and Zoom Out buttons; preset zoom levels; and an area to enter the level of the zoom.

The Dynamic Zoom tool gives you a new control over zooming. With the Dynamic Zoom tool, you click and hold down the mouse button while dragging outward to zoom out, or inward to zoom in.

Loupe Tool

The Loupe tool is a new addition to Acrobat 6 Professional. The Loupe tool allows you to create a viewing area on your PDF that magnifies the selected area in a separate window. Within the Loupe window (see Figure 10.3), you can change the magnification to see even more detail.

Status and Navigation Bars

One of the main areas of navigation is the status bar. Use the status bar, found at the bottom of the document window, to go back and forth between pages, jump to the beginning or end, or go to a specific page.

FIGURE 10.3
The Loupe tool and
window.

By the
Way

To go to a specific page, enter a number in the Page Number field (see Figure 10.4) and press the Return or Enter key. You will automatically go to the page you requested.

FIGURE 10.4
Enter a page num-
ber and jump to
that page.

The other navigation buttons on the status bar are, in order from left to right: First Page, Previous Page, Next Page, Last Page, Previous View, and Next View. The buttons you see on the far right side of the status bar are Single Page, Continuous, Continuous–Facing, and Facing. Use these buttons to quickly change your view of the PDF document.

The Navigation palette does the same as the status bar. You can access this float-ing palette by choosing View, Toolbars, Navigation. Use this when you want to put the capability to change pages in a place more accessible than the bottom of the page.

Hand Tool

The Hand tool acts as your hand does in real life with paper. Use the Hand tool to move your page around.

Layers

Layers capability in Acrobat? Well, if there were layers in the original Adobe application, there may be layers in Acrobat. One of the great additions to an already-great program. Let's say you create this fantastic multilevel floor plan in

Adobe Illustrator and you want to send it out for reviews. Save the Illustrator file as a PDF with layers and all, and you'll see those same layers in Acrobat. To see the layers in Acrobat, click on the Layers tab (see Figure 10.5).

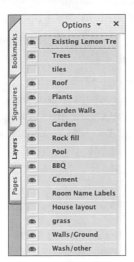

FIGURE 10.5
Layers from the original application are visible in Acrobat.

Pages

Managing your PDF document's pages is quick and easy in Acrobat 6.0 Professional. Jump to a specific page by entering the page in the status bar. Go to the beginning or end of the document by clicking the arrow button in the status bar. You can also arrange how you view your pages in a multiple-page PDF file. Choose whether to view single pages at a time, continuous pages, continuous facing pages, or facing pages (like reading a book).

The Pages pane shows a thumbnail view of each page in the PDF document. Use the Pages pane to delete pages, rearrange pages, or jump to a certain page by double-clicking on it.

Multiple Windows

Work with multiple PDF documents by arranging the pages in various ways. Choose from tiling your multiple windows horizontally or vertically. To bring the active window (the one you are currently working on) to the front, choose Cascade from the Window menu. The active window is placed in front, and the window title is black. All other windows show a gray window title to let you know that they are not active.

Creating PDF Files

Creating a PDF file has now become easier than ever. With Acrobat 6.0 Professional, you can create a PDF from one file, many different files, a Web page or pages, scanned images, or Microsoft Office applications, with one button click.

Create a PDF from a File

Create a PDF from a file by choosing File, Create PDF, From File. You can also choose From File from the pop-up menu in the menu bar. Then simply find the file on your computer and choose Open. After you open the file, to make it into a PDF, you must save the file. The file types you can open in Acrobat to create a PDF are BMP, CompuServe GIF, HTML, JPEG, JPEG 2000, Microsoft Word, PCX, PNG, PostScript/EPS, text file, and TIFF.

To create a PDF from multiple files, choose From Multiple Files from pop-up choices in the Create PDF button on the Tasks toolbar. This launches the Create PDF from Multiple Documents dialog box. Under the Add Files area, click the Choose button to select your files. You can do this multiple times to get all of your files if they aren't in the same folder. If they are in the same folder but not contiguous, hold the (⌘) [Ctrl] key to select the noncontiguous files. After the files are selected, you can arrange them in the Files to Combine area by dragging and dropping them in the order you want (see Figure 10.6). You can also change the order in Acrobat. Then click OK to bind all the pages in one PDF file. Remember to save the combined pages.

FIGURE 10.6
Rearrange the files you added in the Files to Combine area.

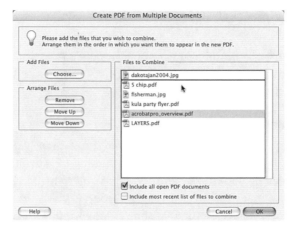

Create a PDF from Microsoft Applications

One valuable feature is one-click PDF creation from Microsoft applications. In Internet Explorer go to the Web site you want to convert to a PDF, and click the Convert Current Web page to PDF File button. This launches the Convert Web Page to PDF dialog box. Enter a name for the PDF file and click the Save button to convert the current Web page to a PDF. In Microsoft Office applications, the Convert to Adobe PDF button is in its own toolbar. If the Convert to Adobe PDF button isn't showing, find it under View, Toolbars, Adobe Acrobat PDFMaker.

Create a PDF from a Web Page

Downloading a Web page or a whole Web site into Acrobat is an easy task. Choose how many levels (children pages or tiers) of the Web site you want to download, or download more later and add the pages to your PDF. Create a PDF from a Web page by choosing From Web Page from the Create PDF button in the menu bar, or choose From Web Page from the submenu of the Create PDF command under the File menu.

When creating a PDF from a Web page, make sure you have the URL ready to enter in the URL text field. You can also set how many levels of the Web site you want to convert (see Figure 10.7). Keep in mind that if you choose to convert the whole Web site or many levels of the Web site, the result could be a huge PDF file. You can convert HTML pages that include forms, links, frames, Flash, graphics with JPEG or GIF, tables, and text files into PDF pages.

> Most Web sites are built hierarchically in different levels. You may have certain links on a home page, which constitutes one layer, but clicking on any of those links may reveal a whole new set of links, which would be another level deeper into the site.

By the Way

FIGURE 10.7
Enter the Web address and the number of levels you want to convert to a PDF.

After the Web page is converted into a PDF file (see Figure 10.8), you can edit and enhance as you see fit.

FIGURE 10.8
A Web site convert-
ed into a PDF docu-
ment.

Editing PDF Files

Now that you have converted files into a PDF, you can edit and alter the files as you wish. Not only can you edit the text in the PDF file, but you also can add comments, stamps, headers and footers, watermarks, backgrounds, sound, movie clips, and more.

The basic editing tools are Hand tool, Select tool (Text, Table, and Image), and Snapshot tool. Use the Hand tool to move your page around. The Select tool simply selects text, tables, or objects so that you can copy and paste. The Snapshot tool copies whatever is within the marquee for pasting later.

The more advanced editing features include the Select Object, Article, Crop, Link, Movie, Sound, TouchUp Text, TouchUp Object, and various Forms tools. To view the Advanced Editing tools, choose Tools, Advanced Editing, Show Advanced Editing Toolbar. Many of the advanced editing tools are covered throughout this chapter.

TouchUp Tools

The TouchUp tools enable you to edit an object as well as text. Use the TouchUp Object tool to edit an existing object. With the TouchUp Object tool you can do only basic edits such as copy, delete, and alter properties. If you need to do more extensive editing, you need to edit in the program the object was created in. When you double-click on a placed object with the TouchUp Object tool, the original application will launch, enabling you to edit the object. When you save, the saved version will update in your PDF file.

The TouchUp Text tool lets you edit text in a PDF document. You first select the text using the TouchUp Text tool, and then enter the new text in the highlighted area (see Figure 10.9). This works only if the font was initially embedded in the PDF file, or if you have the font on your system.

FIGURE 10.9
Editing a PDF with the TouchUp Text tool.

Checking Spelling

You can check the spelling in form fields or comments of any PDF file. To check the spelling of the form fields and comments, choose Edit, Check Spelling, In Comments and Form Fields. You can also edit the dictionary to include odd words such as TIFF and EPS. You can have Acrobat automatically check the spelling as you are typing comments or form fields.

Using Comments

Adding comments is such a breeze in Acrobat. Comments are notes, highlights, or any markings you add to a PDF document to indicate changes. The Commenting tools include Note, Text Edits, Stamp, Highlighter, Cross-Out Text, Underline Text, several drawing tools, Text Box, Pencil, and Attachment tools. The last four of these are under the Advanced Commenting toolbar. Comments can be as simple as a sticky note, or a long explanation. You can also add text edit marks or proofreader marks to the PDF. Sound and movie attachments can be included, as well as stamps to indicate approval, rejection, and more.

Adding Comments

Before adding a comment, decide what kind of comment you want to add. You can insert text edits with the drag of the mouse.

By the Way

> To insert a text edit, first choose the text edit tool from the Commenting Toolbar. Choose the Indicate Text Edits tool and highlight the text you want to show edits on. Then choose from Insert Text at Cursor, Replace Selected Text, Highlight Selected Text, Add Note to Selected Text, Cross out Text for Deletion, and Underline Selected Text. When you choose any of the Text Edits, they automatically change the selected text to your chosen text edits (see Figure 10.10).

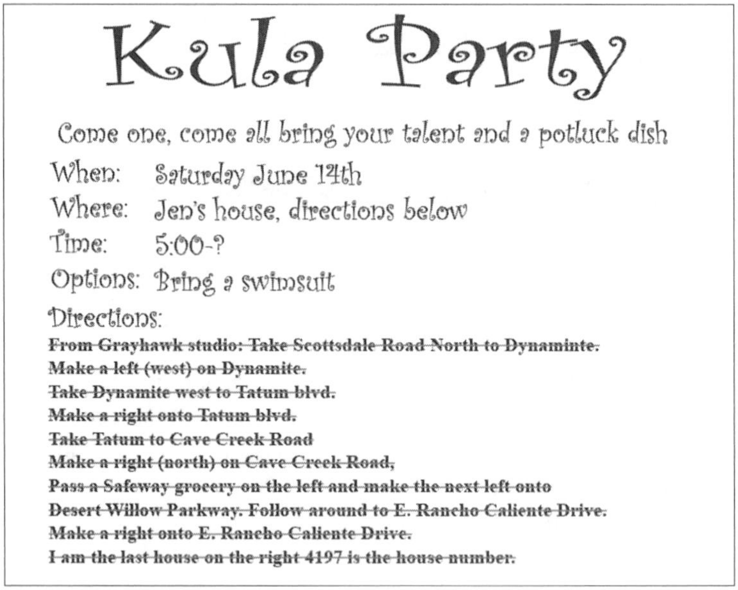

Kula Party

Come one, come all bring your talent and a potluck dish

When: Saturday June 14th

Where: Jen's house, directions below

Time: 5:00-?

Options: Bring a swimsuit

Directions:

~~From Grayhawk studio: Take Scottsdale Road North to Dynaminte.~~
~~Make a left (west) on Dynamite.~~
~~Take Dynamite west to Tatum blvd.~~
~~Make a right onto Tatum blvd.~~
~~Take Tatum to Cave Creek Road~~
~~Make a right (north) on Cave Creek Road,~~
~~Pass a Safeway grocery on the left and make the next left onto~~
~~Desert Willow Parkway. Follow around to E. Rancho Caliente Drive.~~
~~Make a right onto E. Rancho Caliente Drive.~~
~~I am the last house on the right 4197 is the house number.~~

FIGURE 10.10
Adding a text edit to selected text.

Many people simply write a comment on a sticky note and slap it on a printed document. I have even seen sticky notes stuck on a computer screen! To add a sticky note without the mess to your PDF, choose the Note tool from the Commenting toolbar. Click and drag out the size you want the note to be. Don't worry, the note won't show up as a huge yellow page covering your PDF. When the note isn't active, it is a small symbol. You can also resize your note at any time. After creating the note, enter the text for your note (see Figure 10.11).

FIGURE 10.11
A note added to a
PDF document.

Reading Comments from Others

The next step to adding a comment is being able to read the comment. You can read not only the comment you just put on, but also any comments any reviewer may have added to the PDF. To read a note, first choose the Hand tool. Just let the Hand tool rest over the note, and you'll see a pop-up of what the note says. You can also double-click on the note to pop up the note completely. To close the note, click on the box in the upper-right corner of the Note text box. Double-clicking the note symbol again also closes the note.

Commenting Tools

The Basic commenting tools found in the Commenting Toolbar are the Note, Text Edits, Stamp, Highlighter, Cross-out Text, and Underline Text tools.

The Note tool lets you add a note as you would a sticky note to a printed document. Drag out a note, enter your text, and then close the note. Using the Hand tool, you can read the note.

The Text Edit tools highlight a specific area of text, and then you choose a specific edit to apply to the selected text. Choose from Insert Text at Cursor, Replace Selected Text, Highlight Selected Text, Add Note to Selected Text, Cross Out Text for Deletion, and Underline Selected Text.

To add a stamp to a document, you can choose a stamp from the menu, or you can create and use your own stamp. When choosing from the Stamp menu, choose from Dynamic, Sign Here, or Standard Business. Under Dynamic, you can choose from Approved, Confidential, Received, Reviewed, and Revised. In the Sign Here stamp submenu, you'll find Rejected, Accepted, Initial Here, Sign Here, and Witness. Under the Standard Business stamps are Approved, Completed, Confidential, Draft, Final, For Comment, For Public Release, Information Only, Not Approved, Not for Public Release, Preliminary Results, and Void. Under each of those stamp submenus, you can see a preview of what the stamp looks like (see Figure 10.12).

FIGURE 10.12
Samples of various stamps.

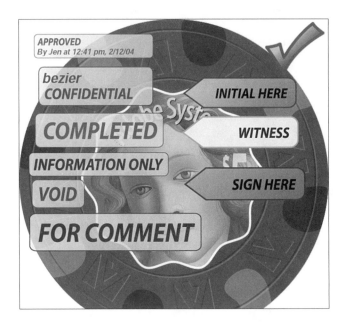

Under the Stamp menu you'll see the commands Create Custom Stamp, Add Current Stamp to Favorites, and Manage Stamps. Before choosing Create Custom Stamp, you first must have created the stamp image in another program, such as Adobe Illustrator or Adobe Photoshop. Then you can follow the steps under the Create Custom Stamp command.

Advanced Commenting Tools

The Advanced Commenting Toolbar can be found by choosing Tools, Advanced Commenting, Show Advanced Commenting Toolbar. The Advanced Commenting tools are Drawing, Text Box, Pencil, and Attachment.

Under the Drawing tools you'll find the Rectangle, Oval, Arrow, Line, Cloud, Polygon, and Polygon Line tools. Use the Drawing tools to add a visual markup to your PDF file. The tools can create a dramatic marking to really show your editing ideas. With the Drawing tools, you can add notes as well.

The Text Box tool lets you create a box that you enter text inside of. You can enhance the text box by accessing the properties of the box. To access the properties, right-click on the text box (Windows), or Ctrl-click (Macintosh) on the box with the Text Box tool as the active tool and choose Properties from the context menu. Under the Properties, change the border color, style, background color, opacity, and thickness of the border.

The Pencil tool is handy for adding free-form sketching and shapes to a PDF document. The handy partner to the Pencil tool is the Pencil Eraser tool. Use the Pencil Eraser tool to remove any sections of the lines you have drawn. The Pencil Eraser tool removes only lines drawn with the Pencil tool, not those drawn with any other Drawing tools.

Add attachments to your PDF with the Attachment tool. The attachments you can add are Attach File, Attach Sound, and Paste Clipboard Image.

> **By the Way**
>
> To attach sound to a PDF, first select the Attach Sound tool. Click with the Attach Sound tool on the PDF where you want the sound symbol to appear. This launches the Record Sound dialog box. You can either record your sound or notes verbally, or choose a sound stored on your computer.

To attach a more advanced sound, such as music from your iPod, you need to use the Advanced Editing tools. The Advanced Editing tools are discussed later in this chapter.

Importing and Exporting Comments

After your PDF document gets passed around for comments from colleagues, you may want to import their comments and then export your own comments.

By the
Way

To import comments, you first must have the document open that you want the comments imported into. Then choose Import Comments from the Document menu. This launches the Import Comments dialog box, where you choose the FDF file on your computer. The comments then show up in the comment window and are added into the document as well.

To export your comments, first make sure you have the file with your comments open. Choose Export Comments from the Document menu. Choose the Save as Type (FDF or XFDF) option, and save the file on your computer. You can also choose to export only certain comments rather than all of your comments. Do this in the Comments pane by (⌘) [Ctrl]-clicking on the specific comments, causing them to be highlighted by a bold rectangle; then use the Export Selected Comments function (see Figure 10.13).

FIGURE 10.13
Selecting certain comments for exporting in the Comments pane.

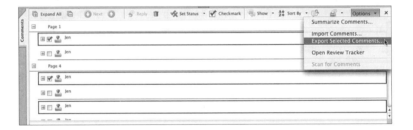

Summarizing Comments

The Summarizing feature allows you to create a PDF file with all the comments shown and organized by date, author, and type. This list shows *only* the comments, not the actual PDF file the comments were created on, unless you choose that option when summarizing the comments.

In the Comments pane, choose Summarize Comments from the Options menu. You then set the organization of how the comments will be displayed. Choose by date, author, type, and page. In the Summarize Options dialog box you can choose to include the original PDF file with the comments (may be a large file), or just the comments.

Reviewing

Acrobat has added the option for you to include others in a reviewing process with PDF documents. You can send a PDF document to your co-workers to get their comments on a file. Use email to start your review or your Web browser to host the review. This is a great way to get instant feedback without waiting for the postal or delivery systems to send paper files back and forth. You can set up an email-based review.

Email-Based Review

Setting up an email-based review is a fairly easy task. First open the PDF file you want to be reviewed. Choose Send by Email for Review under the Review and Comment menu of the Tasks toolbar. Then enter the email addresses of the reviewers and add your email address, and your email program takes care of the process. Acrobat enters instructions in the email on how to review. Simply click the Send button (if necessary) and the review process is on it's way.

Review Tracker

Acrobat also has the capability to track the reviews. Under the Review and Comment menu of the Tasks toolbar is the Track Reviews command. Under the Review Tracker, choose which review you want to track. You'll see the list of any documents you have set up for review. The Review Tracker can also be used to invite more people to your review or send a reminder.

Using Sound and Movies

More advanced sound and the addition of movies can be found in the Advanced Editing tools. The Advanced Editing tools, found under the Tools menu, are Select Object, Article, Crop, Link, Sound, Movie, TouchUp Text, and TouchUp Object. The addition of sound or a movie clip nudges the simple, boring PDF to the next level.

Add Sound

Add sound clips to any PDF file using the Advanced Editing toolbar. Sound can be played when the sound button is clicked, or when a certain action is performed. Use any sounds that can be played in Flash, RealOne, QuickTime, and Windows Media Player. If you are recording your own sounds, make sure you have a microphone attached to your computer. You can add a sound by dragging out a sound button, or add sound to a Page Action or a Form Field.

To add a sound clip using the Sound tool, select the Sound tool from the Advanced Editing toolbar. Drag out the size you want the sound button to be. This launches the Add Sound dialog box. Click the (Choose) [Browse] button to find the sound on your computer. Click OK. To activate the sound, choose the Hand tool and click on the sound box. You can also change the look of the sound icon by altering the Properties of the box.

To change the properties of the sound button, use the Sound tool and (Control-click) [right-click] on the button. Choose Properties from the context menu. You can then change the line style, weight, and color (see Figure 10.14). You can also edit the button in the context menu and change the size as well.

FIGURE 10.14
Editing the proper-
ties of a sound
box.

Add Movies

Movies can be added to any PDF document. Unlike attachments, movies are considered an editing feature. You'll find the Movie tool under the Advanced Editing toolbar. Just as you use other applications to access your sound clips, you need other applications to access your video clips. Adding a movie clip to a PDF is done just as you would add a sound clip. Keep in mind that the larger the movie, the larger your PDF file will be.

To add a movie clip, click and drag out the button for the movie clip. Click the (Choose) [Browse] button to access the movie clip on your computer. Select your movie and click OK. When you click the movie button with the Hand tool, the movie clip will play right inside the PDF document.

Creating Interactivity

Acrobat lets you create amazing interactive documents using various tools. We have already discussed the Sound and Movie tools. Bookmarks, Flash, links, actions, and buttons are all used to create interactive PDF documents. You can make any PDF form interactive as well. Interactivity just lets you go where no PDF has ever gone before.

Adding Bookmarks

Just as you would create a bookmark in your Web browser, you can create bookmarks in your PDF documents. This is quite handy for large PDF files with numerous pages. You can access often-used pages quickly with bookmarks.

To create a bookmark, first go to the page you want to bookmark. Then choose New Bookmark from the Options menu on the Bookmarks pane (see Figure 10.15). I suggest entering a name for the page you are bookmarking that lets you know what the page is about.

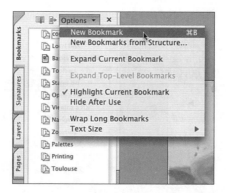

FIGURE 10.15
Choose New Bookmark from the Options menu on the Bookmarks pane.

In large PDF files the bookmarks are really nice for navigating in the PDF. Bookmarks organize your PDF file. You can also access the New Bookmark option by (Control-clicking) [right-clicking] on the PDF page you want to bookmark and choosing New Bookmark from the context menu. Accessing the Pages pane lets you view the whole PDF page in a mini preview. This is also a way of navigating to a certain page, but you really won't know which page is which unless they have very different layouts. That is why bookmarks are so handy for navigating exactly to the area you want.

At any time you can rename, rearrange, or remove bookmarks. By dragging a bookmark above or below another bookmark, you can change the order of the bookmarks. You can also drag a bookmark within a bookmark as a subset of the other bookmark.

Linking and Actions

The Link tool is used to create a button link to other pages in the PDF file. You can also link to other documents or Web sites on the Internet. Within the link you can set the properties of the button as you can for the Sound and Movie buttons. You can not only set the properties, but add an action to the link as well.

You can choose Actions in the Link Properties dialog box (not in the Create Link dialog box). The actions you can choose from are Go to a Page in This Document, Go to a Page in Another Document, Go to Snapshot View, Open a File, Read an Article, Execute a Menu Item, Set Layer Visibility, Show/Hide a Field, Submit a Form, Reset a Form, Import Form Data, Run a JavaScript, Play Media (Acrobat 5 Compatible), Play a Sound, Play Media (Acrobat 6 Compatible), and Open a Web Link. So when you set a link, it can do multiple things.

By the Way

> To set an action to a link, follow these steps. Using the Link tool, drag out a button area for the link. Enter the type of link in the Create Link dialog box. Click OK. Ctrl-click on the link with the Link tool to access the Link Properties dialog box. In the Link Properties dialog box, click the Actions tab (see Figure 10.16). Choose an Action from the pop-up menu and click OK. Use the Hand tool to click on the Link button to see the action activated.

FIGURE 10.16
Click the Actions tab to choose an action for your link.

JavaScript Support

JavaScript allows you to add more interactivity to your PDF forms that you just can't get with Acrobat alone. Use JavaScript with forms, links, and page actions. For those of you who are wondering what JavaScript is, it is a coding for HTML pages. Use it in Acrobat forms for adding up items, costs, and so forth.

To access a JavaScript, choose a button's properties and choose Run a JavaScript from the pop-up menu. Select the desired JavaScript and choose Edit to access JavaScript Editor. In this editor, you can alter the JavaScript code. Click OK when you are done. For more information on JavaScript, see *Sams Teach Yourself JavaScript in 24 Hours* by Michael Moncur.

Providing for Accessibility

Acrobat has added accessibility functions to make using Acrobat easier for vision- and motor-challenged people. The features added include reading out loud, visibility, auto scrolling, keyboard shortcuts, and creating accessible PDF documents.

The Read Out Loud settings are found in Acrobat's preferences. Set the volume, voice type, pitch, words per minute, reading order, and screen reader options.

Visibility can be enhanced by changing the document's color options in the Accessibility area of Acrobat's Preferences. Other visual enhancements are to increase the magnification in the Default Zoom area of Page Display Preferences.

Under the View menu you can set the page to automatically scroll. Use the number keys to control the scroll speed (9 being fast scrolling and 0 being slow scrolling). You can also use the up and down arrows for auto scrolling. The right and left arrows take you to the next and the previous page.

Memorizing keyboard shortcuts is always a great way to enhance your productivity whether you have special needs or not.

> To make your PDF accessible, Acrobat will create a report on the accessibility of your file. Open the PDF you want to make accessible, and choose Add Tags to Document under the Accessibility submenu of the Advanced menu. Before making your file accessible, you may want to run a quick check to see whether there are any problems or things you may need to fix.

By the Way

Using Forms

Forms are probably the most sought-after feature in Acrobat. Use Acrobat to create interactive PDF forms that you can access on a Web site. Forms are created with data fields to be filled out. Form fields can range from buttons, check boxes, combo boxes, list boxes, radio buttons, and signature fields to text fields. Acrobat includes a Forms palette and Form tools. Forms are so popular because you can save a form data within Acrobat Standard or Reader. Your only limitation is that you cannot edit in Standard or Reader. Forms are the best way to get information on your client or from your Web site.

Creating Forms

When you first decide to create a form, you'll need to figure out the type of data you'll need. After you determine the data, the form fields will be easy to add. Use a design program to create your actual form. When choosing a size, keep in mind the computer screen and how it will be seen. In the design program create the text, labels, and any graphic elements.

Typically, you'll start creating a form in another application such as Adobe Illustrator or Microsoft Word. After you've created a PDF for the form you started in the other program, use the Form tools to create form fields to complete your PDF form.

By the Way

To create a text field, use the Text Field tool from the Forms toolbar. Drag out a box to the size that you want the text field to be. This launches the Text Field Properties dialog box (see Figure 10.17). Set the General, Appearance, Options, Actions, Format, Validate, and Calculate tabs to your liking, and then click the Close button to set the text field.

FIGURE 10.17
As you set the various properties of the Text Field tool, it automatically updates on your form.

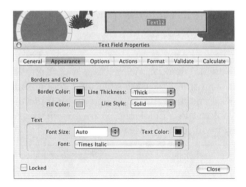

After you create the form's graphic appearance, save the file as a PDF and open it in Acrobat to add the actual form fields. First you have to understand about the Text Fields and their properties.

Text Field Properties

These are the tabs in the Text Field Properties dialog box:

▶ **General**—Under the General properties set the name of the field and the Tool tips. Tool tips are the little notes that come up when you rest your cursor on an item such as the Text field. The Form Field properties you set are whether the box is visible, hidden, visible but not printable, or hidden but printable. Set the orientation to 0, 90, 180, or 270 degrees. Also choose whether to check the Read Only and Required check boxes.

▶ **Appearance**—In the Appearance tab set the Border Color, Fill Color, Line Thickness, and Line Style. Under the Text, choose the Font, Font Size, and Text Color.

▶ **Options**—Choose the Alignment for the text field in the Options tab. Enter a Default Value. Check or uncheck the following boxes: Multi-line, Scroll Long Text, Allow Rich Text Formatting, Limit of ___ Characters, Password, Field Is Used for File Selection, Check Spelling, and Comb of ___ Characters.

▶ **Actions**—Set an action for the Text Field just as you would in a link. Choose your action and the settings.

▶ **Format**—Choose from a format category pop-up: None, Number, Percentage, Date, Time, Special, or Custom.

▶ **Validate**—Check the radio button to specify whether the field value is validated, to indicate whether a field value is within a certain range, or to run a custom validation script.

▶ **Calculate**—Under the Calculate tab choose whether the field is not calculated, or if it is calculated, choose whether it is the sum, product, average, minimum, or maximum of a group of fields that you pick. You can also choose a simplified field notation, or a custom calculation script.

Form Fields

The Form fields come in various appearances and functions. Each function is used for specific effects. Buttons are used to create an action. You press a button and something happens, such as going to another page, or different fields appearing. Check boxes are used to narrow down selections. A combo box is used like a pop-up menu. You see a list of choices and pick one from the box. The list box is similar to the combo box, and you choose one option from the menu. Radio buttons are used to choose an option. You pick one option or the other by clicking the radio button. In the signature field you enter a digital signature or, in a printed form, sign your name. The text fields are used to enter such things as names, addresses, items, costs, and totals.

Open a PDF that has the form base already created in another graphic program. Using the Text Field tool, drag out the size for your text fields. In the Text Field Properties, enter the properties for the text field, such as border or background color. After adding the text fields, add buttons, check boxes, and more (see Figure 10.18).

FIGURE 10.18
A form originally created in Adobe Illustrator and finished in Acrobat.

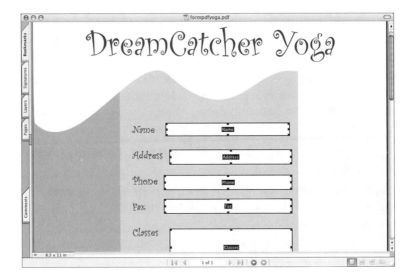

Buttons

Probably one of the most fun things to do with Acrobat is to create interactive buttons. Acrobat has a Button tool in the Forms menu on the Advanced Editing toolbar. Use the Button tool to drag out the size of the button. Enter the properties that you want for the button. Be sure to make an Action for the button, or the point of having a button is lost. If you want a more exciting look for your button, use Adobe Illustrator to create a fantastic button and then use Acrobat to activate it (see Figure 10.19).

Add options to your buttons by altering their look and how they act. Choose the Icon and Label state: Label Only, Icon Only, Icon top Label Bottom, Label Top Icon Bottom, Icon Left Label Right, Label Left Icon Right, and Label Over Icon.

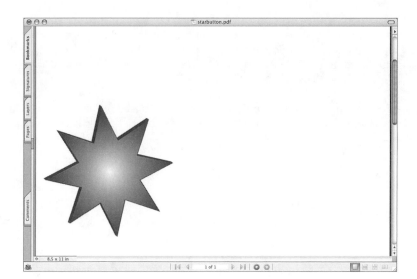

FIGURE 10.19
A button created in Adobe Illustrator and then activated in Acrobat.

List Boxes and Combo Boxes

Use the combo box to list various choices for the form field. A list box is very similar in that it offers choices in a menu pull-down form. The big difference between the two is that you use the combo box for adding text where a list box can't add text. Also the combo box is great for fewer choices. The options you'll find in the list and combo boxes are Item, Export Value, Add, Delete, Up/Down, Sort Items, Multiple Selection (List Box Only), Check Spelling, Item List, and Commit Selected Value Immediately.

Radio Buttons and Check Boxes

Radio buttons and check boxes are used for selecting or deselecting certain variables. The options you'll find under radio buttons and check boxes are Button/Check Box Style, Export Value, Button/Check box Is Checked by Default, and Buttons with the Same Name and Value Are Selected in Unison.

Calculations

Calculations are great for figuring out a total of items, total cost, adding in taxes, and so on. As with spreadsheet programs, you can set up a range of calculations in the Field Properties dialog box. The calculations you can set are adding, multiplying, averaging, and figuring out the minimum and maximum.

To set a calculation field, first pick the type of calculation, and then select which fields you want to calculate. To set the field for calculation, use the Text Field tool to create the box for the calculation. In the Text Field Properties dialog box, click on the Calculate tab. In the Calculate tab, choose from Sum (+), Product (x), Average, Minimum, or Maximum. After you set your value, click the Pick button. This launches the Field Selection dialog box (see Figure 10.20). This dialog box lists all the fields used in your PDF file. Here you can choose which fields will be calculated.

FIGURE 10.20
Choose the fields for calculation in the Field Selection dialog box.

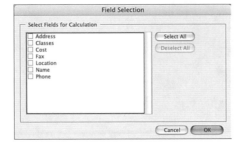

Importing/Exporting Form Data

Now that you are getting the hang of forms, you'll need to know how you can import and export the data from the forms. The key to getting your data is having your fields match word for word. To export your FDF data, choose Export Forms Data from the Forms submenu of the Advanced menu. Enter a name for your form data file and click Save.

Import your form data by choosing Import Forms Data from the Forms submenu of the Advanced menu. Locate your file and click Select. Make sure you have the correct and matching file open so that the data will be brought in to the file.

Security

Use Acrobat's security to protect your files from unwanted access. When you create a PDF file, it isn't protected until you set the protection. Security commands are located in a submenu of the Document menu. Under the Security submenu choose from Restrict Opening and Editing, Encrypt for Certain Identities Using Certificates, or Display Restrictions and Security.

Restrict Opening and Editing

When you choose Restrict Opening and Editing, the Password Security–Settings dialog box opens. Within this dialog box, you can set the Compatibility version of Acrobat. The lower the version, the lower the encryption level. The higher the version of Acrobat, the higher the encryption level.

You can check the box to require a password to open the document. When you choose this option, you'll be asked for a password to enter. If you choose this option, you always have to use a password to open the document.

Permissions options include using a password to restrict printing and editing of the PDF and its security settings. With the Permissions check box, you set the password and choose whether you allow any printing, low-resolution printing, or high-resolution printing. You also set whether changes will be allowed, including Inserting, Deleting, and Rotating Pages; Filling in Form Fields and Signing; Commenting, Filling in Form Fields and Signing; and Any Except Extracting Pages. Other check boxes include Enable Copying of Text, Images, and Other Content; Enable Text Access for Screen Reader Devices for the Visually Impaired; and Enable Plaintext Metadata.

You have three tries to open a password-protected PDF file. After three tries the document closes, and you have to reopen it to try the password again.

Encrypt for Certain Identities

If you choose the option Encrypt for Certain Identities Using Certificates, the Document Security–Digital ID Selection dialog box launches. Select the Digital ID file from the pop-up menu and enter the User Password. Another choice is to Find Your Digital ID File, or Create a New Digital ID File.

Display Restrictions and Security

Choosing the Display Restrictions and Security choice in the Security submenu launches the Document Properties dialog box. In this dialog box, you can set the Security Method (choose No Security, Password Security, or Certificate Security). If you choose to change the Security Method by clicking the Change Settings button, you'll get the Permissions options dialog box as you did in the Restrict Opening and Editing function. The Document Properties dialog box displays the security settings and shows the details of the PDF document (see Figure 10.21).

FIGURE 10.21
The Document
Properties dialog
box displaying the
security and restric-
tions settings.

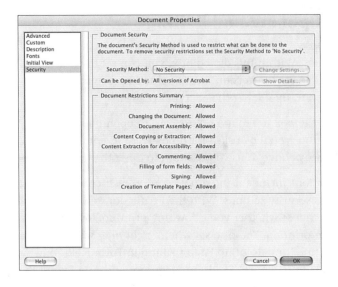

Digital Signatures

More than ever, people want to use digital signatures to replace hand signatures.
Using a digital signature saves a ton of time and money because you don't have
to ship documents back and forth. A digital signature can be an actual handwrit-
ten name, text, or a graphic symbol. After you have a digital signature, you can
verify that the signature is authentic.

Acrobat has a Self-Sign Security feature. This program handles the digital signatures. Set up a signature for signing using the Select My Digital ID File command
in the My Digital ID Files submenu of the Manage Digital IDs submenu under the
Advanced menu.

**By the
Way**

> To create a profile for a digital signature, start with the Select My Digital ID File com-
> mand. In the Select My Digital ID File dialog box, choose the New Digital ID File but-
> ton. Click the Continue button to continue. In the Create Self-Signed Digital ID dialog
> box, enter your name, organization name, and email address. Then choose a pass-
> word to launch the New Self Sign Digital ID File dialog box. Make sure you choose
> the folder in which you want to save the digital signature information, and then click
> Save.

After you set up your profile, you can edit the profile to set how your signature
will be used in a PDF file.

Create a Digital Signature

Now that you have learned how to create a profile, you'll need to add your actual signature or image for the digital signature. First you'll need to scan in your actual signature or use any image and save it as a PDF file. In Acrobat's Preferences dialog box, you select Digital Signatures from the list on the left. Click the New button to add your scanned signature. This launches the Configure Signature Appearance dialog box. In this dialog box enter a Title, and under Configure Graphic choose the PDF File button. In the Select Picture dialog box, click the Browse button, choose your scanned PDF file, and then click OK. In the Select Picture dialog box, you'll see a small preview of your signature. Click OK three times while clicking your heels together, and you have a saved digital signature.

Digitally Sign Your Document

The signature you have saved can now be applied to any PDF document.

To sign your PDF document with your digital signature, click the Signatures tab on the left side of the window (housed with Pages, Layers, and Bookmarks). Under the Options menu in the Signatures pane, choose Create a Blank Signature Field, and then drag out a box to hold your signature. The Digital Signature Properties dialog box comes up. Select the style for the box. Click Close. Then choose Sign Signature Field from the Options area of the Signature window. Click the Continue Signing button after you have read the alert. This brings up the Apply Signature to Document dialog box. Enter your password and then click the Sign and Save button. Your digital signature appears in the box you dragged out (see Figure 10.22).

By the Way

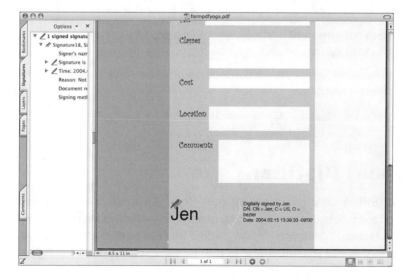

FIGURE 10.22
A digital signature on a PDF document.

Certified PDF

After you digitally sign a document, you may want to certify the PDF document. Doing this lets you exercise some control over the editing of the file.

1. To certify your PDF, choose Save As Certified Document under the File menu. A Save As Certified Document dialog box then comes up.

2. In this dialog box you are told that you need a Digital ID to certify the document. You can get a Digital ID from Adobe Partner, or click OK if you already have a Digital ID. After you click OK, you set the allowable actions.

3. Choose from the following: Disallow Any Changes to the Document, Only Allow Form Fill-In Actions on This Document, or Only Allow Commenting and Form Fill-In Actions on This Document.

> These will take affect only after you save and close the document. It is also a good idea to lock the certifying signature so that it can't be cleared or deleted by anyone.

4. Click the Next button. A warning dialog box comes up, alerting you of any potential problems or suggestions.

5. Click the Next button. Then choose the visibility of the Certification (Show Certification on Document or Do Not Show Certification on Document).

6. Drag out the area where you want the certification to appear on your document.

7. Click OK and, using your mouse, indicate the area on your document.

8. Choose the Digital ID in the next dialog box.

9. Enter your password in the Save As Certified Document–Sign dialog box. From the pop-up choose a reason why you are signing.

10. Click Sign and Save As (or choose Sign and Save and you'll overwrite the original document).

11. Enter a name and location and click Save.

Acrobat Distiller

Acrobat Distiller used to be a separate program of Acrobat. Now it is rolled in with Acrobat 6.0. It still runs as it did, but you can access it in Acrobat under the Advanced menu. When you choose Distiller, the program starts up. Before Acrobat 6, you had to use Distiller to convert many file types into PDF files.

Distiller is mainly used to convert a PostScript file (created by another application) into a PDF file. To convert a PostScript file to a PDF using Distiller, you can simply drag the PostScript file on top of the Distiller icon, or with Distiller active, open the PostScript file. You can also adjust the settings in Distiller to make the PDF the way you want.

PDF Presentations

Presentations are not limited to PowerPoint. I love using Acrobat for a slide show presentation. You even get to use fancy transitions between the slides!

By the Way

To create a slide show presentation with Acrobat, first pick the files you want to be in the slide show. Make sure that all the files are PDFs. In fact, you can use the Create PDF from Multiple Files function to convert the files and open them together as one bound PDF file.

To create a multiple-paged PDF, choose From Multiple Files from the Create PDF submenu of the File menu. Select the files you want by clicking the Choose button in the Add Files area. You can pick more than one file at a time by holding the Shift key while selecting the first and last file of a string of contiguous files, or by holding the (⌘) [Ctrl] key while selecting noncontiguous files.

Arrange the files in the order in which you want them to appear in the Files to Combine area. After you have all the files arranged, click OK.

To make the slide show appear as a slide show, first go to the preferences to set your Full Screen preferences. Choose Full Screen Navigation options and click OK. In the Full Screen Navigation Preferences, set the Advance time, Loop options, and any Transitions you might want. To run the slide show (see Figure 10.23), choose Full Screen from the Window menu or press (⌘-L) [Ctrl+L]. This command toggles between running the slide show and stopping the slide show.

One really nice perk of using Acrobat to create a slide show is that you can send the file to anyone and that person can view it. You only need Reader (available free online at www.adobe.com) to view the slide show.

Full Screen Preferences

Creating a slide show is pretty easy. Now let's clean it up by editing the Full Screen preferences. Choose File, Preferences (Windows) and Acrobat, Preferences (Macintosh), or press (⌘-K) [Ctrl+K]. Choose Full Screen from the choices on the left. Here is where you can set how the slide show functions:

FIGURE 10.23
A full-screen slide show in Acrobat.

- ▶ **Full Screen Navigation**—Enter a value in seconds for how quickly or slowly the slides automatically advance. Check the Loop After Last Page box to have the slide show run continually. Keep the Escape Key Exits box checked so that you can quickly get out if you forget the keyboard shortcut. The last option in this area is Left Click to Go Forward One Page; Right Click to Go Back. These are just nice keyboard commands to navigate your slide show manually.

- ▶ **Full Screen Appearance**—Under this Full Screen preference, you can specify to Ignore All Transitions. Set the default transition, mouse cursor function, and background color.

Transitions

Transitions are a wonderful way to advance from one page of your slide show to the next. Use transitions to enhance your presentation. When choosing a transition, keep in mind what your slides look like. For example, if you have mostly text, or tables, using a dissolve transition looks rather sloppy and confusing. When you choose a transition, it will be used between all slide transitions. You can't choose a different one for each slide. If you are looking for variety, choose the Random Transition. This option randomly uses the various transitions (there are 50) between slides (see Figure 10.24).

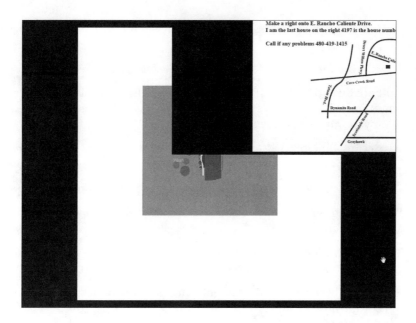

If some day you decide you don't want the transitions anymore, go to Full Screen Preferences and check the Ignore All Transitions option, or choose No Transition from the Default Transition pop-up menu. Remember that you can also change the background color from the default black to any color you want.

Printing and Saving PDF Files

After creating a fantastic PDF, you need to make sure that it is saved. Actually, you should be saving periodically so that you don't ever lose any information. Saving a PDF file is pretty routine and easy. Choose Save from the File menu to save over the original file, or choose Save As to save the file with a different name. Another choice is to Save As Certified Document. This option was discussed earlier in this chapter.

You may wonder about printing your PDF. As with any other file, you can print out your PDF documents.

Saving

When you create a PDF from most means, the first time you choose Save, you'll get the Save As dialog box. You don't have to save every file as a PDF. These are the file format choices:

- ▶ **PDF**—Portable Document Format, or PDF, is easily read by any user who has Adobe Reader (free program found at www.adobe.com).

- ▶ **EPS**—Encapsulated PostScript is used when working with design or page layout programs.

- ▶ **HTML**—Use this file type to save documents for the Web.

- ▶ **Graphic formats**—JPEG, JPEG 2000, PNG, and TIFF are all graphic type formats that you can save a PDF as. When you save a PDF as any of these formats, you will lose the text editing capability.

- ▶ **PostScript**—Similar to EPS, PostScript is mostly used to change the printing options of a file.

- ▶ **RTF**—Rich Text Format will let you use the file in a word processing application.

- ▶ **Word**—Use this format to save the file so that you can take it back into Microsoft Word.

- ▶ **Text**—Use this format for plain or accessible text to save a file that retains the text, but not the text's formatting.

- ▶ **XML**—Use this format and XML Data Package Files for forms and managing document workflows.

Saving a file as anything other than a PDF can offer many options under the Save As dialog box. If you choose to change the default settings under any of the other formats, click the Settings button to see your options (see Figure 10.25).

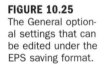

FIGURE 10.25
The General optional settings that can be edited under the EPS saving format.

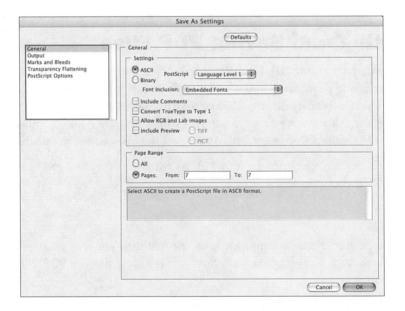

Reverting

The Revert command under the File menu lets you take the document you are working on back to the last saved version. If you realize that you have made some errors and Undo just won't get you back, choose Revert to revert to the last saved version of the document.

Printing

Print any PDF file by choosing the Print command under the File menu. This launches the Print dialog box. In the Print dialog box choose the Printer, Presets, and Copies & Pages. If you are connected to multiple printers, choose the printer you want to use from the pop-up menu. Choose from standard presets, or if you have saved your own presets, choose one of your own. On the Macintosh under Copies & Pages, you have more options to choose from:

- ▶ **Copies and View**—In this area choose All Pages, Current View, Current Page, or From a certain page To a certain page.

- ▶ **Subset**—In the Subset area choose from All Pages in Range, Even Pages, or Odd Pages.

- ▶ **Print What**—Use this setting to choose the Document, Document and Comments, or Form Fields Only.

- ▶ **Page Scaling**—With Page Scaling, choose None, Fit to Paper, Shrink Large Pages, Tile Large Pages, or Tile All Pages.

- ▶ **Auto-Rotate and Center**—This check box will rotate the page to fit the paper and center the document on the page.

The Printing Tips button launches the troubleshooting area on printing for Acrobat at Adobe's Web site.

Advanced Printing Options

In the Advanced Print Setup dialog box (click the Advanced button to get there), choose from the following: Output, Marks and Bleeds, Transparency Flattening, and PostScript Options. Under the Output options set are Color, Screening, Flip, Printer Profile, Apply Working Color Spaces, Apply Proof Settings, Simulate Overprinting, Use Maximum Available JPEG2000 Image Resolution, Emit Trap Annotations, and Ink Manager.

In the Marks and Bleeds setup, choose to Emit Printer Marks or All Marks. The Marks Style pop-up menu lets you pick the style of printer's marks. Check or uncheck Crop Marks, Trim Marks, Bleed Marks, Registration Marks, Color Bars, and Page Information.

In the Transparency Flattening area, you set the Quality/Speed slider (higher for vector-based images and lower for raster-based images). Enter Rasterization Resolution for Line Art and Text and for Gradient and Meshes in pixels per inch. The other options you can check or uncheck are Convert All Text to Outlines, Convert All Strokes to Outlines, and/or Clip Complex Regions.

The PostScript Options you can choose are Font and Resource Policy, Print Method, Download Asian Fonts, Emit Undercolor Removal/Black Generation, Emit Halftones, Emit Transfer Functions, Emit PS Form Objects, and/or Discolored Background Correction.

Printing with Comments

When printing, you can choose to print the PDF file with Comments. Choose Print with Comments from the File menu. This brings up the Summarize Options dialog box. In the Summarize Options dialog box choose a Layout (Document and Comments with Connector Lines on Separate Pages, Document and Comments with Connector Lines on Single Pages, Comments Only, or Document and Comments with Sequence Numbers on Separate Pages). Next choose how to sort the comments, by Author, Date, Page, or Type. Then you can choose to include all comments, or only the comments currently showing. The last option is to choose Font Size (Small, Medium, or Large). After you click OK, you get the Print dialog box. Enter any of the settings and click Print to print the file with comments.

Printing Color Separations

Use Adobe Acrobat to print out your color separations for a color PDF document. In the Print dialog box, click the Advanced button to access your color separations options. Under the Color pop-up menu in the Output options, choose Separations. You can even get as defined as choosing which plates to print. When printing with separations, you'll get one black, one cyan, one yellow, and one magenta file. Printing separations lets you see whether the different plates register (line up) with each other. If the plates are off in any way, you'll get gaps in the printing and may need to use trapping to fix any problems.

If you want to see what the separations will look like before choosing Print, choose Separation Preview from the Advanced menu. This launches the Separation

Preview dialog box (see Figure 10.26), where you can see each plate on its own by unchecking the other plates. The preview is directly on your PDF document.

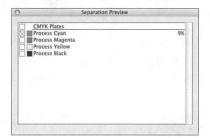

FIGURE 10.26
The Process Cyan box checked shows only the cyan plate in preview.

Transparency Flattener Preview

Under the Advanced menu is the Transparency Flattener Preview. Choose this to launch the Flattener Preview dialog box. In this dialog box choose from the following Preview settings:

▶ **Rasterize Complex Regions**—This option previews the areas that will be rasterized according to the Raster/Vector slider. If you have a highly complex image, choose the Clip Complex Regions to avoid stitching problems.

▶ **Transparent Objects**—This option previews objects with transparency, transparency blending modes, or opacity masks. Certain styles and effects created may also have transparency previews. These objects need to be viewed to check for trapping problems.

▶ **All Affected Objects**—This option previews all objects that interact with transparency. Use this to check for any problems with trapping.

▶ **Expanded Patterns**—This option shows any patterns that will be expanded that use transparency.

▶ **Outlined Strokes**—This option shows any outlined strokes that will be expanded that use transparency.

Other options include the following:

▶ **Convert All Text to Outlines**—Use this to keep the text size consistent and ensure that since the text is changed to vectors, the file can be printed regardless of the fonts on the printer.

▶ **Convert All Strokes to Outlines**—Use this to keep the size of all the lines consistent.

▶ **Clip Complex Regions**—Use this to ensure a smoother blend between vector and raster objects stitching.

Use the Flattener settings slider to adjust for more rasters or vectors. Set the rasterization resolution, and other settings. The preview is the Transparency Flattener Preview window. Click the Refresh button to see your preview settings applied.

Preflight

Preflight refers to the analyzing of a document for printing. Preflighting checks for any problems before sending a file to the print shop or service bureau.

By the Way

> Choose Preflight from the Document menu to activate the Preflight command. This launches the Preflight: Profiles dialog box. Under this list you can choose a preset profile or edit a preset profile as you want by choosing the file and clicking the Edit button. After you have chosen your profile, click the Analyze button to check the file.

There are a bunch of preflight profiles to choose from. Click on one and click Edit to see the rules and conditions of that particular profile (see Figure 10.27). Each profile has certain rules and conditions. You also can create a new profile by clicking the New Profile button at the lower left of the Preflight: Edit Profiles dialog box.

FIGURE 10.27
The preflight rules and conditions are listed when you choose a particular profile.

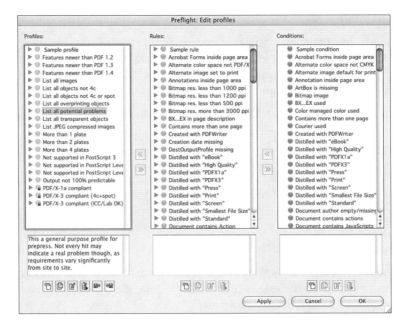

After you have either chosen or created the Preflight profile, click the Analyze button to check the current file. It may take a few minutes to analyze the file, depending on the file size. After the file is analyzed, you'll see the Preflight: Results dialog box (see Figure 10.28). In the Preflight: Results dialog box, you'll see any problems with the file listed. Then with the results listed, you can decide whether and how to fix the files.

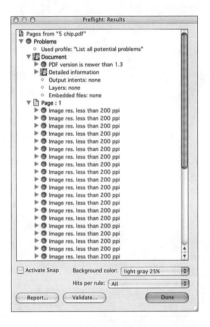

When using Preflight on a document, you may not encounter any problems with the document. If that is the case, you may want to validate the file so that the printer knows that there are no problems with that particular file.

> To validate a file, click the Validate button at the bottom of the Preflight: Results dialog box. This will launch a warning box asking whether you want to continue. The warning also indicates that a Validation stamp will be appended to the document and that when you click OK the document will be saved. Click OK. You'll get a message telling you the Validation was successful. Click Done.

By the Way

Creating PDF/X-1a–Compliant Files

After you have a preflight validated file, you can create a PDF/X-compliant file. Use this when sending a file out for a professional print job. PDF/X is a form of the PDF format created by the International Organization for Standardization. The intent is to make the printing process streamlined by getting rid of unneeded info in a PDF document.

To create a PDF/X-1a–compliant file, follow these steps:

1. Choose the Preflight command from the Document menu.

2. In the listing of Preflight profiles, choose the PDF/X-1a profile and analyze your file.

3. After the file is analyzed, save the file.

4. Choose the Preflight option under the Document menu.

5. Click the PDF/X button.

6. Click the Save As PDF/X-1a button to save the file as a PDF/X-1a–compliant file. This launches the Preflight: Save As PDF/X1-a dialog box.

7. Enter the ICC color profile and any other information you want in this dialog box (see Figure 10.29).

FIGURE 10.29
In the Preflight: Save As PDF/X-1a dialog box, enter your information and click Save.

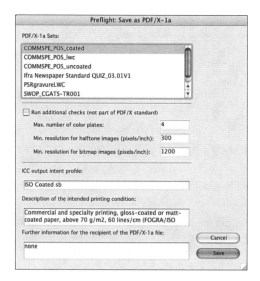

eBooks

Adobe Systems has combined eBook Reader into Adobe Reader. Now you can read eBooks using Reader or Acrobat 6.0. eBook Reader tries to make reading books on your computer much like reading the traditional paper bound manuscript. You have bookmarks and can add notes or comments to any pages without actually damaging the pages. You can also purchase books, borrow books, or lend books as with a traditional library.

To download an eBook, check out the Adobe eBook Mall (digitalmediastore.adobe.com) or eBooks Central (www.adobe.com/epaper/ ebooks/main.html). Here you can choose from thousands of eBooks and eDocs. You can download free eBooks as well.

Before downloading any eBooks, you must activate your Adobe eBook Reader account by accessing the Adobe DRM Activator.

To activate the DRM (Digital Rights Management), choose Adobe DRM Activator from the eBook Web Services submenu of the Advanced menu. This will lead to the activation process. When it's finished, you'll get a message saying your Adobe software has been activated (see Figure 10.30).

By the Way

FIGURE 10.30
Dialog box letting you know that your software has been activated.

Now that your software has been activated, you can access the eBook areas. Shop for eBooks as you would shop for anything online. Choose to buy, then checkout. If shopping through Adobe, you'll need to create an account.

Read an eBook as you would any book. Use the status bar at the bottom to turn pages, or access your keyboard shortcuts. You can also use your Palm or other mobile devices to read and access eBooks.

CHAPTER 11

Using Version Cue

Introduction to Version Cue

Back in Part I of the book, "The Creative Suite," we discussed the role of Version Cue in an Adobe workflow. In its simplest form, Version Cue is a file manager that makes it easy to find the files you're looking for. On a more complex level, Version Cue can act as an asset management system that monitors file usage, tracks versions, and provides write-protection to files. The beauty of Version Cue is that it's so easy to use, no matter how simple or complex a role you ask it to play.

Version Cue was built with small workgroups in mind. Even large design companies don't have everyone working on every project—rather, usually smaller groups of anywhere from 1 to 20 people collaborate on any one project. Version Cue is also useful on many levels for even one person working alone.

If you're working alone, here are some things Version Cue can help you do:

▶ Keep files organized in "projects"

▶ Search for (and find) the right file without necessarily having to open it

▶ Store "versions" of files and instantly access older versions of a file

▶ Back up older projects for archival purposes (and easily access them when needed)

If you're working in a group, here are some things Version Cue can help you do (in addition to those just mentioned):

▶ Automatically lock files when you are working on them to keep others from accidentally overwriting your changes

▶ Instantly see who is working on a file

▶ Search for files in coworker's projects (where you have user access to do so)

Is Version Cue for Me?

Before we even get started, you may be wondering whether Version Cue is really something you need. The truth is, Version Cue isn't for everyone. As you read through this chapter, you may think that it's not for you. Maybe you are still using QuarkXPress and haven't made the switch to InDesign just yet. Version Cue requires you to think about your workflow differently, and maybe you feel that adapting to those changes doesn't justify the benefits you get with using Version Cue.

In either case, my advice is that you read through the chapter and get a grasp on the concepts and basic functionality of Version Cue. Remember that Version Cue is also a version 1.0 product, and it can only get better. My suggestion is to use it for the projects in Part III of this book, "The Projects." It's easy to follow along, and using Version Cue will certainly make it easier to understand the benefits as well as discover how to use Version Cue in a real workflow. After you've completed the projects, you'll be able to make a clear decision on whether Version Cue is right for you.

Version Cue Terminology

To help you better understand the concepts and uses for Version Cue, I will define several terms here, to avoid confusion later in the chapter:

▶ **Managed Workflow**—In a *managed workflow* the files (or *assets*) are tracked in such a way that users can see who is working on any specific file, as well as access additional information about the managed files themselves. Managed workflows also offer file-protection, which prevents users from accidentally overwriting files that others may be working on (see the bulleted item "Check Out/Check In").

▶ **Workspace**—A Version Cue *workspace* is essentially an area set aside on a computer that stores and tracks your files. You can have only one workspace for each computer, so you can think of a workspace as a hard drive—or even a computer. In Version Cue, you can access a workspace that's on your computer, or one that's on someone else's computer or on a server.

By the Way

> Don't confuse a Version Cue workspace with the Workspaces feature found in InDesign and Photoshop—those features are used to save palette positions on your screen.

▶ **Project**—A Version Cue *project* is a collection of folders and files used for a particular purpose. Projects live inside the Version Cue workspace and they are a way to organize your work. For example, you might create a Version Cue project for your company's annual report, and another project for an ad campaign you're working on. Or you might have different projects set up for different clients.

▶ **Assets**—*Assets* are defined as files used in your project. Photoshop files, Illustrator files, InDesign files, and GIF files are all examples of assets.

▶ **Check Out/Check In**—In a managed workflow, opening a file to edit it is called *checking out* the file. When a file is checked out, it's locked so that others can't edit the file (and unknowingly overwrite edits that someone else is making at the same time). *Checking in* a file is the process of releasing the file so that others can edit it. Think of it almost like a library book: When you check out the book, you have it with you, and when you check the book back in, others can then use it. Version Cue usually refers to a checked-out file as *In Use* and a checked-in file as *Available*. One important thing to note is that when someone has a file checked out, other people can still open and view the file, but they won't be able to save a version of it.

Getting Started with Version Cue

Earlier in the book (Chapter 4, "The Key That Makes It All Work: Integration"), I went through the steps necessary to turn on and activate Version Cue on your computer. If you haven't already completed these steps, here's a brief review:

1. *Turn on the Version Cue workspace on your computer.* On a Mac, you can do this via the Adobe Version Cue option in System Preferences. On Windows, you can do this via the Adobe Version Cue option in Control Panels.

2. *Activate the Version Cue user interface inside each of the Suite applications.* For Photoshop, choose the Enable Version Cue Workgroup File Management option in the File Handling section of Preferences. In Illustrator, choose the Enable Version Cue option in the File Handling & Clipboard section of Preferences. In InDesign, choose the Enable Version Cue option in the File Handling section of Preferences. Note that in InDesign, Version Cue will be activated the next time you launch the application (in Illustrator and Photoshop, Version Cue functionality is active immediately).

Adobe suggests that you periodically restart Version Cue, because this runs a self-checking routine that will not only check the integrity of your Version Cue database file, but also make repairs to it, should it be corrupt in some way.

By the Way

You can have your Version Cue workspace located on your own computer, or have it running on a server (a central computer that is accessible by others as well). You can also access workspaces on other people's computers (if you have the rights to do so). It's important to remember that if you activate the workspace on your computer and allow others in your group to share your workspace, the performance of your own computer may be slowed if you have a large number of people accessing your computer continually. In such cases, using a workspace on a dedicated server might be better. Also note that for larger workgroups, you should allocate more RAM to Version Cue (in the Version Cue Control Panel or System Preferences).

By the Way

> Version Cue doesn't require any specific server software, and can run in multiple OS environments. For example, you could install a Version Cue workspace on a Windows machine, and access that workspace from a Mac.

Using Version Cue

Version Cue doesn't have an actual user interface itself—nor is it a program that you actively launch in order to use it. Rather, Version Cue functionality is accessible through the user interface of the applications that support it—Photoshop, Illustrator, InDesign, and GoLive. Additionally, you can make changes to Version Cue's settings via an advanced administration feature using your Web browser (such as Internet Explorer or Safari).

To use Version Cue, click on the Version Cue button in the Open or Save dialog of any of the applications that support it (see Figure 11.1). You're then presented with the Version Cue browser dialog box. It's from here that you can access most of Version Cue's functionality (see Figure 11.2).

FIGURE 11.1
The Version Cue button, as it appears in an application's Open or Save dialog box.

By the Way

> You can also access Version Cue from InDesign's and Illustrator's Place dialog box, although not from Photoshop's Place dialog box.

Creating Projects

You can create Version Cue projects right from the Version Cue browser dialog box. From the Project Tools pop-up menu, choose New Project (see Figure 11.3). Choose a location where you want your new project to live. If you're just working by yourself on your own computer, this will always be your computer, but if you're working with other people, you have the ability to create projects on other computers, or on a server. Name your project and enter as much information about the project as you can (see Figure 11.4). Don't worry—you can always update your comments later by choosing Edit Properties from the Project Tools menu (see Figure 11.5). Finally, choose whether your project should be public. Version Cue lets you decide which of your projects other people can see, and which they can't. Click OK to create the projectA new project in Version Cue is always created with three folders (see Figure 11.6). These are the documents folder, which is where you will store all of your print-based assets, and the web-content and web-data folders, which are used for storing Web assets (and which GoLive is already set up to use for creating and managing Web sites). If you want, you can always add your own folders by using the Create New Folder button in the Version Cue Browser window. New folders should always be added inside one of the three folders mentioned previously.

FIGURE 11.3
Choosing to create
a new project from
the Project Tools
menu.

FIGURE 11.4
Creating a new
Version Cue
project.

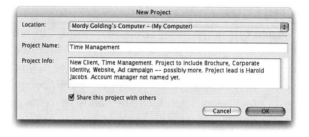

FIGURE 11.5
Choosing to edit
the properties of
an existing project.

FIGURE 11.6
By default, Version Cue creates three folders within a project.

Adding Files to a Version Cue Project

There are basically two ways to add files into a Version Cue project. The first way is to simply save a file into the project directly. Choose File, Save (or File, Save As for existing files), and click on the Version Cue button to switch to the Version Cue browser, if it isn't already open (see note). Enter a comment for the file, navigate to your project file's documents folder, and click Save.

Your application's Save and Open dialog boxes are "sticky," meaning that they remember if you were last using Version Cue and automatically open the Version Cue browser. To access local files on your computer, simply click on the Local Files button to return to the standard Open or Save dialog box (see Figure 11.7).

By the Way

FIGURE 11.7
The Local Files button.

The second way to add files into a Version Cue project is to manually add files by placing them in your My Documents/Version Cue (Windows) or Documents/Version Cue (Mac OS) *ProjectName* folder. Then access the Version Cue browser (through a supported application) and choose Synchronize from the Project Tools menu. This method is perfect for when you need to add several files at once to your project.

You can also add entire folders to a project by using the Synchronize command, but empty folders will be synchronized.

Finding Files in Version Cue

One of the most powerful features in Version Cue is its capability to quickly search for and find the files you're looking for. Unfortunately, you can't search across multiple projects, so make sure you've navigated inside a project file and then click on the Search tab on the Version Cue window. You can then enter any text to search for (see Figure 11.8). Version Cue will look at a file's name and it's metadata for anything that matches and will provide you with a list of files. Version Cue offers both a text-based list view and a visual thumbnail view, to help you better identify your files (see Figure 11.9). Version Cue's thumbnail view can show just about any kind of file—even native Photoshop, Illustrator, and InDesign files. You'll also notice that as you hover your mouse over each of the files, a small tip will pop up showing some of the metadata of that file (see Figure 11.10). All of this makes it easy to find the file you're looking for without necessarily having to open multiple files—which can save huge amounts of time.

FIGURE 11.8
Searching for a file in Version Cue.

FIGURE 11.9
The buttons in the upper-right corner of the dialog toggle between list and thumbnail view.

List View ⌐ ⌐ Thumbnail View

FIGURE 11.10
Rolling your mouse
pointer over a
file reveals its
metadata.

How Version Cue Works

Whether you have your workspace set up to run on a server or on your own machine, it's important to realize that Version Cue is acting very much like a server itself. When you open a file from Version Cue and work with it, here's what's really happening:

▶ The file is copied from the workspace to your Documents folder (My Documents on Windows). The original file sits untouched in the Version Cue workspace (allowing others to access it as well). The file exists locally on your machine now, so you're not working on a file over a network connection (usually a bad thing anyway), and you get better (read: faster) performance.

▶ The application you're using opens this local file. In the document's title bar, the word "Available" appears (see Figure 11.11), meaning that the file is available for you to edit (and available to others as well).

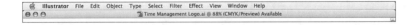

FIGURE 11.11
The status of the
file is displayed in
the document's title
bar. In this case,
you can see that
the file is
"Available."

▶ When you make an edit to the file, Version Cue locks the file in the workspace, and changes the status of the file to "In Use by Me" within your application. Others can open and view the file but will see it as "In Use by *Your Name*," and they won't be able to save a version of the file (see Figure 11.12).

FIGURE 11.12
Others can see that the file is currently locked and in use by you.

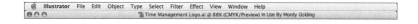

▶ When you save your file using the File, Save command, Version Cue is saving the local file that is on your machine. The file is still shown as locked and in use by you, and the file is not copied back to the Version Cue workspace.

▶ When you choose File, Save a Version, you're prompted with a dialog box to enter comments for this version (see Figure 11.13), and the file is saved and copied back to the Version Cue workspace. The lock on the file is released. The file is now shown as "Available" again, and others can now save versions of the file.

FIGURE 11.13
Entering comments while saving a version of a file.

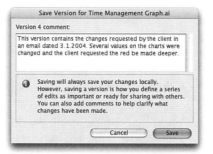

Working with Versions

Version Cue keeps track of all the versions of a file that you save. For example, if you save a version of a file five times, your Version Cue workspace has five separate files, each saved with a version of your file (Version Cue keeps track of which is the latest version). You never see those versions—you just work with one file—but those versions are available to you at any time. To access a previous version of your file, open the file and choose File, Versions. You'll then be presented with a list of all the versions of that file, each with a thumbnail along with the comments you made when you saved the version (see Figure 11.14). You can click on the View Version button to compare any of those versions to the current one, or you can click on the Promote to Current Version button to make an older version of your file the current latest version (great for clients or managers who love to change their minds).

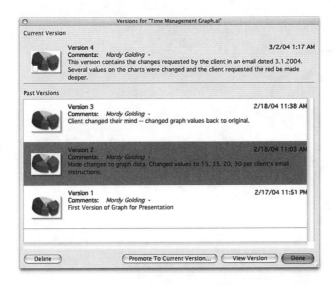

FIGURE 11.14
Viewing the different versions of a file.

As you probably figured out on your own, saving a lot of versions can quickly eat up file space on your hard drive (or your server's hard drive). That's why it's important to use the Save command to make smaller incremental changes, but to use the Save a Version command only when you need to create a new version of the file itself. It's also possible to delete versions of a file that you no longer need, which is covered next in the "Administrating Version Cue" section.

By the Way

Administrating Version Cue

Several features in Version Cue are defined as "advanced" features—those that aren't needed by every individual working on a project. These tasks are usually reserved for an administrator, or someone who is in charge of the project.

As mentioned earlier, Version Cue itself doesn't have a user interface, and to specify settings and perform tasks with Version Cue as an administrator, you will use your Web browser (such as Internet Explorer or Safari).

If you're on a Mac, open your System Preferences and click the Version Cue button. If you're on Windows, open your Control Panel, and double-click on the Version Cue icon. If it isn't already on, turn Version Cue on.

Click on the Advanced Administration button at the bottom of the window. This will launch your Web browser (the Version Cue administration utility is all HTML-based). When prompted to log in to the system (see Figure 11.15), log in as a system administrator by using the following information:

Login: system

Password: system

FIGURE 11.15
Logging into the Version Cue Administration utility.

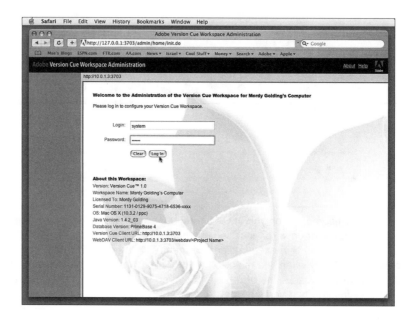

If you're working in an environment where security is a concern, you may want to change the default password of system, but make sure you remember what you've changed it to. If you forget your password, there's no way to get back in.

You then are presented with the administration tools for Version Cue. Here you perform several tasks, including creating projects, adding and editing users, removing old versions of files, and various more advanced tasks such as backing up and retrieving projects and setting workspace preferences (see Figure 11.16).

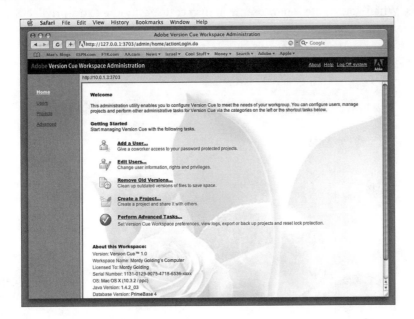

FIGURE 11.16
The Version Cue administration tools, as they appear in Apple's Safari browser.

By default, Version Cue does not require you to add users to a project. All users who have access to a workspace can also access any new projects within that workspace (unless otherwise specified).

By the Way

Rather than running to the Version Cue Control Panel each time you want to perform administration tasks, bookmark the page in your Web browser. Making changes in Version Cue will then be as easy as going to your favorite Web site.

Did you Know?

Adding and Editing Users

You can specify which users have access to your projects, and what rights they have to the files within those projects (see Figure 11.17). Click on the Users button on the left of the screen to specify new users, and to duplicate or delete existing users. When you create a new user, you also can specify the exact privileges for that user (see Figure 11.18).

FIGURE 11.17
Adding a new user.

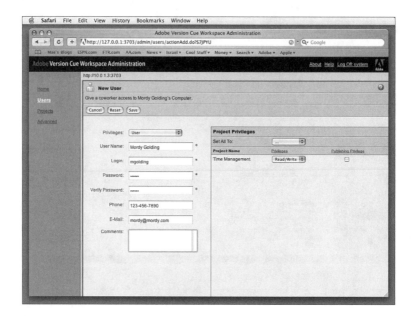

FIGURE 11.18
Specifying the privileges of a user.

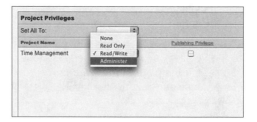

Adding and Editing Projects

We learned earlier in the chapter how to create Version Cue projects from within an application, but they also can be created here. Above that, you can manage existing projects by duplicating them, backing them up, exporting them, or deleting them. You can access all of these features by clicking on the Projects button on the left of the screen (see Figure 11.19).

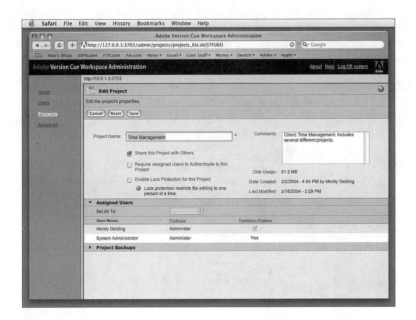

FIGURE 11.19
Editing a Version
Cue project.

Advanced Tasks

Some tasks are performed less frequently, but are equally important when using Version Cue. You can access these features by clicking on the Advanced button at the left of the screen.

Workspace Preferences

By default, the workspace of a computer takes on the name of the computer itself. However, you may want to customize the name of the workspace so that others may be able to recognize it more easily. Clicking on Preferences enables you to change the name of the workspace itself (see Figure 11.20).

Reset Lock Protection

When you first create a project, you can use the option "Enable Lock Protection for This Project," which prevents a user from saving a version when that file is already in use by another user. The Reset Lock Protection feature is needed only when this option is turned on.

At times a file may be locked out because it's in use by a user, even though the user didn't intend for that to happen. For example, a user may have edited a file and performed a Save instead of performing the Save a Version command. In that case, the file remains locked and others can't open and edit the file until that user saves a version and releases the lock on the file. If that user has already gone home for the day, that could present a problem.

The Reset Lock Protection feature can override the locked file and release it (see Figure 11.21) so that others can make edits to the file. In that case, any changes that the original user may have made will not be incorporated into the version.

FIGURE 11.20
Changing the name of your Version Cue workspace.

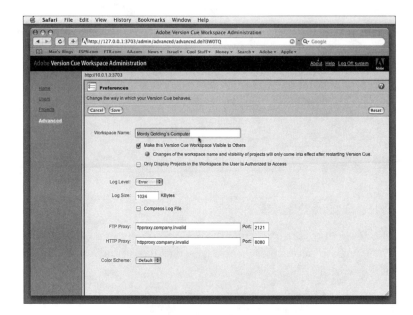

FIGURE 11.21
Resetting Version Cue's lock protection.

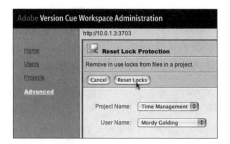

Removing Old Versions

As alluded to earlier in the chapter, saving many versions of a file could easily take up megabytes of hard drive space. If there are versions of a file that you know are not going to be needed, you can delete them with the Remove Old Versions feature. Doing this periodically can help prevent you from running out of room on your computer or server.

Backing Up Version Cue Workspaces

When a project is completed, you can back up that project so that it no longer appears in your Version Cue browser window. You can restore it at any time using the administration tools as well. This process can also be used to archive old jobs that you want to hold on to.

The Relationship Between Metadata and Asset Management

It's often overlooked, but what makes Version Cue so useful is how it uses metadata to save precious time. That's why it's so important to enter comments when you save a version of a file or when you create a project. The more information you enter for a file, the easier it will be for you to find that file when you do a search in Version Cue. In the past, you may have spent valuable time opening and closing large files trying to find just the one you were looking for, whereas Version Cue can give you enough information to know which file to open in the first place.

All of Adobe's applications—including Version Cue, of course—use the XMP standard for storing metadata. Although it may seem insignificant to you, it's actually quite important to the world of graphic design. The XMP standard utilizes XML (another standard in itself) and is compatible with other industry asset management systems. It can be scripted, meaning that metadata can be added to batch files automatically. Most of all, it offers you peace of mind, knowing that any file you work with will be able to be used by others.

Thinking Different

No, this isn't a discussion about Steve Job's advertising antics, but rather it's an important discussion about the things you need to think about when working in a managed workflow. Because human nature is to resist change, it takes some effort to really adapt to using Version Cue in your workflow.

It's important to remember the difference between saving a file and saving a version of a file. Until recently, you would always save a file when you were done with it. But in a managed workflow, saving a file just updates the working copy of the file on your computer, and doesn't unlock the file on the server. So even though you've saved the file, others still see a locked file that is in use by you. If they choose to view the file, they won't see your most recent edits either.

Saving a file is great for making incremental saves (ensuring that you don't lose your work) and for making small changes to a file as you're working on it. When you've made your changes and want to release the file for others to use, you have to use the Save a Version command, which not only saves the file, but also copies it back to the server and unlocks the file.

We also mentioned how Version Cue uses the metadata of a file to speed up the process of finding your files and versions. No one likes to spend extra time putting comments or notes into a file when they are working, but doing so can save valuable time later in the process. It can also help coworkers find files you've worked on.

In Closing

There's no question that Version Cue is a valuable tool—the question, though, is whether it fits within your workflows and whether it meets your needs. Try to use Version Cue as you go through Part III of the book and see whether you can grasp all it has to offer. Then decide whether it's something that fits you and your work.

PART III

The Projects

CHAPTER 12

Creating a Corporate Identity

The Project

In this project we'll create a logo, a business card, a letterhead and an envelope for a fictitious company called Time Management. The company gives classes and seminars on how business people can better manage their time. The company takes pride in the fact that it can compete with established companies that have been around for many years. The company needs a modern look, but it still must appeal to large corporations that are used to a classic look. The company's tagline is "Rush Less, Relax More."

Setting Up a Version Cue Project

By now you should have turned on Version Cue and set it up for use. If not, refer to Chapter 11, "Using Version Cue," for information on doing so.

> You don't have to use Version Cue for these projects, but I've included the steps here for those who are interested in using it.

By the Way

Start off by creating a new Version Cue project. You can do this from the Open dialog, or from the Version Cue Administrator utility. Call the project Time Management.

Creating the Logo

The first step is going to be creating the logo. It's best to create logos in Illustrator because vector art is scalable to any size. It's also easier to repurpose the art for print or Web use, as well as easily apply spot colors, if necessary.

The logo we're going to create for Time Management will consist of some type and an icon. Begin by launching Illustrator and creating a new CMYK document.

Choose a Typeface

Choosing a typeface is obviously one of the most important parts of designing a logo. Although it might be fun trying to find a totally cool and different font to use, remember that a logo has to be clear and readable. It's not just by coincidence that so many logos are set in fonts like Helvetica or Garamond. We can add little tweaks to the type afterward to give it a unique look.

Use the Type tool to set the words `Time Management`, and try applying different fonts to get the look you want (see Figure 12.1). I chose Chaparral Pro Regular because I thought that a serif font would give it a more sophisticated look, yet the square serifs give it a more modern feel.

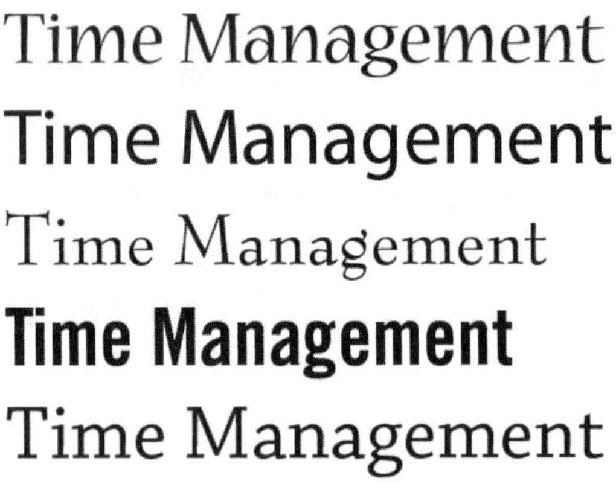

FIGURE 12.1
I usually stack different type treatments and then eliminate the ones that don't work, leaving me with a choice few to make a final decision.

Time Management

Time Management

Time Management

Time Management

Time Management

I set the type at 32-point and set the tracking amount to –20. I turned on Illustrator's Optical Kerning as well (see Figure 12.2). Logos always seem to look better when the letters are hugging each other (not touching, though).

FIGURE 12.2
Setting the tracking and the kerning so that the characters are cohesive and look better as a unit.

Time Management

Next we'll want to tweak the text to give it a unique appearance. In the word Time, we can make adjustments to the "T" and "i" by removing the dot over the "i" and bringing the two character much closer together. To make these modifications, we need to convert the text to outlines. This is usually a good idea anyway with a logo, making it easier to send the logo to others without worrying about fonts. The last thing you would want is to have your logo look completely different just because the person who opened it on her computer didn't have your exact font.

When you convert text to outlines (Type, Create Outlines), all the characters are grouped together. Because there are two words here, first ungroup them, select the word Time and group it, and then select the word Management and group that separately. This will make it easier to move the words around.

Using the Direct Selection tool, select the lowercase "i" in the word Time by clicking anywhere inside the letter (not on the path itself). You'll notice that the entire letter is selected—both the base and the dot. That's because characters are originally created as compound paths. With the "i" selected, choose Object, Compound Paths, Release. Now deselect the "i" and then click on just the dot and delete it. Select the "T" and, holding the shift key, drag it to the right so that it sits right up against the "i" (see Figure 12.3).

Time Management

FIGURE 12.3
The final type treatment with the stylized word Time.

While we're creating text, type in the tagline, **Rush Less. Relax More.** and set it to Chaparral Pro Regular, 14-point. Convert it to outlines as well. Leave it on the side and we'll position it later.

Create an Icon

To add a graphic element to our logo, we'll create a simple logo that can quickly help identify the kind of company Time Management is. Rather than something lavish, a simple striking piece of art will work best here, so that it can be used as a design element elsewhere if needed. In this case I've decided to create a stopwatch.

Did you
Know?

It's always a good idea to plan your art in advance and try to anticipate ways it will be used—and build it to work for all uses. You never know where or when the art may be needed.

Start by dragging out a horizontal guide and a vertical guide, effectively creating a crosshair (where they both meet). This will be our center point (see Figure 12.4).

FIGURE 12.4
Creating a center point using two guides.

Select the Ellipse tool and (Option-click) [Alt-click] on that center point to draw a circle numerically. Enter a value of 0.5 inches for both the Width and the Height. Press the "D" key to set the circle to the default white fill, black stroke setting. With the circle still selected, press the "S" key to select the Scale tool, and while holding both the Shift and (Option) [Alt] keys, drag out a copy of that circle, slightly larger than the first one. Be sure to click and start dragging to create the circle *before* you press the modifier keys. Change the Stroke weight to 0.5-point for the larger circle and send it to the back (see Figure 12.5).

Now we'll create the tick marks. Use the Line tool to create a single tick mark, giving it a fill of none and a stroke of 1 point (see Figure 12.6). With the line selected, press the "R" key to select the Rotate tool and (Option-click) [Alt-click] on the center point of the circle (where the two guides meet). Enter an Angle value of **15** degrees and press the Copy button (see Figure 12.7). You'll notice that a copy of the tick mark now appears to the left of the original. Now press the "D" key repeatedly until you've created all the tick marks (see Figure 12.8).

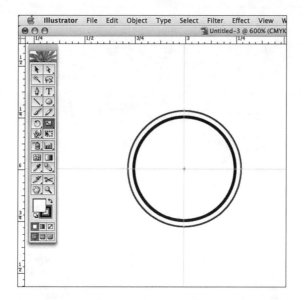

FIGURE 12.5
The two circles.

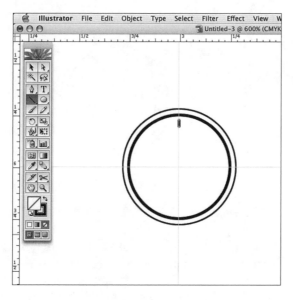

FIGURE 12.6
Creating a single tick mark.

FIGURE 12.7
Setting a rotation value for the tick mark, using the center of the circle as the origin point.

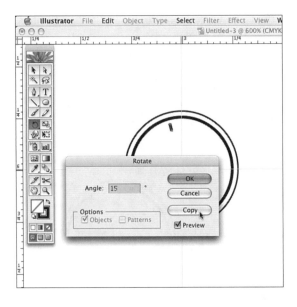

FIGURE 12.8
Pressing (⌘-D) [Ctrl-D] repeatedly to create all the tick marks.

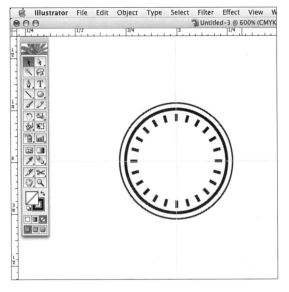

To make the watch look more interesting, make a section of it black and color the tick marks white in that area, bringing the tick marks to the front of the stacking order (see Figure 12.9).

FIGURE 12.9
Creating a reverse section, coloring some tick marks white, and bringing them to the front.

To finish the look, add a rectangle just above the circle, to look like a button. Then, select all the elements of the stopwatch and group them. Then rotate the watch 15 degrees to give it some movement (see Figure 12.10).

FIGURE 12.10
Rotating the icon on an angle.

Save the Logo

Now drop the icon between the words Time and Management, using the Selection tool to move the objects around. Bring the tagline into place to complete the look of the entire logo treatment (see Figure 12.11).

Save the logo into Version Cue as a native Illustrator file (.ai), giving it a comment describing what it is (see Figure 12.12). If you have enough RAM, you can leave Illustrator running, but if your computer has less than 512MB of RAM, quit Illustrator so that you won't be slowed down when working in Photoshop and InDesign.

Preparing the Photo

The next step will be finding the right photo to use. The client wants something that will grab a reader's attention, and we thought using a photograph in our identity might add some punch. So we'll launch Photoshop to try to find the right image.

> The images I'm looking through can be found in the Goodies/Illustrator CS/Illustrator Stock Photos folder on the Resources and Extras CD that comes with the Creative Suite.

By the Way

Find the Right Image

We'll begin our search by opening Photoshop's File Browser. Navigate to the Illustrator Stock Photo collection and flag the photos you think are appropriate. After you've gone through the collection, choose to view only Flagged images (see Figure 12.13). I personally like the image of the guy running while talking on the phone—it shows movement and has a business tone. Double-click on the image to open it.

FIGURE 12.13
Using the File Browser to choose from the images you've flagged.

Adjust the Image

We aren't going to be printing the stationery items in color, so Choose Image, Mode, Grayscale to convert the photo to grayscale mode (see Figure 12.14).

Notice how dark the image is. Choose Image, Adjustments, Shadow/Highlight to enhance the photograph. I think the default Shadows setting of 50 is too much, so drag the slider down to about 30 (see Figure 12.15).

FIGURE 12.14
Converting the image to grayscale.

FIGURE 12.15
Using the Shadow/Highlight command to adjust the image.

The image has a very soft appearance with all the motion blur in the photo, so I'm going to apply the Unsharp Mask filter to make the man who is running appear to pop just a bit to the front (see Figure 12.16).

Save the Image

We're done with the image for now, so you can save it to your Version Cue project as well. Save it as a native Photoshop file (.psd) and add a comment (see Figure 12.17).

I know it takes an extra few seconds to add a comment to a file when you save it into Version Cue, but remember that a few seconds now can save you several minutes later when you're trying to find a particular file. It also helps when other people in your department need to use your assets for other projects.

FIGURE 12.16
Unsharp Mask, set
to 100, using a
Radius of 1.3 and
a Threshold of 7.

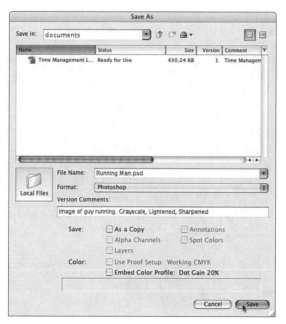

FIGURE 12.17
Saving the file, with
version comments,
into the Version
Cue project.

Designing the Business Card

Now that the design elements are complete, we can lay out and design the stationery. Although it's possible to create business cards inside of Illustrator (and in many cases, it makes sense to do so), for this example we will use InDesign. Start by launching InDesign.

I like to start designing the business card first, because it's normally used most often and because the business card is small and thus forces you to think and design clearly. If you create other items first, you may find that your design won't work in such a small space.

Create a New Document

Create a new document, setting the width to 3.5 inches and the height to 2 inches. Set your margins to 0.125 inches all around and click on the More Options button to set a bleed of 0.125 inches all around as well (see Figure 12.18).

FIGURE 12.18
Setting up a new document in InDesign.

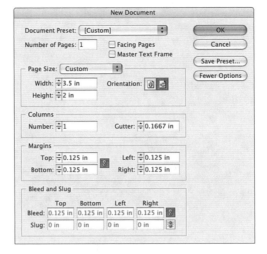

Because business cards are so common, you can save a document preset with these specifications to use again later. Simply click on the Save Preset button and specify a name. The next time you want to create a business card, you'll be able to choose the preset from the Document Preset pop-up.

Place the Photoshop file from Version Cue (see Figure 12.19). We'll have it bleed off the top of the card, so drag a horizontal guide to the 0.75-inch mark and use the Selection tool to resize the picture frame so that it bleeds off the top (see Figure 12.20). Switching to the Direct Selection tool, resize the image so that it's cropped nicely at the top of the card (see Figure 12.21).

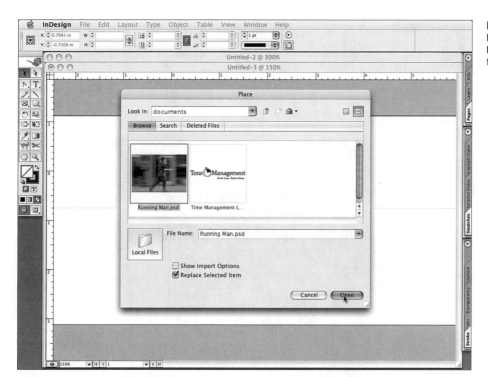

FIGURE 12.19
Placing the Photoshop image from Version Cue.

FIGURE 12.20
Resizing the image frame to bleed off the top of the card.

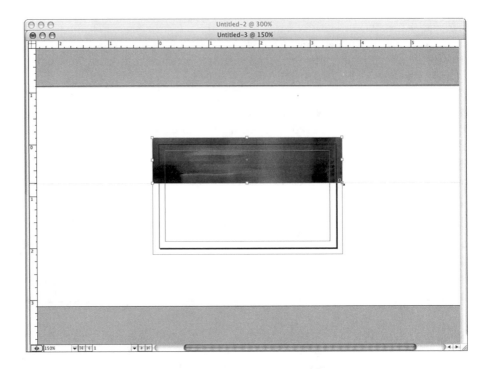

FIGURE 12.21
Cropping the image perfectly into the frame.

Enter the additional text information on the card. I used 8-point Warnock Pro Regular and 11-point leading (see Figure 12.22).

Now we can place the Illustrator logo from Version Cue. So that we can see the artwork better, choose View, Display Performance, High Quality Display. Scale the logo so that it fits nicely within the image (see Figure 12.23). Obviously, the dark background makes the logo difficult to read. Additionally, the tagline doesn't really fit where we have it—it will most likely fit better at the lower-right corner of the card.

FIGURE 12.22
Adding the informational text to the card.

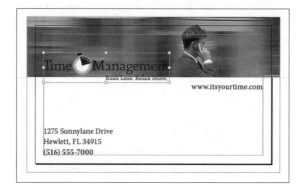

FIGURE 12.23
Scaling and positioning the logo within the photo.

Now we'll edit the logo for our needs by selecting it and opening the Links palette. Click on the Edit Original icon to automatically open the logo file in Illustrator.

In Illustrator, delete the tagline from the file and select the words Time and Management and give them a fill of white. We don't want to save these changes because we want to keep the original logo. Instead, choose Save As from the File menu and give the file a different name, adding a comment that this logo is colored white and has the tagline removed.

Switch back to InDesign. In the Links palette, with the logo selected, click on the Relink button, and choose the logo you just created with the white letters. When you click OK, the logo should now appear correctly in the layout (see Figure 12.24).

Finally, add the tagline at the bottom right of the card (12-point Chaparral Pro Regular) and save the file into Version Cue. This should give you the final version of the business card (see Figure 12.25).

FIGURE 12.24
The white logo replaces the black one.

FIGURE 12.25
The final business card.

Designing the Letterhead

Next we'll design the letterhead, which is very similar in design to the business card we just made. Create a new document in InDesign that is set to letter size 8.5×11 with a margin of 0.375 inches all around and a bleed of 0.125 inches all around as well.

Rather than redoing all the work we did for the business card, simply open the business card file and copy all the contents from it. Then switch back to the letterhead document and paste (see Figure 12.26).

Select the text and change it to 10-point type on 14-point leading. Then select the tagline and change it to 24-point type. Scale the photo and the image so that they fit correctly at the top of the page (drag a horizontal guide to the 2-inch mark to help). The letterhead is now complete (see Figure 12.27), so save it into Version Cue and add a comment to the file.

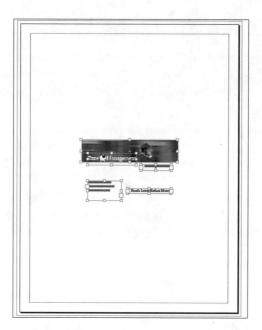

FIGURE 12.26
The business-card
elements pasted
into the letterhead
file.

FIGURE 12.27
The final letter-
head.

Designing the Envelope

Finally, we'll create a standard #10 envelope. Create a new InDesign file, set to 9.5 inches wide and 4.125 inches tall. Set the margins to 0.375 inches, and we don't need a bleed because we won't be using the photo in this design.

Did you Know?

> As I mentioned earlier when we created the business card, you might consider saving the envelope settings as a document preset so that you can quickly create standard envelopes in the future.

First, copy and paste the text from the business-card file and remove the phone number (not necessary for an envelope). Next, choose File, Place and choose the original Time Management logo that we created—the one with the black letters and the tagline. Position the text and the logo in the upper-left corner of the envelope and save the file to Version Cue (see Figure 12.28).

FIGURE 12.28
The final #10 envelope.

Congratulations, you've just created a complete corporate identity!

CHAPTER 13

Creating a Brochure

The Project

In this project, we'll create a tri-fold brochure for the Time Management company. We've already created the company's corporate identity in the preceding chapter, and we can use some of those assets in this project as well.

Planning the Layout in InDesign

A tri-fold brochure is an 8.5×11-inch sheet of paper that's folded twice. The result is a piece that has six panels and can fit inside a standard #10 envelope. When you are laying out the brochure in InDesign, you'll need to arrange the panels so that the job will look correct when it is folded and printed.

Launch InDesign and create a new file. In the New Document dialog, specify the following options (see Figure 13.1):

- ▶ Set the number of pages to 2.
- ▶ Uncheck the Facing Pages option.
- ▶ Specify a Letter-size page (8.5×11 inches) with an orientation set to landscape (wide).
- ▶ Set your number of columns to 3 and specify a gutter of 0.5 in.
- ▶ Set the margins to 0.25 in all around and set the bleeds to 0.125 in all around.

Save the file into your Version Cue project.

FIGURE 13.1
Specifying the doc-
ument settings for
the brochure.

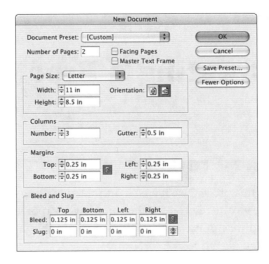

FIGURE 13.1
Specifying the doc-
ument settings for
the brochure.

Import the Text

Before beginning the actual design and layout, I like to label the individual panels, making it easier to visualize the final piece (see Figure 13.2). Most important,
this step keeps you from accidentally mixing up the panels.

FIGURE 13.2
Labeling the panels
in the layout. You'll
delete these later
in the project.

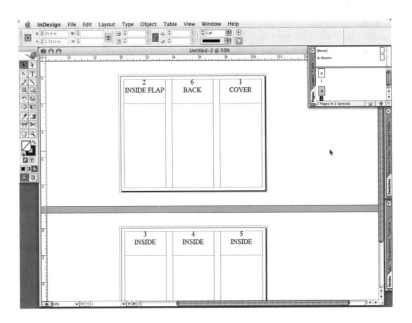

The next step is to bring in the text. For many jobs, you'll receive text files from a word processing program (Microsoft Word, for example). Of course, at times you'll also receive text that you'll have to copy and paste from an email, and there will be plenty of times when you'll have to type the text yourself directly into InDesign. For now, I'm going to place a Word file, but you can add text you want to for this project.

> If you don't feel like typing any words, simply draw a text frame and choose Type, Fill with Placeholder Text.

Did you Know?

The text will flow from page 3 to page 4, so after placing the first box on the column for page 3, click on the out link box and then click in the column for page 4 (see Figure 13.3).

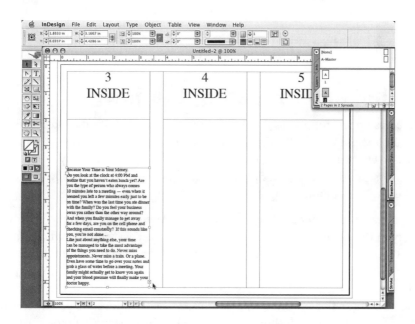

FIGURE 13.3
Placing the text from an external file.

The quote will be a separate text block, so cut and paste it into it's own new text block. Do the same for the headline as well (see Figure 13.4).

FIGURE 13.4
Separating the
quote and the
headline into their
own text blocks.

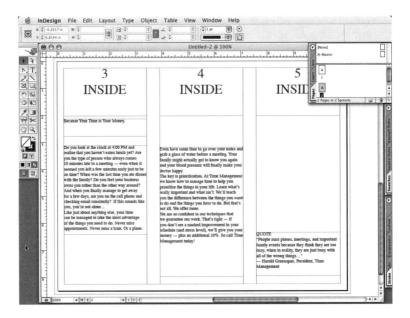

Finding and Preparing the Images

We'll be using several photos in the brochure, and we'll start off by launching
Photoshop to use the File Browser to find just the right images. As we did in the
preceding chapter's project, use the File Browser to flag the images you like, and
then choose to view only your flagged images (see Figure 13.5). In this brochure
we're going to need four images.

We'll start with the image of the man running. We used him for our corporate
identity in the preceding chapter, but for the brochure we want the image in full
color. Open the image, and similar to what we did in the previous project, use the
Shadow/Highlight command with a shadow setting of 30 to lighten up the photo
a bit. Apply the Unsharp Mask filter as well, using a setting of 100 for the
amount. Because this brochure will be printed, choose Image, Mode, CMYK Color,
and then save it as a Photoshop (.PSD) file into your Version Cue project (see
Figure 13.6).

Next, open the image of the two businessmen standing on the clock. The image is
fine the way it is, so you just want to convert the image to CMYK and then save it
as a PSD file into your Version Cue project as well.

FIGURE 13.5
Showing just the images that you've flagged in the File Browser.

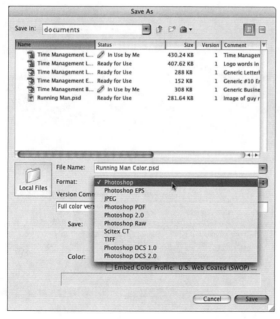

FIGURE 13.6
Choosing to save the file as a Photoshop file (.PSD).

Do the same for the image with the airplane. Eventually we'll do further editing of the plane, but for now we'll just convert it to CMYK and save it as a PSD file into our Version Cue project.

Silhouette the Clock

We're going to wrap the brochure header around the image of the clock, so we'll create a silhouette to get rid of the background. Open the clock image; double-click on the Background layer and press OK to rename it Layer 0. Then convert the image to the CMYK colorspace.

Because of the highlights near the edges of the clock, using the Extract filter won't be of much use here, and neither the Magic Wand nor the Magnetic Lasso will work well here either. Instead, select the Polygonal Lasso Tool and click repeatedly around the edge of the clock to select it (see Figure 13.7). After you've selected the entire clock, choose Select, Inverse (see Figure 13.8) to select everything except the clock, and then press Delete to remove the background. You should now see the checkerboard transparency grid behind the clock (see Figure 13.9). Save the file as a .PSD into your Version Cue project.

FIGURE 13.7
Using the Polygonal Lasso tool to select the clock. By using short line segments, you can choose what appears to be a circular shape.

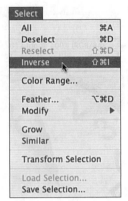

FIGURE 13.8
Choosing to invert your selection.

FIGURE 13.9
The clock with the background removed.

Designing the Cover

Switch back to InDesign and we'll begin designing the brochure, starting with the cover. Press (⌘-D) [Ctrl+D] and place the color version of the running man on the cover panel (see Figure 13.10). Delete the label we made earlier to identify the cover, and then adjust the picture frame and scale the image to fit within the cover (see Figure 13.11). Remember to allow the image to bleed off the page.

FIGURE 13.10
Choosing to place the color image of the running man. In this example, Version Cue is set to view files as thumbnails.

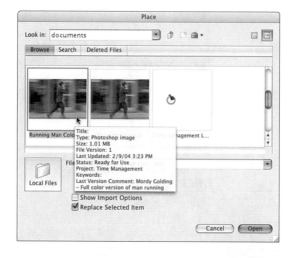

FIGURE 13.11
The image, correctly scaled and positioned on the cover.

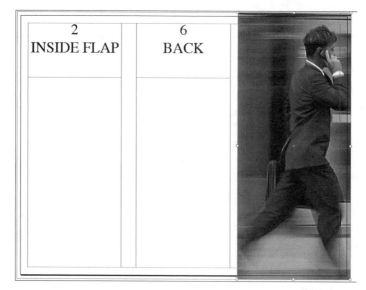

Add the Text and the Logo

Next, we'll add the text headline and logo to the cover. Type the words **Get Your Life Back On Track**, pressing (Shift-Return) [Shift+Enter] after each word (making each word sit on its own line). Set the text to Warnock Pro Regular, 30-point on 32-point leading, with Optical kerning (see Figure 13.12). Position the text in the upper-left corner of the cover and give the text a fill of white.

FIGURE 13.12
The text headline added.

Draw a rectangle that spans the cover and that is 1 inch in height (use the Control palette at the top of the screen to help you). Specify a stroke of none, and a color of 50% black (which will look gray), but then open the Transparency palette and specify the Multiply blend mode (see Figure 13.13). This will make the bar appear to simply darken an area of the underlying photo. We're going to place the company logo in this bar.

Press (⌘-D) [Ctrl+D] again to place the Time Management logo. Choose the first version we created—the one that had the black text and the tagline in it. Scale the logo to 85% and position it on top of the bar you just created (see Figure 13.14). Switch to High Quality Display so that you can better see what you're doing.

FIGURE 13.13
Adding the rectangle, which will eventually darken the area of the photo under it.

FIGURE 13.14
Placing the scaled logo on top of the bar.

Edit the Logo to Make It Reverse

The logo text will have to appear in reverse, so choose Window, Links, and with the logo selected click on the Edit Original button on the Links palette to open the logo in Illustrator (see Figure 13.15). In Illustrator, select all the text (not the watch icon) and change the Fill color to white (see Figure 13.16). Then choose File, Save As to save the file with a different name into your Version Cue project. Remember to add a comment indicating that the text is white and the logo *does* include the tagline.

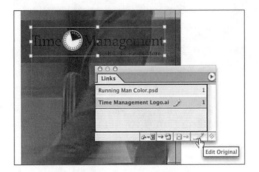

FIGURE 13.15
Using the Edit Original feature to edit the placed logo.

FIGURE 13.16
Coloring the text white inside of Illustrator.

Switch back to InDesign and, with the logo selected in your layout, click on the Relink button in the Links palette to choose the new reverse logo. The comments you made when saving the file into Version Cue will help you make sure that you're choosing the correct logo (see Figure 13.17). When you return to your InDesign file, you'll now see the correct logo on the cover.

FIGURE 13.17
The useful comments that are available when you're placing files take the guesswork out of choosing the correct file.

While you're already there, complete the back cover by placing the regular logo and adding the contact information (I copied it from the letterhead we created in the preceding chapter). Page 2 (the inside flap) will remain blank, because the company will use it to print specific city and date information on seminars, which is subject to change throughout the year (see Figure 13.18).

FIGURE 13.18
One side of the brochure, completed.

Designing the Inside of the Brochure

Now let's move to the inside of the brochure. Switch to page 2 of your InDesign document. We'll start laying out the bottom first by dragging out a horizontal guide to the 6-inch mark. This will leave us with a 2.5-inch area at the bottom of the page. Draw a rectangle to fill that entire area, remembering to bleed the edges off the page (see Figure 13.19). Specify a stroke of none and a fill of 50% black. Choose Object, Arrange, Send to Back to send the rectangle to the bottom of the stacking order.

> If you have your own text, you can place it, or you can type the text you see in Figure 13.19.

By the Way

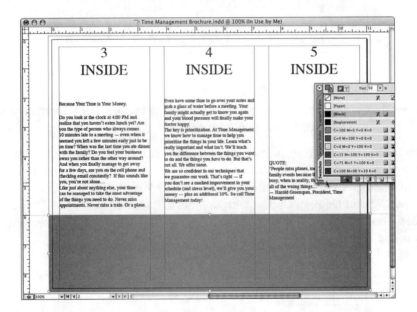

FIGURE 13.19
Creating a gray rectangle at the bottom of the page.

Place the image of the two businessmen standing on a clock from your Version Cue project, and position it to the far left of the page. Scale it so that it fits correctly (see Figure 13.20).

FIGURE 13.20
Adding the photo
collage of the two
men and the clock.

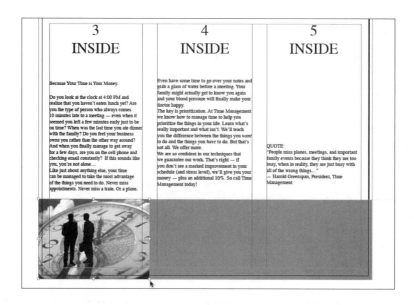

FIGURE 13.20
Adding the photo
collage of the two
men and the clock.

Define Style Sheets

Now we'll style and lay out the text for the inside of the brochure. You can also delete the labels you created to identify the panels.

Open the Paragraph Styles palette and (Option-click) [Alt-click] on the Create New Style button to create and define a new style. Choose Basic Character Formats and give the style a name of Body. Specify Warnock Pro Regular, 11-point type on 16-point leading, Optical kerning, and a Tracking value of –10 (see Figure 13.21). Choose Indents and Spacing, and then specify a Space Before amount of 8 points and click OK to create the style.

FIGURE 13.21
Defining a para-
graph style for the
body copy.

We'll create another style for the quote. Create a new style (as you did previously), name it Quote, and specify Warnock Pro Regular, 22-point on 28-point leading with Optical kerning and a Tracking value of –10. Click OK to create the style.

Now select the body copy and apply the Body style sheet you defined (see Figure 13.22). Apply the Quote style sheet for the quote text as well.

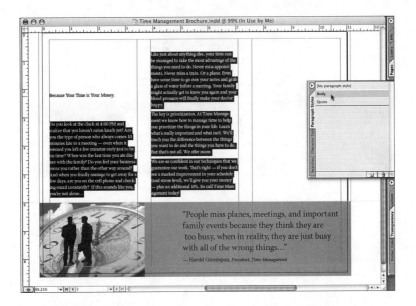

FIGURE 13.22
Applying the styles to the text.

Apply a Text Wrap

The next step will be to place the photo of the clock, and then wrap the headline around it. Begin by setting the headline text to Warnock Pro Regular, 30-point type on 36-point leading. Turn on Optical kerning and set the Tracking to –10. You can define the headline as a new paragraph style if you'd like.

Now place the image of the clock. Position the clock so that nearly half of it falls off the page (see Figure 13.23). Crop the image frame so that you see only the image that will show and the bleed, and choose Window, Type & Tables, Text Wrap to open the Text Wrap palette (see Figure 13.24). With the image of the clock still selected, choose the Wrap Around Object Shape option in the Text Wrap palette. Then choose Alpha Channel in the Contour Type pop-up and set the offset to 0.125 in (see Figure 13.25).

FIGURE 13.23
Positioning the
image of the clock.

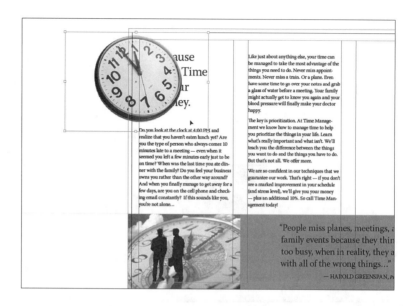

FIGURE 13.24
The Text Wrap
palette.

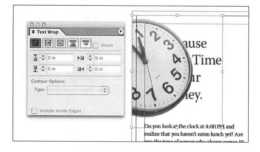

FIGURE 13.25
Applying the text
wrap.

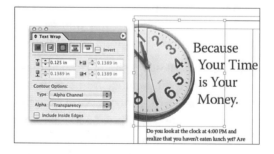

To add a little more pop to the page, add a soft drop shadow to the clock by
choosing Object, Drop Shadow (see Figure 13.26).

Add a Background

Finally, we'll add the photo of the plane landing to add a background to the page and fill out the design. The image of the plane also reinforces the president's quote in the bar across the bottom.

Place the image and position it over the middle and right panel. After you've positioned it where you want it, send it to the back of the stacking order by pressing (⌘-Shift-[) [Ctrl+Shift+[] or by choosing Object, Arrange, Send to Back (see Figure 13.27).

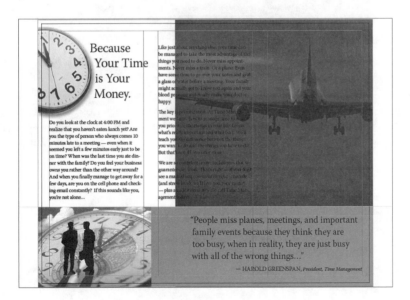

Because the image gets in the way of the text in the middle column, we'll create a fade so that the image of the plane blends into the background of the page. We're going to use Photoshop to create the fade, so select the plane. Then (Control-click) [right-click] and choose Graphics, Edit Original from the contextual menu that pops up (see Figure 13.28).

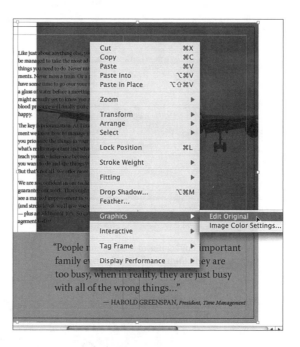

Now that we're in Photoshop, we'll use a gradient as a selection to create the fade. Double-click on the Background layer and then press OK to rename it Layer 0. If your Foreground and Background colors are not set to black and white already, press the "D" key to set them back to their default black and white settings.

Press the "Q" key on your keyboard to enter Quick Mask mode. Then choose the Gradient tool, specify the Foreground to Background gradient, and position your cursor directly over the tail of the plane. Press and hold the Shift key while you drag the mouse toward the left of the image (see Figure 13.29). Let go of the mouse when you're near the edge of the image (see Figure 13.30).

FIGURE 13.29
Getting ready to create the gradient.

Now press the "Q" key again to exit Quick Mask mode. The gradient you just created is now a selection. Press the Delete key to execute the fade (see Figure 13.31).

FIGURE 13.30
The finished gradient, still in Quick Mask mode.

From the File menu, choose Save a Version to save this change as a new version in your file. This will allow you to go back to the version without the fade, if you would need to do so later. It will also automatically update your image in your Version Cue project. Add a comment regarding the changes you've made to the file, and click the Save button (see Figure 13.32).

Upon returning to InDesign, you'll see that the image is now automatically updated. To make the gray bar across the bottom visually appealing, select it and choose the Multiply blend mode from the Transparency palette. Select the text in the quote and choose white for the fill color to make it more readable. Copy and paste the reverse logo from the cover, and place it under the plane (see Figure 13.33).

FIGURE 13.31
The completed
fade.

FIGURE 13.32
Saving a version of
the Photoshop file.

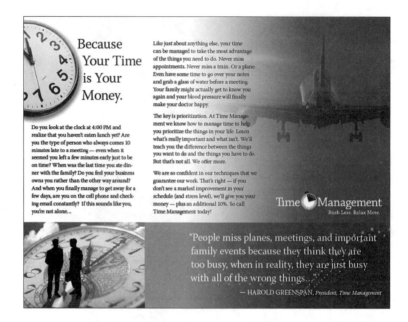

Congratulations, you've just completed a tri-fold brochure! You can either print a proof or create a PDF file to send to your manager or client for comments or approval.

CHAPTER 14

Creating an Ad Campaign

The Project

In this project, we will create a print advertising campaign for the Time Management company. After designing the ads, we'll create a PDF file to send to the client for comments. Next we'll pretend we're the client, and use Acrobat to make comments on the campaign (we'll be our own critic!). Then we'll go back to InDesign and see how to generate a PDF/X-1a–compliant file, which is an ISO standard format used in the advertising industry.

By the Way

Once again, we'll be using Version Cue to help us keep track of the assets for this project. You can continue to use the same Version Cue project that you set up in Chapter 12, "Creating a Corporate Identity."

Choosing and Preparing Images in Photoshop

All of those sayings that you hear people repeat endlessly, such as "image is everything" or "a picture is worth a thousand words" prove quite true in the world of advertising. Advertisers know that they have only a few precious seconds to attract people's attention before they move on to something else.

In this campaign, we're going to create a series of three ads, and each ad will play up a specific image. The first ad will feature an image of a train, sporting a headline of "Never Miss Another Train." The second ad will feature an image of a plane with a headline reading "Never Miss Another Plane." The final ad will show an image of people in a business meeting and will read "Never Miss Another Meeting."

We'll start looking for photos as we have done in previous projects—by using the File Browser in Photoshop. Flag the files you want to use and open them by double-clicking on them (see Figure 14.1).

FIGURE 14.1
Choosing to view
only the flagged
images in the
Photoshop File
Browser.

Create a Cohesive Look

Because each of these images differs from the others, we're going to apply a specific look to them so that you can easily identify that they are all part of the same
campaign. One simple way to do that is to apply a stylized filter to all of them, or
give them all similar color hues. In this case, we're going to add some noise—*Yo,
Photoshop in da house!* No, not that kind of noise. I'm talking about the Noise filter, which will give the images a grainy texture, similar to a mezzotint.

Record and Use an Action

In fact, because we'll be applying similar settings to all three images, let's create
an action to help save some time.

Start with the image of the train. Choose Window, Actions to open the Actions
palette. Click on the Create New Action button and name the action Mezzotint.
When you click the Record button in the New Action dialog, you'll notice that the
Record button at the bottom of the Actions palette is on (see Figure 14.2). Don't
be alarmed, but Photoshop is now watching every move you make. Choose

Image, Mode, CMYK to convert the image from RGB to CMYK. After you've applied the color mode change, you can see that it was added to the Action in the Actions palette (see Figure 14.3). Now choose Filter, Noise, Add Noise. I specified 10% for the amount, and checked the Gaussian and Monochromatic options (see Figure 14.4). Click OK. The Noise filter is now added to the action as well.

FIGURE 14.2
Photoshop's indication that you're being watched.

FIGURE 14.3
The color mode change appears in the Mezzotint action.

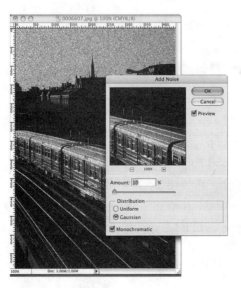

FIGURE 14.4
Adding noise to the image, to give it a mezzotint-like feel.

In the Actions palette, click on the Stop button (see Figure 14.5). Now, you'll be able to "replay" the techniques you just applied to the other images. First, save the train image into your Version Cue project. Remember to add a comment that alludes to the fact that this file has a mezzotint effect applied to it.

FIGURE 14.5
Stopping the recording of the action.

Now open the image of the plane. Select the Mezzotint action in the Actions palette and click once on the Play button. Sit back and watch the file convert itself to CMYK and apply the Noise filter. When it's done, save it to your Version Cue project. Do the same for the image of the people in the meeting.

By the Way

The action you created will remain in Photoshop, and you can either modify it later for another task or delete it.

After all of your images are saved into your Version Cue project, you can quit Photoshop. The next step is to lay out the ads in InDesign.

Setting Up Pages in InDesign

Launch InDesign and create a new file. In the New Document dialog (see Figure 14.6), specify the following options:

Set the number of pages to 3.

Uncheck the Facing Pages option.

Specify a letter-size page (8.5×11) with an orientation set to portrait (tall).

Set the number of columns to 2 and specify a gutter of 0.375 in.

Set your margins as follows: top, 8.375 in; bottom, 1 in; left, 0.375 in; right, 0.375 in.

Set your bleed to 0.125 in all around.

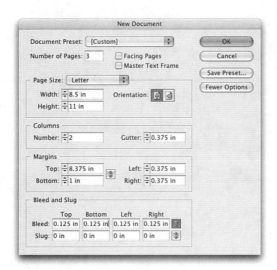

FIGURE 14.6
Specifying document options.

> **By the Way**
>
> You may be wondering how I knew to set up all of these specific options before we even started designing the piece. I'm psychic. The truth is I started out with a regular document and then made changes as I designed the piece using the Layout, Margins & Columns and the File, Document Setup settings. To make it easier to follow along, I've already given you the final settings, but when you're creating your own projects, you'll probably use the method I just described.

Setting Up a Master Page

Because we want the ads to appear as a series, they will all be similar in layout, and only the content will be different in each ad. Rather than applying the same design elements to different pages, we'll use a master page that will contain the common elements. This is beneficial not only when creating the files, but also when making edits. For example, when the client asks for the logo to be made larger, you can make the change on the master page and all the other pages will update automatically.

Double-click on the term A-Master in the Pages palette to switch to that master page (see Figure 14.7). Start by dragging a horizontal guide to the 8-inch mark, which will be where the photo will end. Drag a second horizontal guide to the 10 5/8-inch mark, which will be the baseline for the logo (see Figure 14.8).

FIGURE 14.7
Switching to the A-Master page.

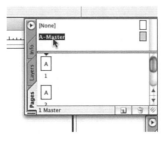

FIGURE 14.8
Placing guides for alignment.

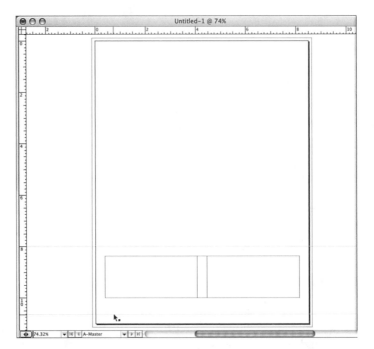

Place the Common Design Elements

Now that we have the guides in place, choose File, Place and import the Time Management logo from your Version Cue project. Use the Control palette to scale the logo by 80%, and position it so that it rests along the baseline you created, in the lower-right corner of the page. Then, using the Type tool, drag out a new text box, enter **www.itsyourtime.com**, and style it 14-point Warnock Pro Regular. Align that to the baseline as well, in the lower-left corner of the page (see Figure 14.9). Now that you've completed the master page, switch back to page 1 of your document.

FIGURE 14.9
The completed master page.

Placing the Photos

Now the fun begins. Place the train photo from your Version Cue project, and scale and position it so that the image fills the entire upper portion of the ad. The bottom of the picture box should meet the guide at 8 inches, and the top and sides of the image should bleed off the page (see Figure 14.10).

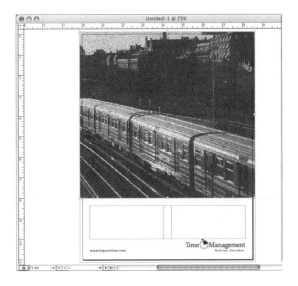

Placing the Text

As mentioned in the preceding chapter, you can place a text file, or you can just
type the text yourself inside InDesign. Add the body copy for the ad, and create a
paragraph style using Warnock Pro Regular, 12.5-point text on 18-point leading,
with Optical kerning turned on. Apply the paragraph style to the body text (see
Figure 14.11). I used two text boxes, linked together to create the two columns.

The final element that has to be added is the headline. Use the Type tool to drag out a new text box, and type the words **Never Miss Another Train**. Press (Shift-Return) [Shift+Enter] after each word, effectively forcing each word to be on its own line. Set the text to Warnock Pro Regular, 60-point text on 60-point leading with Optical kerning and a tracking value of –10 (see Figure 14.12).

Position the headline text over the photo, making sure that the left side of the headline aligns with the left side of the text box in the right column (see Figure 14.13). Change the fill color of the text to white and you're done.

Now that you've completed the first ad, save the file into your Version Cue project and then repeat the process for the remaining two ads on the other two pages of your document—the plane and the meeting—changing the headlines to reflect the photos (see Figure 14.14).

FIGURE 14.14
The completed ad
campaign.

Exporting a PDF File for Review

Now that the designs are complete, we can send the campaign off for approval. Whereas in the past you might have created large (and expensive) color proofs to present to your client (and then waited for faxed corrections), today's fast-paced world demands the use of e-mail and PDF files.

Choose File, Export and select Adobe PDF as the format, and then click Save. Because we're going to e-mail this file for approval, choose the Screen PDF preset in the Export PDF dialog box (see Figure 14.15), and click Export.

FIGURE 14.15
Choosing the
Screen preset,
which will optimize
the PDF for
onscreen viewing.

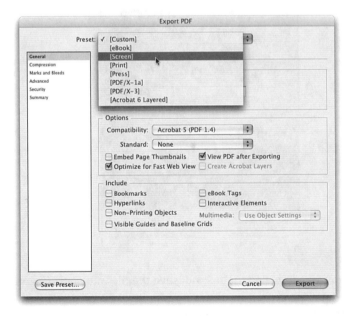

You can then send an e-mail to your manager or client and attach the PDF file that you just created to your e-mail.

Adding Comments to the File in Acrobat

Are you up for a little role-playing adventure? I am. Let's make believe that we're now the manager or client who just received the PDF of the ad campaign. Double-click on the PDF file to open the file in Adobe Acrobat 6 Professional (see Figure 14.16).

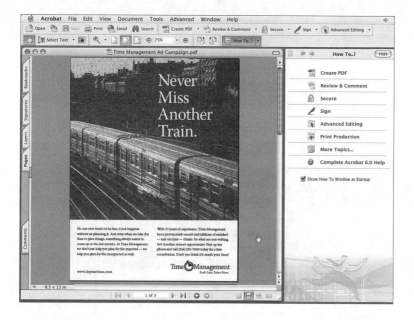

FIGURE 14.16
Viewing the file in Acrobat.

> If the PDF file opened in the Adobe Reader (the free viewer), close it and then manually launch Acrobat 6 Professional and choose File, Open to choose the PDF file.

Did you Know?

Step through the three pages of the PDF file to see the three ads. You like it (and make a mental note to give the designer who created it a raise), but a few small things have to be changed. First, the logo is too small (of course), so click on the Review and Comment button in the toolbar across the top to reveal the Commenting toolbar (see Figure 14.17). Choose the Note tool and then click on the logo to create a comment. In the note that pops up, write that you'd like to see the logo enlarged. Now click on the headline to add a second note. Turns out that the lawyers didn't approve of the word "never" in the headline and would rather see it say "Don't" instead. Add that comment into the new note you just created. Finally, click on the Stamp tool and choose the Dynamic, Reviewed option to stamp your action on the document (see Figure 14.18). Save the PDF file and e-mail it back to your very hard-working designer who really does deserve that raise.

FIGURE 14.17
Opening the Commenting toolbar.

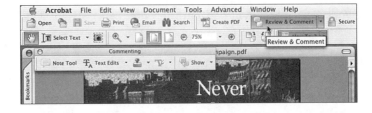

FIGURE 14.18
The PDF file with the comments added.

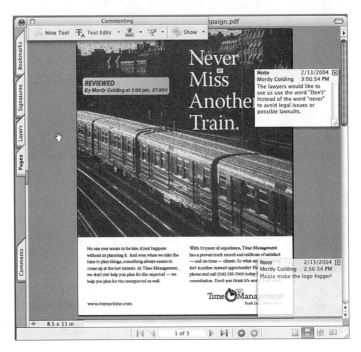

Making Changes in InDesign

Turning back into a designer, you check your e-mail to see that you got the PDF file back. You open it and read the comments (and roll your eyes at the "bigger logo" comment) and then open the source InDesign file from your Version Cue project.

Change the headlines to read "Don't Miss Another Train," and so on, and switch to the A-Master page to make the logo a teensy bit larger (remember that the change will automatically propagate to all the pages).

Saving a Version and Exporting It As a PDF/X-1a–Compliant File

Rather than saving the file, you want to create a new version of the InDesign file (so that you can track these changes later, or even revert to the original version if you'd like). Choose File, Save a Version and enter a comment that describes the changes you've made (see Figure 14.19).

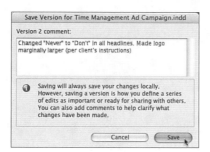

FIGURE 14.19
Saving a version of the InDesign file.

To send the ad to the publisher, you'll want to export a PDF/X-1a–compliant file. With the file still open in InDesign, choose File, PDF Export Presets, [PDF/X-1a] to export your file as a PDF/X-1a–compliant file (see Figure 14.20).

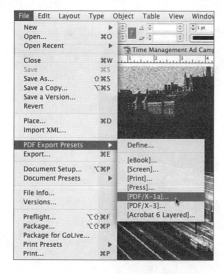

FIGURE 14.20
Choosing to export a PDF/X-1a–compliant file.

Congratulations! You've just created and completed an entire ad campaign.

CHAPTER 15

Creating a Web Banner

The Project

In this project, we'll create a Web banner that the Time Management company can use to help promote its business online. Things that are important to ad banner advertising are a clear message, eye-catching graphics, and small file size. With the Adobe Creative Suite, you have all the tools necessary to achieve those goals. We'll start off in Illustrator and then use ImageReady to add some interactivity. The final format will be a 468×60-pixel animated GIF file.

> In this task specifically, we won't be using Version Cue. ImageReady has no direct support for Version Cue, and the work-flow doesn't require its services.

By the Way

Creating a New Illustrator File

Begin by launching Illustrator and creating a new file. From the New Document dialog, choose 468×60 from the Size pop-up menu and choose Pixels as your unit of measurement. For Color Mode, choose RGB (see Figure 15.1).

FIGURE 15.1
Creating a new doc-
ument in Illustrator
CS.

By the Way

Like it or not, designing for the Web is very much a "by the numbers" process. You're usually concerned with exact pixel dimensions, exact colors, exact position- ing, and more. As you'll see throughout this project, we'll be performing tasks with exact values. Especially with Web graphics, it's a discipline that will undoubtedly result in better-looking graphics and, ultimately, more free time on your hands.

Next, we'll set up a few things in Illustrator to make the task of designing Web graphics easier and more precise:

▶ Choose Object, Crop Area, Make to set crop marks at the exact size of the document. Doing this will ensure that the graphic will export at the correct size.

▶ Open your Web-safe color palette by choosing Window, Swatch Libraries, Web. This way, we can choose Web-safe colors when designing the banner.

▶ Choose View, Pixel Preview. This will allow you to view your images as they would appear in a Web browser, with correct antialiasing applied.

▶ Press (⌘-R) [Ctrl+R] to turn on your rulers. This will assist us in positioning items.

▶ Finally, open your Transform palette by choosing it from the Window menu. The Transform palette will help us edit and position graphics perfectly.

With your file set up this way (see Figure 15.2), you can be assured that you'll be creating high-quality Web graphics. Now would also be a good time to save your file with the name of your choice.

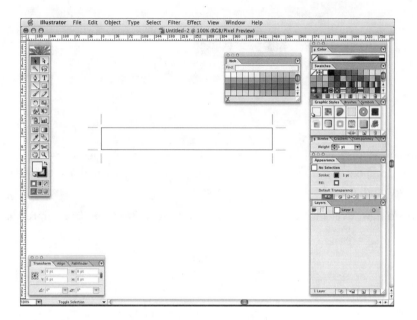

Adding the Headline

We're going to split the ad into two sections. The left side will eventually contain a photo; the right side, the logo. Select the Rectangle tool and click once anywhere on your artboard to create a rectangle numerically. Enter **234 px** for the Width and **60 px** for the Height and click OK (see Figure 15.3). Give the rectangle a black fill and no stroke. With the rectangle still selected, click on the lower-left box of the proxy in the Transform palette, and enter a value of **0** for both the X and the Y coordinates. This will position the black rectangle perfectly in the left half of the banner (see Figure 15.4).

FIGURE 15.3
Drawing a rectangle numerically.

FIGURE 15.4
Using the
Transform palette
to position the rec-
tangle.

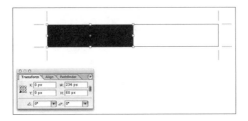

Double-click on Layer 1 in your Layers palette and rename the layer **Placeholder**.
This rectangle will really be replaced with a photo when we're done, but we need
it now to make it easier to create our design.

Create a new layer in the Layers palette and name it **Headline** (see Figure 15.5).

FIGURE 15.5
Creating a new
layer for the head-
line.

**Did you
Know?**

> Using layers when creating Web graphics that will eventually be animated is extreme-
> ly important. By taking the extra few seconds to organize your art in Illustrator in the
> design stage, you can save a lot more time later in the animation and optimization
> stage.

Select the Type tool and click on your artboard to create a point text object (don't
click on the rectangle). Enter the words **Never Miss Another Plane** and style it
with 20 pt Warnock Pro Regular. Turn on optical kerning and specify a tracking
value of **-10**. Color the text white and position it in the center of the black rectangle (see Figure 15.6).

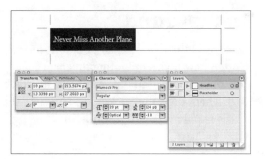

FIGURE 15.6
Positioning the headline text over the placeholder rectangle.

Adding the Logo

Create a new layer and name it **Logo**. Then open the Time Management logo file you created way back in our first project. Press (⌘-A) [Ctrl+A] to select everything and copy the logo. Then close the file and paste the logo into the banner file.

With the logo selected, click on the lock icon in the Transform palette and specify a Width of **200 px** for the logo. Position the logo in the center of the white area of the banner (see Figure 15.7)

FIGURE 15.7
Scaling and positioning the Time Management logo.

When we first created the logo, we grouped the elements together. Because we're going to animate the tagline separately, ungroup the logo so that the tagline is no longer grouped with the words of the logo. Create a new layer and name it Tagline. Select the tagline itself and you'll notice in the Logo layer a small box indicating that something on that layer is selected (see Figure 15.8). Click and drag that small box up into the new Tagline layer. This will move the tagline itself into the new layer.

FIGURE 15.8
Moving the tagline into the correct layer by dragging the selection dot in the Layers palette.

Adding a Background

The white background behind the logo just isn't doing it for me, so let's add a colored background. Create a new layer and name it **Background**. Draw a rectangle that is a bit larger than the banner itself, and choose a fill color from the Web palette (see Figure 15.9). Then, drag the Background layer to the bottom of the stacking order in the Layers palette (see Figure 15.10).

FIGURE 15.9
Drawing and coloring the rectangle for the background.

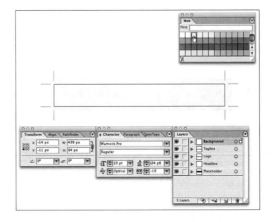

FIGURE 15.10
Moving the Background layer behind all the other layers.

By the Way

I've instructed you to create the background rectangle larger than the document itself to illustrate how the crop marks will affect the file when it's exported. Even though the art extends past the crop marks, the document will open in ImageReady at the correct document size.

Save the Illustrator file.

Exporting a Photoshop File

Now we're ready to take the banner into ImageReady. Although ImageReady is capable of opening native Illustrator files, we can take advantage of some advanced functionality by exporting a PSD file right from Illustrator.

> When you open a native Illustrator file in ImageReady, the file will get flattened into a single layer. However, if you export a Photoshop (PSD) file from Illustrator, you can preserve layers, clipping masks, editable text, opacity levels and blend modes, slices and optimization settings, and more.

By the Way

Choose File, Export and select Photoshop (PSD) from the Formats pop-up; then click Export. You'll be presented with the Photoshop Export Options dialog box (see Figure 15.11). Choose Screen (72 ppi) for the resolution, and choose to export as Photoshop CS with the Write Layers choice and the Preserve Text Editability and Maximum Editability options checked.

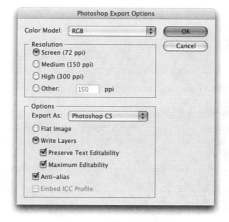

FIGURE 15.11
The Photoshop Export Options dialog box.

At this point you're done with Illustrator. You can close the file and quit the application.

Opening the File in ImageReady

Launch ImageReady and choose File, Open to open the Photoshop file that you just exported from Illustrator.

Take a look at the Layers palette. Notice how all the layers you so carefully named and arranged in Illustrator now appear exactly the same, here in ImageReady. This will make it a lot easier to build the animation. Start off by clicking on the eyeballs to hide the Logo, Tagline, and Placeholder layers (see Figure 5.12).

FIGURE 15.12
Hiding the Logo, Tagline, and Placeholder layers.

Placing the Photo

Choose File, Place and click on the Choose button. Find and place the image of the plane that we've been using throughout these projects.

By the Way

The image of the plane can be found in the Goodies/Illustrator CS/Illustrator Stock Photos folder on the Resources and Extras CD. The name of the file is 0004912.jpg.

After the image is placed, rename its layer to **Photo** and position it so that the layer appears directly under the Placeholder layer (see Figure 15.13).

Obviously, the photo is useless where it currently sits, so we'll scale it and position it properly. We can do this precisely by making sure that the Photo layer is highlighted and then choosing Edit, Transform, Numeric.

In the Position section, uncheck the box marked Relative. This will allow you to position the photo with absolute values that correspond to the document, not the image itself. Leave the values set to 0,0.

We want the image to be the same dimensions as the placeholder was, so in the Scale section, enter a width of **234** pixels and click OK (see Figure 15.14). You'll notice now that the image is correctly scaled and aligned to the left side of the banner (see Figure 15.15).

FIGURE 15.13
The Layers palette, after the photo has been placed.

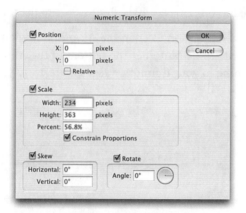

FIGURE 15.14
Scaling and positioning the image of the plane.

FIGURE 15.15
The image correctly scaled and positioned.

Correcting the Text

If you remember back in the last project (the ad campaign), the client requested that the headlines be changed from Never Miss... to Don't Miss..., so we'll have to make the change here as well. A text change this late in the design process would normally be quite disruptive in some workflows, but because we exported our file from Illustrator as a Photoshop file, the headline text was preserved as live text.

Choose the Type tool, highlight the word Never, and change it to read **Don't** (see Figure 15.16). So much for disruptive workflows.

FIGURE 15.16
Changing text in a
Web banner has
never been easier.

Go ahead and hide the Headline layer now, because we don't want it to appear in the first frame of the animation.

Creating the Animation

To make the banner visually exciting, we'll animate the photo so that it appears as if the plane is taking off. This is where things start to get fun.

First, choose Window, Animation to open the Animation palette. Next, click on the Duplicates Current Frame button at the bottom of the Animation palette. This will add a second frame to your animation (see Figure 15.17).

FIGURE 15.17
Adding a second
frame to the
animation.

In the Layers palette, highlight the Photo layer and then choose the Move tool. Hold the Shift key and drag the image of the plane upward until you can no longer see the wheels of the plane (see Figure 15.18). You may need to move the image several times in small increments.

FIGURE 15.18
Moving the image
upward in the sec-
ond frame so that
the plane is no
longer visible.

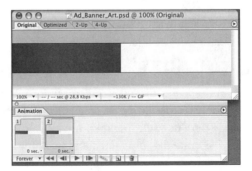

Back in the Animation palette, highlight the second frame in the animation and click on the Tweens Animation Frames button at the bottom of the palette (see Figure 15.19). Choose to add five frames and click OK (see Figure 15.20). You'll see that ImageReady automatically creates the intermediate frames for you (see Figure 15.21). If you click the Play button at the bottom of the Animation palette, you'll see the animation in action.

FIGURE 15.19
Clicking on the Tween button in the Animation palette.

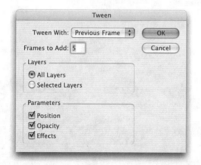

FIGURE 15.20
Choosing to add five frames to the animation.

FIGURE 15.21
The Animation palette with the tweened frames added.

Whenever you're ready, click on the Stop button to stop the animation from playing. We'll now finish the rest of the frames. Highlight the last frame (frame 7) and show the Headline layer in the Layers palette (see Figure 15.22).

Duplicate the seventh frame to create an eighth frame. In the Layers palette, choose to show the Logo layer (see Figure 15.23).

Duplicate the eighth frame to create a ninth frame. In the Layers palette, choose to show the Tagline layer (see Figure 15.24).

You can click Play again to see the animation in action. Click the Stop button before you continue.

FIGURE 15.22
Showing the
Headline layer in
the seventh frame
of the animation.

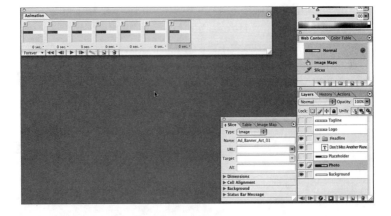

FIGURE 15.23
Showing the Logo
layer in the eighth
frame of the
animation.

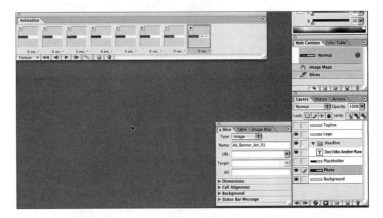

FIGURE 15.24
Showing the Tagline
layer in the ninth
frame of the
animation.

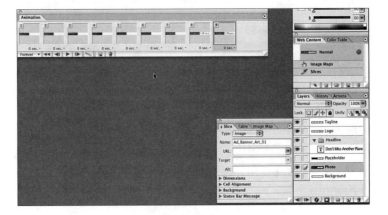

Set the Timing of the Frames

As is often said, timing is everything—and in animation, timing is key. Think of the playing of your animation as an important sentence in a speech. You have to add pauses and adjust the timing so that your emphasis and points are understood.

The first few frames are of the plane flying away, so those can go quickly; but you want to make sure that the animation pauses long enough that people can see the name of the company too. In the animation palette, highlight the first frame and choose a frame delay of 0.1 seconds (see Figure 15.25). Choose the same value of 0.1 seconds for frames 2 through 6. For frame 7, choose a frame delay of 0.5 seconds. For frame 8, choose a frame delay of 1 second. For the final frame, choose a 2-second frame delay (see Figure 15.26).

FIGURE 15.25
Choosing a frame delay for the first frame.

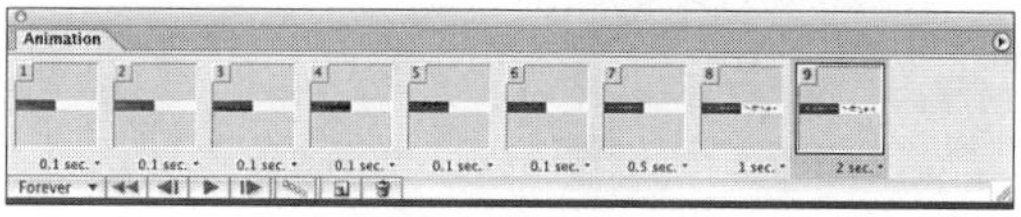

FIGURE 15.26
All the frames with specified frame delays.

Now play the animation again and see the difference.

Optimizing and Exporting the Animation

The final step is to optimize the file so that we can export it at the smallest file size possible, and still make it look good. Click on the 4-Up tab in the document window to see the banner with four different optimization settings. We know that we want to use the GIF format for final delivery, so use the Optimize palette to view the banner as a GIF with 64, 32, and 16 colors (see Figure 15.27). Pick the one you like; choose File, Save Optimized As and you're done!

Congratulations, you've just created an animated Web ad banner!

FIGURE 15.27
Choosing from different optimization settings.

CHAPTER 16

Creating a Web Page

The Project

In this project, we'll create a single Web page for the Time Management company. Other pages will be linked to this page, so we'll create a navigation bar that will allow users to visit the other pages in the site. We'll also utilize some other elements we've created in previous projects.

By the Way

> Of all the applications we've used so far, GoLive has the most robust support for Version Cue, so if you've been following along with Version Cue this far, great. By *robust support*, I mean that Version Cue is integrated so well into GoLive that you'll forget Version Cue is even there. The only "gotcha" is that ImageReady has no direct support for Version Cue, and because ImageReady is used often in Web workflows, it makes life a bit tedious (as we'll see during this project).

Creating the Navigation Bar

Let's start this project by creating the navigation bar for the Web site.

Launch Photoshop and open the original RGB image of the man running. Then open the original Time Management logo you created in Illustrator. When you open the file, you'll be presented with a dialog box asking how you want to rasterize the file (see Figure 16.1). Set the resolution to 72dpi and the Mode to RGB Color and click Open.

Now create a new Photoshop file that's 600 pixels wide by 130 pixels high. Set the Resolution to 72dpi and the Color Mode to RGB Color, 8 bit (see Figure 16.2). Switch to the running-man image, select all, and copy. Then come back to the new file you created and paste. Position the image (using the Move tool) so that the guy's head is closer to the right side (see Figure 16.3). Rename the new layer (that was automatically created when you pasted the image) **Running Man**.

FIGURE 16.1
Rasterizing the
Illustrator file
(remember that
Illustrator's native
file format is PDF).

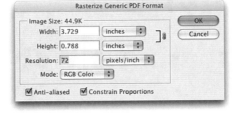

FIGURE 16.2
Creating a new
Photoshop file.

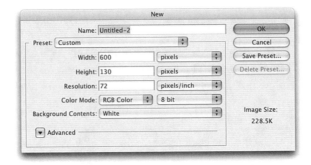

FIGURE 16.3
Positioning the
image.

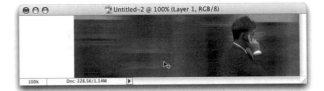

As we've done before to this image in previous projects, choose Image, Adjust,
Shadow/Highlight to brighten up the image. Especially on the Web, we want our
graphics to sing.

Next, we'll fade the image out to the left. Press G to switch to the Gradient tool;
press Q to enter Quick Mask mode and drag a gradient from right to left (see
Figure 16.4). Press Q again to exit Quick Mask mode, and press the Delete button
to create the fade (see Figure 16.5).

By the Way

If your gradient settings are anything other than the default setting, you'll need to
choose a Black to White gradient and choose Linear as the type of gradient.

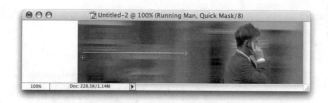

FIGURE 16.4
Dragging out a gradient with the Gradient tool.

FIGURE 16.5
The image with the fade applied.

Let's add a bar across the bottom (where we'll put the buttons). Create a new layer above the Running Man layer and call it **Button Bar**. Press the M key to switch to the Rectangular Marquee tool, and choose Fixed Size from the Style pop-up in the Tool Options bar (see Figure 16.6). Specify a Width value of **600** pixels and a Height value of **20** pixels. When you click in the document, you'll see that your selection is automatically constrained to that size. Drag it down so that it rests at the bottom of the file (see Figure 16.7).

FIGURE 16.6
Choosing the Fixed Size option from the Tool Options bar.

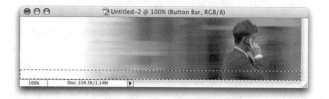

FIGURE 16.7
Creating your selection.

Press I to select the Eyedropper tool, and click on the area of the running man's back to sample a color (see Figure 16.8). Now press (Option-Delete) [Alt-Delete] to fill your selection with the color you just sampled. As an added touch, set the

Button Bar layer to the Multiply blend mode, which gives the bar a unified look with the image (Figure 16.9).

FIGURE 16.8
Sampling a color from the back of the man's jacket.

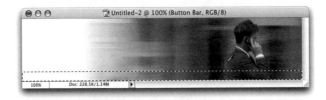

FIGURE 16.9
Setting the button bar to the Multiply blend mode.

Switch to the file of the logo, and copy and paste that into the new file as well, positioning it on the left side of the image, just above the button bar. Using the Rectangular Marquee tool (you may need to set the mode back to Normal if Fixed Size is still chosen in the Tool Options bar), select the tagline and delete it, because we'll be using the tagline elsewhere in the design of the site (see Figure 16.10).

FIGURE 16.10
Removing the tagline from the logo.

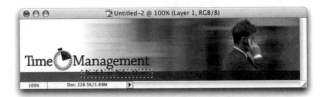

Add the Buttons

Now we'll add the text for the buttons. Press the T key to select the Type tool, and click anywhere in the file to create a new text layer. Type the words **CONTACT US**, style it 14-point Chaparral Pro Bold, and color it white (see Figure 16.11). In the Layers palette, change the Opacity for the text layer to 40%. This will give a dimmed appearance to the text, and we'll create rollovers for it when we're in ImageReady. Position the text (using the Move tool) so that it appears at the far right of the bar (see Figure 16.12).

FIGURE 16.11
Entering the text for the first button.

FIGURE 16.12
Positioning the text in the button bar, to the far right.

In the Layers palette, select the text layer and choose Duplicate Layer from the palette menu (see Figure 16.13). Alternatively, you can drag the text layer itself onto the Create New Layer icon to duplicate the layer. Use the Move tool to position the new text to the left, and change the text to read **CLIENTS**. Repeat this step to add three more text layers, reading **SEMINARS**, **SERVICES**, and **HOME** (see Figure 16.14).

FIGURE 16.13
Duplicating a text layer and changing the text.

Save your image into your Version Cue project, but we're going to do something a little different this time. Instead of saving it into your project file's Documents folder, navigate to your project's Web-Data\SmartObjects folder (see Figure 16.15). As you'll see later, this will make it easier for us to track these files in GoLive.

Add Rollovers

With the navigation bar file still open in Photoshop, click on the Jump to ImageReady button (see Figure 16.16), which will launch ImageReady (if it isn't already open) and open the navigation bar file.

FIGURE 16.16
Using the Edit in ImageReady feature.

Before we can add any rollovers, we'll need to create slices. Using the Slice tool, draw slices so that each button is a separate slice (see Figure 16.17). It's also a good idea to create a slice for the logo.

FIGURE 16.17
Specifying Web slices with the Slice tool.

Switch to the Slice Select tool and click on the slice for the HOME button. Open the Web Content palette and you'll notice that the slice that you selected is now highlighted. Click on the Create Rollover State button at the bottom of the palette to create an "over" state (see Figure 16.18).

FIGURE 16.18
Adding a rollover
state to the select-
ed slice.

Now change the Opacity level for the HOME text layer back to 100% in the
Layers palette (see Figure 16.19). This will cause the word HOME to appear to
"light up" when you move your mouse over the word.

FIGURE 16.19
Changing the
Opacity level of the
HOME layer for the
rollover.

In the Web Content palette, highlight the SERVICES slice and create a rollover state for that slice as well. Then change the Opacity level of the SERVICES layer. Repeat the process until all the text buttons have rollovers applied to them.

> If you know the URL links ahead of time, you can specify them here in ImageReady. Otherwise, you can also specify them later in the workflow, when you're in GoLive. Since we're designing a single page in this project, we won't specify URL links for the button slices.

Choose File, Save and then click the Jump To button at the bottom of the toolbox to open this file in Photoshop. We're doing this extra step because we want to check a new version of this file into Version Cue and there's no way to do that directly from ImageReady.

Save a Version

Now that you're back in Photoshop, choose File, Save a Version, and enter a comment stating that you've added rollovers to the navigation bar. We're done with both Photoshop and ImageReady for now, so you can quit both of those applications.

Creating Additional Web Graphics

We'll need to create two more graphical elements to use on our Web page, and we'll use Illustrator to create them. If it isn't already open, launch Illustrator, and we'll create a text header as well as an image of a clock, similar to what we did for the brochure.

Create a Text Header

Create a new RGB file (the size of the file doesn't matter), and turn Pixel Preview on. Using the Type tool, enter the words **Rush Less. Relax More.** Set the text to 18-point Chaparral Pro (see Figure 16.20).

FIGURE 16.20
Setting the text header in Illustrator CS.

Save the file as a native Illustrator file (AI), into the `Web-Data\SmartObjects` folder in your Version Cue project.

Add the Clock and Text

Next, create a new RGB file, type the words **Because Your Time is Your Money**, and set the text to Warnock Pro Regular, 30-point on 36-point leading.

Choose File, Place and find the image of the silhouetted clock that you created in an earlier chapter for the brochure. Uncheck the Link option (see Figure 16.21) and click the Place button. This will embed the image itself instead of placing a link to the graphic. Because the file is a native Photoshop file, Illustrator will offer two options: to convert the Photoshop image to Illustrator objects (layers) or to embed a single flattened image. In this case, we're going to choose the latter option (see Figure 16.22).

FIGURE 16.21
Unchecking the Link button when placing it will embed the image into your file. Linked images that are already placed can be embedded via an option in the Links palette.

FIGURE 16.22
Illustrator offers two options when embedding a Photoshop file.

Scale the image of the clock 50% and position it to the left of the text. Adjust the text so that it appears to wrap around the edge of the clock (I just added spaces before some of the words). If you feel like it, select the image of the clock and add a soft drop shadow as well (see Figure 16.23).

FIGURE 16.23
The final graphic, with a soft shadow added to the clock.

Save the document as a native Illustrator file (AI), into the `Web-Data\SmartObjects` folder in your Version Cue project. We're done with Illustrator for now, so feel free to quit the application at this point.

Laying Out the Page in GoLive

Now it's time to pull everything together. Launch GoLive and dismiss the startup screen that pops up. Choose File, Connect to Version Cue (see Figure 16.24), and select your project file. GoLive will then automatically create a site for your project and open the Site window (see Figure 16.25). This is actually the last time you'll be thinking about Version Cue, because from here on, GoLive practically takes care of everything.

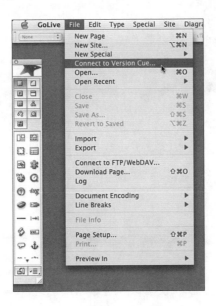

FIGURE 16.24
Choosing to connect to Version Cue.

FIGURE 16.25
The GoLive CS Site window with the Time Management project site loaded.

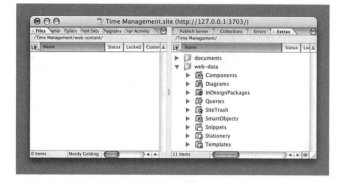

We'll begin by creating a new Web page. First (Control-click) [right-click] in the left side of the Site window to bring up the contextual menu, and then choose New, HTML Page (see Figure 16.26). Check in the file and rename the file **index.html**. Double-click on the page file to open it.

FIGURE 16.26
Creating a new HTML page.

Drag a layout grid onto the page. Because you're making an edit to the file, GoLive will prompt you to Check Out the file (which you should do). With the grid selected, click on the Align Center button (see Figure 16.27). Switch to the Smart group of tools in the toolbox, and drag a Smart Photoshop object onto the upper left of the grid (see Figure 16.28).

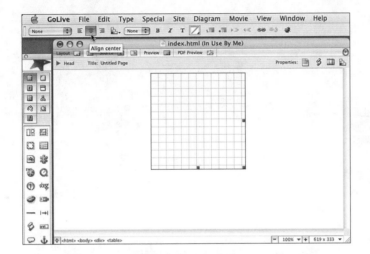

FIGURE 16.27
Aligning the grid to the center.

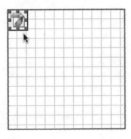

FIGURE 16.28
Adding a Smart Photoshop object.

With the Smart Object selected, point and shoot to the navigation bar you created, which you saved into the SmartObjects folder, to define it as the source for the Smart Object (see Figure 16.29). Click OK in the Variable Settings dialog that appears, because we won't need to use Variables for this project. In the Save for Web dialog that appears next, set the slice optimizations for each of the slices and click Save. Choose to save the contents in the site's Root folder (see Figure 16.30) and check in the files. You'll also be asked to check in the JavaScript that is used for the rollovers. You should now see the navigation bar in your layout (see Figure 16.31).

FIGURE 16.29
Choosing the
Navigation file as
the source for the
Smart Object.

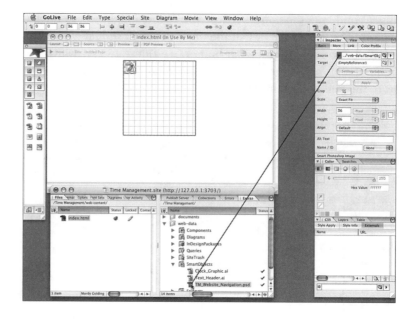

FIGURE 16.30
Saving the compo-
nents of the Smart
Object in the Root
folder.

FIGURE 16.31
The navigation bar
as it appears in the
layout.

Drag another Smart Object into your layout, this time for an Illustrator graphic,
and use the clock graphic as the source. Because GoLive sees the native Illustrator
file, it will ask whether you want to have the object converted to a bitmap format
or other vector formats that are supported on the Web. In this case, we're going to
choose Bitmap Format. Optimize the file in Save for Web, and click the Save button to save the image in the root folder (as we did earlier).

The graphic is too big, so grab one of the corners of the graphic while holding the Shift key and make the image smaller (see Figure 16.32). To better match the way we used the graphic in the brochure, we'll crop it so that only a portion of the clock is visible. With the clock graphic selected, click on the Crop Image icon in the Inspector palette and draw a box around the area of the image you want to remain (see Figure 16.33). Click on the Crop Image button in the main toolbar to crop the image, and the image will appear cropped.

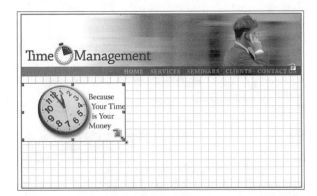

FIGURE 16.32
Scaling the Smart Object to be smaller.

FIGURE 16.33
Specifying the crop area.

Drag out one more Illustrator Smart Object, and this time link it to the text header you created. Save it the same way you saved the previous Illustrator graphic, and position the graphic on your page (see Figure 16.34). We're now ready to add some text.

Switch back to the Basic group of tools and drag out a Layout Text box. Add some copy (I copied and pasted the first paragraph of text from the brochure file in InDesign) and apply the Paragraph tag (see Figure 16.35).

FIGURE 16.34
Positioning the text header.

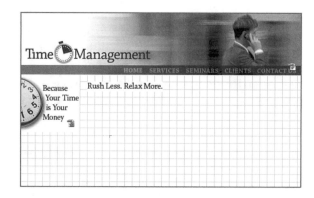

FIGURE 16.35
Adding copy and applying the Paragraph tag.

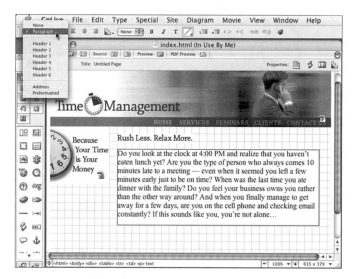

Place an Ad Banner at the Bottom of the Page

If you'd like, place an additional graphic at the bottom of your Web page—the ad banner we created in Chapter 15, "Creating a Web Banner." You can choose to place either the ImageReady source file, or the final GIF file you created.

Preview the Web Page

Save the file and close the window. Then check the file in (you can use the contextual menu by right-clicking on the file to do this). This releases the file so that others who have access to your project can open and edit it.

Click on the Preview button at the top of the document window to see what your page will look like in a Web browser. Notice how the rollovers work when you run your mouse cursor over the buttons in the navigation bar (see Figure 16.36).

FIGURE 16.36
The final Web page in Preview mode, where you can see the page as it would appear in a browser, as well as test the rollovers.

Congratulations, you've created a Web page!

CHAPTER 17

Creating a Business Presentation

The Project

In this final project, we'll create a business presentation for the Time Management company. The presentation will be designed in InDesign, and we'll use Illustrator to create some eye-catching charts. The executives would like to distribute this presentation to potential clients, but they don't want competitors to use the content; so we'll create a secure PDF as the final delivery format. The client will also require the graphics in a format they can use in PowerPoint, for internal presentations.

If you've been following along this far with Version Cue, great! For this project, we'll continue to use the same Version Cue project we created way back in Chapter 12, "Creating a Corporate Identity."

Creating an InDesign Document

Begin by launching InDesign and creating a new document. Standard presentations are 10 inches wide by 7.5 inches tall, and you should set the margins to be 0.5 inches all around. Specify two pages, with Facing Pages turned off (see Figure 17.1).

We're not going to add anything to the pages just yet, though. The nature of business presentations practically demands the use of master pages, and we'll set those up first.

FIGURE 17.1
Creating a new document in InDesign CS.

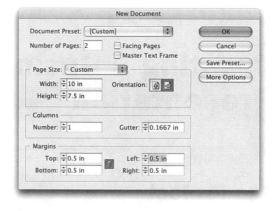

FIGURE 17.2
Choosing to create a new master page.

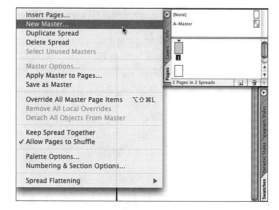

Design Two Master Pages

We're actually going to create two master pages. The first will be used for graphs and charts, the second for bulleted lists.

Open the Pages palette, and from the flyout menu choose New Master (see Figure 17.2). Give it a Prefix of **B**, name it **Graphs** and click OK.

The first thing we want to do is create a background, so place the color version of the photo with the guy on the cell phone running. Scale and crop the image so that it fills the entire page (see Figure 17.3). Then, with the image still selected, choose Object, Feather and specify a value of 1 inch. This will give the background a nice soft edge effect. Finally, open the Transparency palette and change the Opacity value of the image to 30% (see Figure 17.4).

FIGURE 17.3
Cropping and positioning the image on the page.

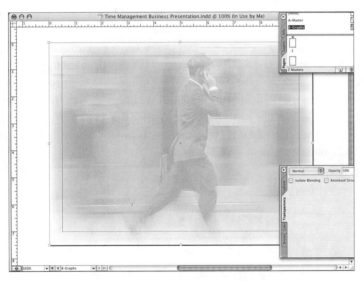

FIGURE 17.4
Adding a feathered edge, and changing the opacity value.

Next we'll do a few things by the numbers.

Draw a rectangle—any size—on your artboard. With the rectangle selected, go to the Control palette and click on the upper-left corner of the proxy. Then enter the following values: X=**0.5 in**; Y=**0.5 in**; W=**9 in**; H=**0.75 in**. Color the rectangle with a black 1 pt stroke and a fill of yellow (see Figure 17.5).

FIGURE 17.5
Adding the back-
ground for the
header.

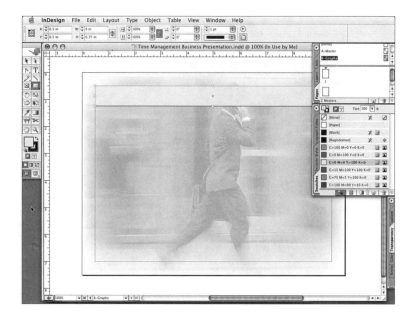

Switch to the Type tool and click once inside the yellow rectangle to convert it to a
text frame. Then type in the words **HEADLINE GOES HERE...** and press (⌘-Shift-C)
[Ctrl+Shift+C] to center the text. Select the text and set the font to Warnock Pro
Semibold at 36 pt with Optical kerning. Finally, choose Object, Text Frame
Options and set the Vertical Justification to Center (see Figure 17.6). Using the
Selection tool, select the yellow text frame and apply the Multiply blend mode
from the Transparency palette (see Figure 17.7).

FIGURE 17.6
Adding and styling
the placeholder for
the header.

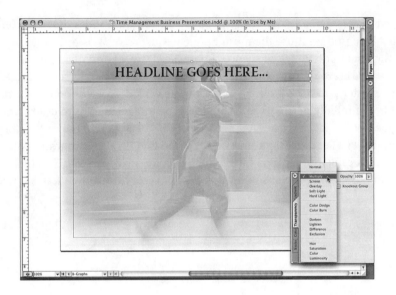

FIGURE 17.7
Setting the blend
mode to Multiply.

Press the M key to switch to the Rectangle tool, and draw another box on your artboard. Press the D key to color it with a black stroke and no fill, and, using the Control palette again, enter the following values: X=**0.5 in**; Y=**0.5 in**; W=**9 in**; H=**5.75 in**. This gives us a nice border for our slide.

Lastly, place the Time Management logo in the lower-right corner of the page to complete this master page (see Figure 17.8).

FIGURE 17.8
Adding the border
and the logo.

We need to create one more master page for presentation slides that will contain bulleted lists, and we'll use the master page we just created as a starting point. From the Pages palette flyout menu, choose New Master and assign it a Prefix of **B**, name it **Bulleted List**, base it on "B-Graphs," and click OK (see Figure 17.9). On this master page, draw out a new rectangle with a stroke of none, and position it in the middle of the page. Using the Type tool, convert it to a text frame and type in a bullet character followed by the words **Bullet Item 1**. Set the text to Warnock Pro Regular, 38 pt type on 40 pt leading. In the Paragraph palette, specify a Space Before setting of 0.125 in. Select the text with the Type tool and copy and paste a few copies so that you have several lines of text (see Figure 17.10).

FIGURE 17.9
Basing a new master page on a previous one.

FIGURE 17.10
Adding the placeholder for a bulleted list.

We're now ready to move on to filling the presentation with content. In the Pages palette, double-click on Page 1 to switch to that page.

> If you want to reuse this design for future presentations, you might want to save the file—as it is now—as an InDesign template.

Add the Content

We'll start with the easy one first. Drag the Bulleted List master page to the first page of your document to apply that master page (see Figure 17.11).

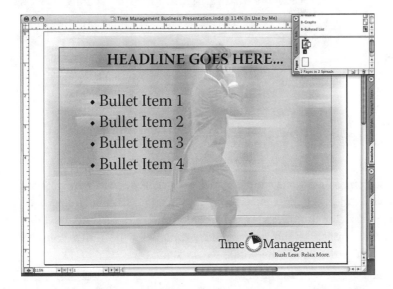

FIGURE 17.11
Applying the Bulleted List master page to the first page.

First, we'll edit the header. You'll notice that you can't select the header because it's an element that appears on a master page. In order to "override" the object to make a change to it, press (⌘-Shift) [Ctrl+Shift] while clicking on the header text. You'll now be able to change the text for that object to read **PROFESSIONAL SERVICES**.

Let's do the same for the text box below so that we can add our own bulleted text list. After you've applied the override, change the bullets to read **All-Day Seminars**, **One-on-One Consultations**, **Customized Daily Planners**, and **Post-Seminar Support** (see Figure 17.12).

Save your file into your Version Cue project.

FIGURE 17.12
The final bulleted
list slide.

Creating a Pie Chart

If you've had to create business presentations before, you know how dull and boring those corporate graphs can look. Well, with the Adobe Creative Suite in your hands, you can make those executives sit up in their leather chairs and take interest in the cool graphics you can create—especially with Adobe Illustrator. Let's start by launching Illustrator and creating a new document that is 9 inches by 5.75 inches (the size of the border we created).

By the Way

> Because this is a presentation that will be viewed onscreen, you can choose RGB for the color mode for this graph, which will allow your colors to appear more vibrant onscreen.

Choose the Pie Graph tool (see Figure 17.13) and click once on the artboard to bring up the Graph dialog. Enter a value of **4 in** for both the Width and the Height (see Figure 17.14). In the Graph Data window that appears, enter values of **20**, **30**, **10**, and **40**. Click the Check Mark button to see the values updated in the pie graph itself (see Figure 17.15).

Close the Graph Data window and switch to the Direct Selection tool. Select each pie wedge individually and fill it with a color of your choice. Set the Stroke to none.

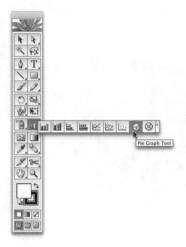

FIGURE 17.13
Choosing the Pie
Graph tool.

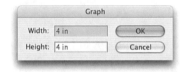

FIGURE 17.14
Specifying the size
of the graph.

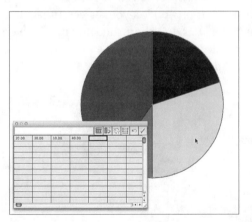

FIGURE 17.15
Adding values to
the graph.

When you're done, choose the Selection tool and select the entire graph. Press the "X" key to put the focus on the Stroke attribute, and then press the "/ "(slash) key to set the Stroke color to none (see Figure 17.16).

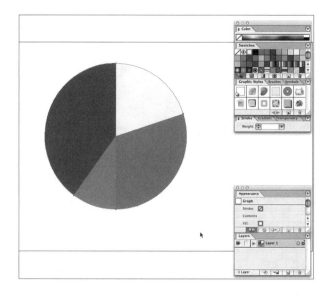

I'll bet you're thinking that the graph doesn't look very exciting at this point, and I'd have to agree with you. So we'll add some punch by applying a 3D effect. With the graph still selected, choose Effect, 3D, Extrude & Bevel. Position the dialog so that you can see your artwork on your screen (if possible) and click the Preview button. You'll see your dull chart suddenly turn into an eye-catching 3D chart. Change the Extrude Depth to 75 pt and rotate the "X" axis to 55° (see Figure 17.17). Click OK and deselect the graph.

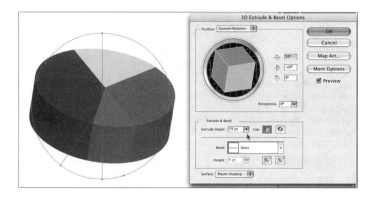

To add emphasis to one of the pie wedges, switch to the Direct Selection tool and drag one of the wedges out from the center. Because the 3D is applied as a live effect, the graph will update to show that wedge in an "exploded" view (see Figure 17.18).

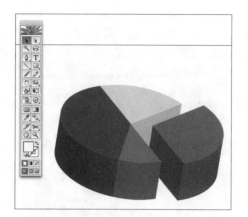

For a final effect, use the Selection tool to select the entire graph and choose
Effect, Stylize, and Drop Shadow to add a nice drop shadow to the pie graph (see
Figure 17.19).

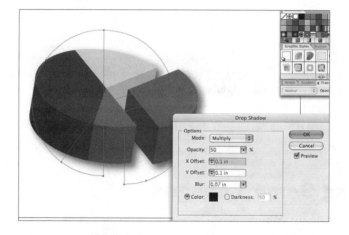

Save the graph file as a native AI file into your Version Cue project. Remember to
include a comment when you save the file. Close the Illustrator file and switch
back to InDesign.

Creating the Chart Slide

After you're back in InDesign, switch to page 2 of the document and apply the
Graph's master page. Then place the Illustrator pie graph that you just created.
Center it nicely inside the border, and change the header to read MARKET SHARE
DATA (see Figure 17.20).

FIGURE 17.20
Completing the
Graph slide.

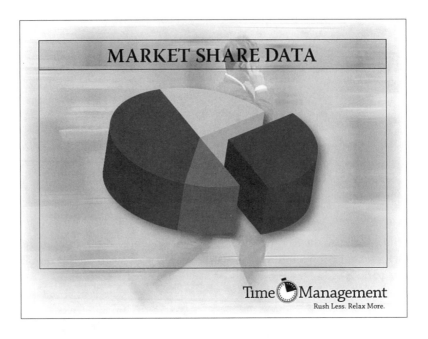

> To keep the project simple and within the scope of this book, we just created a sim-
> ple graph in Illustrator, but of course you could also create legends, add text and val-
> ues, and include other information as well.

By the Way

Choose File, Save a Version to save the file, adding a comment about the added
slides you created.

Making Some Changes

Just when you're thinking that you have some time to actually go and grab some
lunch, you get an e-mail from your manager or client saying that the numbers
have changed for the graph. So much for your lunch plans, right? Maybe not.

Suppose that the e-mail says you need to change the values of the graph to 15,
35, 20, 30. The first thing you'll do is open the Presentation file in InDesign. Then
select the placed graph and from the Links palette, click on the Edit Original button (see Figure 17.21). This action will launch Illustrator (if it isn't already open)
and automatically open the graph file for you.

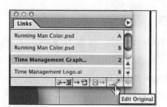

FIGURE 17.21
Using the Edit
Original button in
InDesign's Links
palette.

Using the Selection tool, select the graph and choose Object, Graph, Data, and enter the new values into the Graph Data window. Click on the Apply button to update the graph, and then close the Graph Data window.

Now choose File, Save a Version, and add a comment about the change you just made (see Figure 17.22). Close the Illustrator file.

FIGURE 17.22
Choosing to save a
version of the
graph file.

If you're not playing along using Version Cue, just save the file as you would normally.

Now switch back to InDesign and you'll see the graph update automatically with the new values. If I were you, I'd head out to lunch before another e-mail from the client comes your way....

Change a Version

Well, you come back from lunch only to notice another e-mail from the client apologizing for the earlier e-mail, but the original graph numbers that he supplied were the correct ones—not the ones he e-mailed you right before lunch. Before you reach for the antacid tablets, remember that we've been using Version Cue extensively in this project (for those of you who haven't, keep reaching for those tablets), and we're going to let Version Cue do the work for us.

Start off the same way we made the changes to the graph by selecting the graph in your InDesign layout and using Edit Original to open it in Illustrator.

Choose File, Versions (see Figure 17.23) and you'll be presented with the "Adobe Engineers, I Owe You One" dialog (at least that's what I like to call it). You'll see a list of all the versions you've created for this file, along with thumbnails and comments to help you see the changes that were made to each of the versions (see Figure 17.24). Click on Version 1 to highlight it, and click on the Promote to Current Version button at the bottom of the dialog (see Figure 17.25). Quit Illustrator and return to InDesign; once again, the graph will update automatically to the correct version.

FIGURE 17.23
Choosing to view the versions of a file.

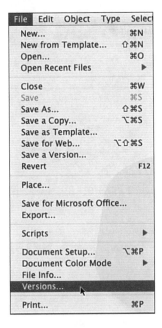

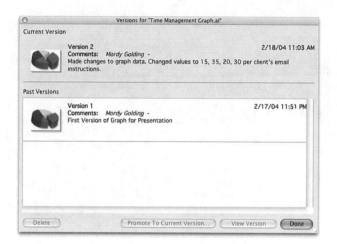

FIGURE 17.24
The Versions
dialog.

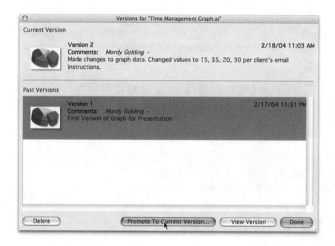

FIGURE 17.25
Promoting Version
1 to the current
version.

Save a version of the InDesign file, noting that the presentation has now been updated with the original values in the graph.

Exporting a PDF from InDesign

Well, it seems everything is finally approved on the presentation, so we'll export a PDF from InDesign. Choose File, Export; give the file a name; click Save; and choose the Acrobat 6 Layered preset in the Export PDF dialog box (even though we don't have layers in our document). To save some time, check the View PDF After Exporting box and click Export (see Figure 17.26).

FIGURE 17.26
Exporting a PDF
from InDesign CS.

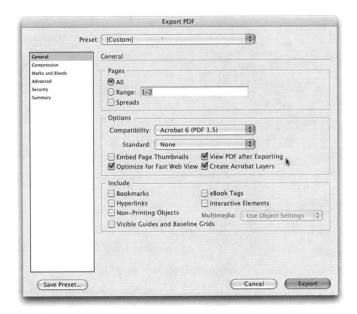

Adding the Finishing Touches

With the file open in Acrobat, we can specify certain settings to make the PDF file more suitable for presentations. Choose File, Document Properties, and from the list on the left, choose Initial View. In the Window Options section, check the box marked "Open in Full Screen Mode" (see Figure 17.27). This will cause the PDF to automatically open in Full Screen mode.

Specify Page Transitions

One of your jobs as a designer, of course, is to make your presentation as engaging as possible. We've already added some nifty graphics (I've always wanted to use the word *nifty* in a book), and another way to add a little spice to the presentation is to add page transitions. Rather than simply moving from one page to the next, a page transition animates the movement of one page to another.

To set page transitions, choose Document, Pages, Set Page Transitions (see Figure 17.28). You can choose from a laundry list of different transitions (there's also a Randomize setting, which will pick different transitions for you as the presentation is viewed). If you'd like, you can even have the pages turn by themselves (useful for a kiosk-like presentation that won't be given by an individual). After you're done, click OK.

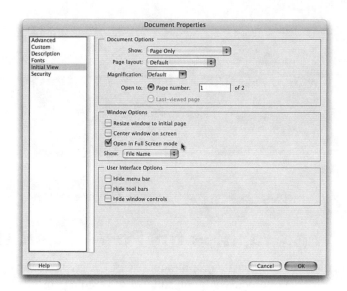

FIGURE 17.27
Setting the PDF file
to open in Full
Screen mode.

FIGURE 17.28
Setting the transi-
tion options for the
presentation.

Save Secure PDF

Finally, we're going to password-protect the file so that others can't change the
content of the presentation. Choose Document, Security, Restrict Opening and
Editing to open the Password Security–Settings dialog (see Figure 17.29). Add a
password for permissions and set both the Printing and the Changes settings to
None. Click OK.

Save your PDF file and you're done!

FIGURE 17.29
Setting the PDF file to require a password in order to print or make changes (or even copy elements from the document).

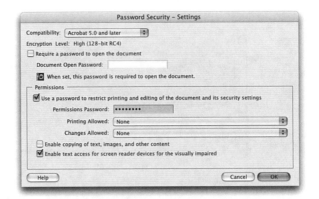

Exporting Graphics for PowerPoint Use

At times you'll be asked to create graphics for use in PowerPoint (part of the Microsoft Office suite of products). If you still want to create your nifty graphics in Illustrator (there's that *"nifty"* word again!), you certainly can.

After you create your graphics in Illustrator, choose File, Save for Microsoft Office, and Illustrator will save your file in the standard PNG format, which can be placed directly into PowerPoint (and the graphics will look great!).

Congratulations, you've just completed a spectacular business presentation!

APPENDIX A

Final Output: Sending Your Files to Print

Getting It Printed

Creating artwork on your computer is really only half the process. It's not like you'll be inviting everyone to your home or office to see what you've created on your screen—a client may not be too keen on that. Rather, after your design is complete and approved, you'll need to send it to a printer to create the final piece.

Naturally, each job is different. In some cases your final product will be a Web site or a PDF, but most jobs require a printed piece as the final product. This chapter specifically covers jobs that are printed by an offset printer.

Plenty of jobs are simply run off on a copying machine or even a laser printer. For the most part, this chapter does not address those kinds of jobs, although some concepts do apply.

By the Way

The Love-Hate Relationship Between Designers and Printers

Ask some printers what they think of graphic designers and they may answer, "They are the root of all evil." Other printers get along with designers just fine, so what's all the fuss about? In reality, the issue stems from designers who aren't familiar with the printing process, its capabilities, or its limitations.

The biggest complaint from printers is that designers create art that is very difficult to print—and in many cases, they design art that can't be printed reliably at all.

As a designer, you have only to gain by learning more about the printing process, and applying that knowledge to the art you design. For example, don't create 5-point white text that knocks out of a process color background. Find out how close you can come to the edge of a page (a printer needs "gripper" space), or if you are creating art that will come to the edge of the page, be sure to add a bleed (extending the art past the edge of the page).

Undoubtedly there's a gray line between what a designer is responsible for and what a printer is responsible for. But when it comes to getting a job done, and there's money on the line—and a client waiting to get the product—you want to make sure that the job is done correctly. And the better shape a file is in when you hand it off to a printer, the happier everyone will be in the end.

I know that many printers value a designer who knows what they are doing, and will even refer design work to them when their clients ask whether they know any good designers. Turns out I've gotten more than just design jobs referred to me over the years—my father-in-law is a printer... <g>

Understanding the Printing Process

When trying to understand graphics, printing, and the technology that makes it all possible, I like to make a comparison to how some of the greatest professional athletes look at the sports they play.

Sandy Koufax is considered one of the greatest left-handed pitchers of all time, and what made him unique was that he understood the underlying physics of what makes a baseball curve, rise, or sink. He likened the human body to a catapult and understood the dynamics of throwing a baseball.

Tiger Woods is arguably the greatest golf player in history—and for good reason. Besides having talent, Tiger studies the physics of the game, and understands why a certain club gives more lift than others, or how the direction the grass grows affects a particular shot.

The point I'm trying to make is that the more you know about your field, the better you can be at it—no matter what it is that you do. In graphic design specifically, knowing about printing makes you a better designer.

Many of today's printers are utilizing digital workflows to save costs and improve quality and turnaround time. Some printers have a CTP system (Computer-to-Plate), which eliminates the need to create film—basically creating plates directly from a computer file. Although these methods present other challenges to printers (trapping, imposition, and so on), use of such a method also puts the responsibility on the designer to create art files that are free of problems (okay, so at least with as few problems as possible).

Understanding Transparency

The transparency features in Illustrator and InDesign have gotten a bad rap since they were initially introduced—and rightfully so. The technology was too new for the older systems that most printers were using, and above all, there was very little information on how it worked, leaving many printers and designers to struggle with the settings. Most people didn't even know that transparency existed, and printers who suggested that users save their files as older Illustrator files ended up causing even more issues. At the end of the day, it was all quite messy.

But transparency has come quite a ways since then. Illustrator CS, InDesign CS, and Acrobat 6 now all share the same flattening code (necessary to process files with transparency), and more important, the transparency features and settings across all of these applications are identical. Adobe has also been extremely active in helping print service providers and printers learn about transparency, and numerous guides and white papers are also available (I reference these later).

A Designer's Checklist

Although it's impossible to list everything that might go wrong in a job, there are several issues that come up more often. As a checklist for yourself when you're creating files, or preparing them to send to a printer, here are some common issues to be aware of:

- ▶ **Make sure that everything is CMYK**—Make sure that you haven't accidentally created artwork in RGB mode. Many times you might use stock photography that you've downloaded from a Web site—and those images are almost always in RGB. Remember that almost all images from a digital camera are RGB—and must be converted to CMYK in Photoshop before they can be sent to the printer.

- ▶ **Remember your fonts**—When you send your files to your printer, make sure that you've included copies of all the fonts you've used in the file. Additionally, try to avoid using off-brand fonts that you've found somewhere on the Internet, or fonts from those "10,000 fonts for $9.99" collections, because they usually end up causing problems.

- ▶ **Use spot and process colors correctly**—If you're printing a job as a four-color process (CMYK), don't provide your printer with a file made up of spot colors. Likewise, if you're printing a spot color job, don't provide your printer with a file that uses process colors. Some jobs combine both spot and process colors as well. If you aren't sure, talk to your printer.

▶ **Make sure that images are high resolution**—Sometimes designers use low-resolution images in their design but forget to replace them with high-resolution versions of the images before they send their files to the printer. Sometimes designers copy files from a Web site, and those images are almost always 72dpi low-resolution images. Make sure that photos taken with a digital camera are also of sufficient resolution.

▶ **Check Illustrator resolution settings**—If you've applied any effects in Illustrator (they appear in the Effects menu), those effects may need to be rasterized at print time. Drop shadows, feathers, Gaussian blurs, and some mapped 3D artwork are examples of effects that get rasterized at print time. To ensure best results, make sure that the Document Raster Effects Setting is set to 300dpi.

▶ **Check Transparency Flattener settings**—In many cases, if you've used native Illustrator CS and InDesign CS files—and PDF 1.4 files or higher—your printer will determine the correct flattener settings. But at times you may be working with EPS files, or your printer may ask you to export older format files—and in those cases, you'll be supplying files to your printer that are already flattened. Flattened files can't be changed, so if they aren't correct, the printer can't fix them.

▶ **Check your stroke weights**—Just because Illustrator and InDesign allow you to specify extremely thin lines, that doesn't mean a printing press will be able to reproduce them. In general, never specify a stroke weight that's less than 0.25-point. Pay attention to logos or other art that is scaled—a logo that has a 1-point stroke that is scaled down to 20% in your InDesign layout will end up with a 0.2-point stroke.

▶ **Check your tints**—Specify tints that won't cause problems on press. Tints lower than 5% or higher than 95% are usually problematic. The truth is, each printing press is different, and printers know what their presses can handle; so it's best to ask your printer for suggestions.

▶ **Add bleed or gripper space**—if your design includes art or a background that is supposed to print all the way to the edge of a page, you have to specify a *bleed*, which is basically extending the art outside the boundaries of the page. This ensures that no whitespace will show when the page is trimmed to the correct size. Where art doesn't come all the way to the edge of the page, you have to leave a certain amount of space, called *gripper space*, along the edges of your page (you can use margin settings to help you stay out of these areas).

In case you were wondering, pages with a bleed don't usually need gripper space because they are printed on larger pages that are trimmed down to the page size you specify.

▶ **Perform general file cleanup**—Throughout the design process, you may choose from many colors, fonts, symbols, and so forth. When your job is complete, it's best to "clean up" your file by deleting unused swatches, brushes, or symbols. Use the Find Font feature in InDesign or Illustrator to make sure that you don't have empty objects with additional fonts in your file.

▶ **Provide a dummy**—I'm not referring to the kind of dummy that a ventriloquist uses. A dummy is a printed mockup that shows a printer how a job should look when it's printed and folded. It doesn't have to be in color or even full size—but it should give the printer a good visual of what you expect. Creating a dummy also helps you—the designer—because you can make sure that the panels fold correctly and are the right size.

InDesign's Package Feature

InDesign's Package feature is a great way to prepare a project to hand off to your printer. This feature (found in InDesign's File menu) creates a folder that contains a copy of your file, along with all the fonts and linked images that are used in your file. It also allows you to easily create a text file with instructions that you can pass on to your printer.

I've found that it's also good practice to send along a PDF version of your file so that the printer can see what the file looks like and compare it to what he sees in InDesign, making sure that everything is correct.

InDesign and Acrobat's Separation Preview Feature

Both InDesign CS and Acrobat 6.0 Professional allow you to view color separations onscreen and also feature a densitometer reading for checking ink coverage. To make sure that your process or spot colors are separating correctly, these are invaluable tools that should be used. If you aren't sure what you should be looking for when viewing separations, speak to your printer.

Resources

Plenty of material on this topic is available, and it would only benefit you to find some time to learn more about the printing process, as well as understanding how art goes from the computer monitor to the printed page (and everything that happens in between).

Here's a list of some resources that I find useful on this subject. Visit www.mordy.com for the latest updated list.

▶ *A Designer's Guide to Transparency for Print Output*, by Adobe Systems Incorporated (www.adobe.com/products/indesign/pdfs/transparency_guide.pdf)

▶ *Adobe InDesign CS Printing Guide for Service Providers*, by Adobe Systems Incorporated (partners.adobe.com/asn/printserviceprovider/assets/IDCS_PrintGuide .pdf)

▶ *Adobe Illustrator CS Printing Guide for Service Providers*, by Adobe Systems Incorporated (partners.adobe.com/asn/printserviceprovider/assets/AICS_PrintGuide 6.pdf)

▶ *Adobe Acrobat 6.0 Professional Output Guide for Print Service Providers*, by Adobe Systems Incorporated (partners.adobe.com/asn/ printserviceprovider/assets/Acrobat6OutputGuide.pdf)

▶ *Professional Printing with Adobe Illustrator CS*, by Adobe Systems Incorporated (www.adobe.com/products/creativesuite/pdfs/ilcsproprint.pdf)

▶ *Pocket Pal: A Graphic Arts Production Handbook*, 18th Edition, by Michael H. Bruno (GATF Press)

▶ *Real World Color Management*, by Bruce Fraser, Fred Bunting, and Chris Murphy (Peachpit Press)

Finally—and I can't emphasize this enough—talk to your printer. An open line of communication between designer and printer is crucial and can save time, energy, money, and mental sanity. If possible, arrange to spend a day or two at a printer and see the process for yourself. Learn about the issues that come up and how they are addressed. The information you will learn will prove more valuable than you can imagine.

Index

H

I

S

T

W